尾田栄一郎

Why am I drinking alone? Didn't someone once sing that if we *imagine* a more peaceful world that we'd have peace? Will you join me? Today's the anniversary of John's death. Wait, I'm actually talking about a dog named John. Anyway, let's start volume 59!

-Eiichiro Oda, 2010

 iichiro Oda began his manga career at the age of 17, when his one-shot cowboy manga **Wanted!** won second place in the coveted Tezuka manga awards. Oda went on to work as an assistant to some of the biggest manga artists in the industry, including Nobuhiro Watsuki, before winning the Hop Step Award for new artists. His pirate adventure **One Piece**, which debuted in **Weekly Shonen Jump** in 1997, quickly became one of the most popular manga in Japan.

ONE PIECE VOL. 59
PARAMOUNT WAR PART 3

SHONEN JUMP Manga Edition

This graphic novel contains material that was originally published in
English in SHONEN JUMP #97–100. Artwork in the magazine may have
been slightly altered from that presented here.

STORY AND ART BY EIICHIRO ODA

English Adaptation/Lance Caselman
Translation/Laabaman, HC Language Solutions, Inc.
Touch-up Art & Lettering/Vanessa Satone
Design/Fawn Lau
Editor/Alexis Kirsch

Printed in the U.S.A.

Published by VIZ Media, LLC
P.O. Box 77010
San Francisco, CA 94107

10 9 8 7 6 5 4 3 2 1
First printing, December 2011

www.viz.com

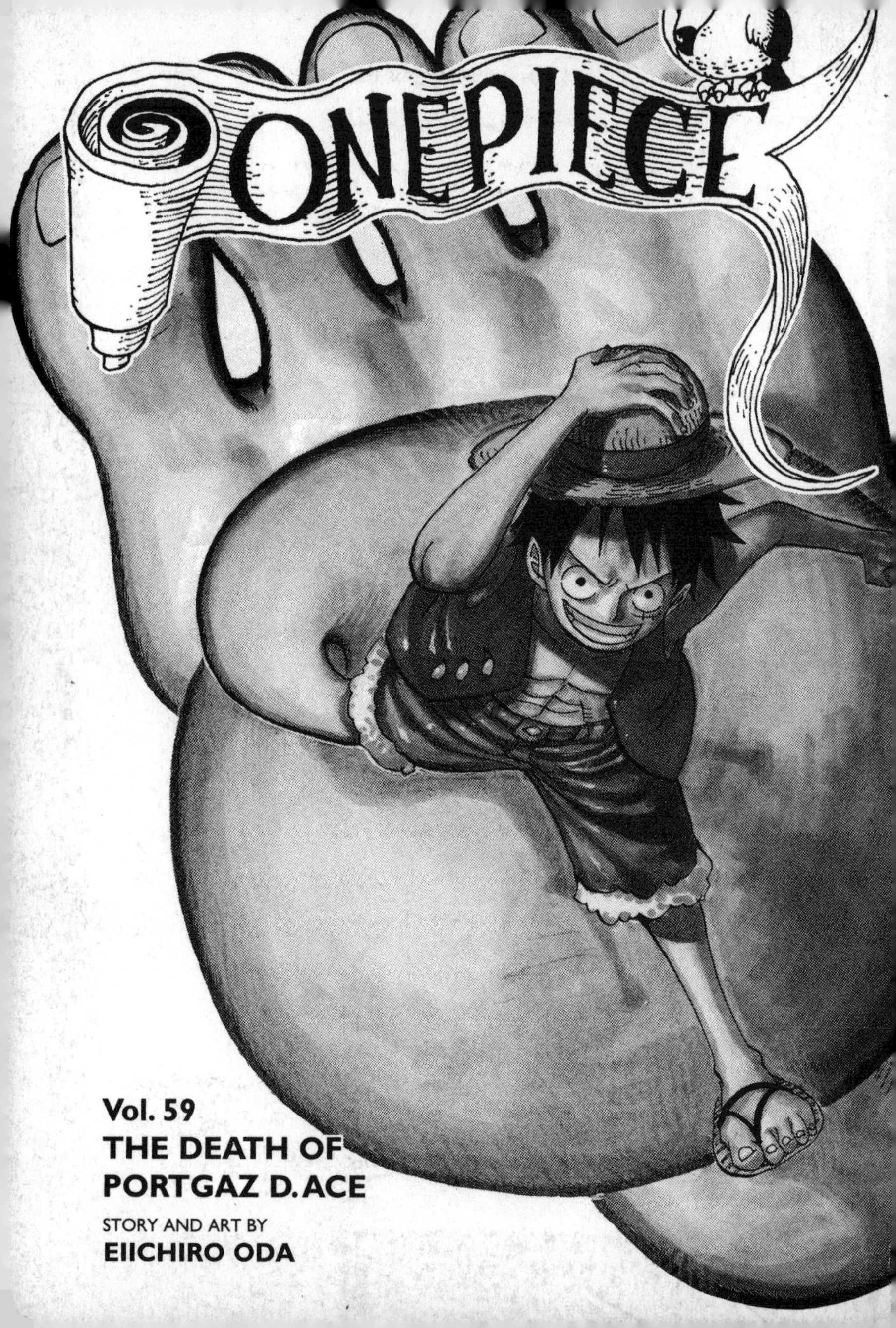
ONE PIECE

Vol. 59

THE DEATH OF PORTGAZ D.ACE

STORY AND ART BY

EIICHIRO ODA

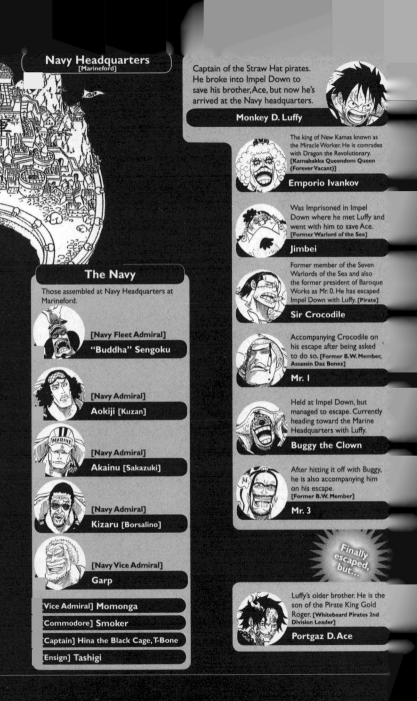

Navy Headquarters
[Marineford]

The Navy

Those assembled at Navy Headquarters at Marineford.

[Navy Fleet Admiral]
"Buddha" Sengoku

[Navy Admiral]
Aokiji [Kuzan]

[Navy Admiral]
Akainu [Sakazuki]

[Navy Admiral]
Kizaru [Borsalino]

[Navy Vice Admiral]
Garp

[Vice Admiral] **Momonga**

[Commodore] **Smoker**

[Captain] **Hina the Black Cage, T-Bone**

[Ensign] **Tashigi**

Captain of the Straw Hat pirates. He broke into Impel Down to save his brother, Ace, but now he's arrived at the Navy headquarters.

Monkey D. Luffy

The king of New Kamas known as the Miracle Worker. He is comrades with Dragon the Revolutionary. [Kamabakka Queendom Queen (Forever Vacant)]

Emporio Ivankov

Was Imprisoned in Impel Down where he met Luffy and went with him to save Ace. [Former Warlord of the Sea]

Jimbei

Former member of the Seven Warlords of the Sea and also the former president of Baroque Works as Mr. 0. He has escaped Impel Down with Luffy. [Pirate]

Sir Crocodile

Accompanying Crocodile on his escape after being asked to do so. [Former B.W. Member, Assassin Daz Bonez]

Mr. 1

Held at Impel Down, but managed to escape. Currently heading toward the Marine Headquarters with Luffy.

Buggy the Clown

After hitting it off with Buggy, he is also accompanying him on his escape. [Former B.W. Member]

Mr. 3

Finally escaped, but...

Luffy's older brother. He is the son of the Pirate King Gold Roger. [Whitebeard Pirates 2nd Division Leader]

Portgaz D. Ace

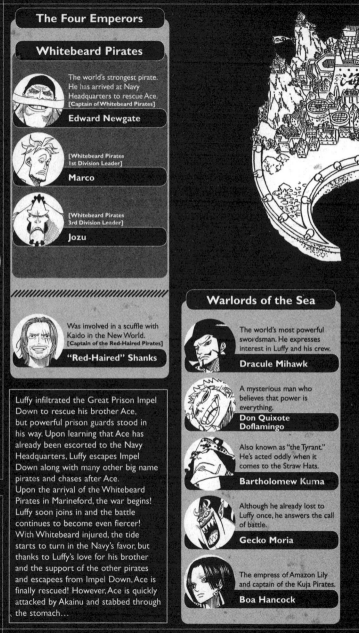

THE STORY OF ONE PIECE

Volume 59

海

The Four Emperors

Whitebeard Pirates

The world's strongest pirate. He has arrived at Navy Headquarters to rescue Ace.
[Captain of Whitebeard Pirates]
Edward Newgate

[Whitebeard Pirates 1st Division Leader]
Marco

[Whitebeard Pirates 3rd Division Leader]
Jozu

Was involved in a scuffle with Kaido in the New World.
[Captain of the Red-Haired Pirates]
"Red-Haired" Shanks

Luffy infiltrated the Great Prison Impel Down to rescue his brother Ace, but powerful prison guards stood in his way. Upon learning that Ace has already been escorted to the Navy Headquarters, Luffy escapes Impel Down along with many other big name pirates and chases after Ace.
Upon the arrival of the Whitebeard Pirates in Marineford, the war begins! Luffy soon joins in and the battle continues to become even fiercer! With Whitebeard injured, the tide starts to turn in the Navy's favor, but thanks to Luffy's love for his brother and the support of the other pirates and escapees from Impel Down, Ace is finally rescued! However, Ace is quickly attacked by Akainu and stabbed through the stomach…

Warlords of the Sea

The world's most powerful swordsman. He expresses interest in Luffy and his crew.
Dracule Mihawk

A mysterious man who believes that power is everything.
Don Quixote Doflamingo

Also known as "the Tyrant." He's acted oddly when it comes to the Straw Hats.
Bartholomew Kuma

Although he already lost to Luffy once, he answers the call of battle.
Gecko Moria

The empress of Amazon Lily and captain of the Kuja Pirates.
Boa Hancock

PARAMOUNT WAR

ONE PIECE

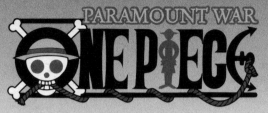

Vol. 59
The Death of Portgaz D. Ace

CONTENTS

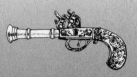

Chapter 574:
THE DEATH OF PORTGAZ D. ACE

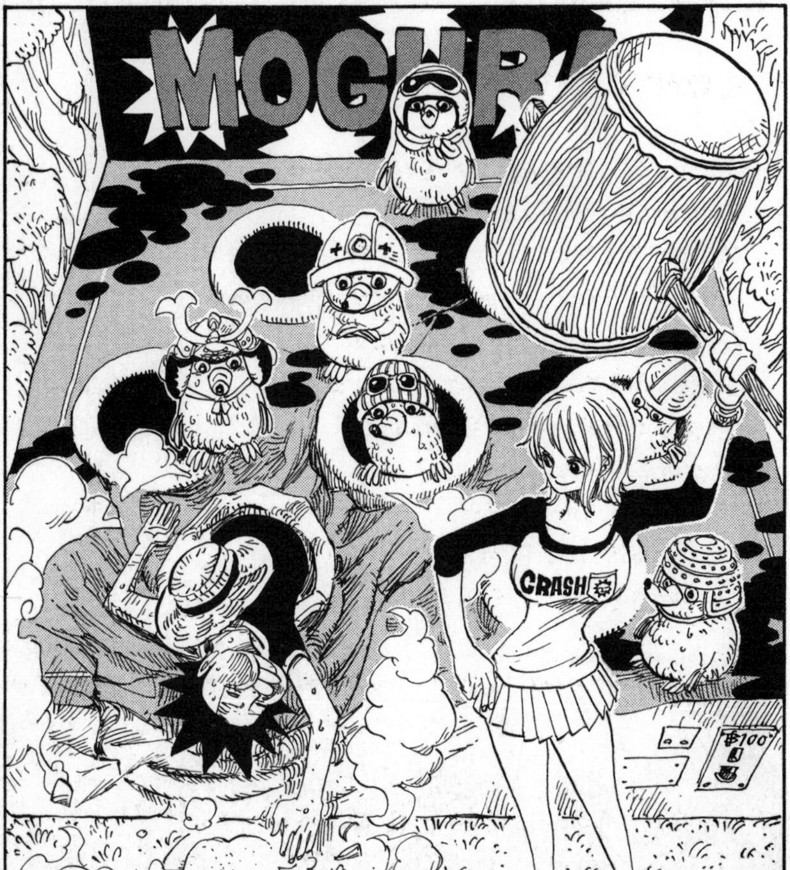
CRASH
฿100

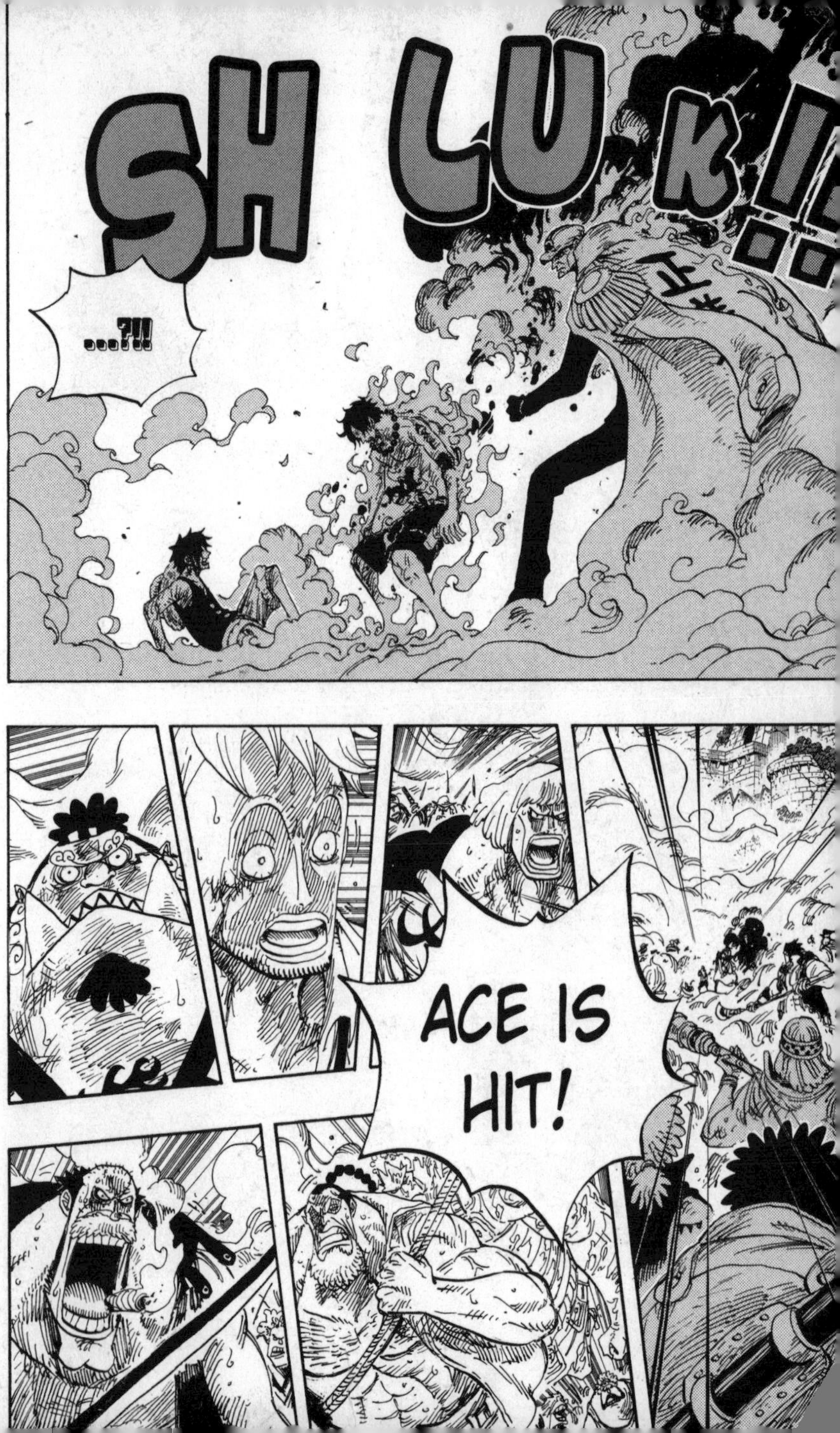
SHLUK!!
...?!!
ACE IS HIT!

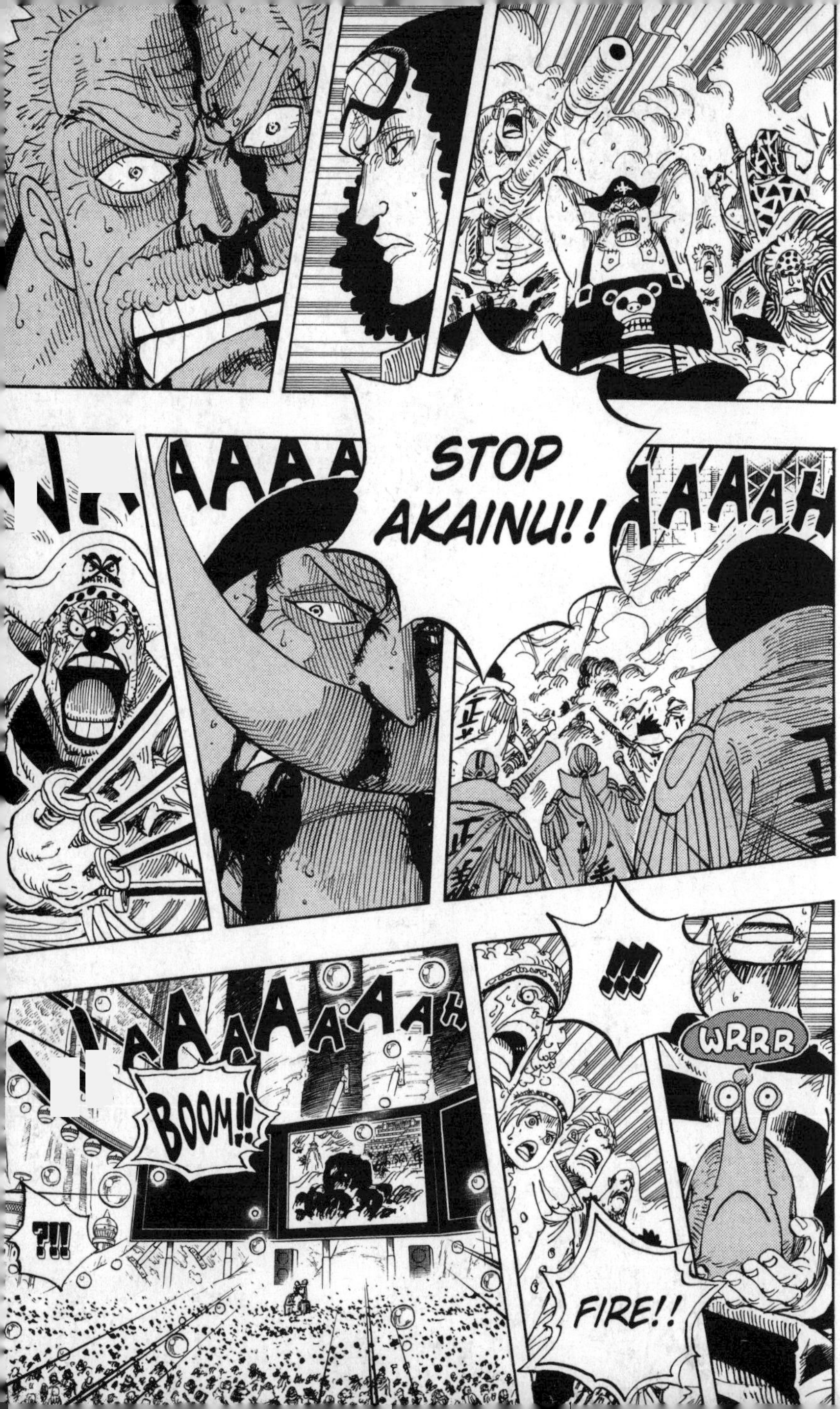
STOP AKAINU!!
AAAAH
AAAA
!!!
WRRR
FIRE!!
AAAAAAAAH
BOOM!!
?!!

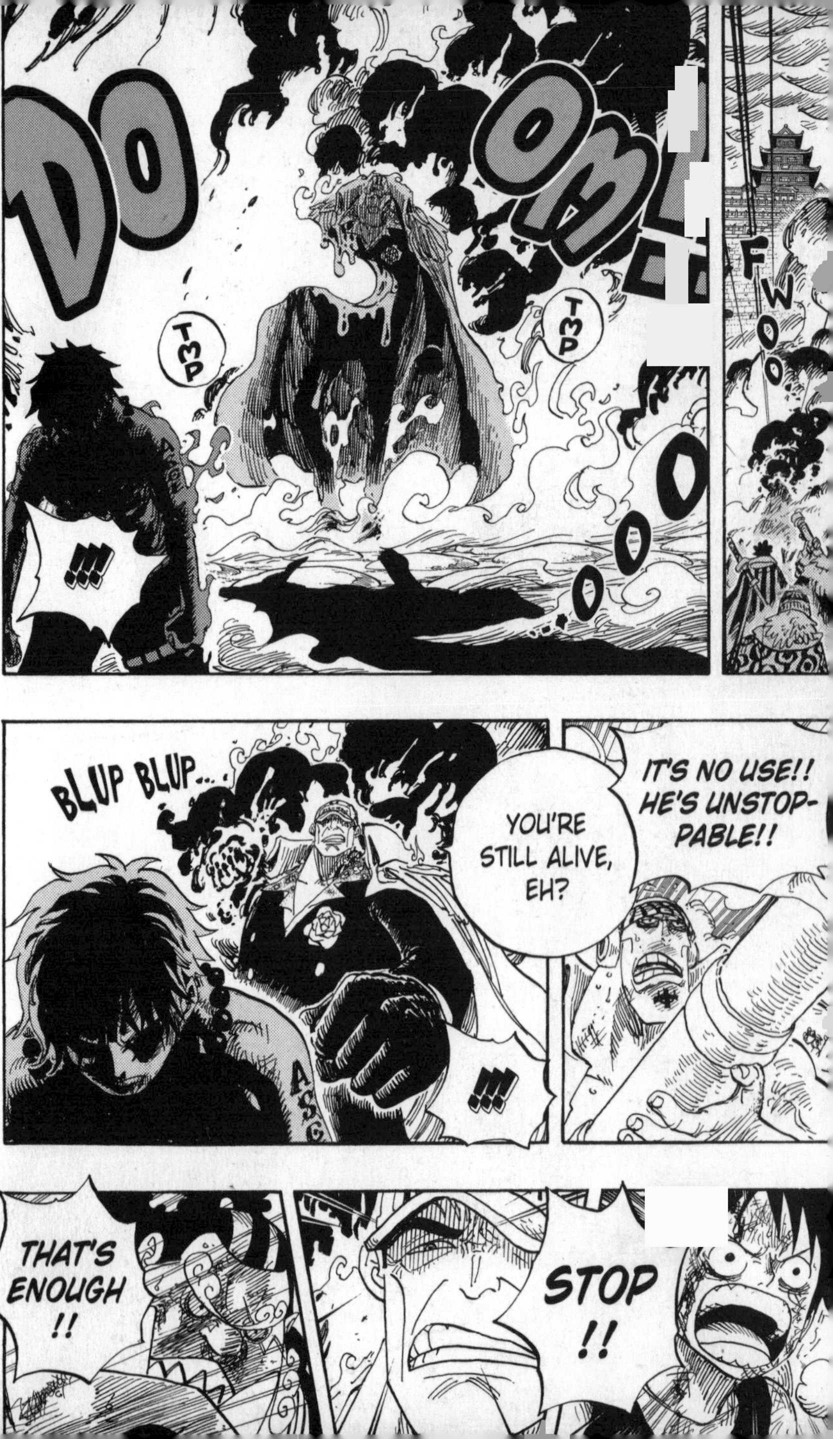
FWOO
DO
OM
TMP
TMP
OOOO
!!!
IT'S NO USE!! HE'S UNSTOP-PABLE!!
BLUP BLUP...
YOU'RE STILL ALIVE, EH?
!!!
STOP !!
THAT'S ENOUGH !!

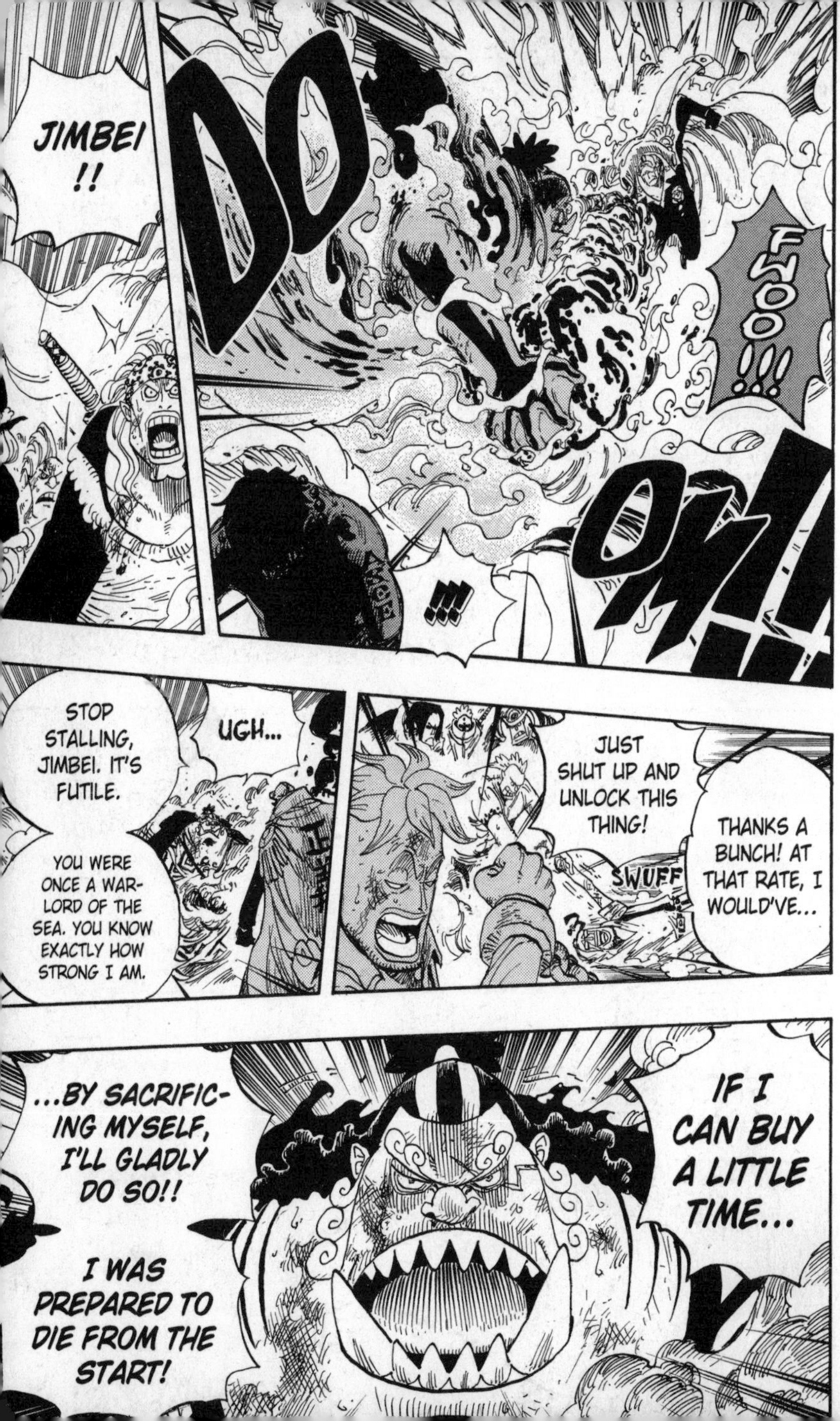
FWOO!!!
DO
ON!!
!!!
JIMBEI!!
THANKS A BUNCH! AT THAT RATE, I WOULD'VE...
JUST SHUT UP AND UNLOCK THIS THING!
SWUFF
UGH...
STOP STALLING, JIMBEI. IT'S FUTILE.
YOU WERE ONCE A WARLORD OF THE SEA. YOU KNOW EXACTLY HOW STRONG I AM.
IF I CAN BUY A LITTLE TIME...
...BY SACRIFICING MYSELF, I'LL GLADLY DO SO!!
I WAS PREPARED TO DIE FROM THE START!

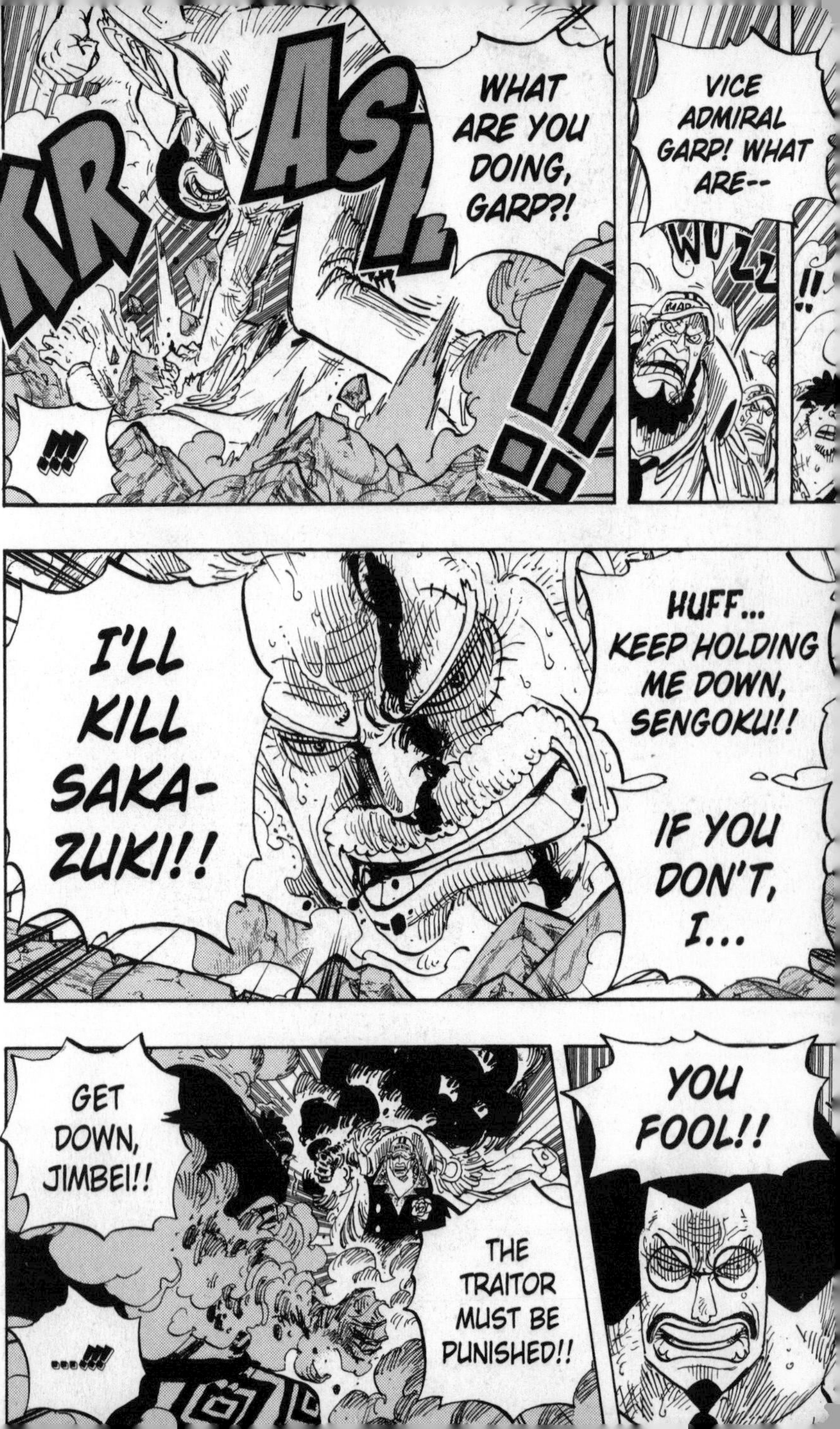
VICE ADMIRAL GARP! WHAT ARE--
WUZZ
!!
WHAT ARE YOU DOING, GARP?!
KR
AS
!!
!!!
HUFF... KEEP HOLDING ME DOWN, SENGOKU!!
IF YOU DON'T, I...
I'LL KILL SAKAZUKI!!
YOU FOOL!!
THE TRAITOR MUST BE PUNISHED!!
GET DOWN, JIMBEI!!
...!!!

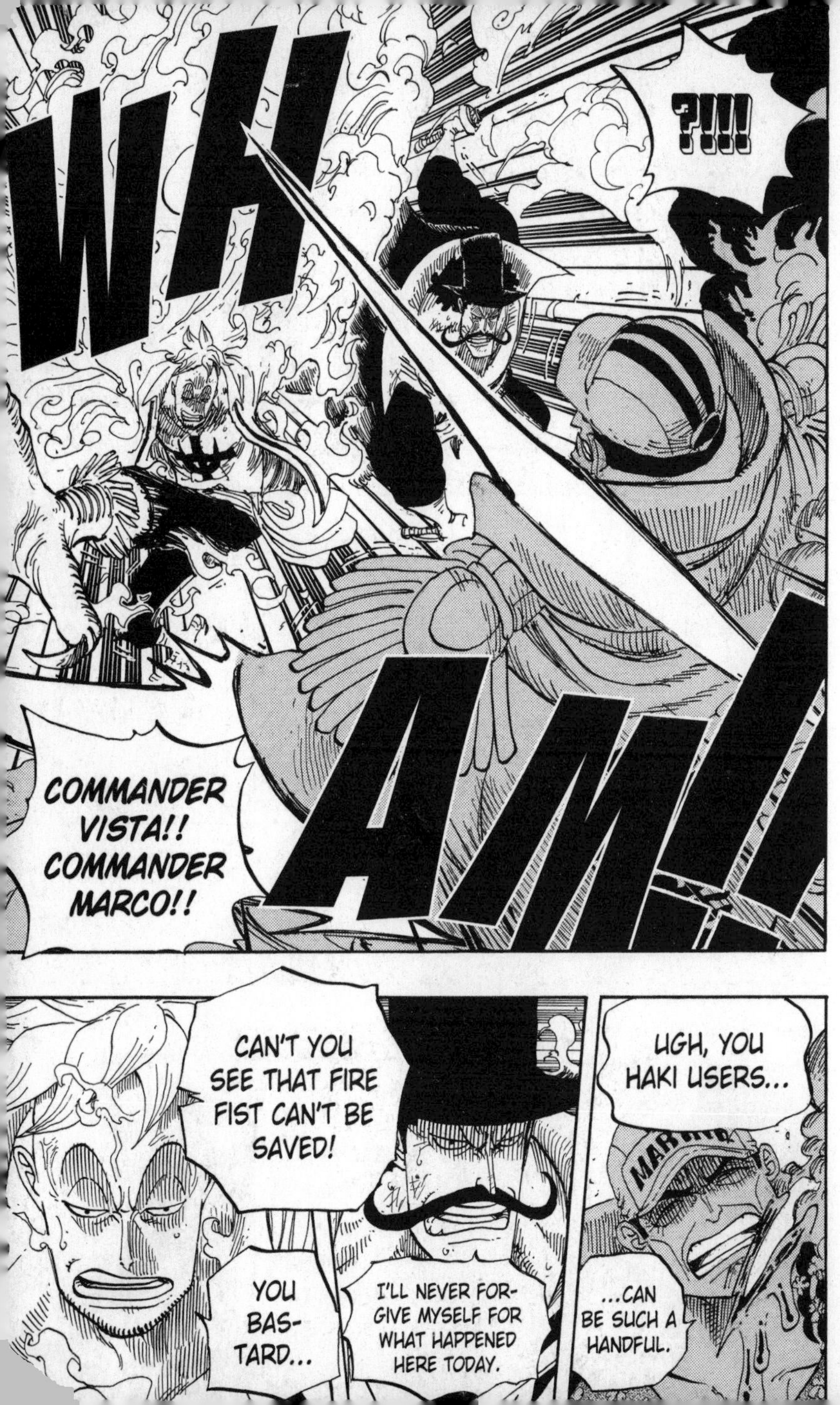
?!!!
WHAM!!
COMMANDER VISTA!! COMMANDER MARCO!!
UGH, YOU HAKI USERS...
...CAN BE SUCH A HANDFUL.
CAN'T YOU SEE THAT FIRE FIST CAN'T BE SAVED!
I'LL NEVER FOR-GIVE MYSELF FOR WHAT HAPPENED HERE TODAY.
YOU BAS-TARD...

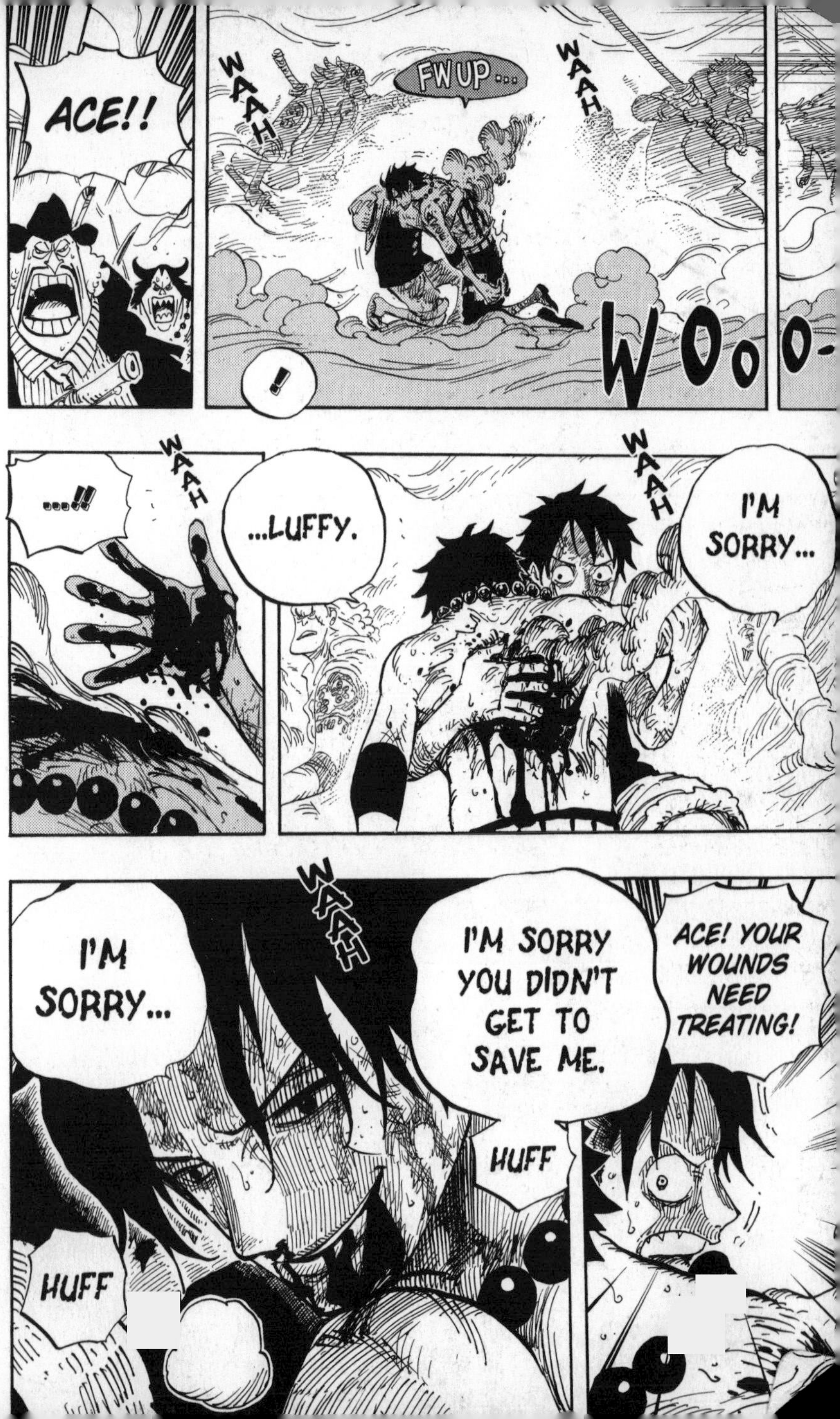
WAAH
FWUP...
WAAH
WOOO-
!
ACE!!
WAAH
I'M SORRY...
...LUFFY.
WAAH
...!!
ACE! YOUR WOUNDS NEED TREATING!
I'M SORRY YOU DIDN'T GET TO SAVE ME.
WAAH
HUFF
I'M SORRY...
HUFF

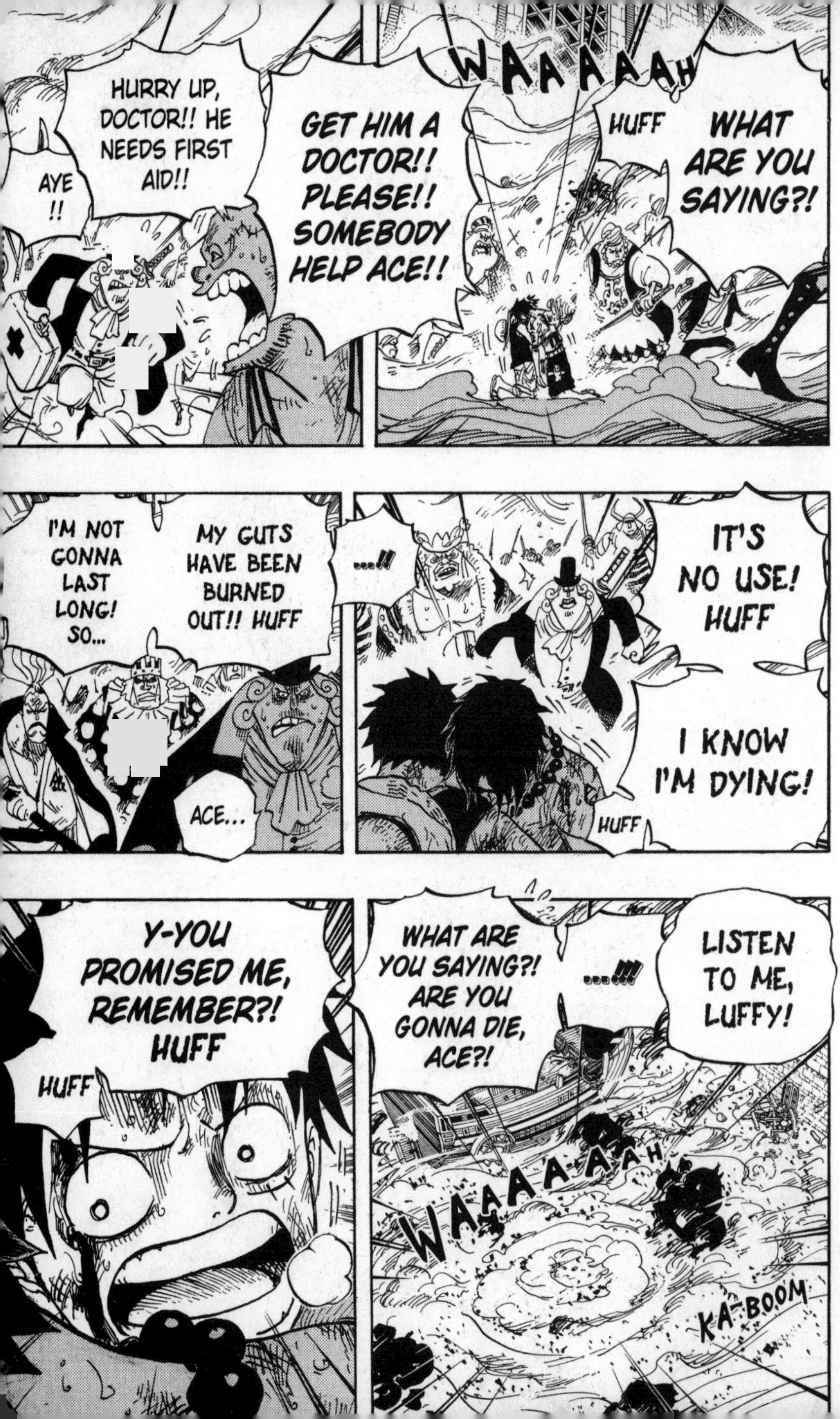
WAAAAAH
HUFF
WHAT ARE YOU SAYING?!
GET HIM A DOCTOR!! PLEASE!! SOMEBODY HELP ACE!!
HURRY UP, DOCTOR!! HE NEEDS FIRST AID!!
AYE !!
IT'S NO USE! HUFF
I KNOW I'M DYING!
HUFF
...!!
MY GUTS HAVE BEEN BURNED OUT!! HUFF
I'M NOT GONNA LAST LONG! SO...
ACE...
LISTEN TO ME, LUFFY!
...!!!
WHAT ARE YOU SAYING?! ARE YOU GONNA DIE, ACE?!
WAAAAAAH
KA-BOOM
Y-YOU PROMISED ME, REMEMBER?! HUFF
HUFF

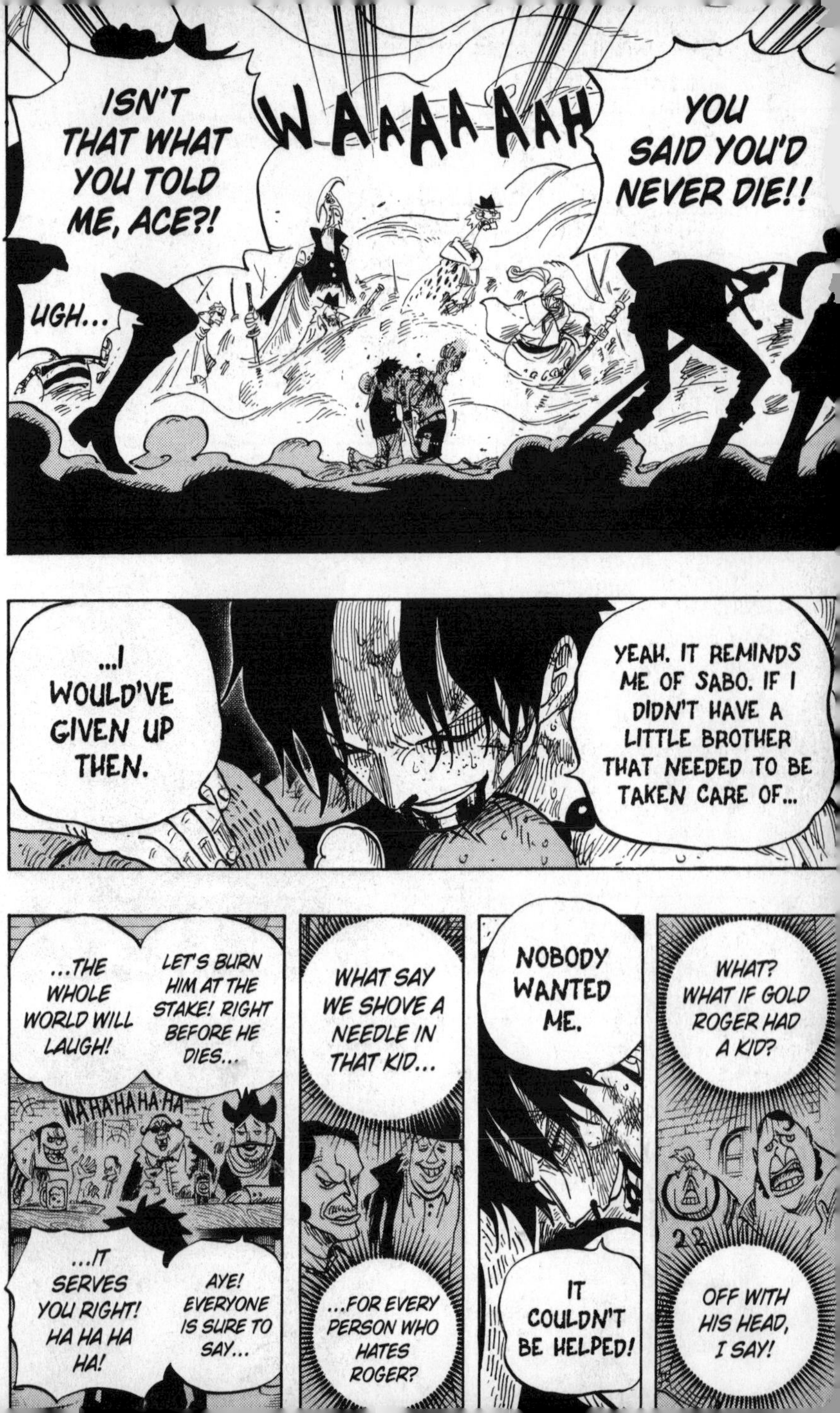
YOU SAID YOU'D NEVER DIE!!
WAAAAAAH
ISN'T THAT WHAT YOU TOLD ME, ACE?!
UGH...
YEAH. IT REMINDS ME OF SABO. IF I DIDN'T HAVE A LITTLE BROTHER THAT NEEDED TO BE TAKEN CARE OF...
...I WOULD'VE GIVEN UP THEN.
WHAT? WHAT IF GOLD ROGER HAD A KID?
OFF WITH HIS HEAD, I SAY!
NOBODY WANTED ME.
IT COULDN'T BE HELPED!
WHAT SAY WE SHOVE A NEEDLE IN THAT KID...
...FOR EVERY PERSON WHO HATES ROGER?
LET'S BURN HIM AT THE STAKE! RIGHT BEFORE HE DIES...
...THE WHOLE WORLD WILL LAUGH!
WAHAHAHAHA
AYE! EVERYONE IS SURE TO SAY...
...IT SERVES YOU RIGHT! HA HA HA HA!

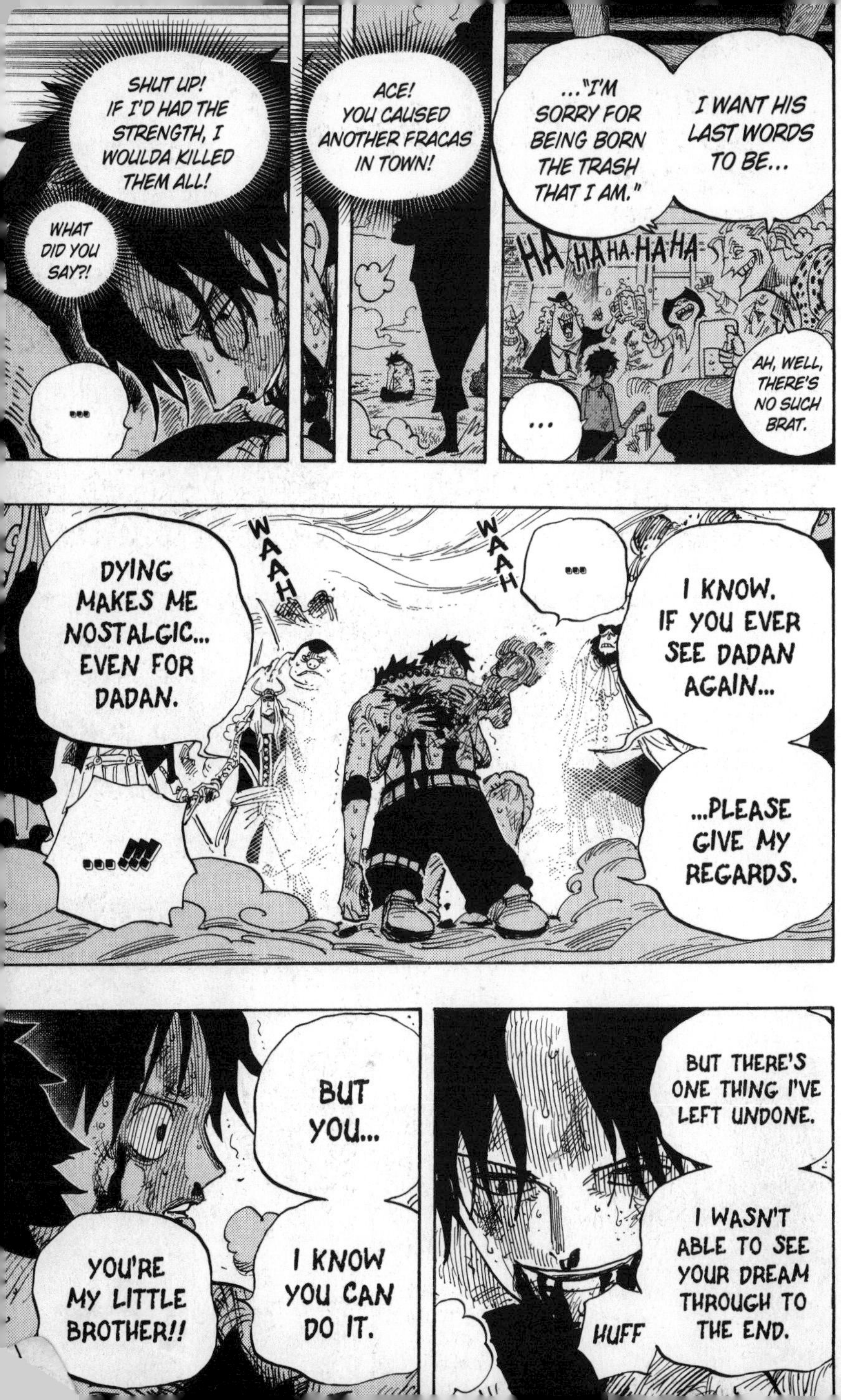
I WANT HIS LAST WORDS TO BE...
..."I'M SORRY FOR BEING BORN THE TRASH THAT I AM."
HA HA HA HA HA HA
AH, WELL, THERE'S NO SUCH BRAT.
...
ACE! YOU CAUSED ANOTHER FRACAS IN TOWN!
SHUT UP! IF I'D HAD THE STRENGTH, I WOULDA KILLED THEM ALL!
WHAT DID YOU SAY?!
...
I KNOW. IF YOU EVER SEE DADAN AGAIN...
...PLEASE GIVE MY REGARDS.
...
WAAAH
WAAAH
DYING MAKES ME NOSTALGIC... EVEN FOR DADAN.
...!!
BUT THERE'S ONE THING I'VE LEFT UNDONE.
I WASN'T ABLE TO SEE YOUR DREAM THROUGH TO THE END.
HUFF
BUT YOU...
I KNOW YOU CAN DO IT.
YOU'RE MY LITTLE BROTHER!!

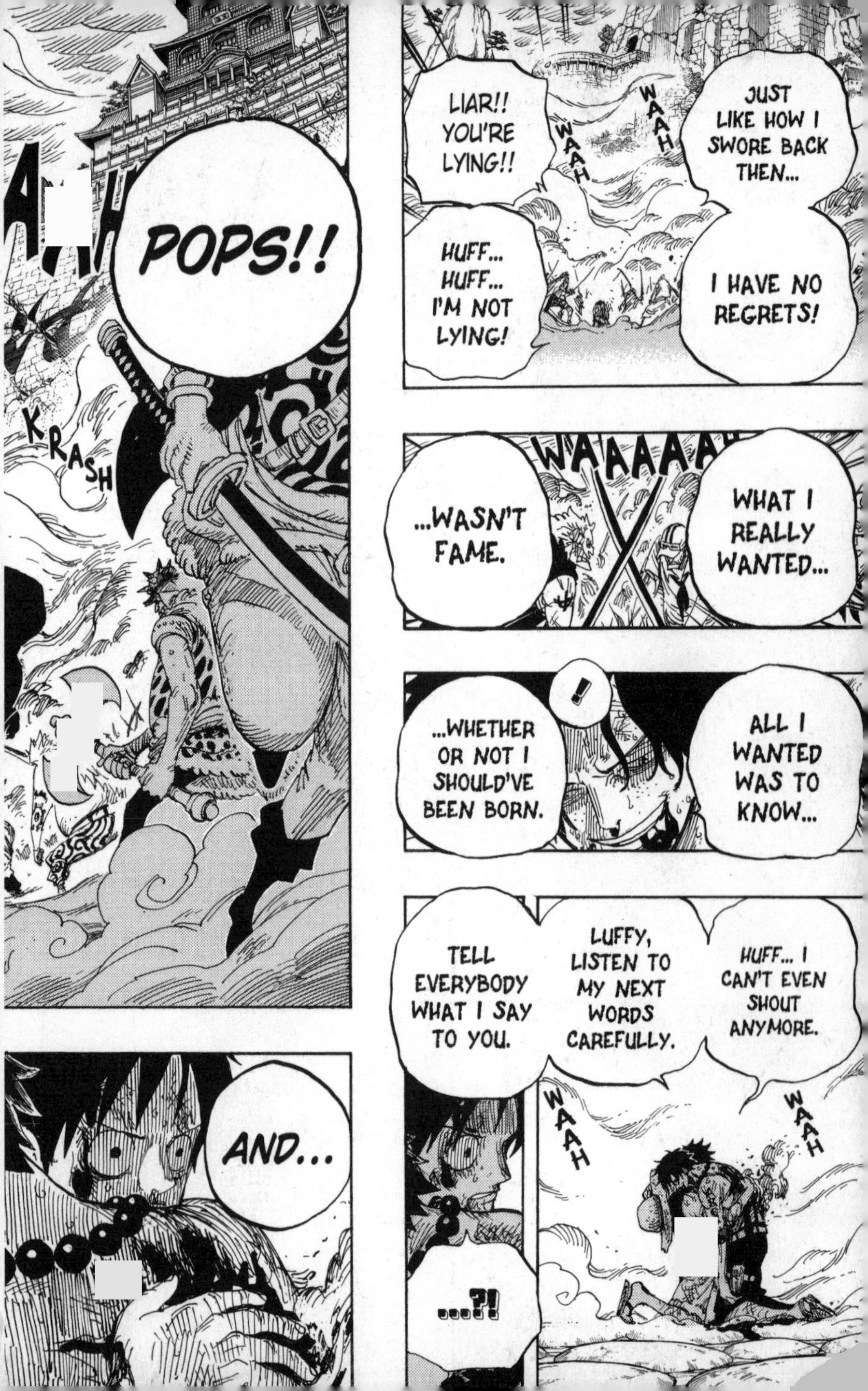

JUST LIKE HOW I SWORE BACK THEN...
I HAVE NO REGRETS!
WAAH
WAAH
LIAR!! YOU'RE LYING!!
HUFF... HUFF... I'M NOT LYING!
WHAT I REALLY WANTED...
WAAAAA
...WASN'T FAME.
ALL I WANTED WAS TO KNOW...
!
...WHETHER OR NOT I SHOULD'VE BEEN BORN.
HUFF... I CAN'T EVEN SHOUT ANYMORE.
LUFFY, LISTEN TO MY NEXT WORDS CAREFULLY.
TELL EVERYBODY WHAT I SAY TO YOU.
WAAH
WAAH
...?!
POPS!!
KRASH
AND...

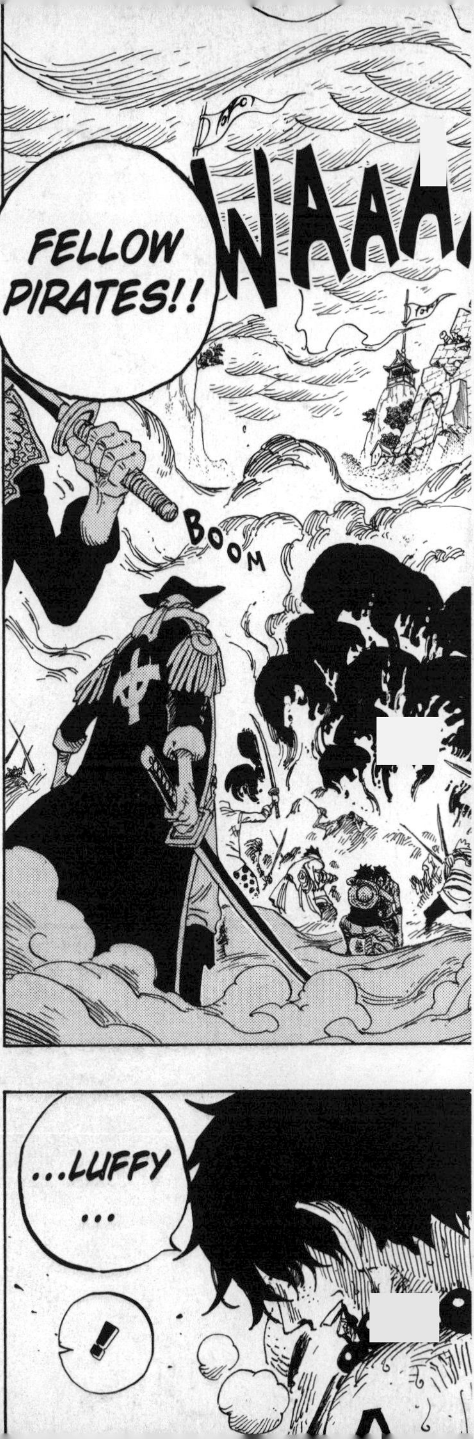
WAAA
FELLOW PIRATES!!
BOOM
...LUFFY ...
!
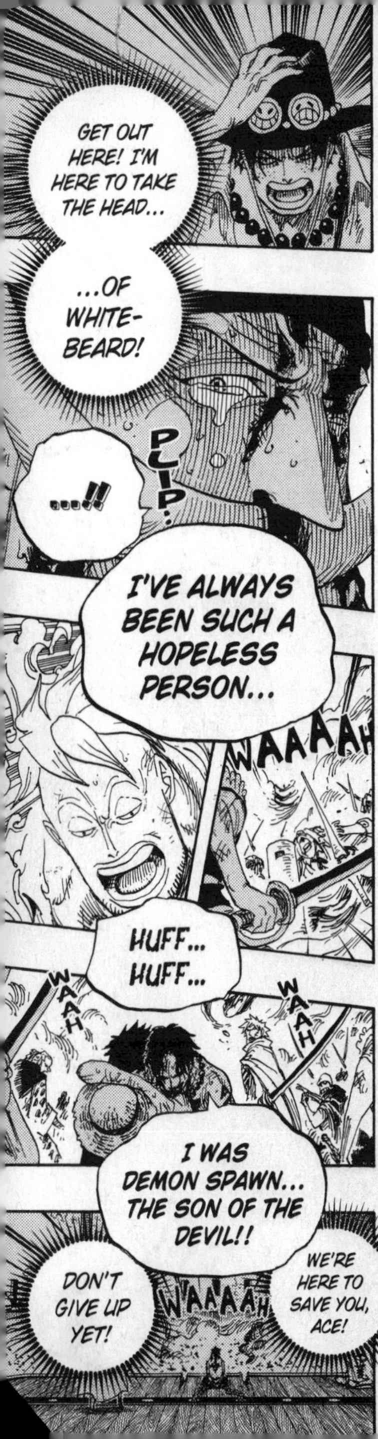
GET OUT HERE! I'M HERE TO TAKE THE HEAD...
...OF WHITE-BEARD!
PLIP
...!!
I'VE ALWAYS BEEN SUCH A HOPELESS PERSON...
WAAAAH
HUFF... HUFF...
WAAH
WAAH
I WAS DEMON SPAWN... THE SON OF THE DEVIL!!
WE'RE HERE TO SAVE YOU, ACE!
WAAAAH
DON'T GIVE UP YET!

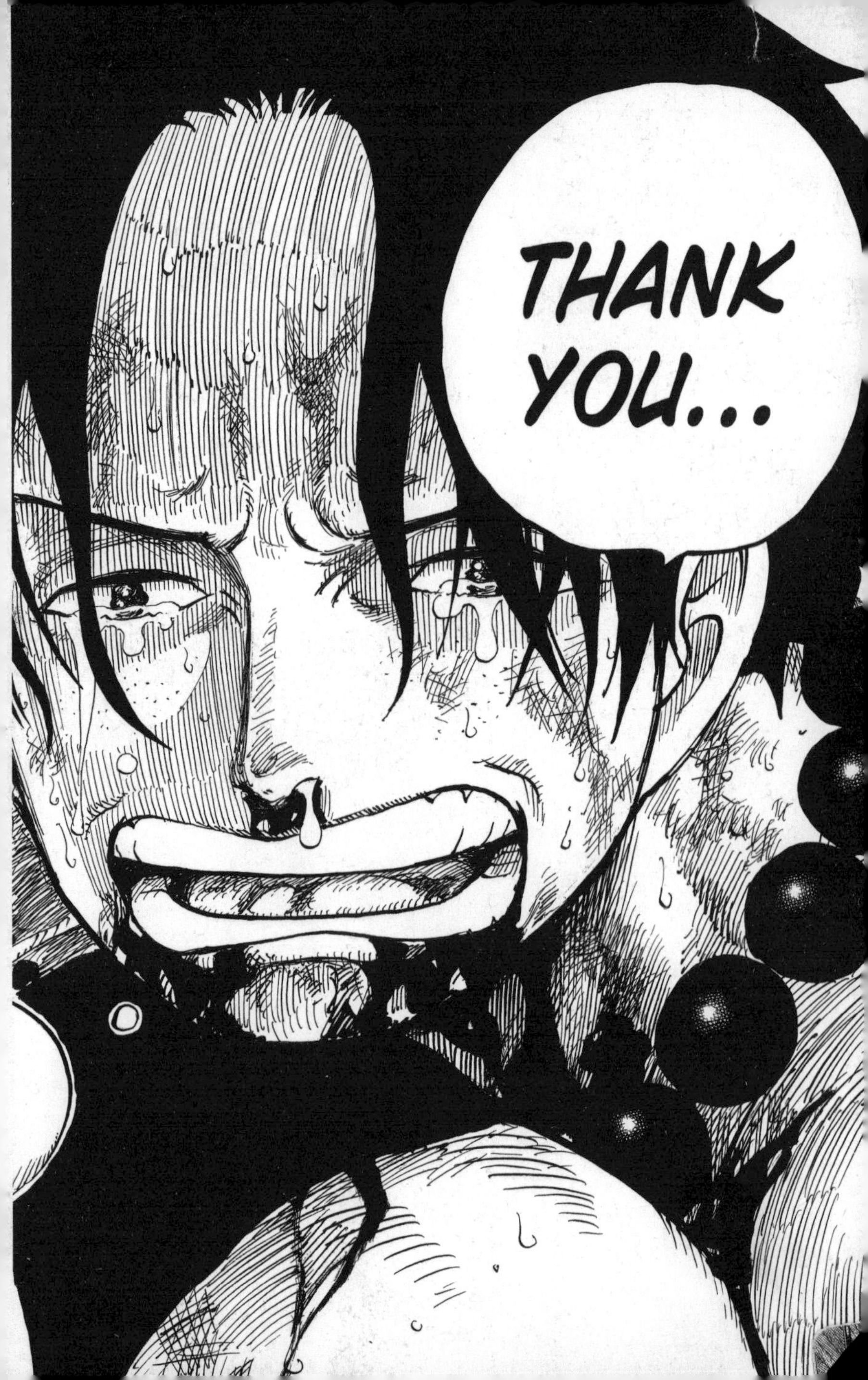
THANK YOU...

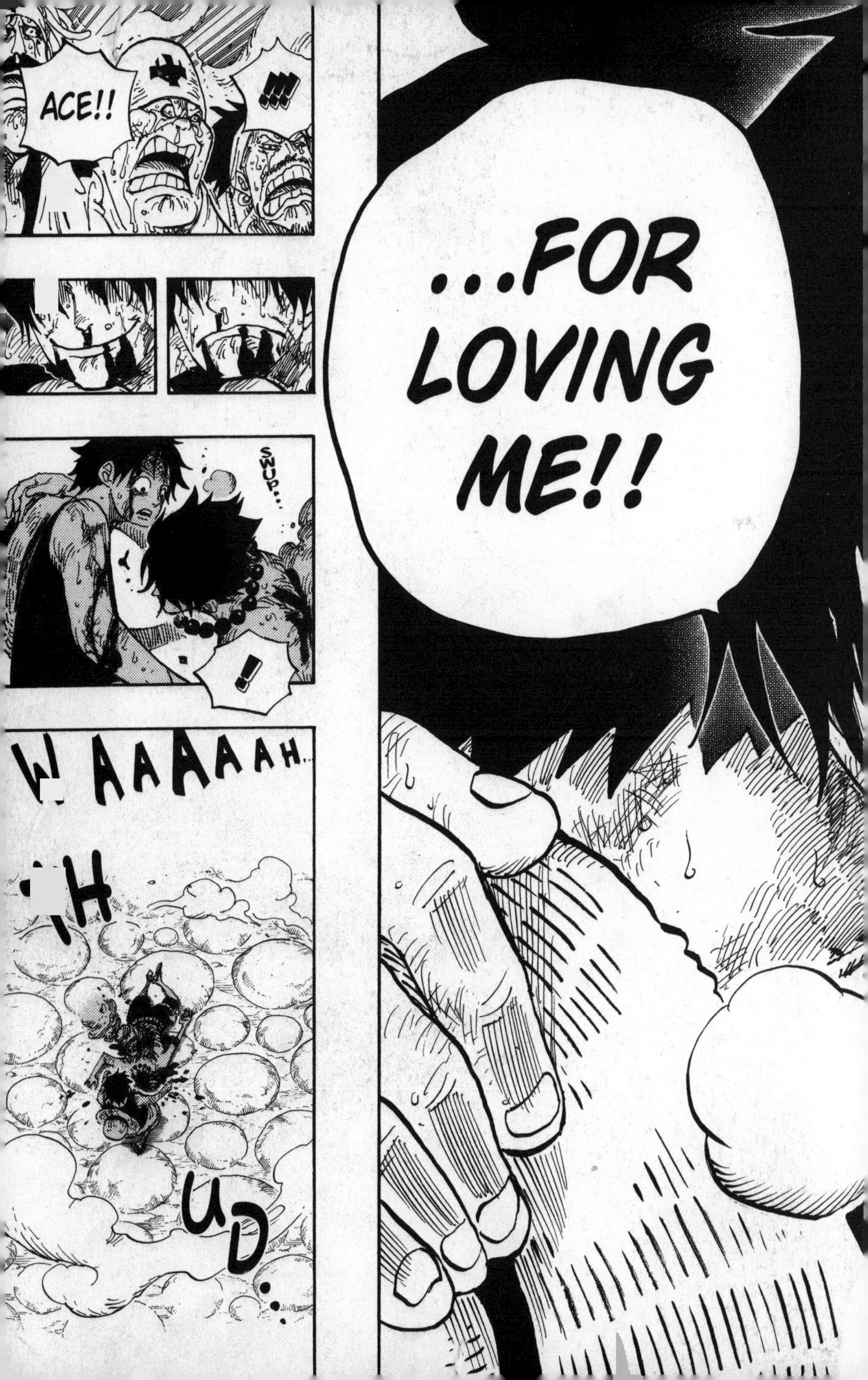
...FOR LOVING ME!!
ACE!!
!!!
SWUP...
!
WAAAAAH...
UD...

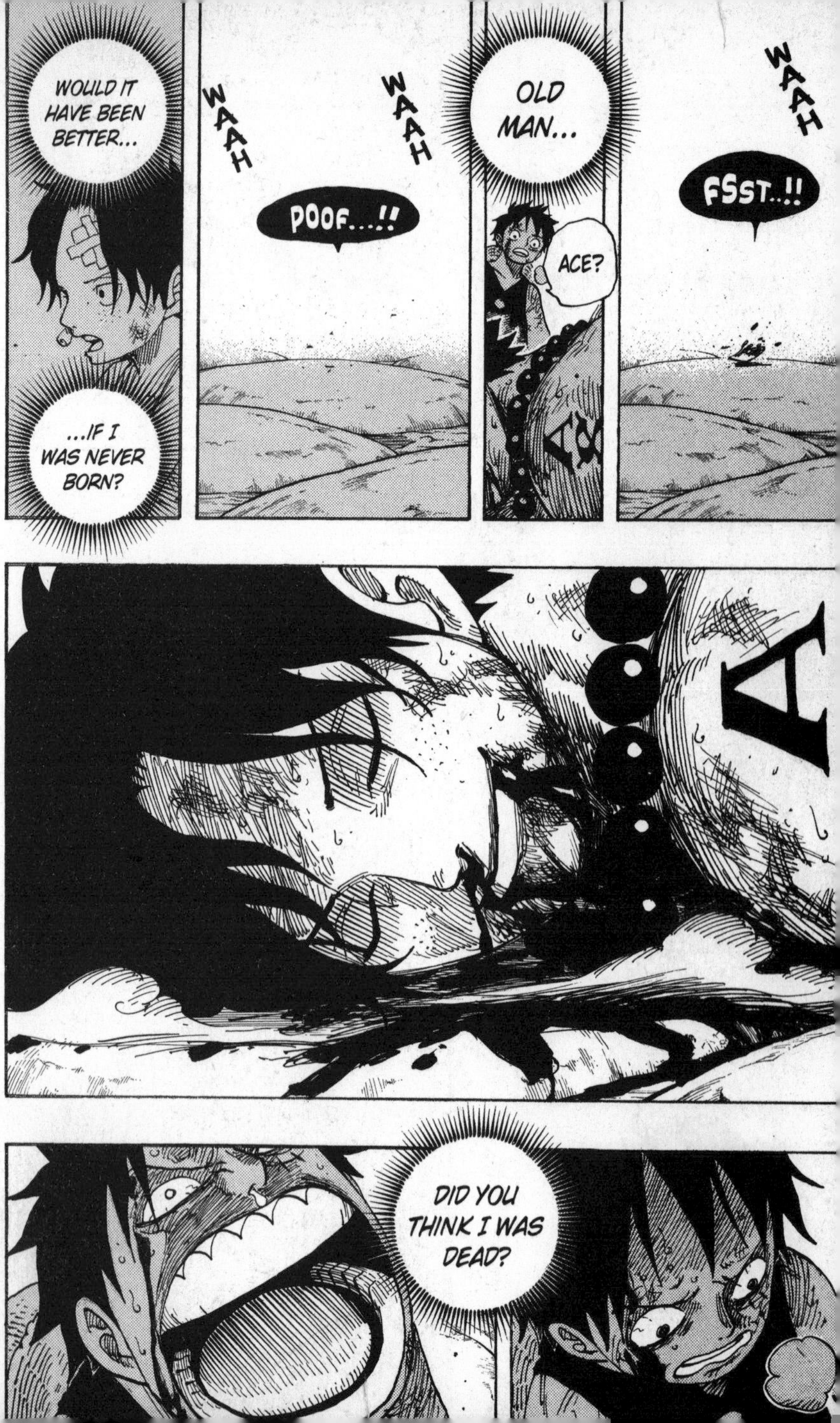
WAAH
FSST..!!
OLD MAN...
ACE?
WAAH
WAAH
POOF...!!
WOULD IT HAVE BEEN BETTER...
...IF I WAS NEVER BORN?
DID YOU THINK I WAS DEAD?

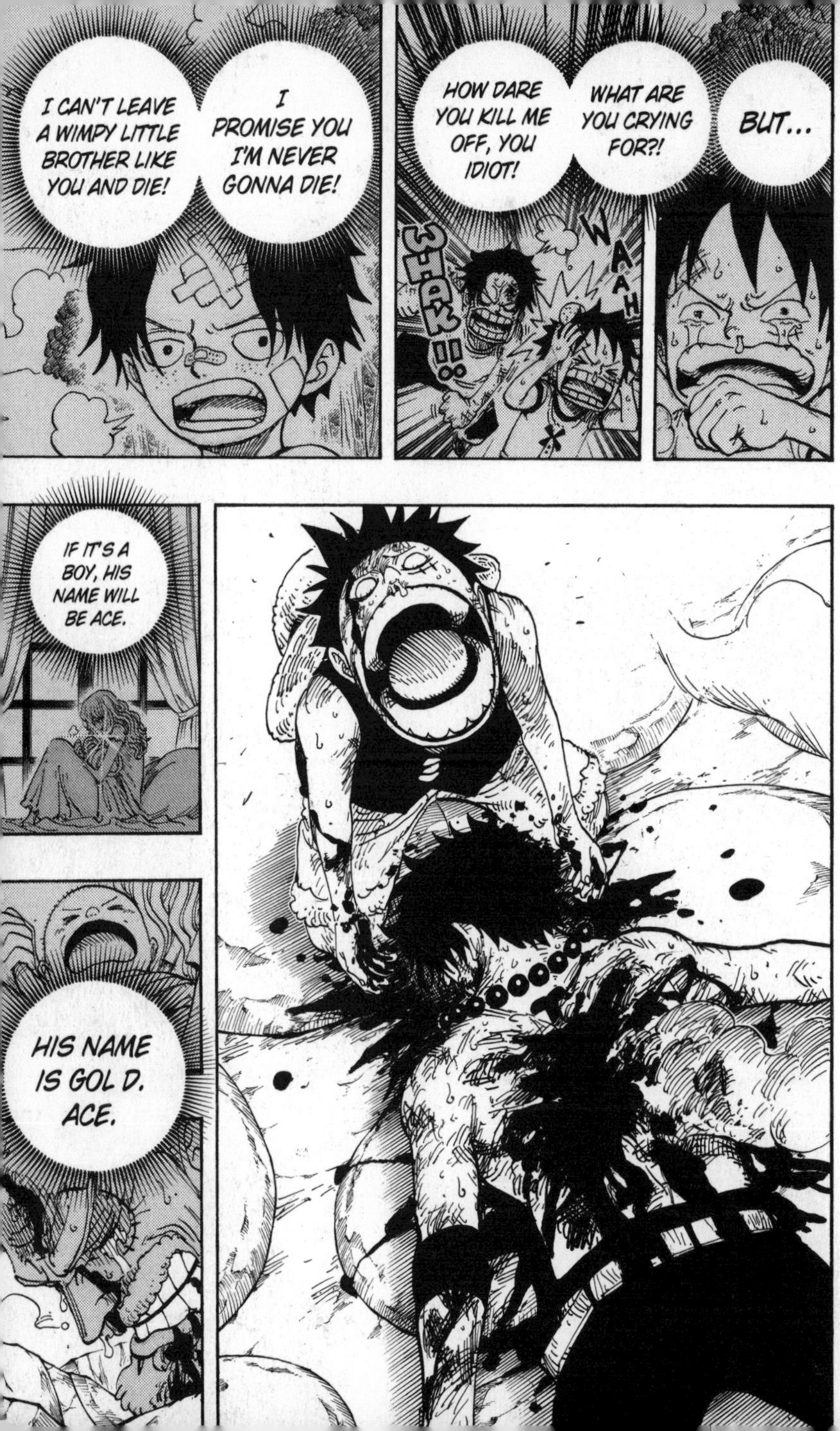
BUT...
WHAT ARE YOU CRYING FOR?!
HOW DARE YOU KILL ME OFF, YOU IDIOT!
WHAK!!
WAAH
I PROMISE YOU I'M NEVER GONNA DIE!
I CAN'T LEAVE A WIMPY LITTLE BROTHER LIKE YOU AND DIE!
IF IT'S A BOY, HIS NAME WILL BE ACE.
HIS NAME IS GOL D. ACE.

Chapter 575: VOICELESS RAGE

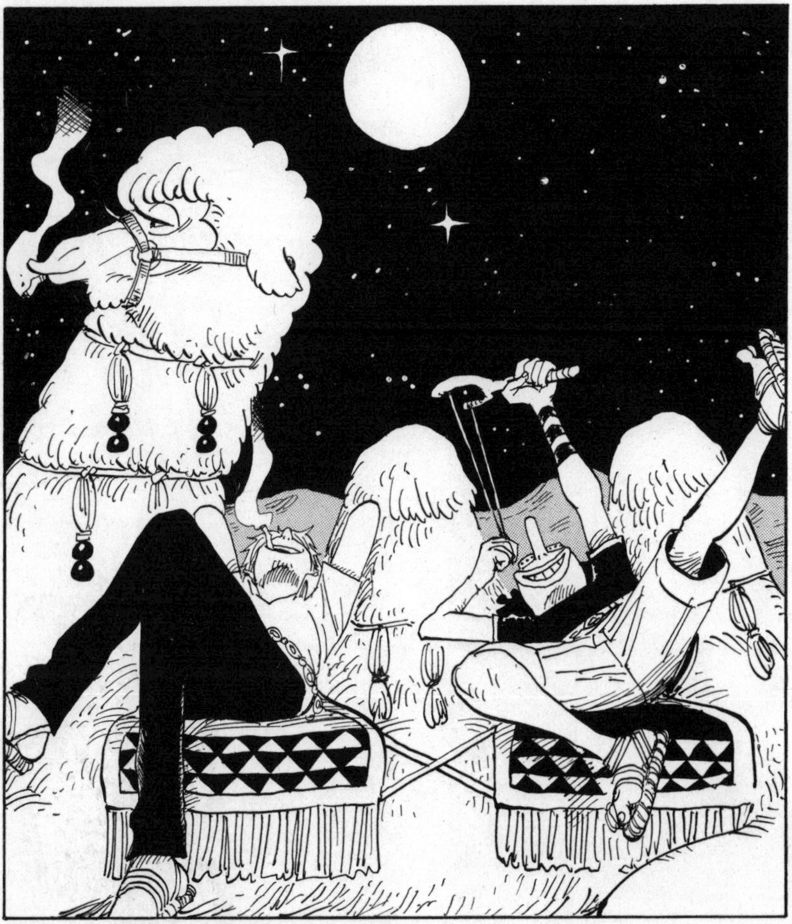

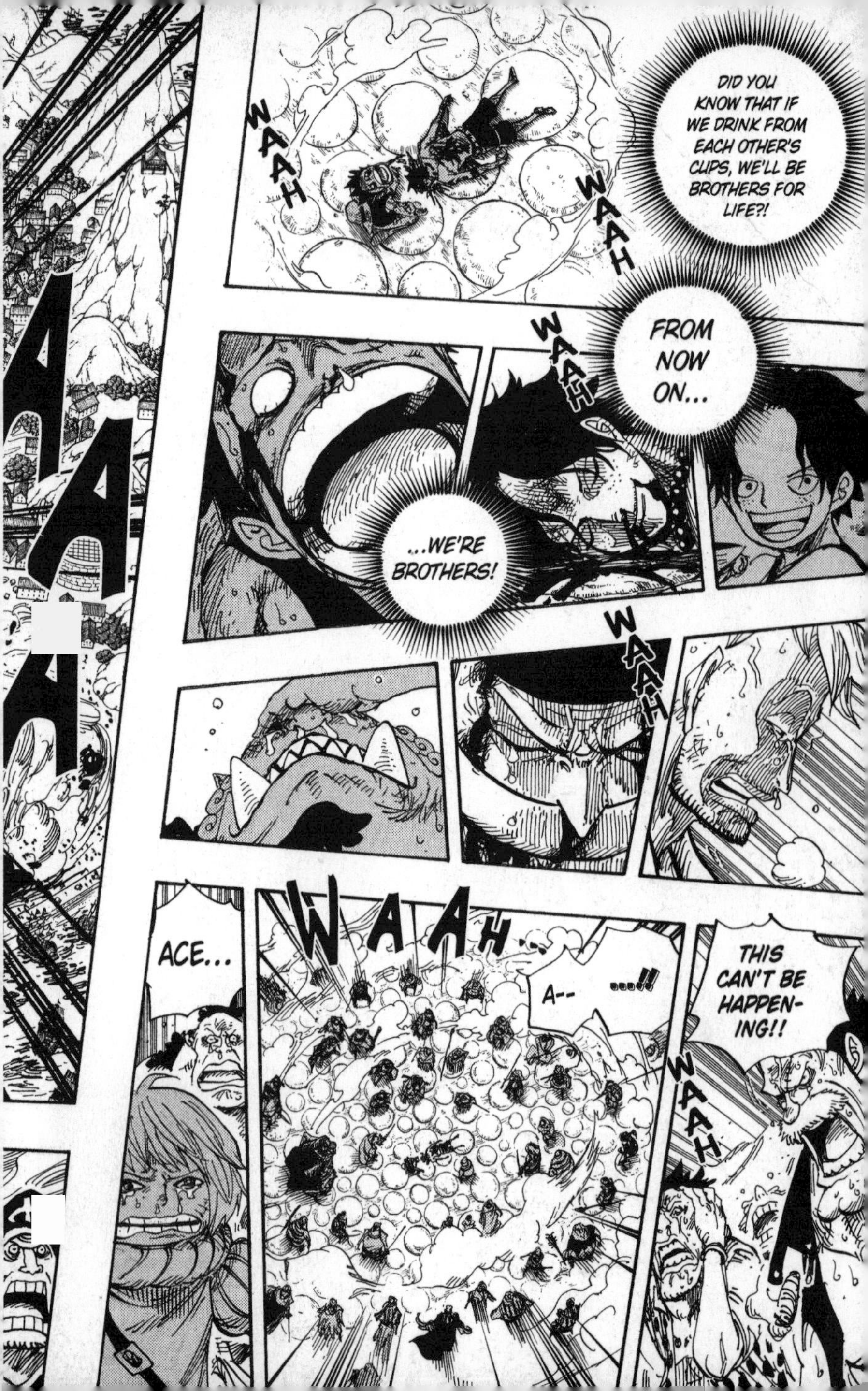
DID YOU KNOW THAT IF WE DRINK FROM EACH OTHER'S CUPS, WE'LL BE BROTHERS FOR LIFE?!
WAAH
WAAH
FROM NOW ON...
WAAH
...WE'RE BROTHERS!
WAAH
THIS CAN'T BE HAPPEN-ING!!
WAAH
WAAH
A-- ...!!
ACE...
A
A
A

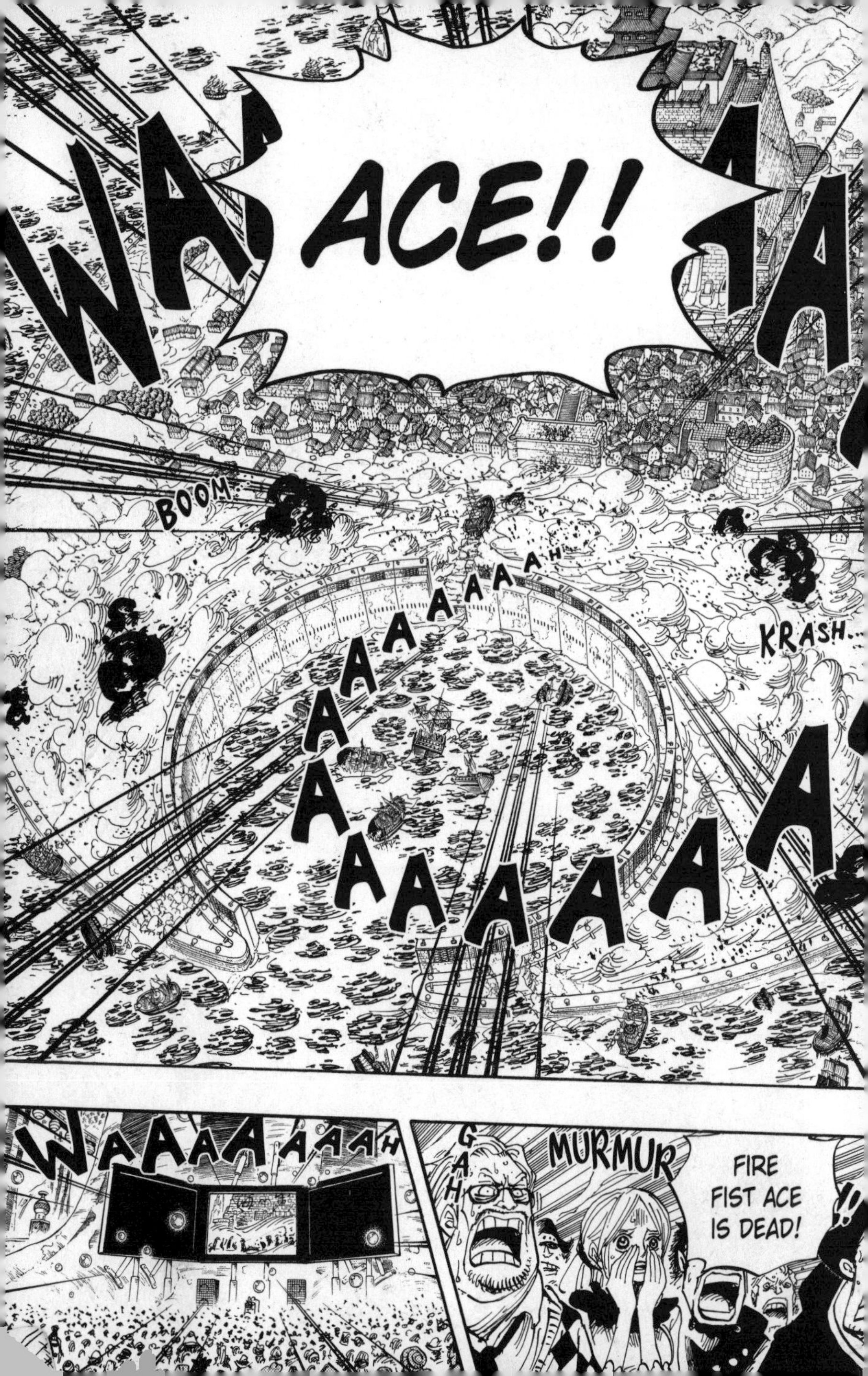
WAA
ACE!!
AAA
BOOM
AAAAAAAAAAAAAAH
KRASH...
AAAAAA
GAH
MURMUR
FIRE FIST ACE IS DEAD!
!!
WAAAAAAAH

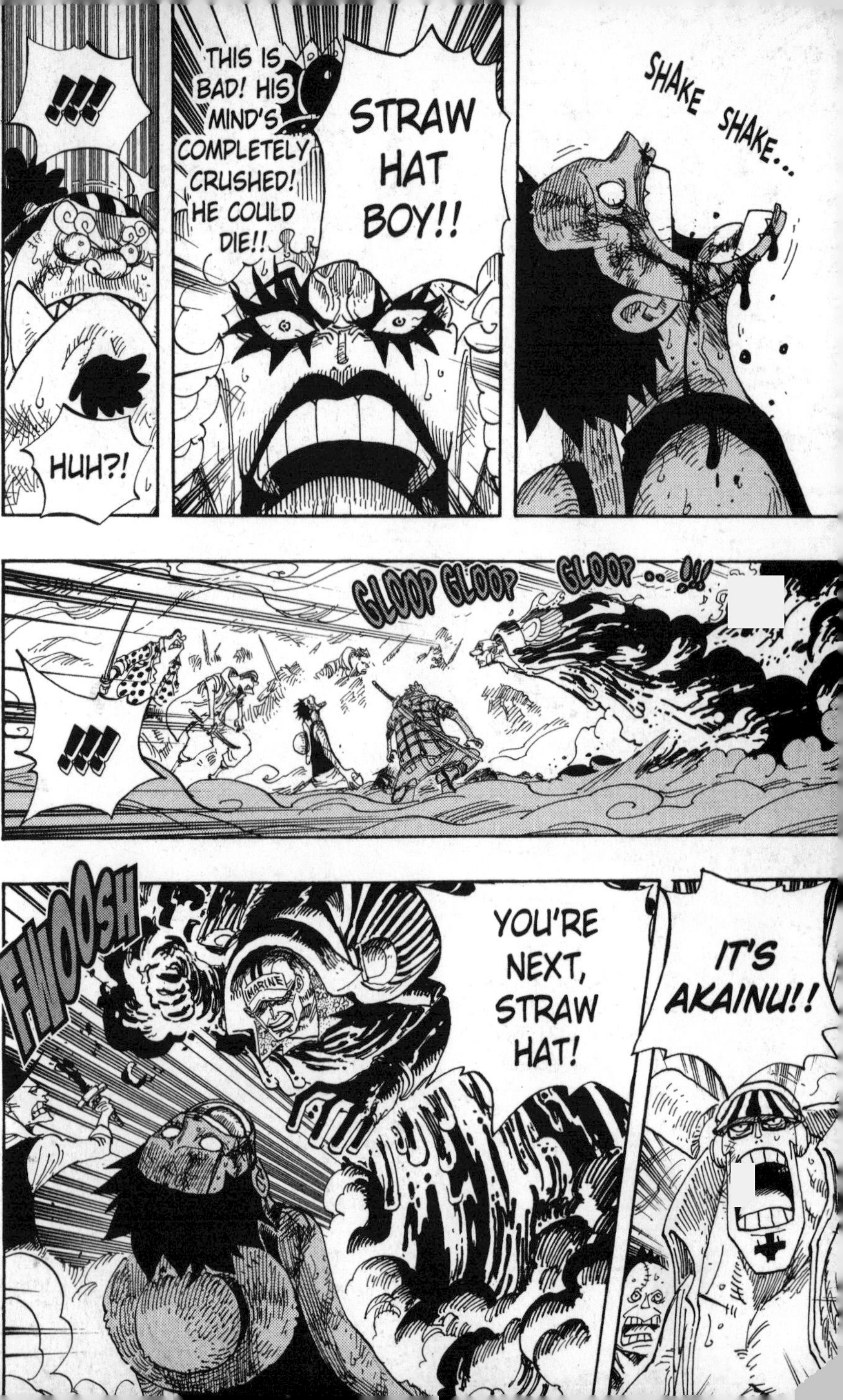
SHAKE SHAKE...
STRAW HAT BOY!!
THIS IS BAD! HIS MIND'S COMPLETELY CRUSHED! HE COULD DIE!!
!!!
HUH?!
GLOOP GLOOP GLOOP..!!!
!!!
IT'S AKAINU!!
YOU'RE NEXT, STRAW HAT!
FWOOSH

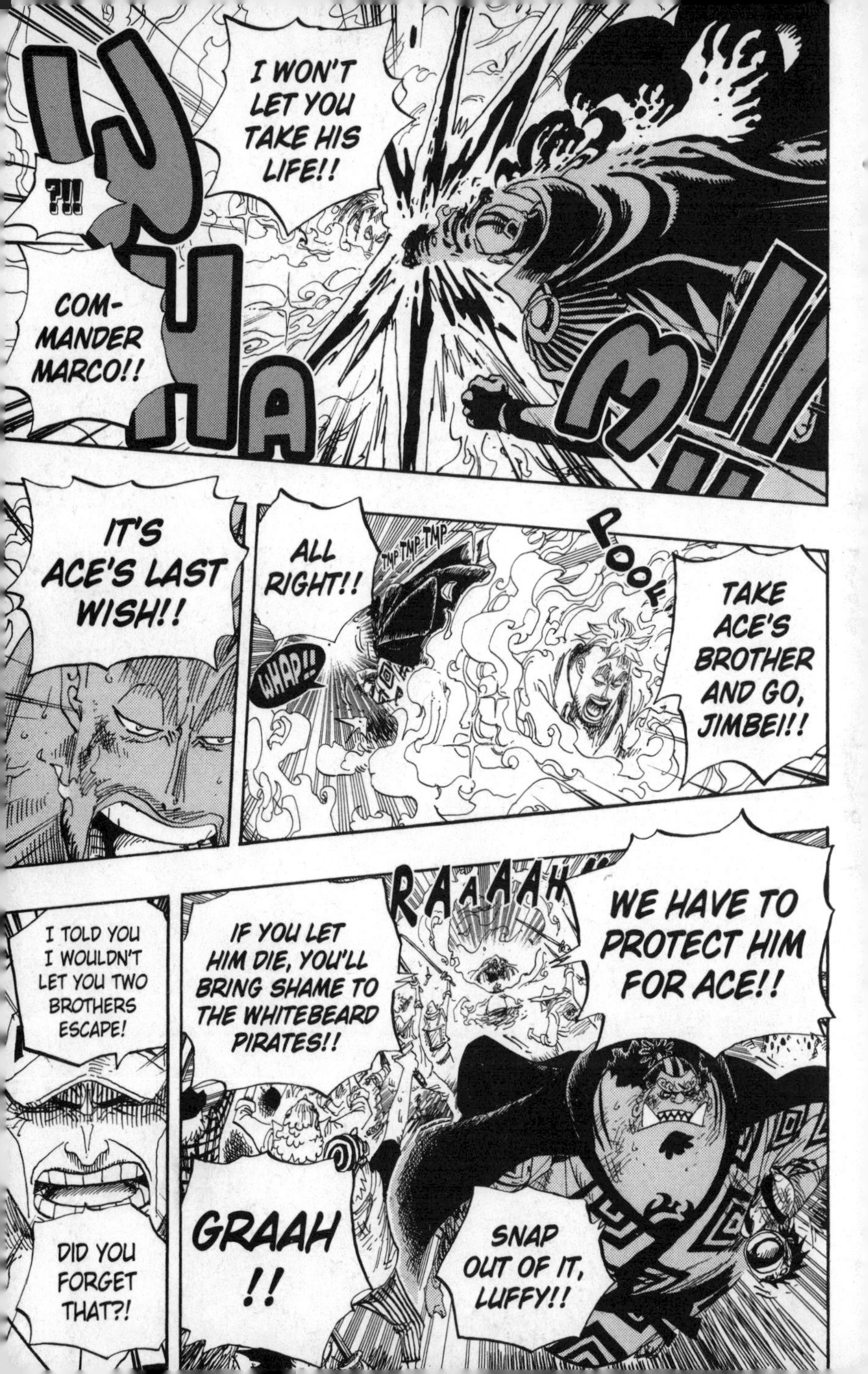
I WON'T LET YOU TAKE HIS LIFE!!
WHAM!!
?!!
COM-MANDER MARCO!!
TAKE ACE'S BROTHER AND GO, JIMBEI!!
POOF
TMP TMP TMP
ALL RIGHT!!
WHAP!!
IT'S ACE'S LAST WISH!!
WE HAVE TO PROTECT HIM FOR ACE!!
RAAAAH
IF YOU LET HIM DIE, YOU'LL BRING SHAME TO THE WHITEBEARD PIRATES!!
SNAP OUT OF IT, LUFFY!!
GRAAH!!
I TOLD YOU I WOULDN'T LET YOU TWO BROTHERS ESCAPE!
DID YOU FORGET THAT?!

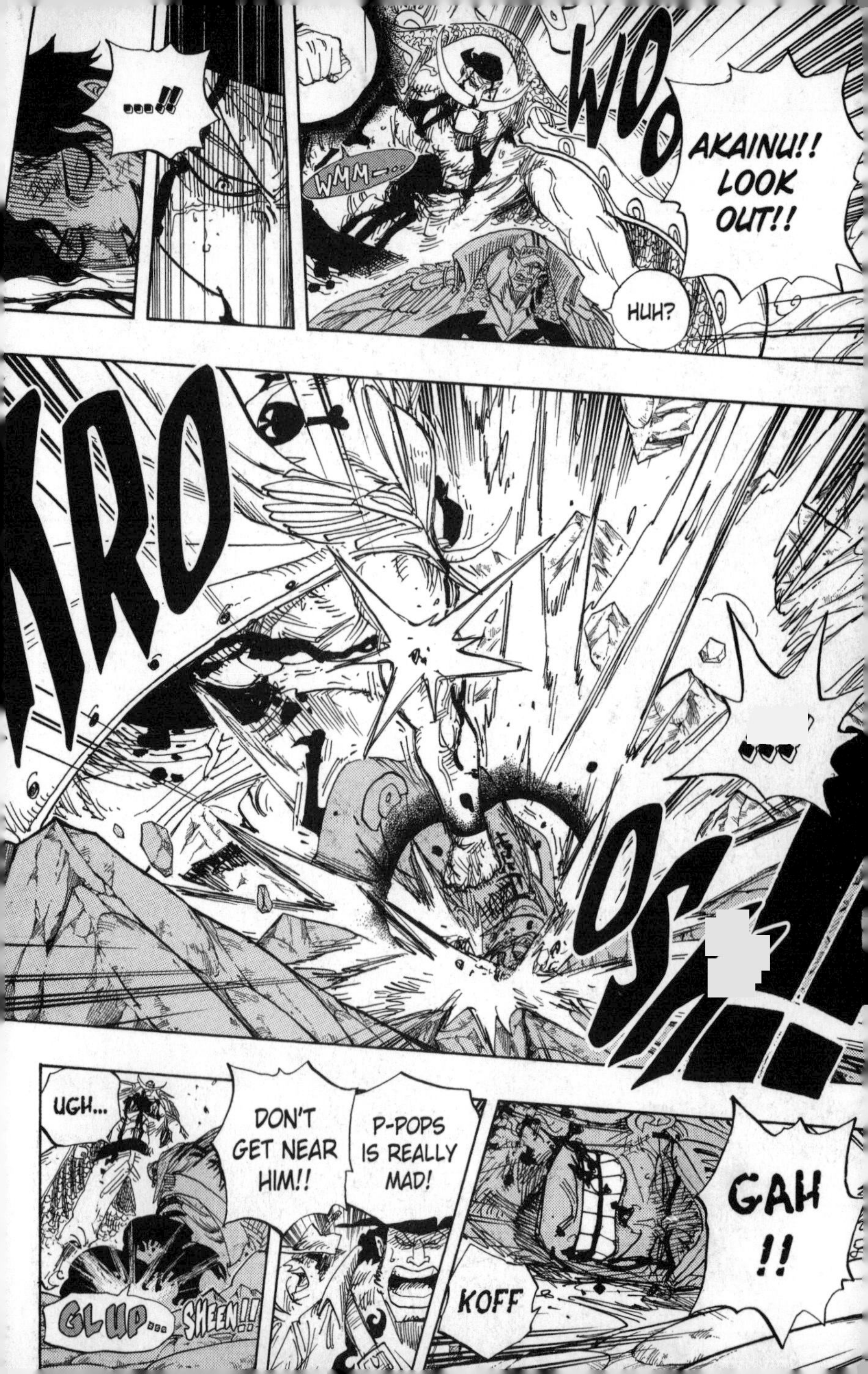

WOO
AKAINU!! LOOK OUT!!
WMM-...
HUH?
...!!
GAH !!
KOFF
P-POPS IS REALLY MAD!
DON'T GET NEAR HIM!!
UGH...
GLUP...
SHEEN!!

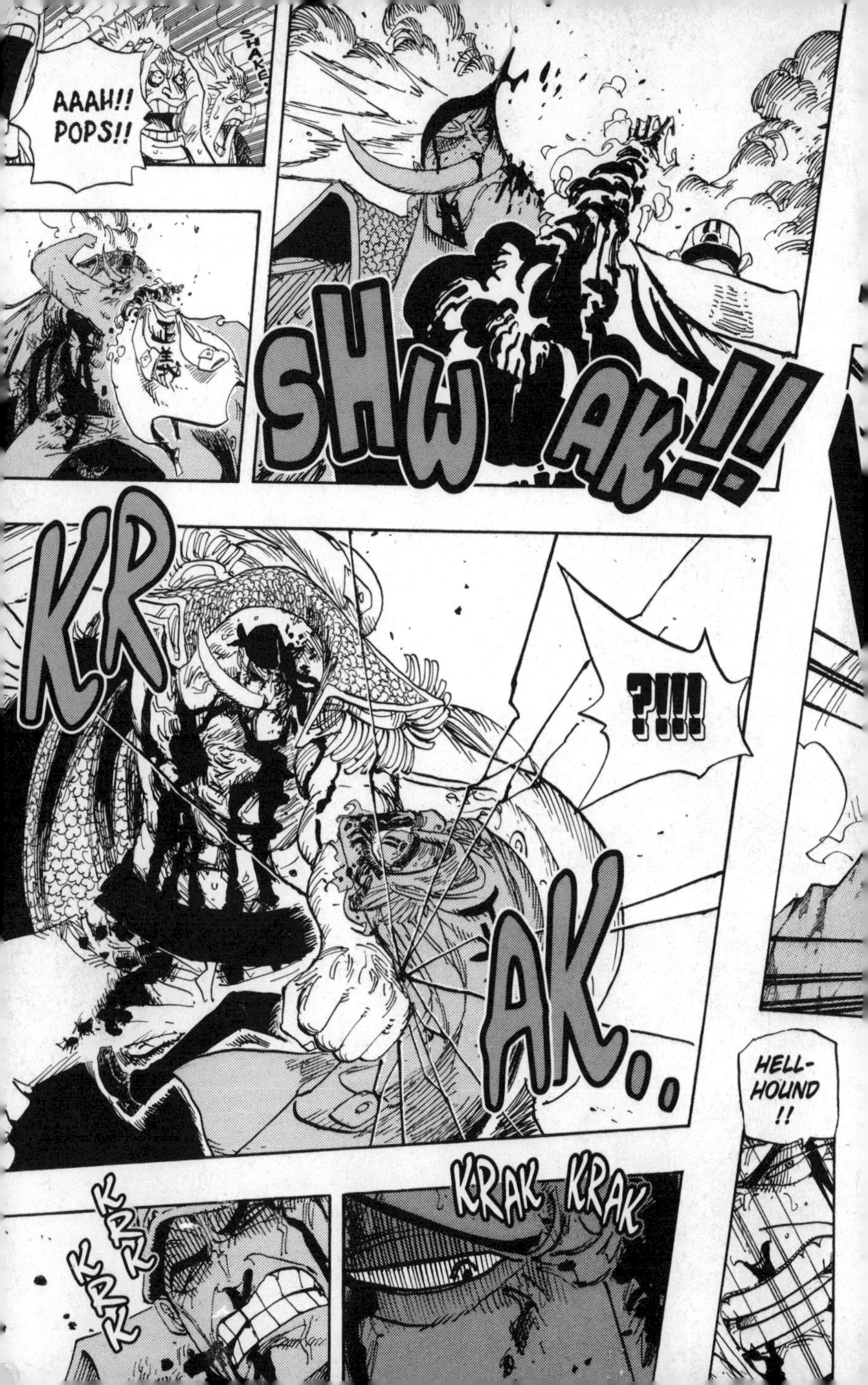
SHWAK!!
SHAKE...
AAAH!! POPS!!
?!!!
KRAK..
HELL-HOUND!!
KRAK KRAK
KRRK KRRK

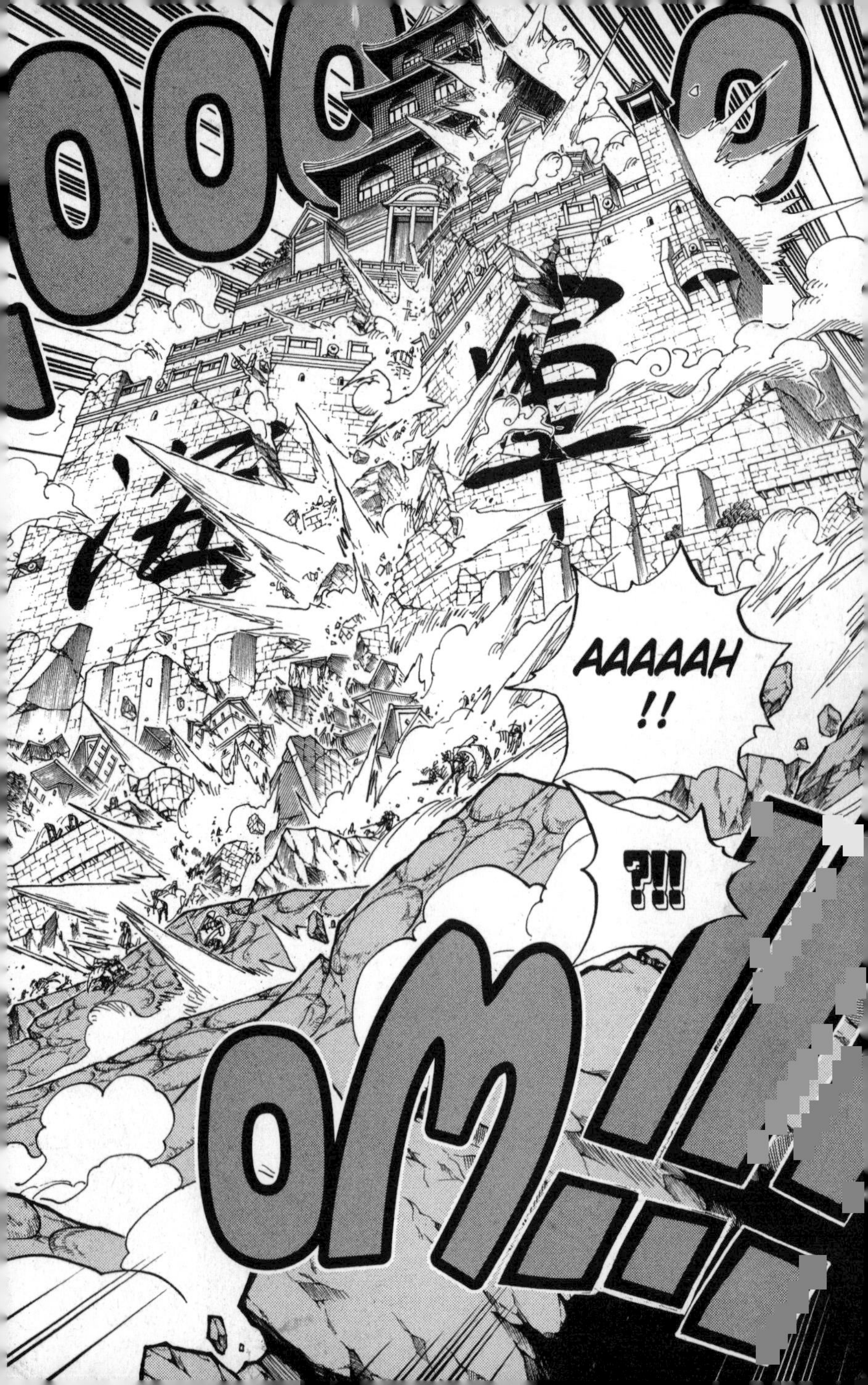
AAAAAH !!
?!!
OOM!!

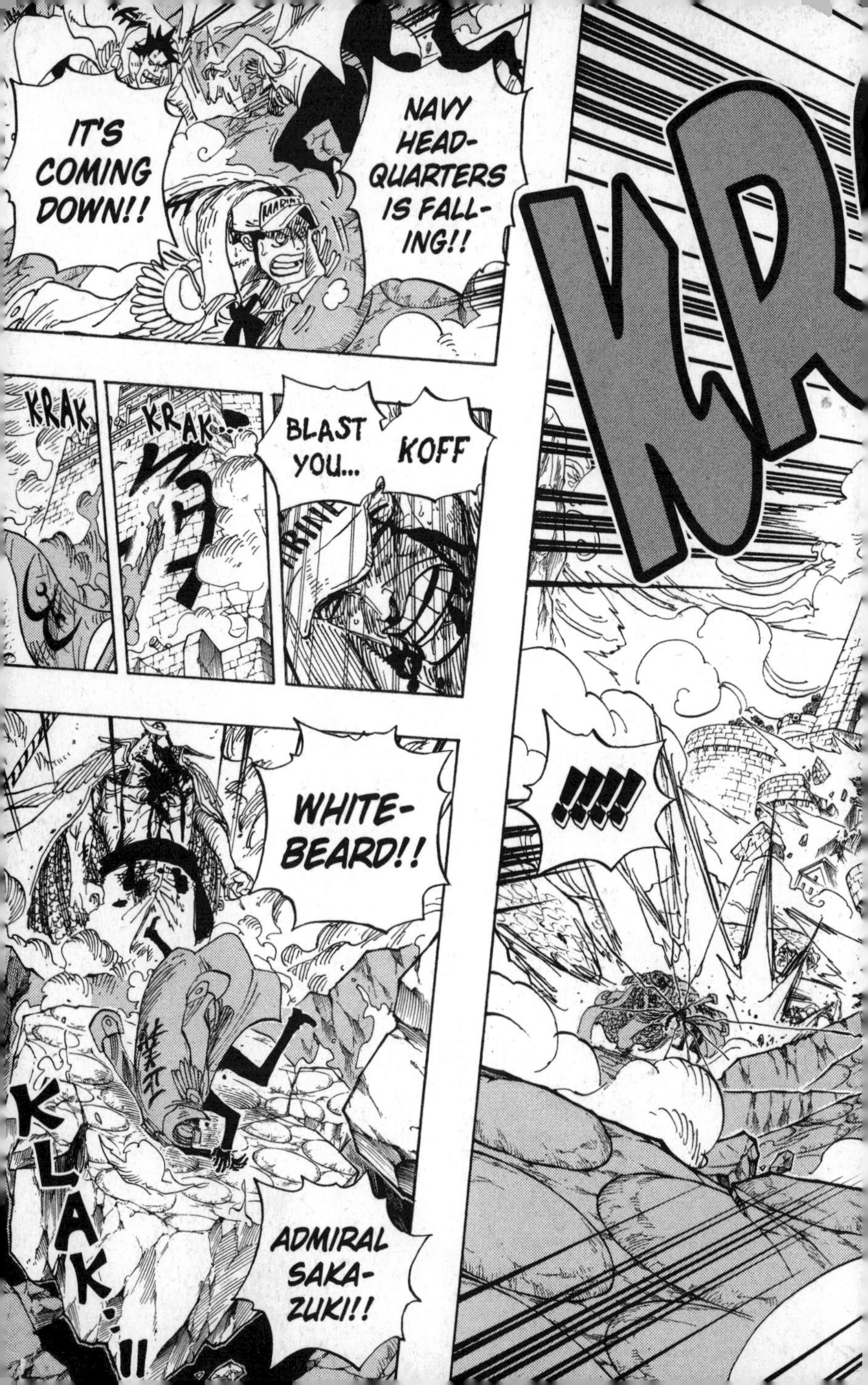
KR
NAVY HEAD-QUARTERS IS FALL-ING!!
IT'S COMING DOWN!!
BLAST YOU... KOFF
KRAK...
KRAK
!!!!
WHITE-BEARD!!
ADMIRAL SAKA-ZUKI!!
KLLAK!!

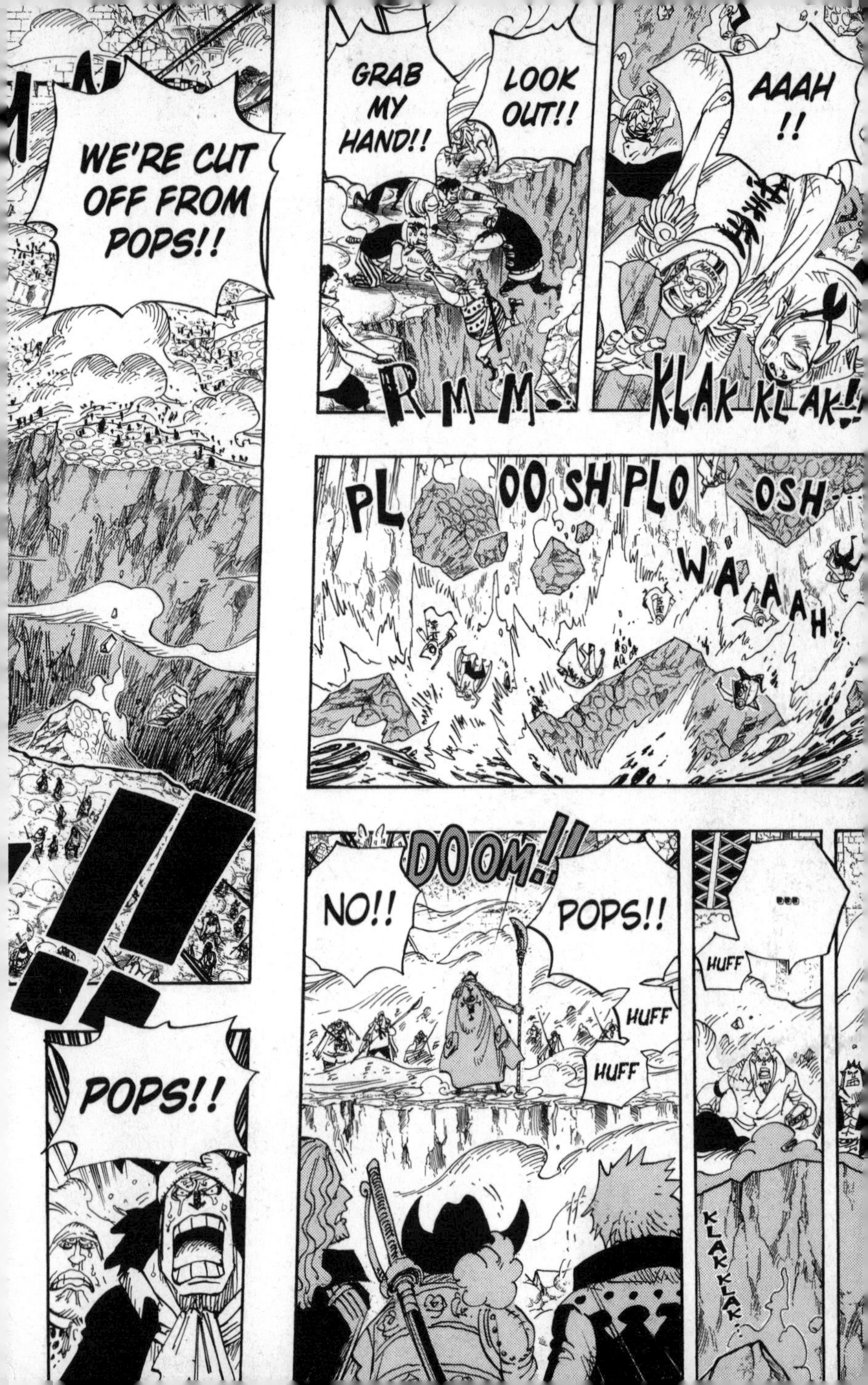
AAAH !!
KLAK KLAK!!
LOOK OUT!!
GRAB MY HAND!!
RMM...
PLOOSH PLOOSH
WAAAAH...
...
HUFF
KLAK KLAK...
DOOM!!
POPS!!
NO!!
HUFF
HUFF
WE'RE CUT OFF FROM POPS!!
!!
POPS!!

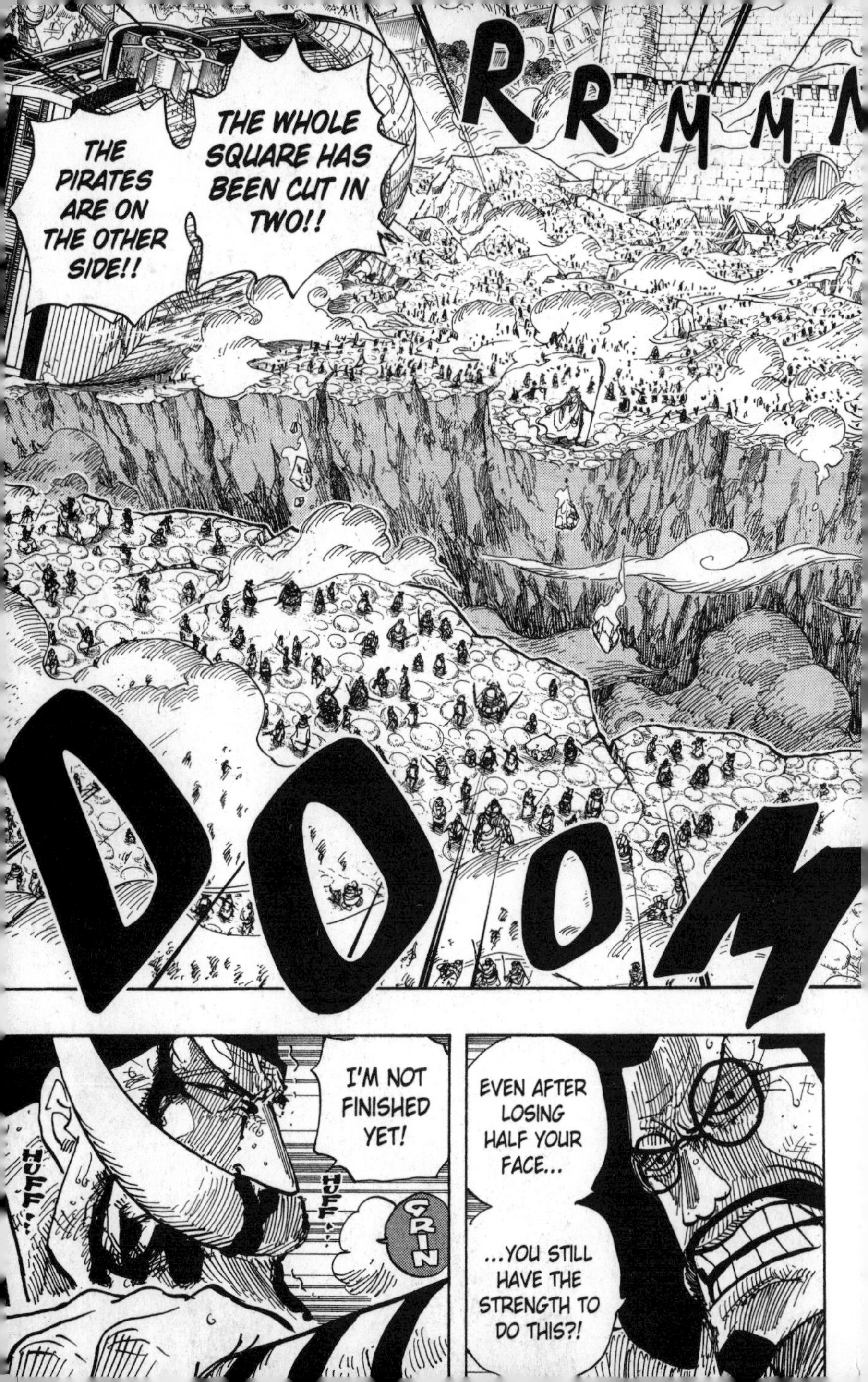
RRMMM
THE WHOLE SQUARE HAS BEEN CUT IN TWO!!
THE PIRATES ARE ON THE OTHER SIDE!!
DOOM
EVEN AFTER LOSING HALF YOUR FACE...
...YOU STILL HAVE THE STRENGTH TO DO THIS?!
I'M NOT FINISHED YET!
HUFF...
HUFF...
GRIN

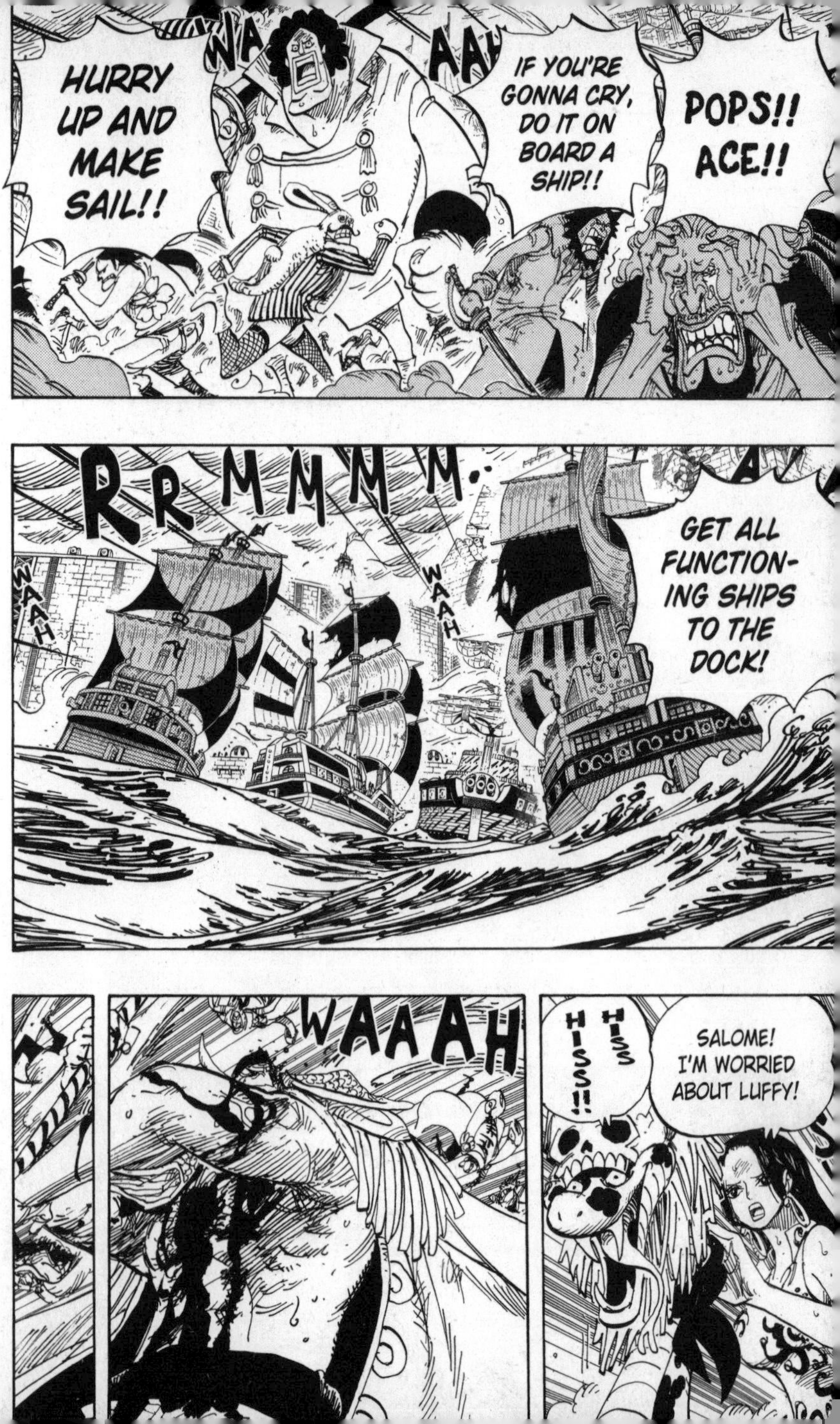
POPS!! ACE!!
IF YOU'RE GONNA CRY, DO IT ON BOARD A SHIP!!
WA AAH
HURRY UP AND MAKE SAIL!!
RRMMMM..
GET ALL FUNCTION-ING SHIPS TO THE DOCK!
WAAAH
WAAAH
SALOME! I'M WORRIED ABOUT LUFFY!
HISS
HISS!!
WAAAH

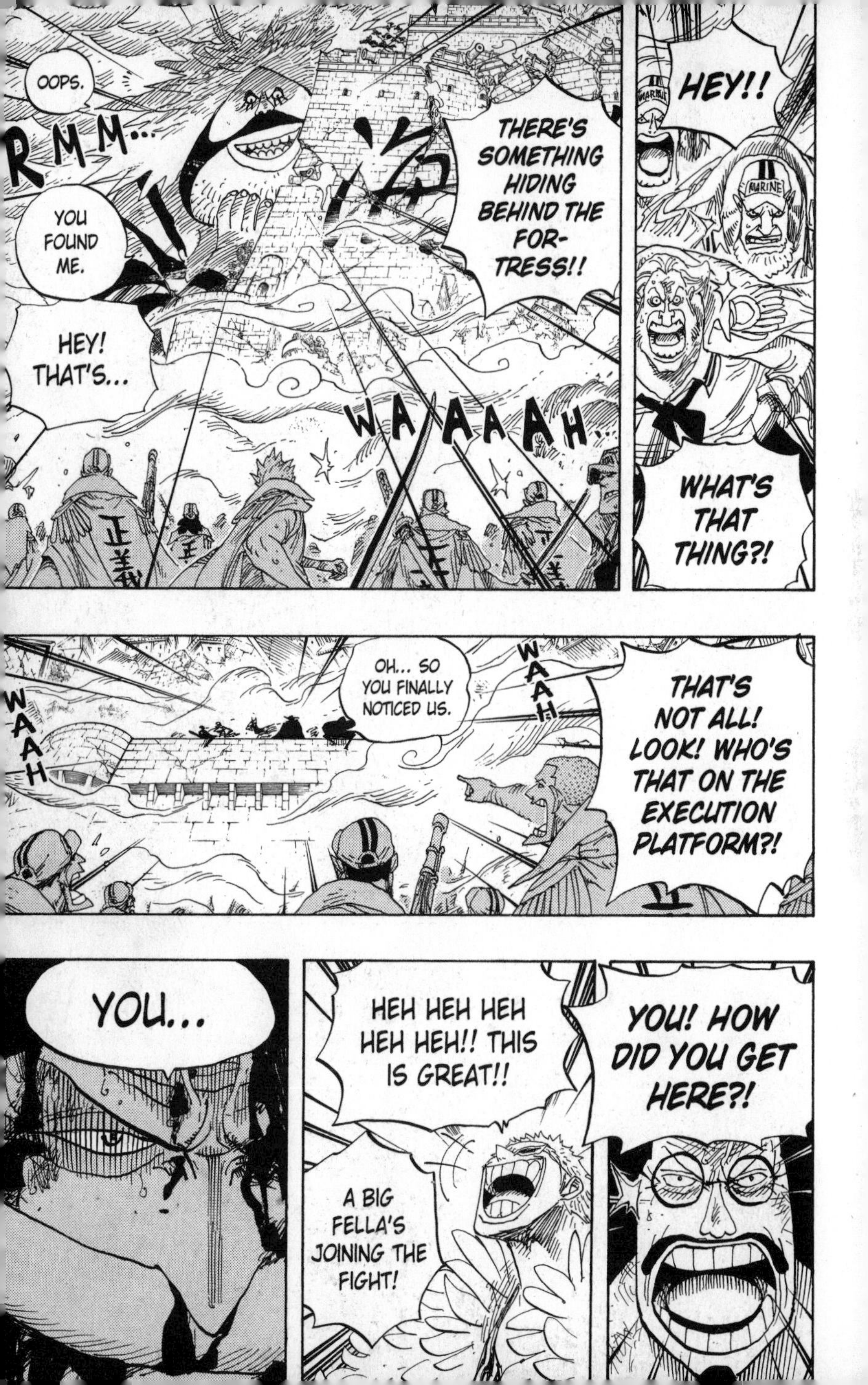
HEY!!
WHAT'S THAT THING?!
THERE'S SOMETHING HIDING BEHIND THE FOR-TRESS!!
OOPS.
RMM...
YOU FOUND ME.
HEY! THAT'S...
WAAAAH...
THAT'S NOT ALL! LOOK! WHO'S THAT ON THE EXECUTION PLATFORM?!
WAAH
OH... SO YOU FINALLY NOTICED US.
WAAH
YOU! HOW DID YOU GET HERE?!
HEH HEH HEH HEH HEH!! THIS IS GREAT!!
A BIG FELLA'S JOINING THE FIGHT!
YOU...

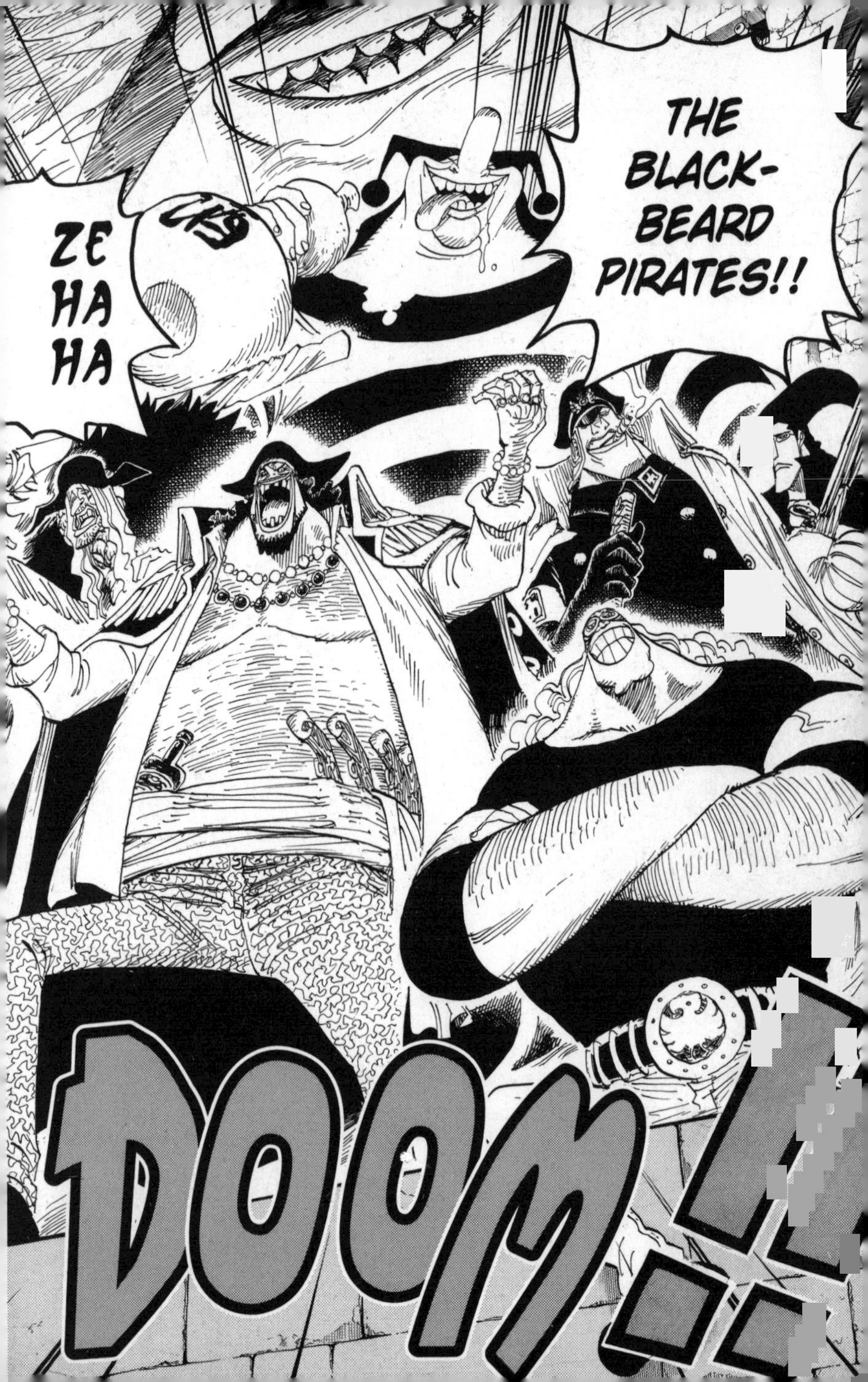
THE BLACK-BEARD PIRATES!!
ZE HA HA HA
DOOM..!!

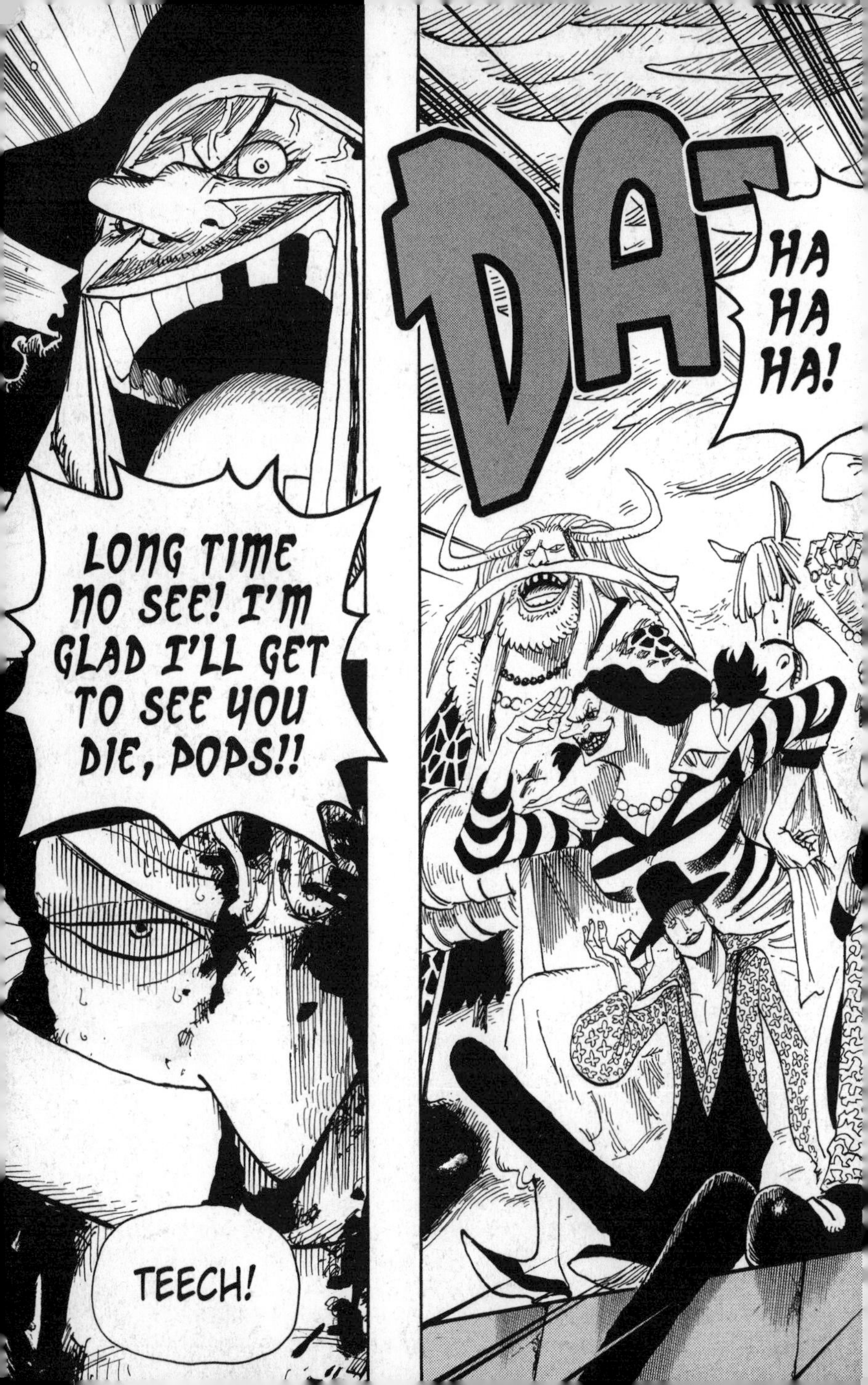
DA
HA HA HA!
LONG TIME NO SEE! I'M GLAD I'LL GET TO SEE YOU DIE, POPS!!
TEECH!

質問コーナー
エスビーエス
SBS

(Ponio, Aichi)

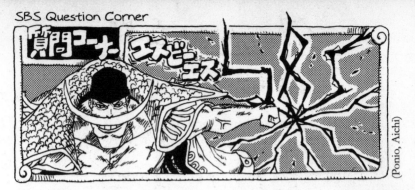

Reader(Q): Hello, Mr. Oda. We can now borrow *One Piece* from the library. If a volume's not available in the neighborhood library, we can have one sent in from another one in the same city through the library's network. Even if the library in your city doesn't have a copy of *One Piece,* you can just put in a request to have them include it. Now even small children can read *One Piece* for free. Anyway let's start SBS.

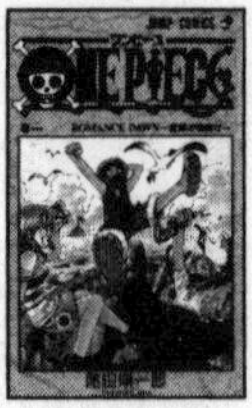

--Faint Hollyhock

Oda(A): *Gasp*!? Oh, it's already started?! You freaked me out! I was reading what you were saying so intently. Wow, they have manga in libraries now?! I see. That's something I didn't expect...and hadn't heard before. Manga in a library?! Well, this should be great for the little kids. Let's go to our local library! Speaking of free stuff, you can go to ONE PIECE WEB on the Internet to see a summary of the stories for free too.

Q: Odattsu!
VSH
(this is so old...) Sit down! Put away your smut rags! This is about old man Garp's disappearing scar! I had lots of free time so I checked through chapter 580 and discovered...25 instances! (BOOM!) Though it's highly subjective, that's how many I found. He doesn't appear that much, but his scar sometimes disappears really obviously. I guess everyone makes mistakes. I'm going to assume that you intend to apologize, so as punishment, I'm going to confiscate your favorite book that you hide behind your cupboard.

--Shimeji SP

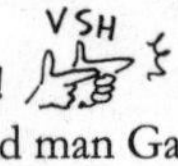

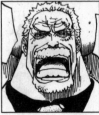

A: Look at it this way... Maybe when his sworn enemies come close to him...his scar actually becomes more visible. Something like that? That's why you don't normally see the scar. It's a special kind of scar that comes out only during special circumstances. WHAT AM I SUPPOSED TO DO WITH THIS?! Maybe it's a mistake when you see the scar! (Okay, that's not true.) Anyway, give me back my book! Give me back my book! I'll be more careful next time so give it back to me!

Chapter 576:
THE GREAT PIRATE EDWARD NEWGATE

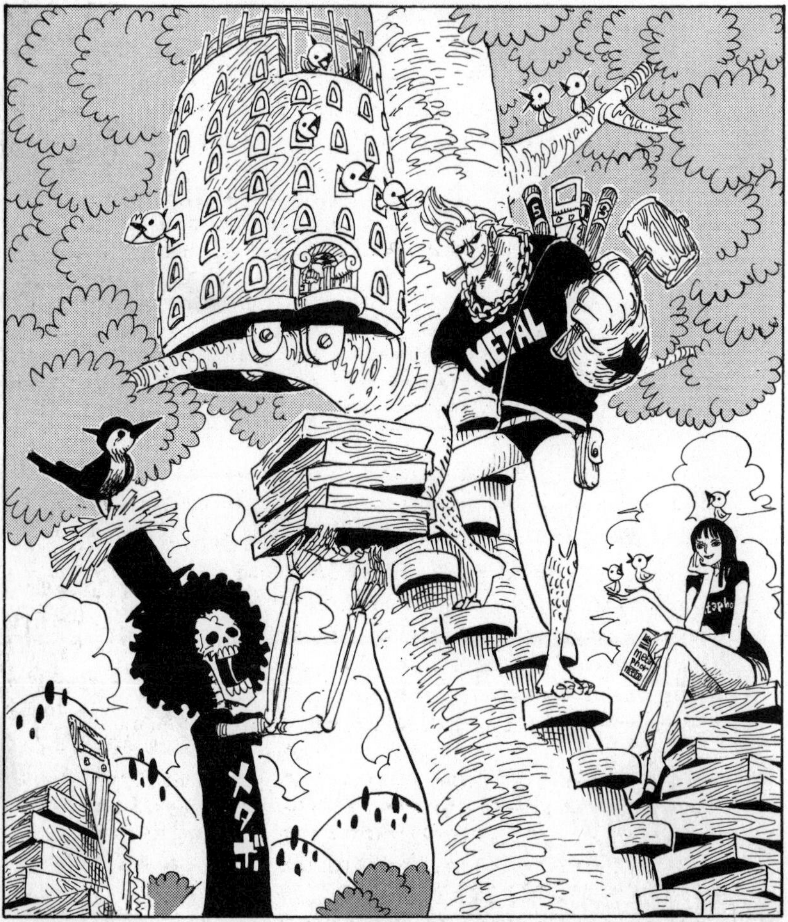
METAL
メタボ

*SHIRT SAYS "METABO." SHORT FOR METABOLIC SYNDROME.

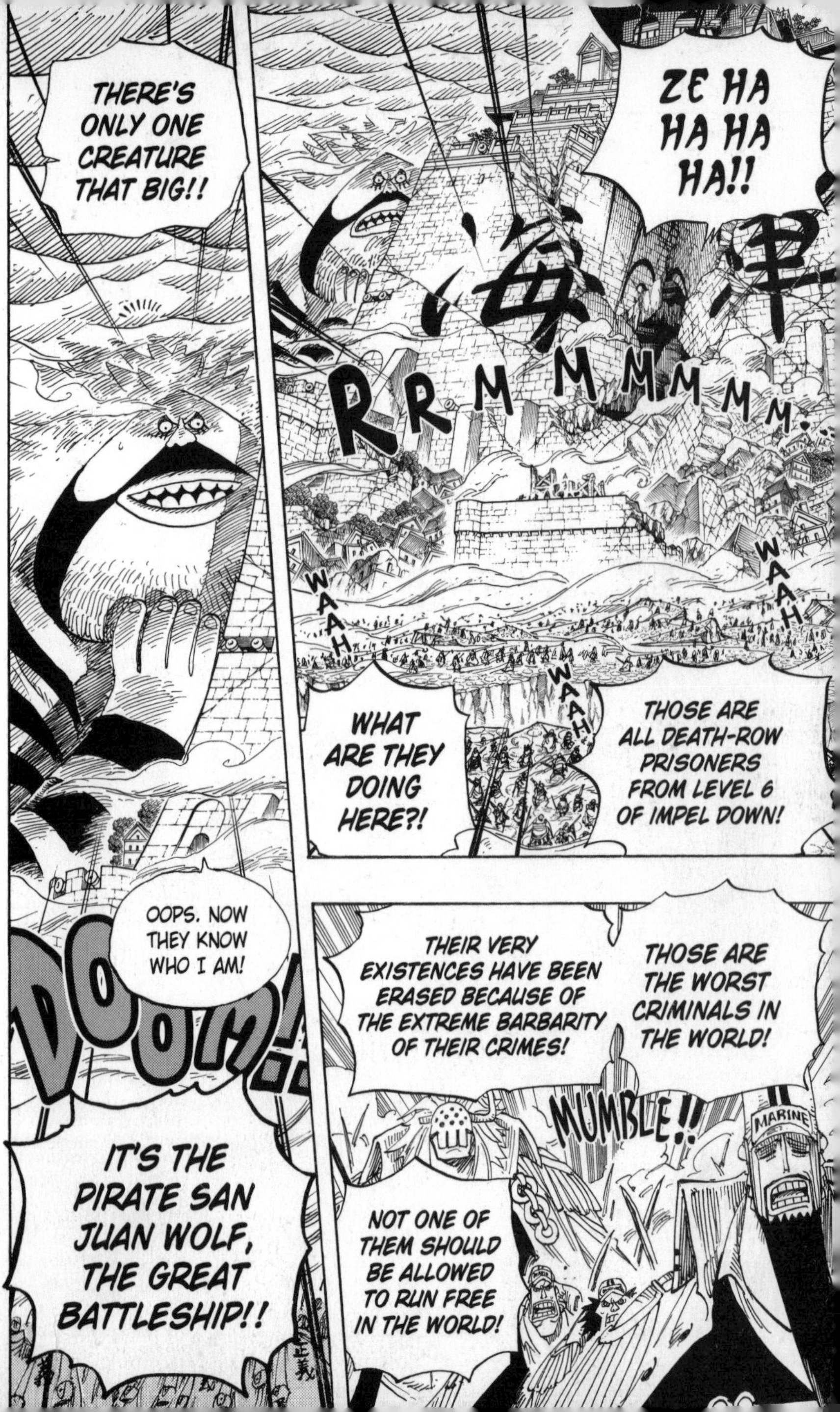
ZE HA HA HA HA!!
海 軍
RRMMMMMMM
WAAH
WAAH
WAAH
THOSE ARE ALL DEATH-ROW PRISONERS FROM LEVEL 6 OF IMPEL DOWN!
WHAT ARE THEY DOING HERE?!
THOSE ARE THE WORST CRIMINALS IN THE WORLD!
THEIR VERY EXISTENCES HAVE BEEN ERASED BECAUSE OF THE EXTREME BARBARITY OF THEIR CRIMES!
MUMBLE!!
MARINE
NOT ONE OF THEM SHOULD BE ALLOWED TO RUN FREE IN THE WORLD!
THERE'S ONLY ONE CREATURE THAT BIG!!
OOPS. NOW THEY KNOW WHO I AM!
DOOM!!
IT'S THE PIRATE SAN JUAN WOLF, THE GREAT BATTLESHIP!!

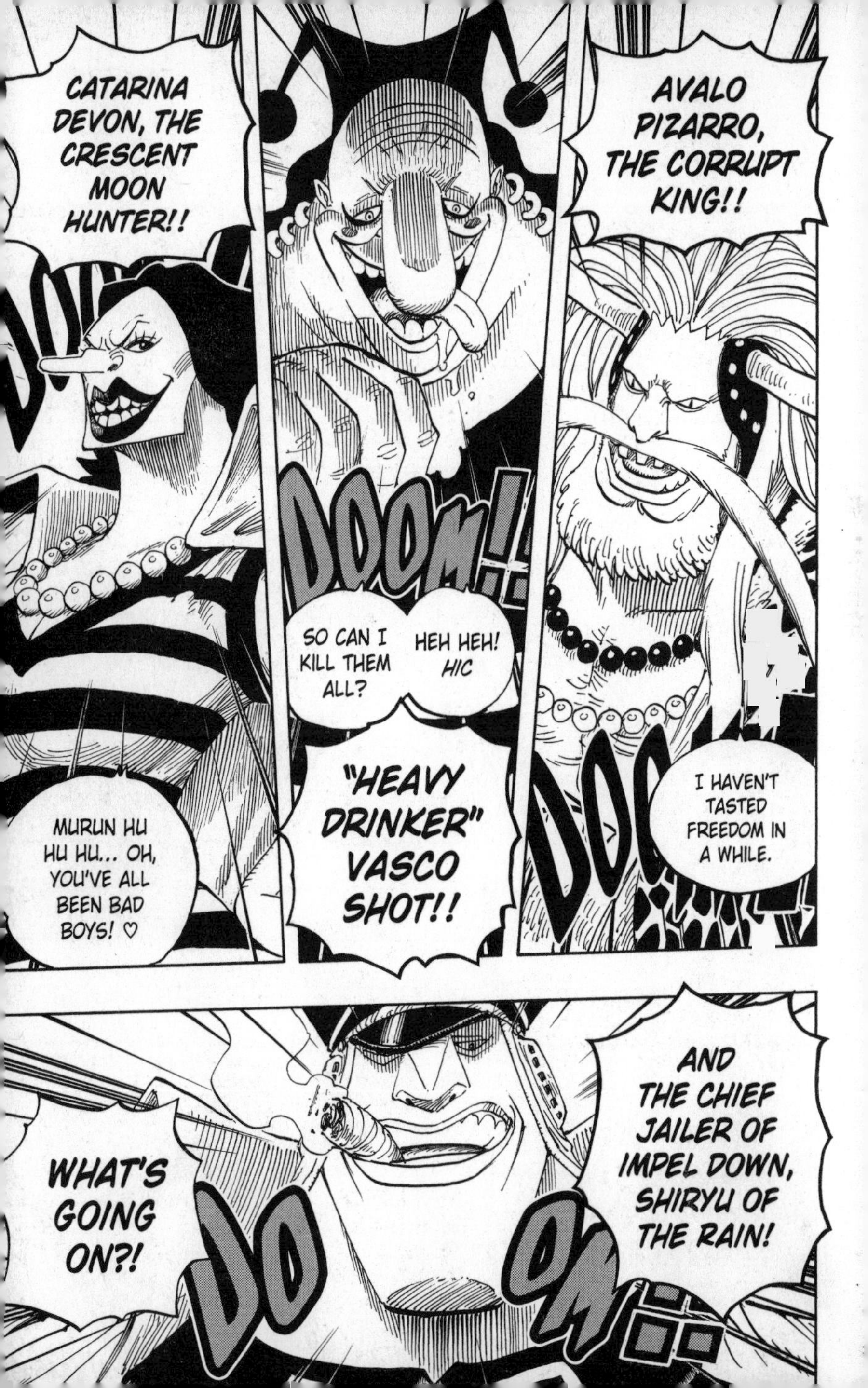
AVALO PIZARRO, THE CORRUPT KING!!
I HAVEN'T TASTED FREEDOM IN A WHILE.
DOOM!!
HEH HEH! HIC
SO CAN I KILL THEM ALL?
"HEAVY DRINKER" VASCO SHOT!!
CATARINA DEVON, THE CRESCENT MOON HUNTER!!
MURUN HU HU HU... OH, YOU'VE ALL BEEN BAD BOYS! ♡
AND THE CHIEF JAILER OF IMPEL DOWN, SHIRYU OF THE RAIN!
DO OM
WHAT'S GOING ON?!

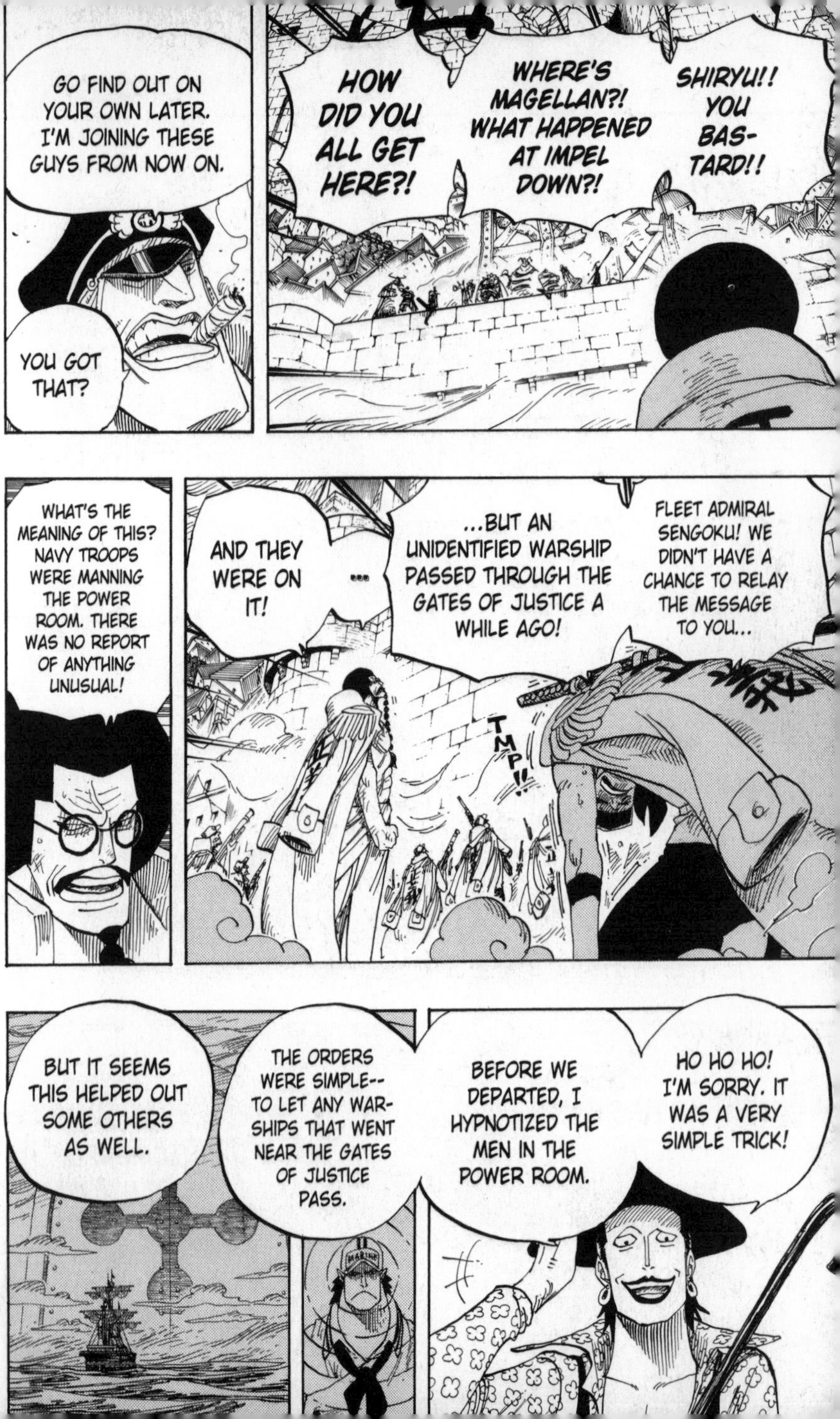
SHIRYU!! YOU BAS- TARD!!
WHERE'S MAGELLAN?! WHAT HAPPENED AT IMPEL DOWN?!
HOW DID YOU ALL GET HERE?!
GO FIND OUT ON YOUR OWN LATER. I'M JOINING THESE GUYS FROM NOW ON.
YOU GOT THAT?
FLEET ADMIRAL SENGOKU! WE DIDN'T HAVE A CHANCE TO RELAY THE MESSAGE TO YOU...
...BUT AN UNIDENTIFIED WARSHIP PASSED THROUGH THE GATES OF JUSTICE A WHILE AGO!
...
AND THEY WERE ON IT!
TMP!!
WHAT'S THE MEANING OF THIS? NAVY TROOPS WERE MANNING THE POWER ROOM. THERE WAS NO REPORT OF ANYTHING UNUSUAL!
HO HO HO! I'M SORRY. IT WAS A VERY SIMPLE TRICK!
BEFORE WE DEPARTED, I HYPNOTIZED THE MEN IN THE POWER ROOM.
MARINE
THE ORDERS WERE SIMPLE-- TO LET ANY WAR- SHIPS THAT WENT NEAR THE GATES OF JUSTICE PASS.
BUT IT SEEMS THIS HELPED OUT SOME OTHERS AS WELL.

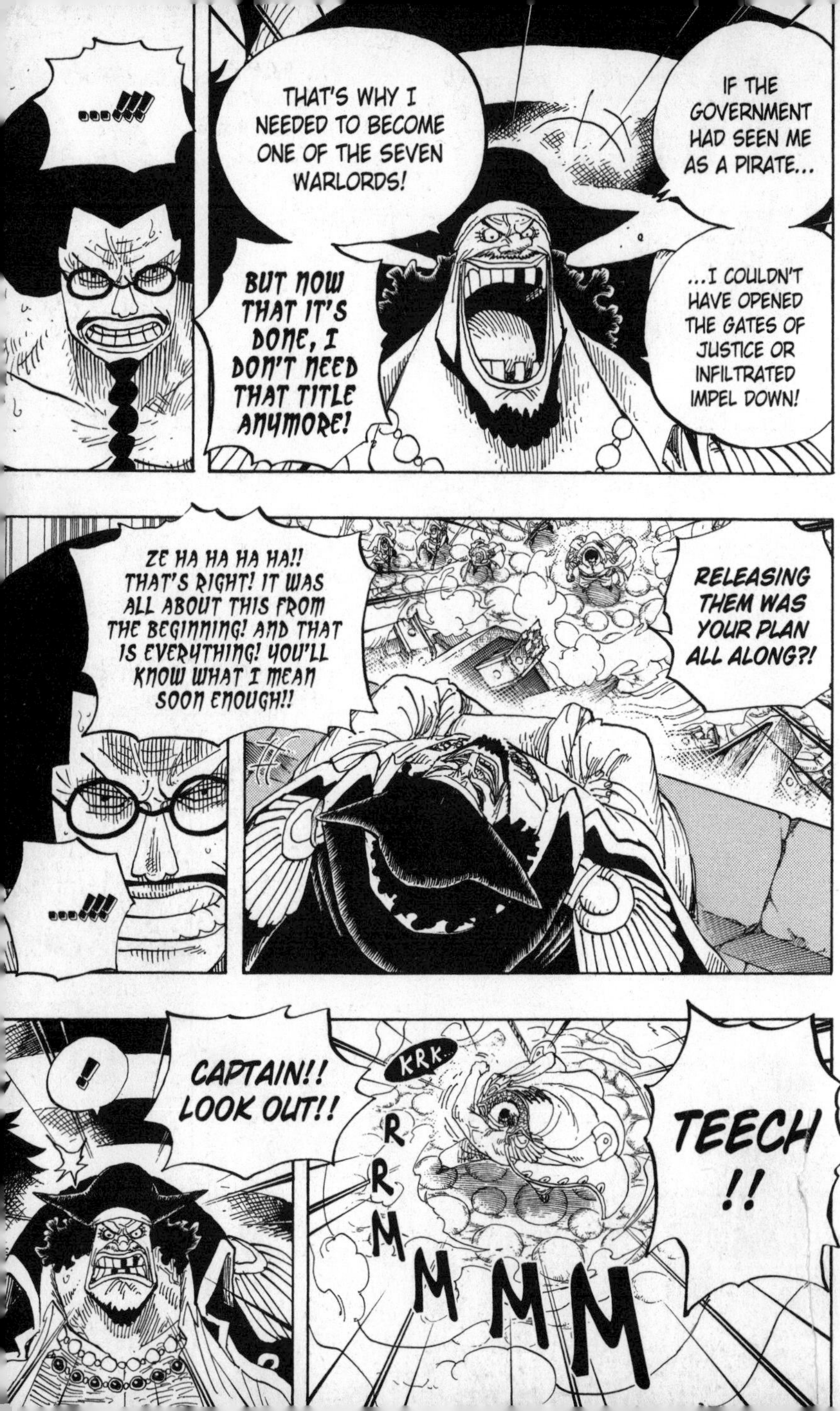
IF THE GOVERNMENT HAD SEEN ME AS A PIRATE...
...I COULDN'T HAVE OPENED THE GATES OF JUSTICE OR INFILTRATED IMPEL DOWN!
THAT'S WHY I NEEDED TO BECOME ONE OF THE SEVEN WARLORDS!
BUT NOW THAT IT'S DONE, I DON'T NEED THAT TITLE ANYMORE!
...!!!
RELEASING THEM WAS YOUR PLAN ALL ALONG?!
ZE HA HA HA HA!! THAT'S RIGHT! IT WAS ALL ABOUT THIS FROM THE BEGINNING! AND THAT IS EVERYTHING! YOU'LL KNOW WHAT I MEAN SOON ENOUGH!!
...!!!
TEECH !!
KRK
RRRMMMM
CAPTAIN!! LOOK OUT!!
!

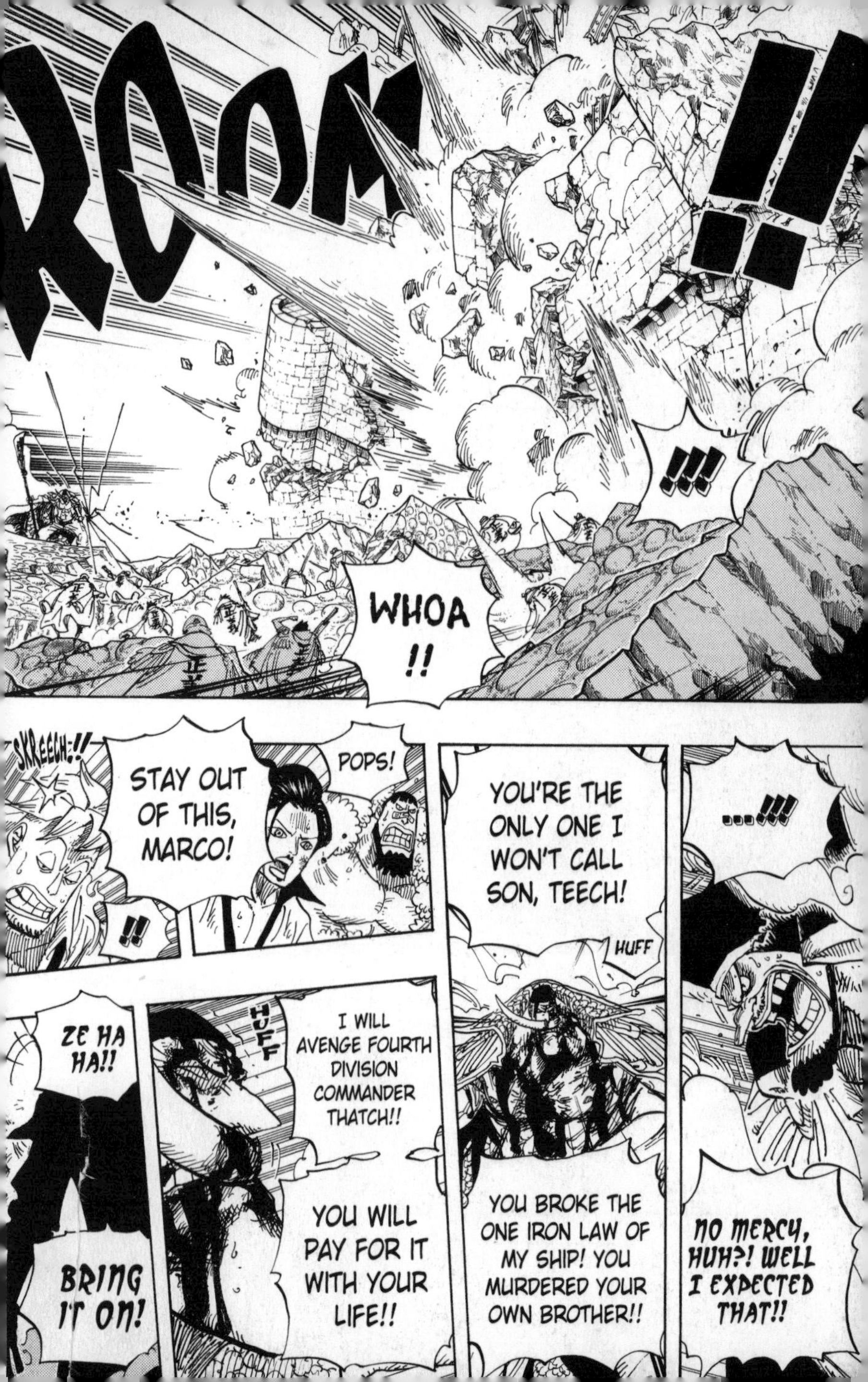
!!
!!!
WHOA !!
...!!!
YOU'RE THE ONLY ONE I WON'T CALL SON, TEECH!
HUFF
POPS!
STAY OUT OF THIS, MARCO!
SKREECH!!
!!
NO MERCY, HUH?! WELL I EXPECTED THAT!!
YOU BROKE THE ONE IRON LAW OF MY SHIP! YOU MURDERED YOUR OWN BROTHER!!
I WILL AVENGE FOURTH DIVISION COMMANDER THATCH!!
HUFF
YOU WILL PAY FOR IT WITH YOUR LIFE!!
ZE HA HA!!
BRING IT ON!

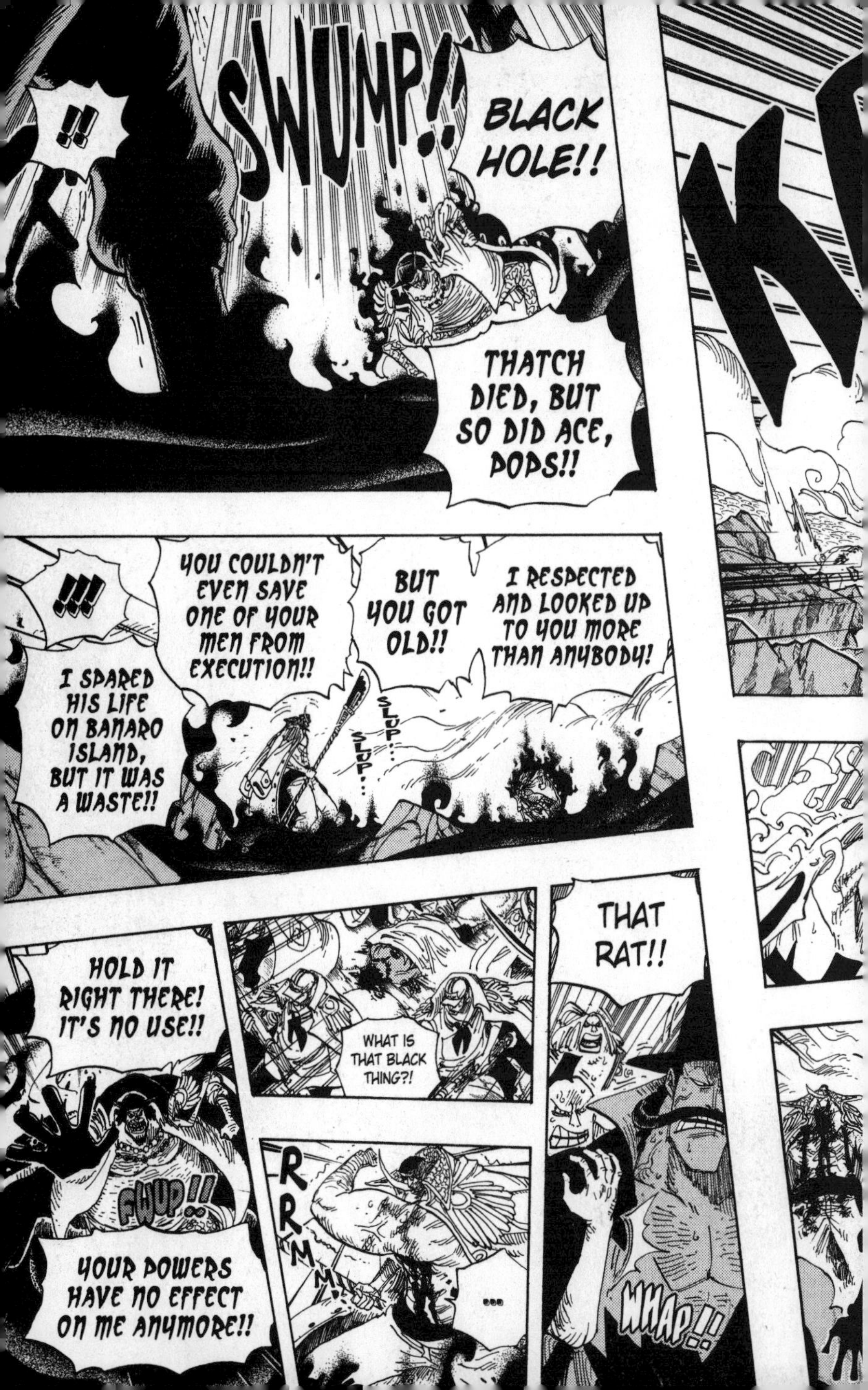
BLACK HOLE!!
SWUMP!!
!!
THATCH DIED, BUT SO DID ACE, POPS!!
I RESPECTED AND LOOKED UP TO YOU MORE THAN ANYBODY!
BUT YOU GOT OLD!!
YOU COULDN'T EVEN SAVE ONE OF YOUR MEN FROM EXECUTION!!
!!!
SLUP...
SLUP...
I SPARED HIS LIFE ON BANARO ISLAND, BUT IT WAS A WASTE!!
THAT RAT!!
WHAP!!
WHAT IS THAT BLACK THING?!
RRRMMM...
...
HOLD IT RIGHT THERE! IT'S NO USE!!
FWUP!!
YOUR POWERS HAVE NO EFFECT ON ME ANYMORE!!

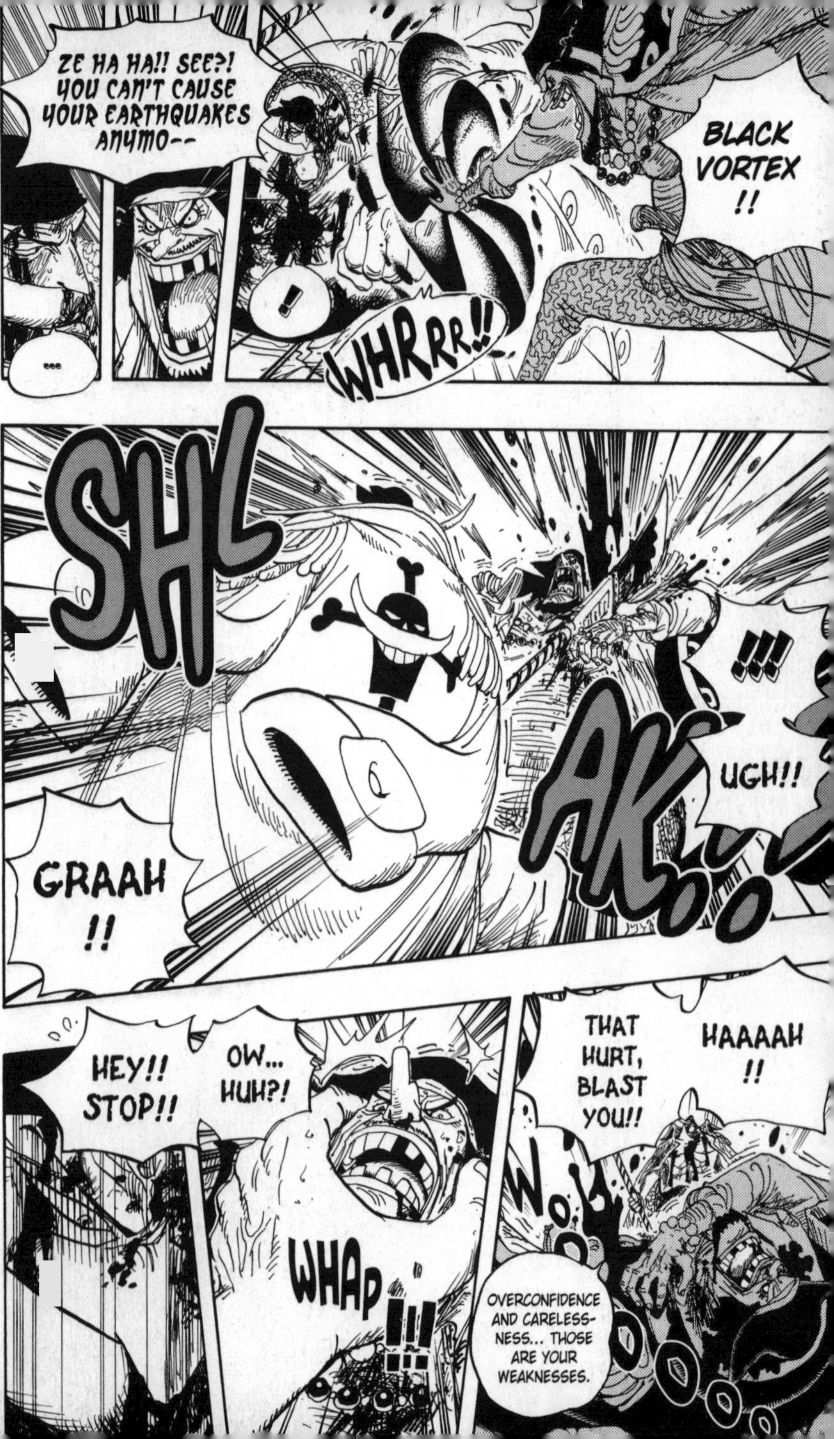
BLACK VORTEX !!
!
WHRRR!!
ZE HA HA!! SEE?! YOU CAN'T CAUSE YOUR EARTHQUAKES ANYMO--
...
UGH!!
!!!
AK...!!
SHL
GRAAH !!
HAAAAH !!
THAT HURT, BLAST YOU!!
OVERCONFIDENCE AND CARELESS-NESS... THOSE ARE YOUR WEAKNESSES.
OW... HUH?!
WHAP!!!
HEY!! STOP!!

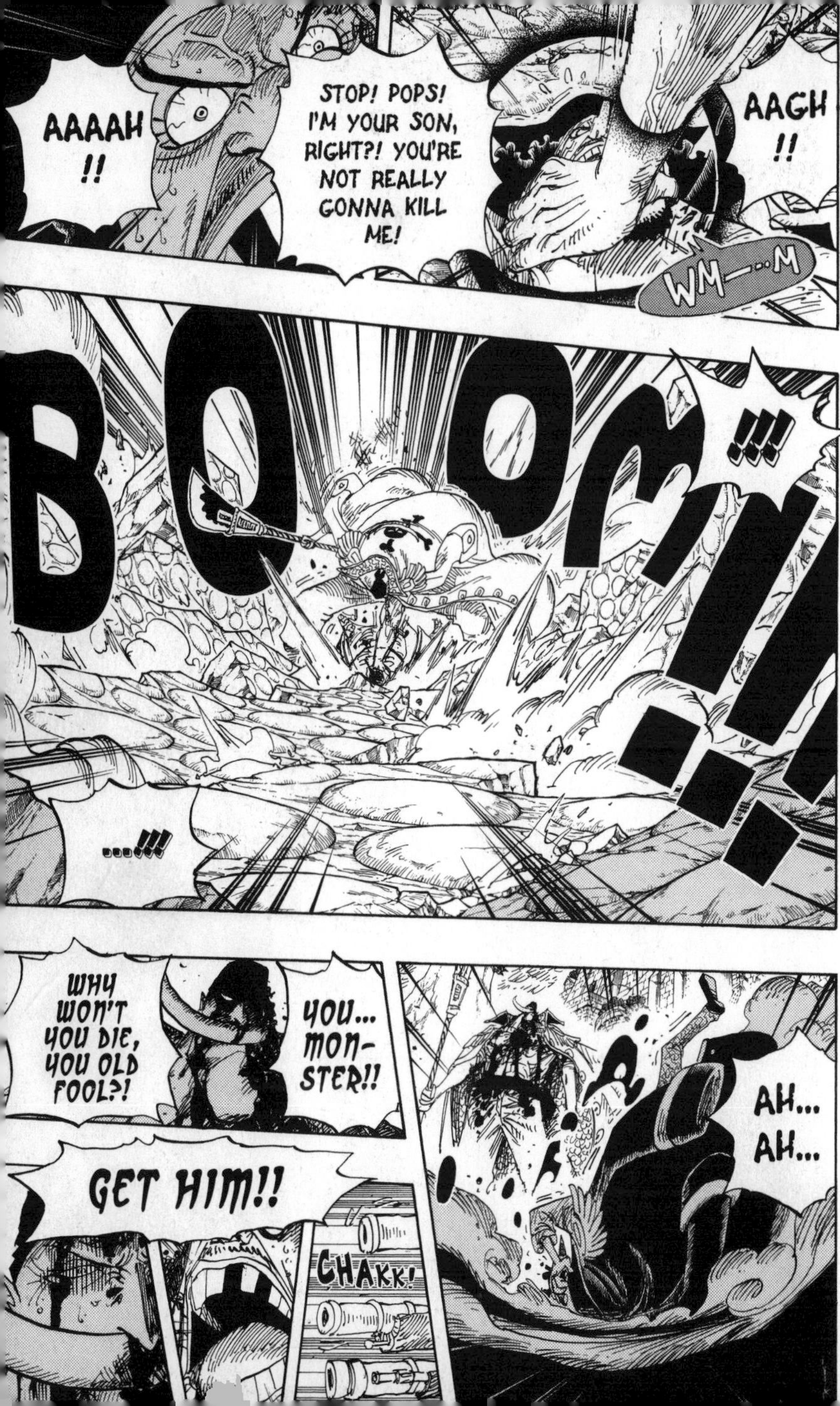
AAGH !!
WM—M
STOP! POPS! I'M YOUR SON, RIGHT?! YOU'RE NOT REALLY GONNA KILL ME!
AAAAH !!
BOOM!!!!
...!!!
AH... AH...
YOU... MON-STER!!
WHY WON'T YOU DIE, YOU OLD FOOL?!
GET HIM!!
CHAKK!

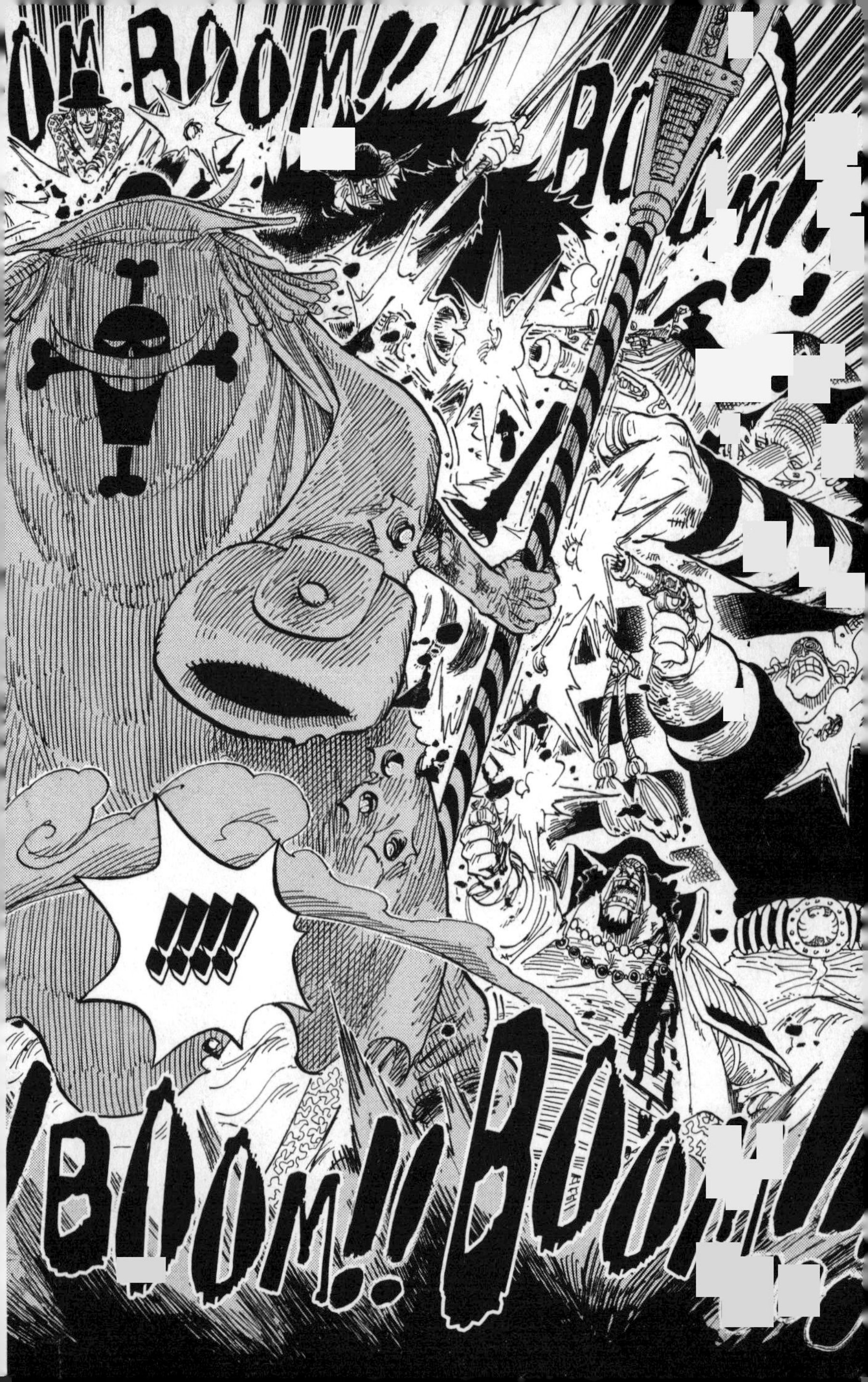
OM BOOM!!
!!!!
BOOM!! BOO

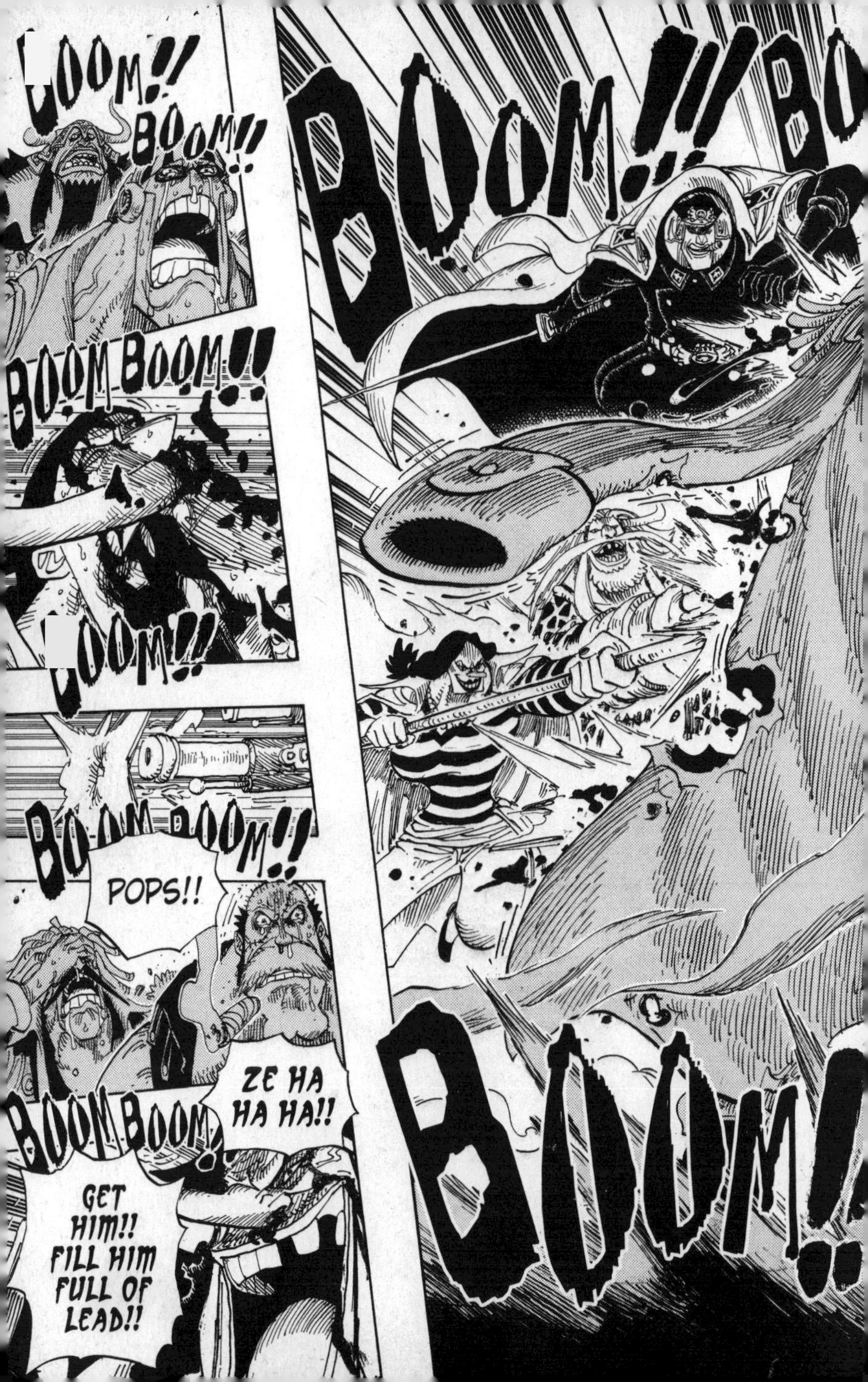
BOOM!! BO
BOOM!!
OOM!!
BOOM!!
BOOM BOOM!!
OOM!!
BOOM BOOM!!
POPS!!
ZE HA HA HA!!
BOOM BOOM
GET HIM!! FILL HIM FULL OF LEAD!!

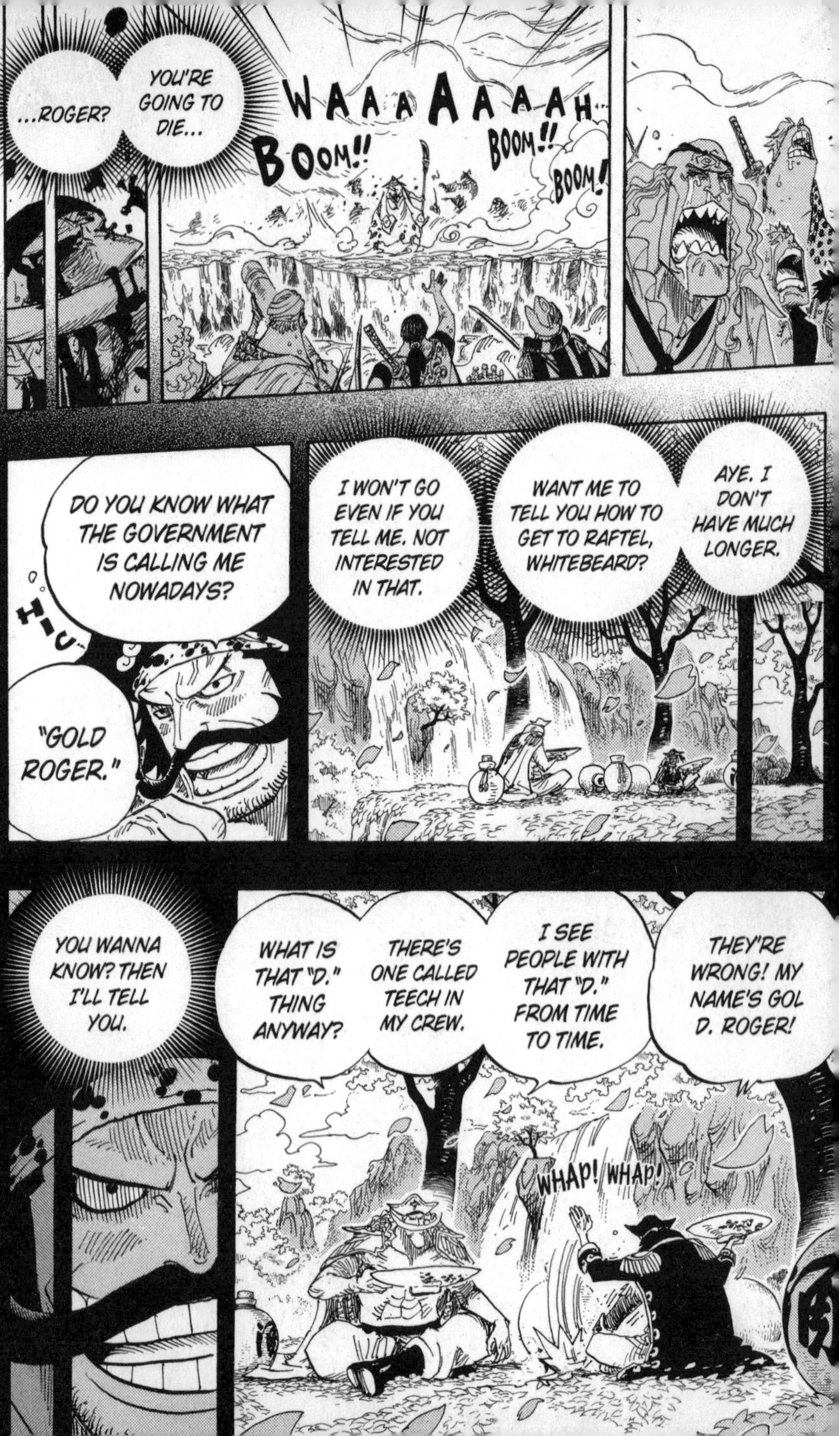
WAAAAAAAH...
BOOM!
BOOM!!
BOOM!!
YOU'RE GOING TO DIE...
...ROGER?
AYE. I DON'T HAVE MUCH LONGER.
WANT ME TO TELL YOU HOW TO GET TO RAFTEL, WHITEBEARD?
I WON'T GO EVEN IF YOU TELL ME. NOT INTERESTED IN THAT.
DO YOU KNOW WHAT THE GOVERNMENT IS CALLING ME NOWADAYS?
HIC
"GOLD ROGER."
THEY'RE WRONG! MY NAME'S GOL D. ROGER!
I SEE PEOPLE WITH THAT "D." FROM TIME TO TIME.
THERE'S ONE CALLED TEECH IN MY CREW.
WHAT IS THAT "D." THING ANYWAY?
WHAP! WHAP!
YOU WANNA KNOW? THEN I'LL TELL YOU.

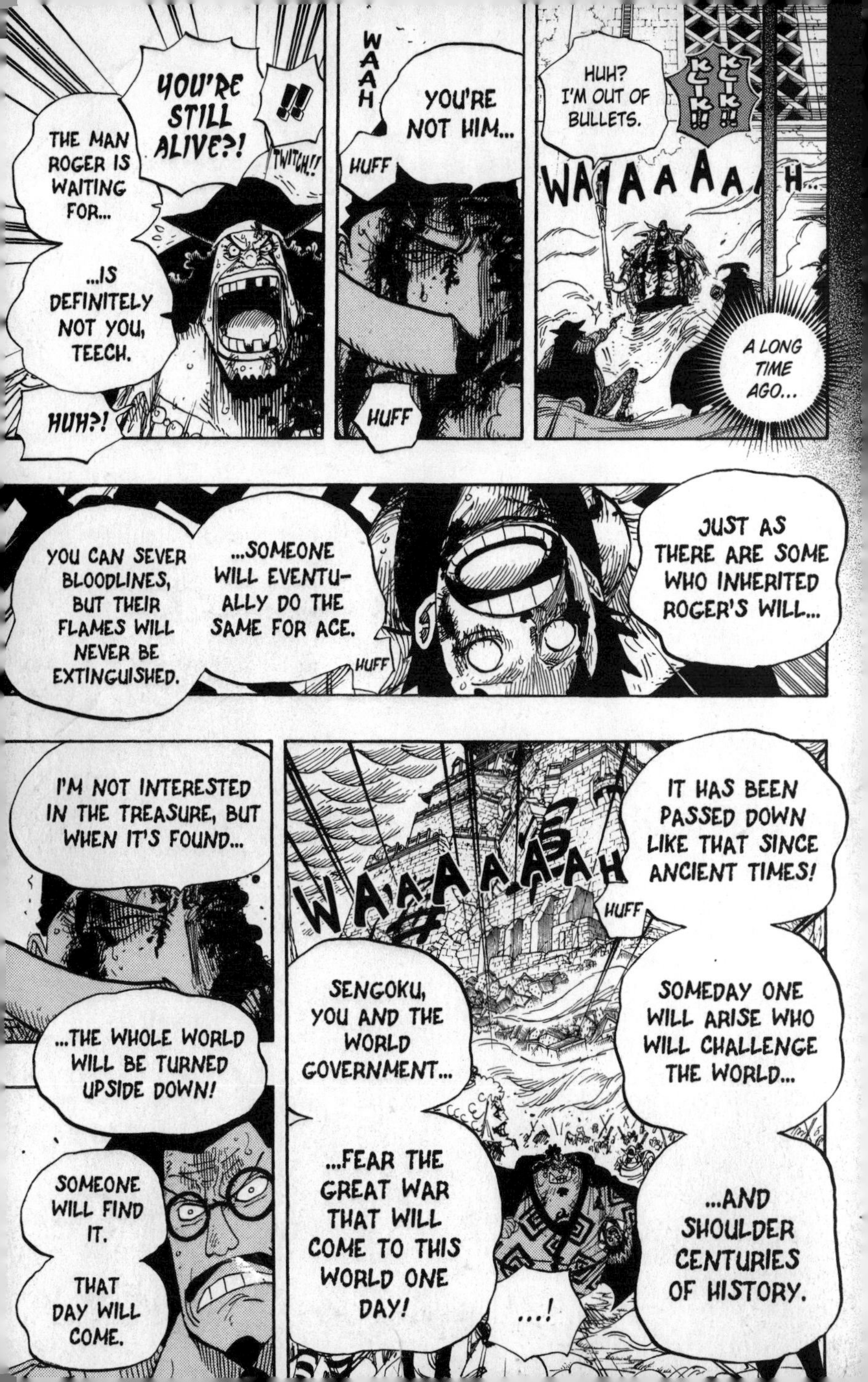
HUH? I'M OUT OF BULLETS.
KLIK!! KLIK!!
WAAAAAAH...
A LONG TIME AGO...
WAAH
YOU'RE NOT HIM...
HUFF
HUFF
YOU'RE STILL ALIVE?!
!!
TWITCH!!
THE MAN ROGER IS WAITING FOR...
...IS DEFINITELY NOT YOU, TEECH.
HUH?!
JUST AS THERE ARE SOME WHO INHERITED ROGER'S WILL...
HUFF
...SOMEONE WILL EVENTUALLY DO THE SAME FOR ACE.
YOU CAN SEVER BLOODLINES, BUT THEIR FLAMES WILL NEVER BE EXTINGUISHED.
IT HAS BEEN PASSED DOWN LIKE THAT SINCE ANCIENT TIMES!
WAAAAAAH
HUFF
SOMEDAY ONE WILL ARISE WHO WILL CHALLENGE THE WORLD...
...AND SHOULDER CENTURIES OF HISTORY.
SENGOKU, YOU AND THE WORLD GOVERNMENT...
...FEAR THE GREAT WAR THAT WILL COME TO THIS WORLD ONE DAY!
...!
I'M NOT INTERESTED IN THE TREASURE, BUT WHEN IT'S FOUND...
...THE WHOLE WORLD WILL BE TURNED UPSIDE DOWN!
SOMEONE WILL FIND IT.
THAT DAY WILL COME.

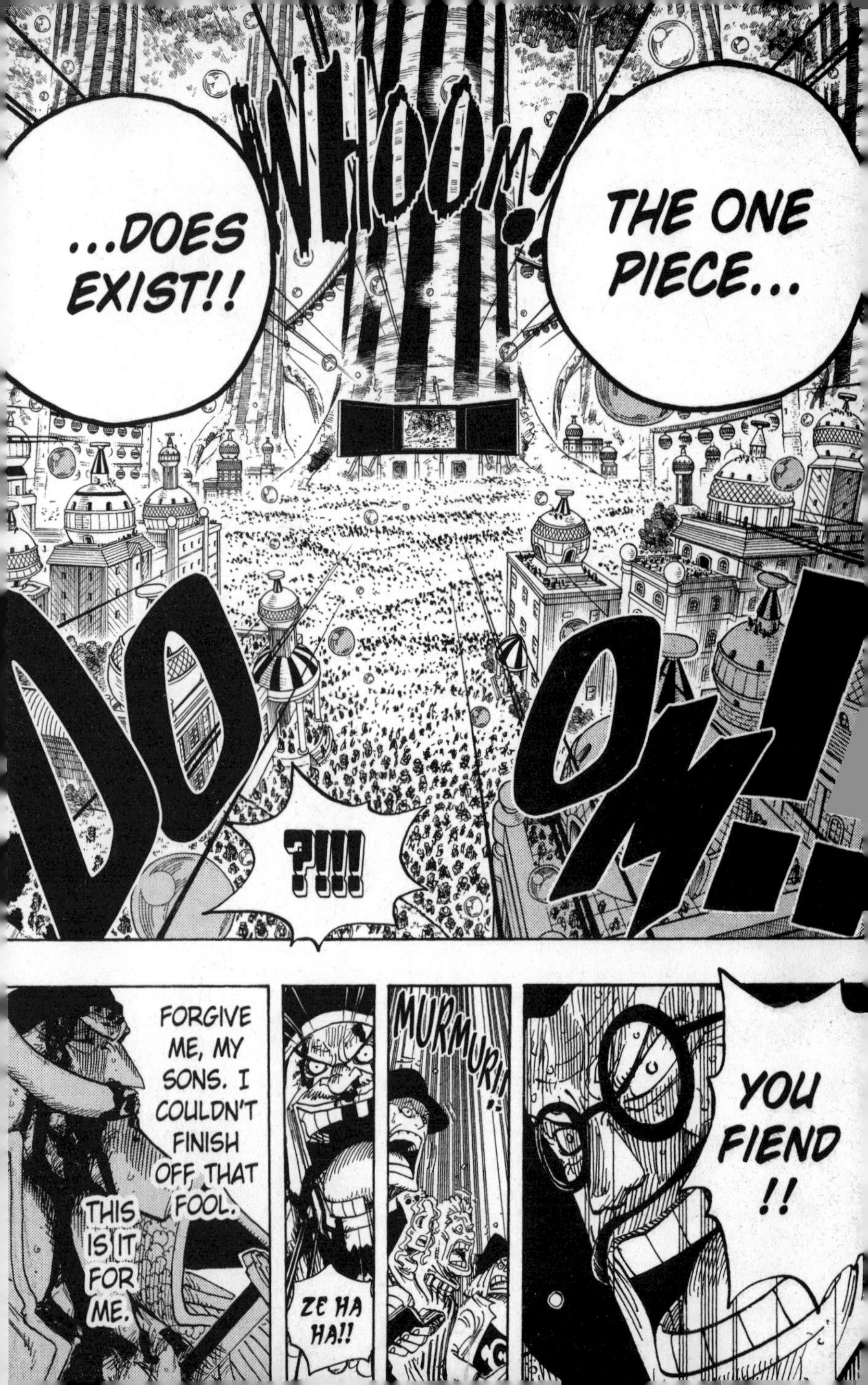
THE ONE PIECE...
WHOOM!!
...DOES EXIST!!
DOOM!!
?!!!
YOU FIEND!!
MURMUR!!
ZE HA HA!!
FORGIVE ME, MY SONS. I COULDN'T FINISH OFF THAT FOOL.
THIS IS IT FOR ME.

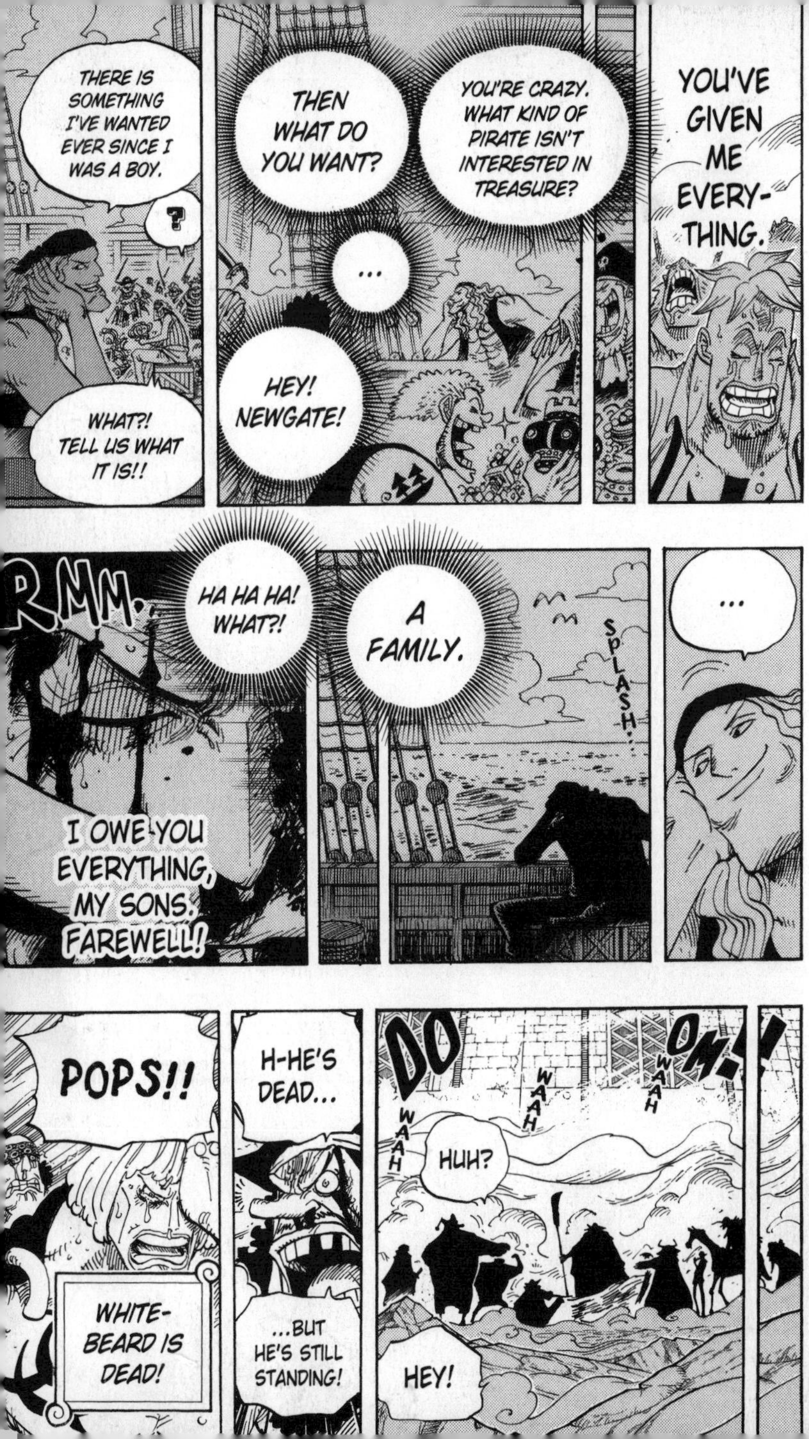
YOU'VE GIVEN ME EVERY-THING.
YOU'RE CRAZY. WHAT KIND OF PIRATE ISN'T INTERESTED IN TREASURE?
THEN WHAT DO YOU WANT?
...
HEY! NEWGATE!
THERE IS SOMETHING I'VE WANTED EVER SINCE I WAS A BOY.
?
WHAT?! TELL US WHAT IT IS!!
...
A FAMILY.
SPLASH...
HA HA HA! WHAT?!
R.MM.
I OWE YOU EVERYTHING, MY SONS. FAREWELL!
DO
OM..!
WAAH
WAAH
WAAH
HUH?
HEY!
H-HE'S DEAD...
...BUT HE'S STILL STANDING!
POPS!!
WHITE-BEARD IS DEAD!

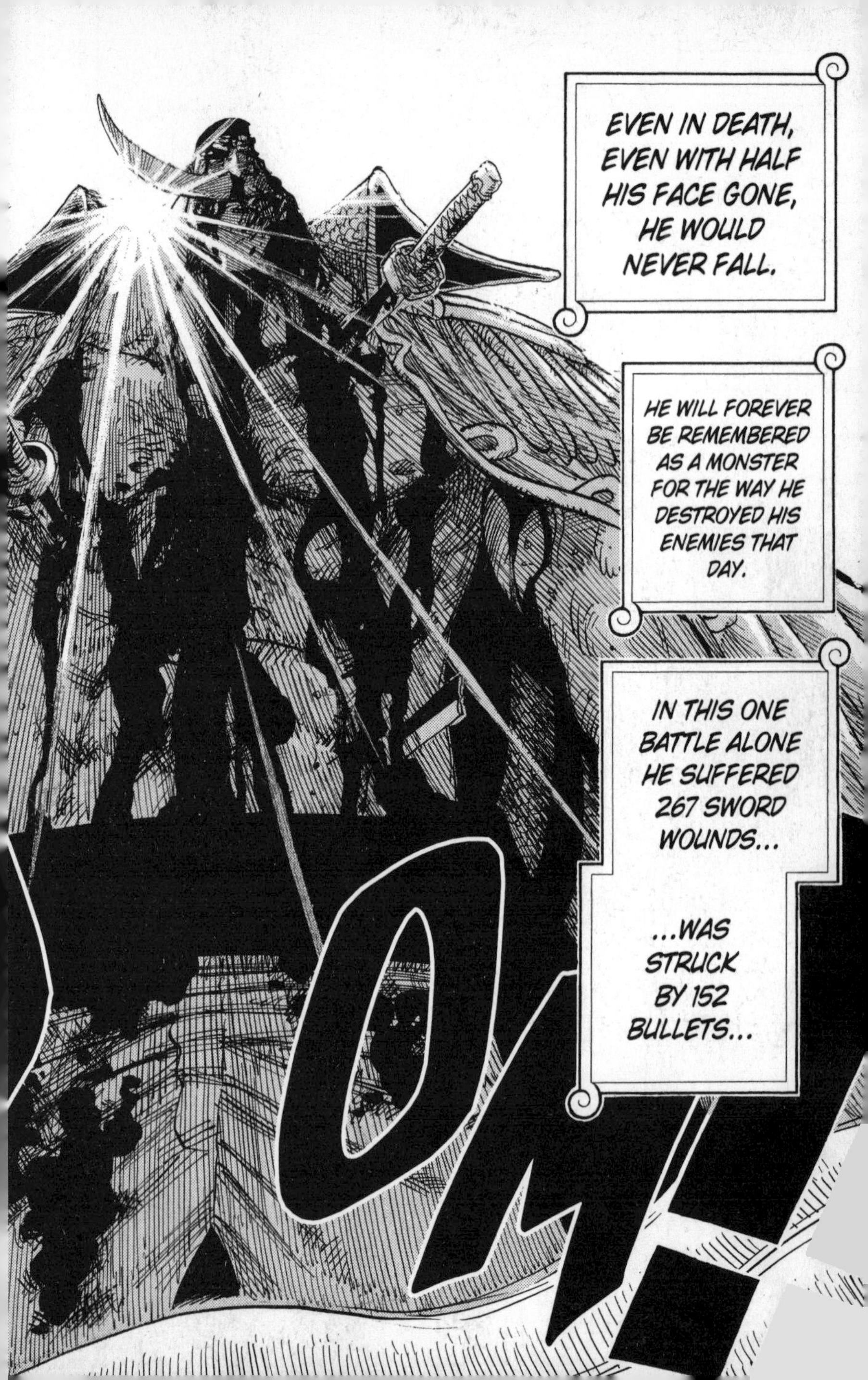
EVEN IN DEATH, EVEN WITH HALF HIS FACE GONE, HE WOULD NEVER FALL.
HE WILL FOREVER BE REMEMBERED AS A MONSTER FOR THE WAY HE DESTROYED HIS ENEMIES THAT DAY.
IN THIS ONE BATTLE ALONE HE SUFFERED 267 SWORD WOUNDS...
...WAS STRUCK BY 152 BULLETS...

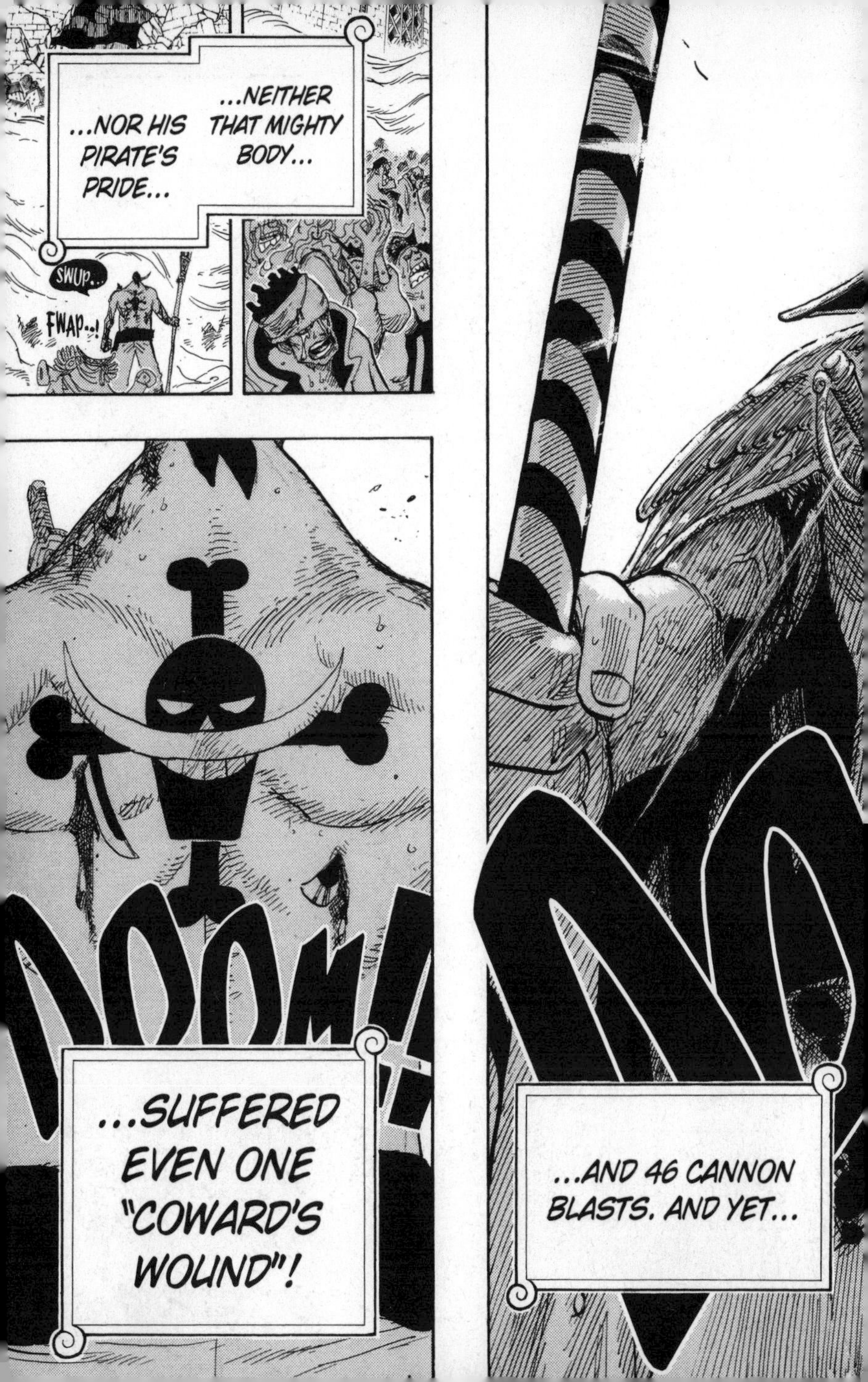
...AND 46 CANNON BLASTS. AND YET...
...NEITHER THAT MIGHTY BODY...
...NOR HIS PIRATE'S PRIDE...
SWUP...
FWAP..!
DOOM
...SUFFERED EVEN ONE "COWARD'S WOUND"!

Chapter 577: OUTRAGEOUS EVENTS ONE AFTER ANOTHER

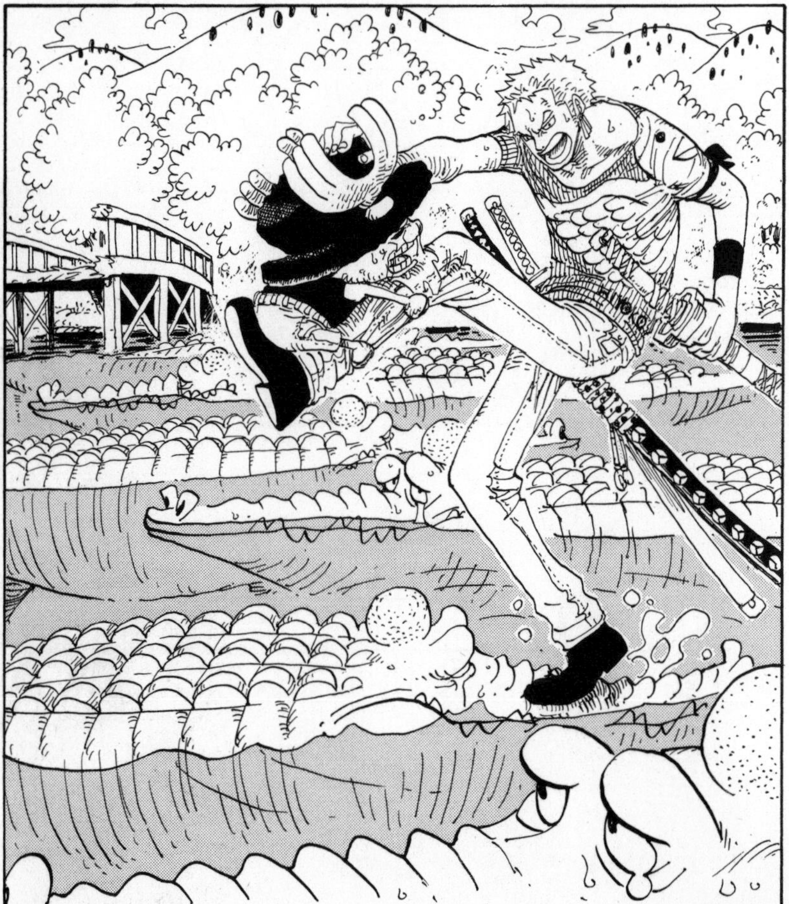

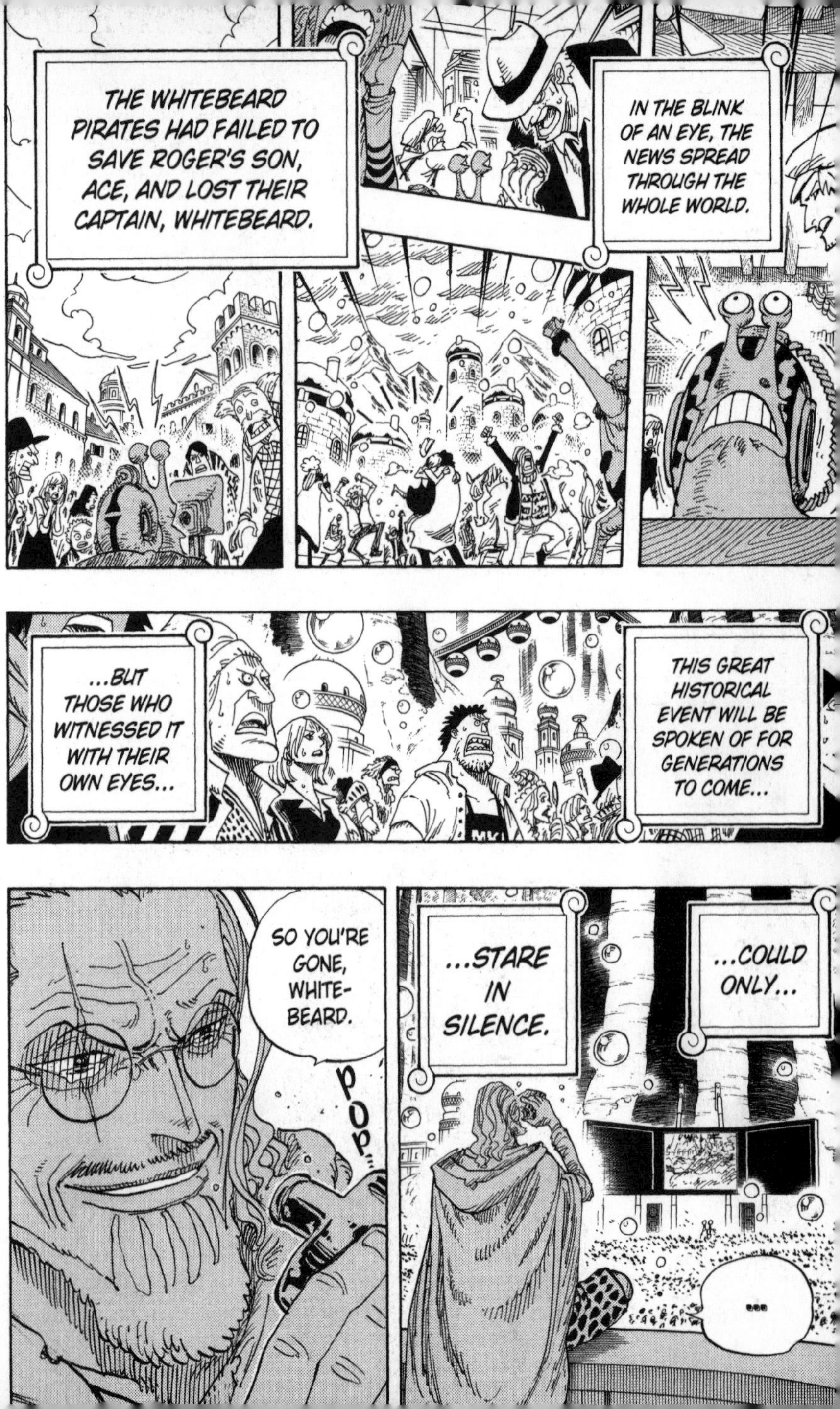
IN THE BLINK OF AN EYE, THE NEWS SPREAD THROUGH THE WHOLE WORLD.
THE WHITEBEARD PIRATES HAD FAILED TO SAVE ROGER'S SON, ACE, AND LOST THEIR CAPTAIN, WHITEBEARD.
THIS GREAT HISTORICAL EVENT WILL BE SPOKEN OF FOR GENERATIONS TO COME...
...BUT THOSE WHO WITNESSED IT WITH THEIR OWN EYES...
...COULD ONLY...
...STARE IN SILENCE.
...
SO YOU'RE GONE, WHITE-BEARD.
POP...

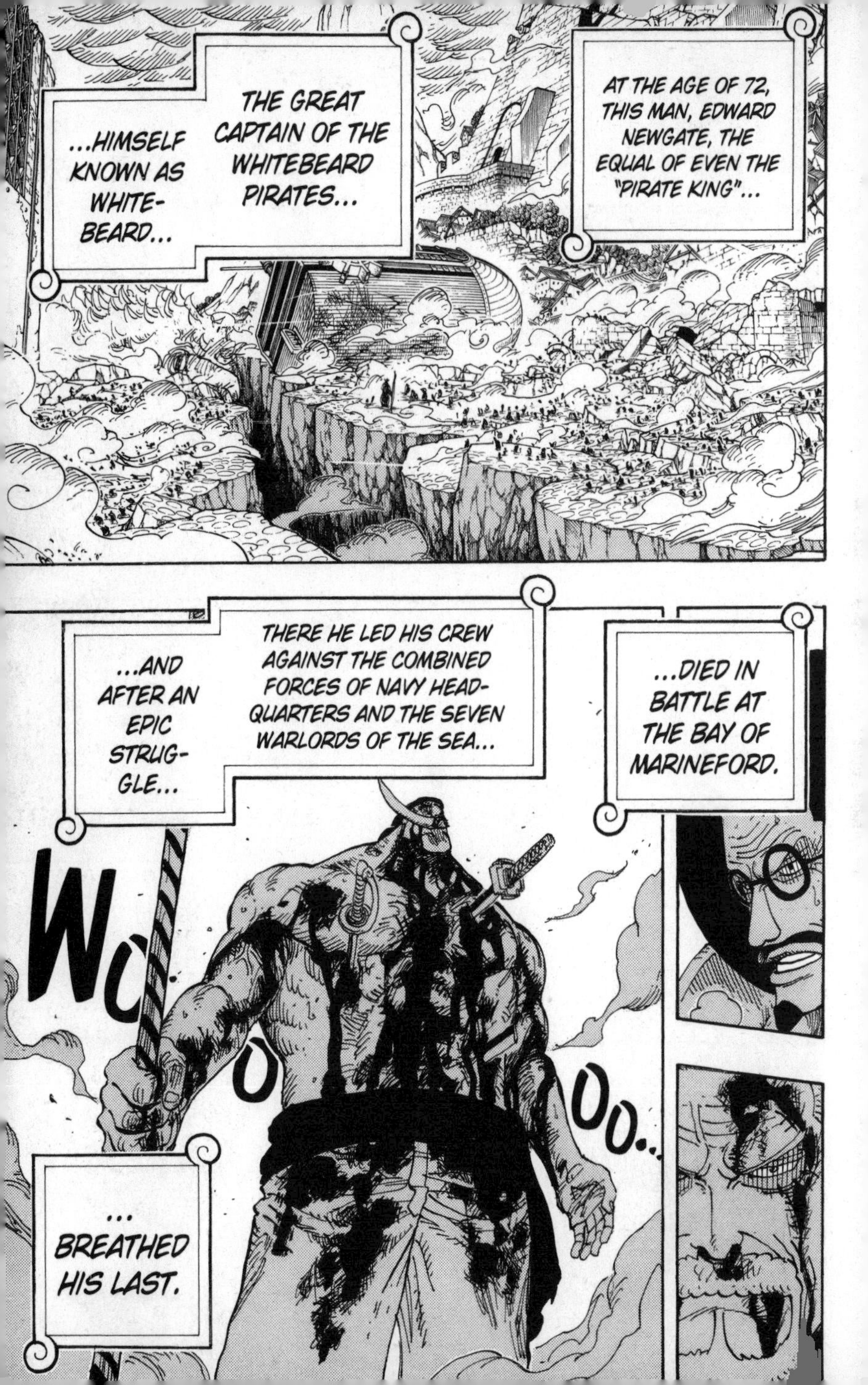
AT THE AGE OF 72, THIS MAN, EDWARD NEWGATE, THE EQUAL OF EVEN THE "PIRATE KING"...
THE GREAT CAPTAIN OF THE WHITEBEARD PIRATES...
...HIMSELF KNOWN AS WHITE-BEARD...
...DIED IN BATTLE AT THE BAY OF MARINEFORD.
THERE HE LED HIS CREW AGAINST THE COMBINED FORCES OF NAVY HEAD-QUARTERS AND THE SEVEN WARLORDS OF THE SEA...
...AND AFTER AN EPIC STRUG-GLE...
WOOOO...
... BREATHED HIS LAST.

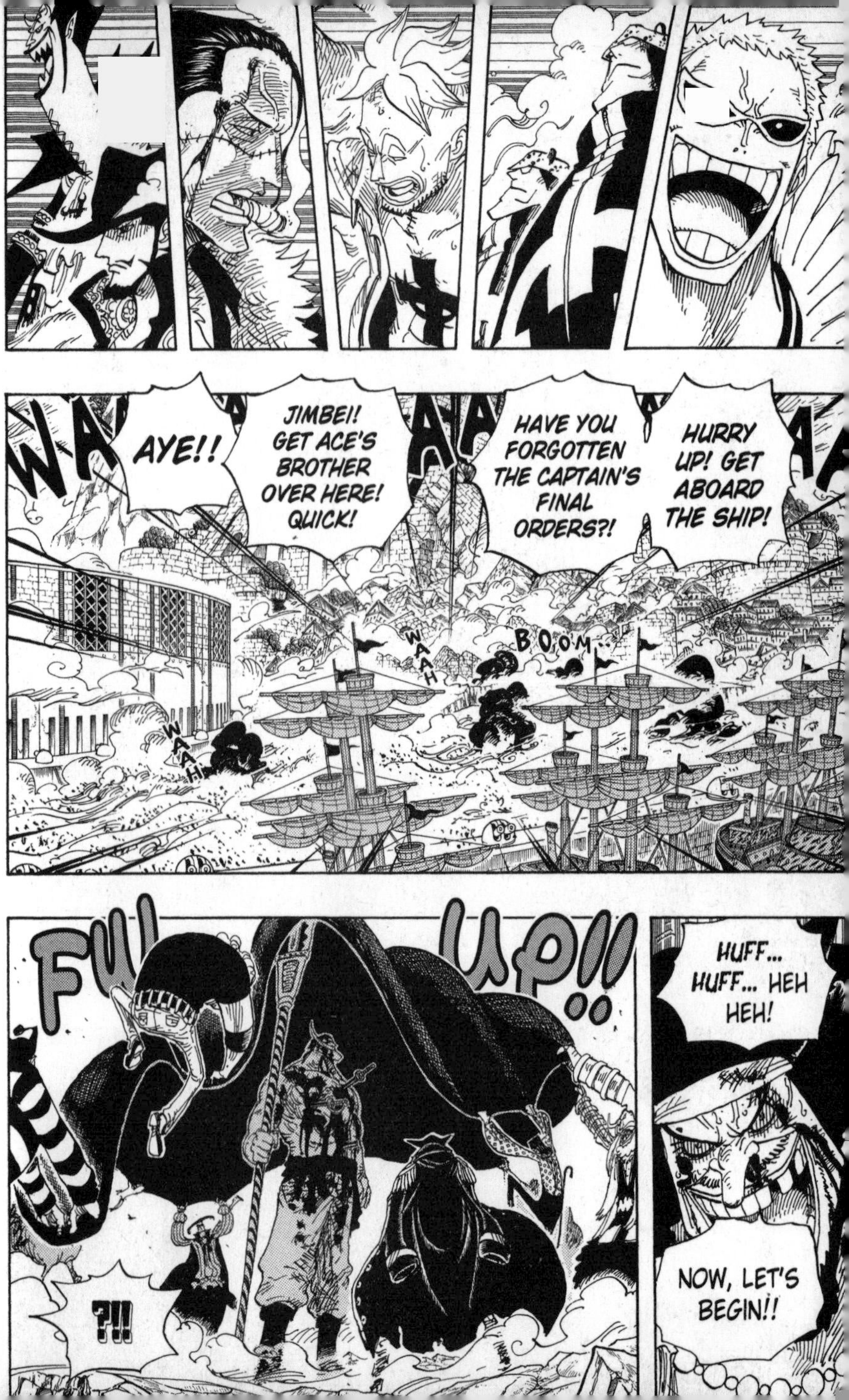
HURRY UP! GET ABOARD THE SHIP!
HAVE YOU FORGOTTEN THE CAPTAIN'S FINAL ORDERS?!
JIMBEI! GET ACE'S BROTHER OVER HERE! QUICK!
AYE!!
BOOM
WAAH
WAAH
HUFF... HUFF... HEH HEH!
NOW, LET'S BEGIN!!
UP!!
FU
?!!

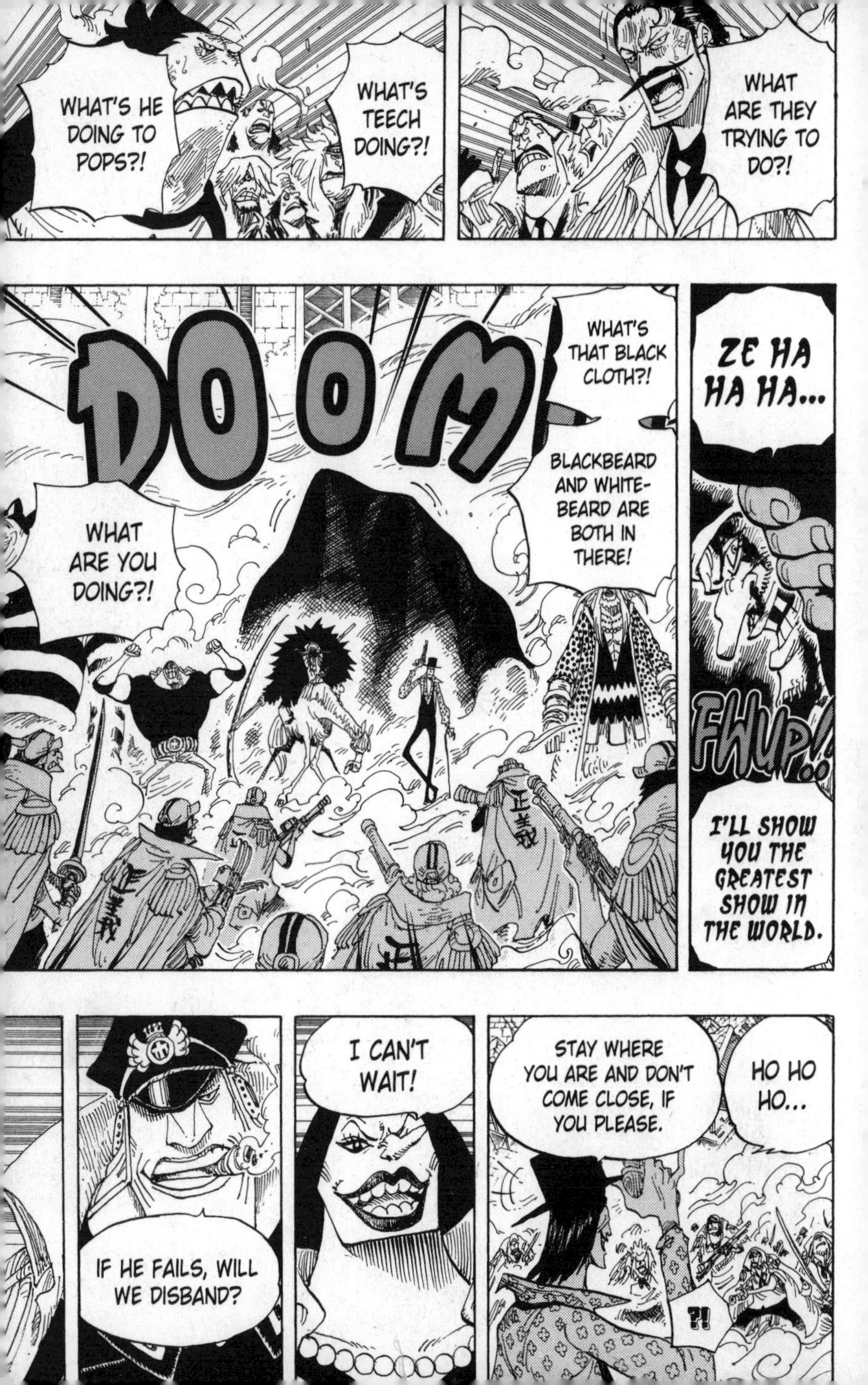
WHAT ARE THEY TRYING TO DO?!
WHAT'S TEECH DOING?!
WHAT'S HE DOING TO POPS?!
ZE HA HA HA...
FWUP!!
I'LL SHOW YOU THE GREATEST SHOW IN THE WORLD.
WHAT'S THAT BLACK CLOTH?!
DOOM
BLACKBEARD AND WHITE-BEARD ARE BOTH IN THERE!
WHAT ARE YOU DOING?!
HO HO HO...
STAY WHERE YOU ARE AND DON'T COME CLOSE, IF YOU PLEASE.
?!
I CAN'T WAIT!
IF HE FAILS, WILL WE DISBAND?

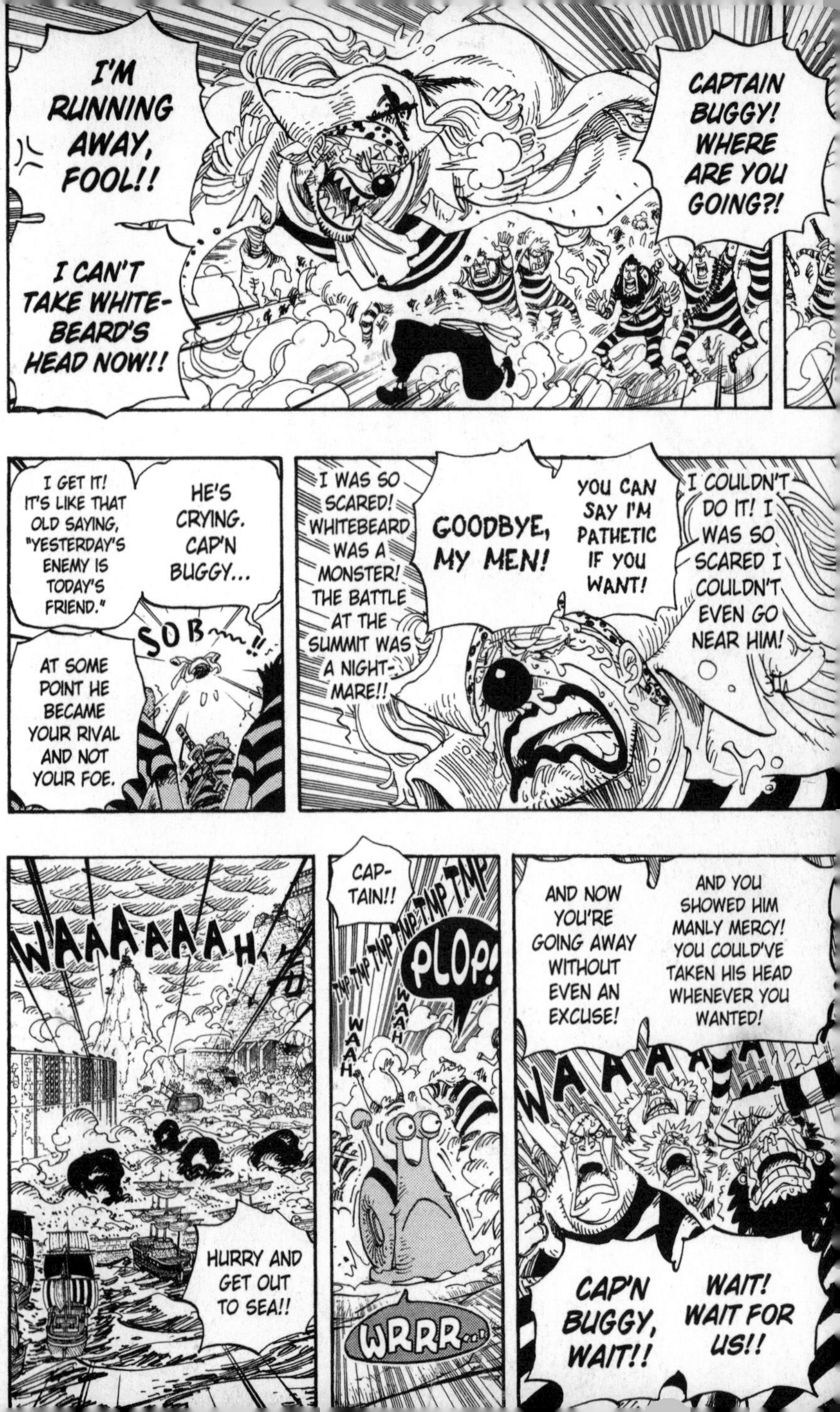

CAPTAIN BUGGY! WHERE ARE YOU GOING?!
I'M RUNNING AWAY, FOOL!!
I CAN'T TAKE WHITEBEARD'S HEAD NOW!!
I COULDN'T DO IT! I WAS SO SCARED I COULDN'T EVEN GO NEAR HIM!
YOU CAN SAY I'M PATHETIC IF YOU WANT!
GOODBYE, MY MEN!
I WAS SO SCARED! WHITEBEARD WAS A MONSTER! THE BATTLE AT THE SUMMIT WAS A NIGHTMARE!!
HE'S CRYING. CAP'N BUGGY...
I GET IT! IT'S LIKE THAT OLD SAYING, "YESTERDAY'S ENEMY IS TODAY'S FRIEND."
SOB~!!
AT SOME POINT HE BECAME YOUR RIVAL AND NOT YOUR FOE.
AND YOU SHOWED HIM MANLY MERCY! YOU COULD'VE TAKEN HIS HEAD WHENEVER YOU WANTED!
AND NOW YOU'RE GOING AWAY WITHOUT EVEN AN EXCUSE!
WAAAAA
WAIT! WAIT FOR US!!
CAP'N BUGGY, WAIT!!
CAP-TAIN!!
TMP TMP TMP TMP TMP TMP
PLOP!
WAAH
WAAH
WRRR..
WAAAAAAH
HURRY AND GET OUT TO SEA!!

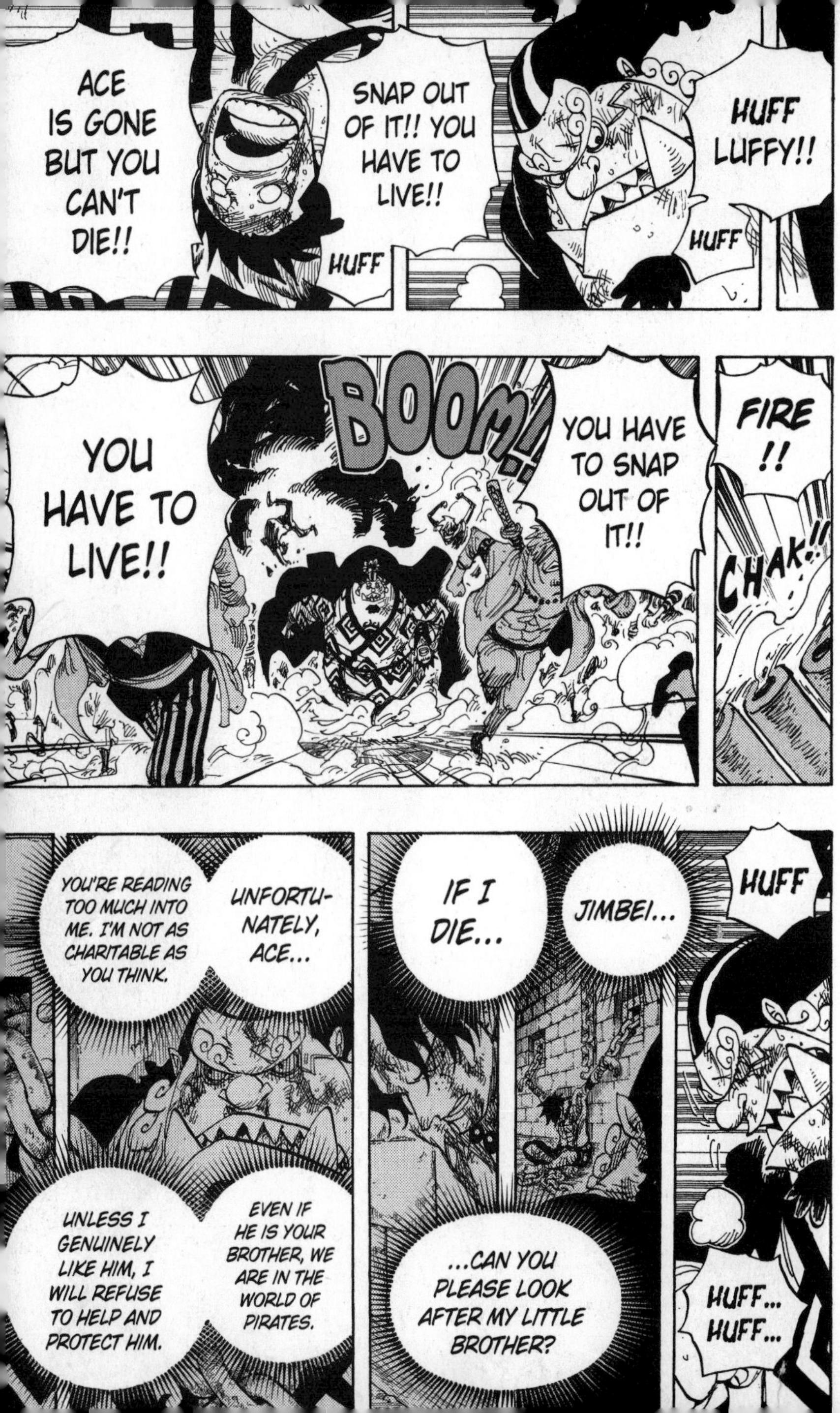
HUFF LUFFY!!
HUFF
SNAP OUT OF IT!! YOU HAVE TO LIVE!!
ACE IS GONE BUT YOU CAN'T DIE!!
HUFF
FIRE!!
CHAK!!
BOOM!!
YOU HAVE TO SNAP OUT OF IT!!
YOU HAVE TO LIVE!!
HUFF
HUFF... HUFF...
JIMBEI...
IF I DIE...
...CAN YOU PLEASE LOOK AFTER MY LITTLE BROTHER?
UNFORTU-NATELY, ACE...
YOU'RE READING TOO MUCH INTO ME. I'M NOT AS CHARITABLE AS YOU THINK.
EVEN IF HE IS YOUR BROTHER, WE ARE IN THE WORLD OF PIRATES.
UNLESS I GENUINELY LIKE HIM, I WILL REFUSE TO HELP AND PROTECT HIM.

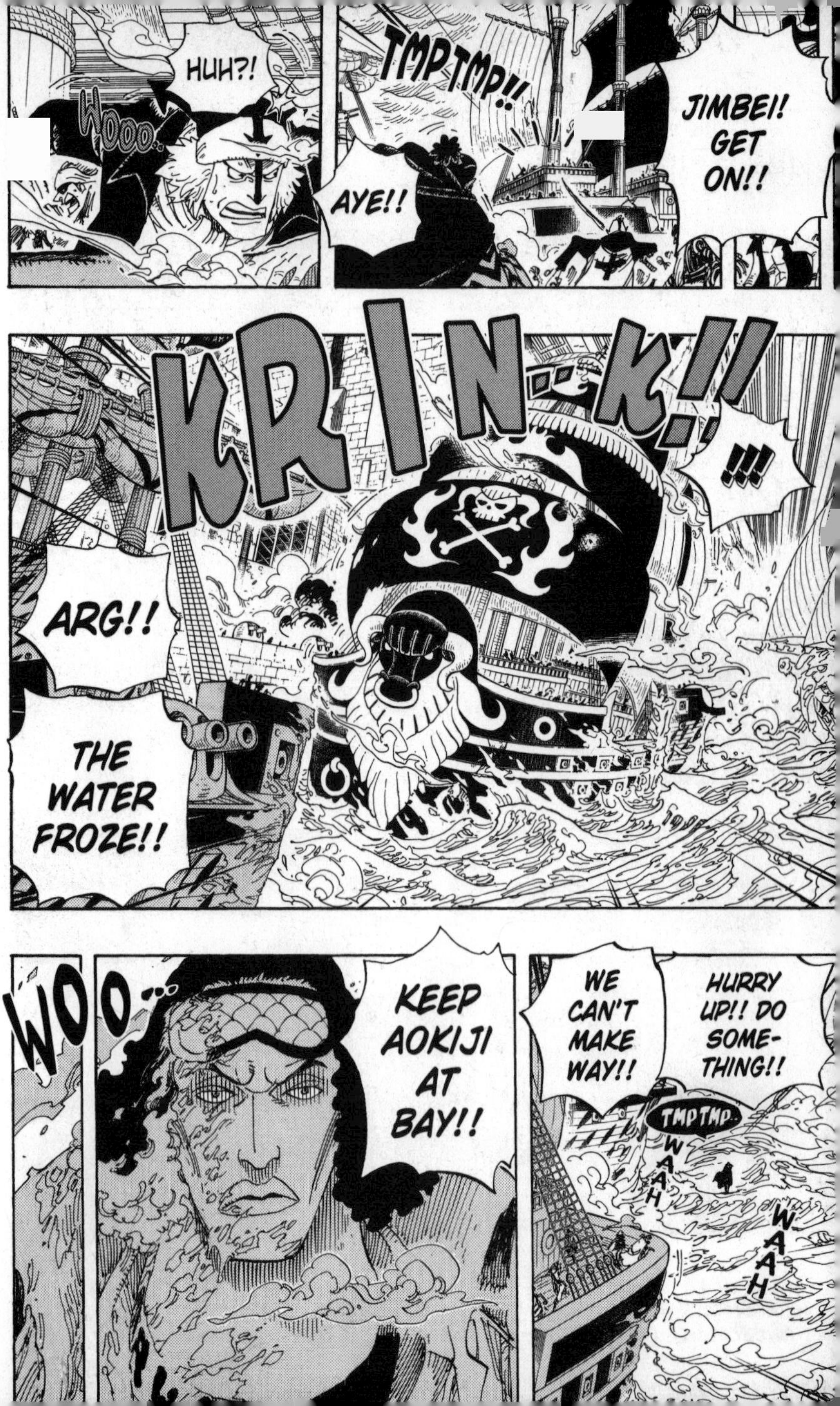
JIMBEI! GET ON!!
TMP TMP!!
AYE!!
HUH?!
WOOO...
KRIN...K!!
!!!
ARG!!
THE WATER FROZE!!
HURRY UP!! DO SOME-THING!!
WE CAN'T MAKE WAY!!
TMP TMP
WAAH
WAAH
KEEP AOKIJI AT BAY!!
WOO...

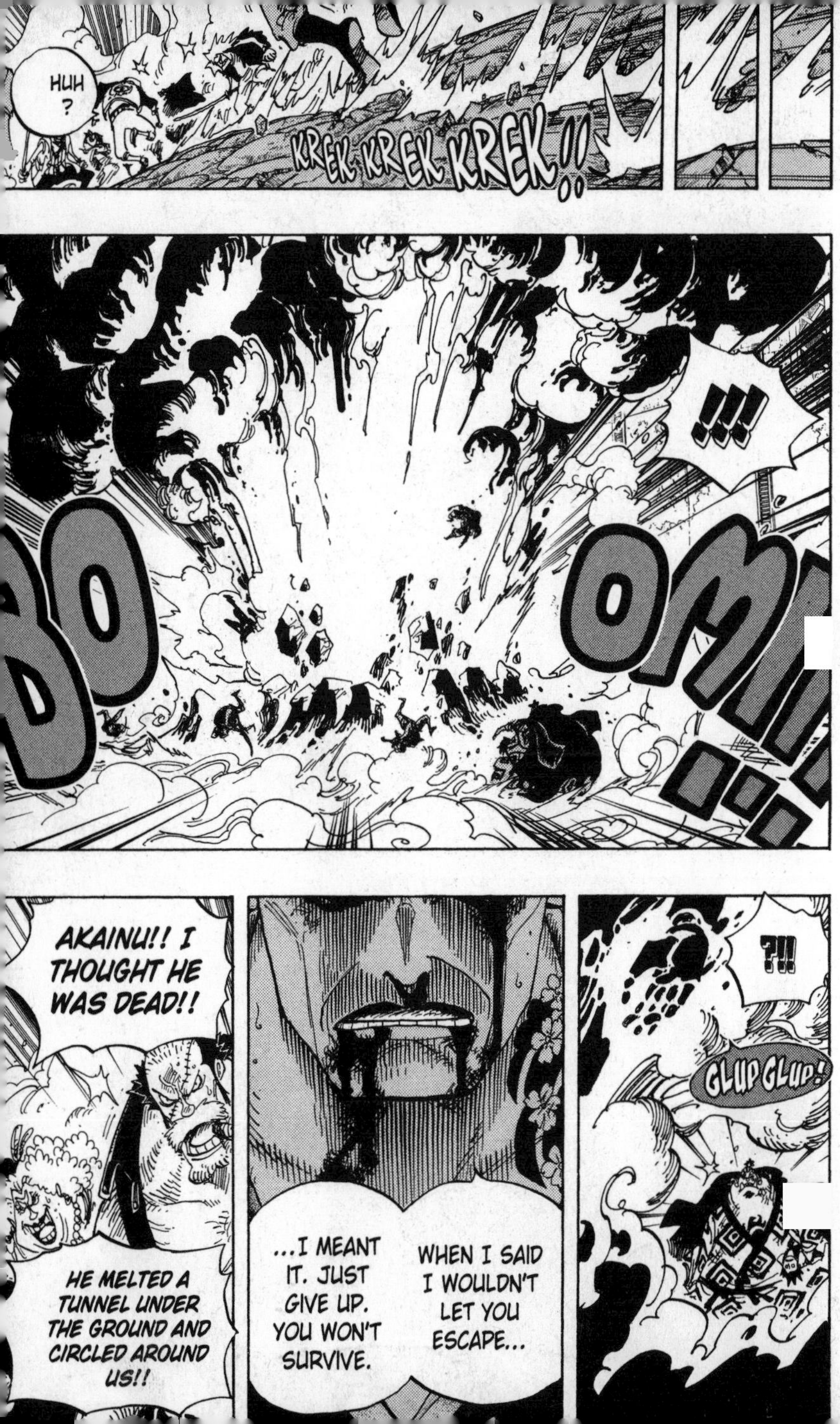
HUH ?
KREK KREK KREK!!
!!!
BOOM...
?!!
GLUP GLUP!
WHEN I SAID I WOULDN'T LET YOU ESCAPE...
...I MEANT IT. JUST GIVE UP. YOU WON'T SURVIVE.
AKAINU!! I THOUGHT HE WAS DEAD!!
HE MELTED A TUNNEL UNDER THE GROUND AND CIRCLED AROUND US!!

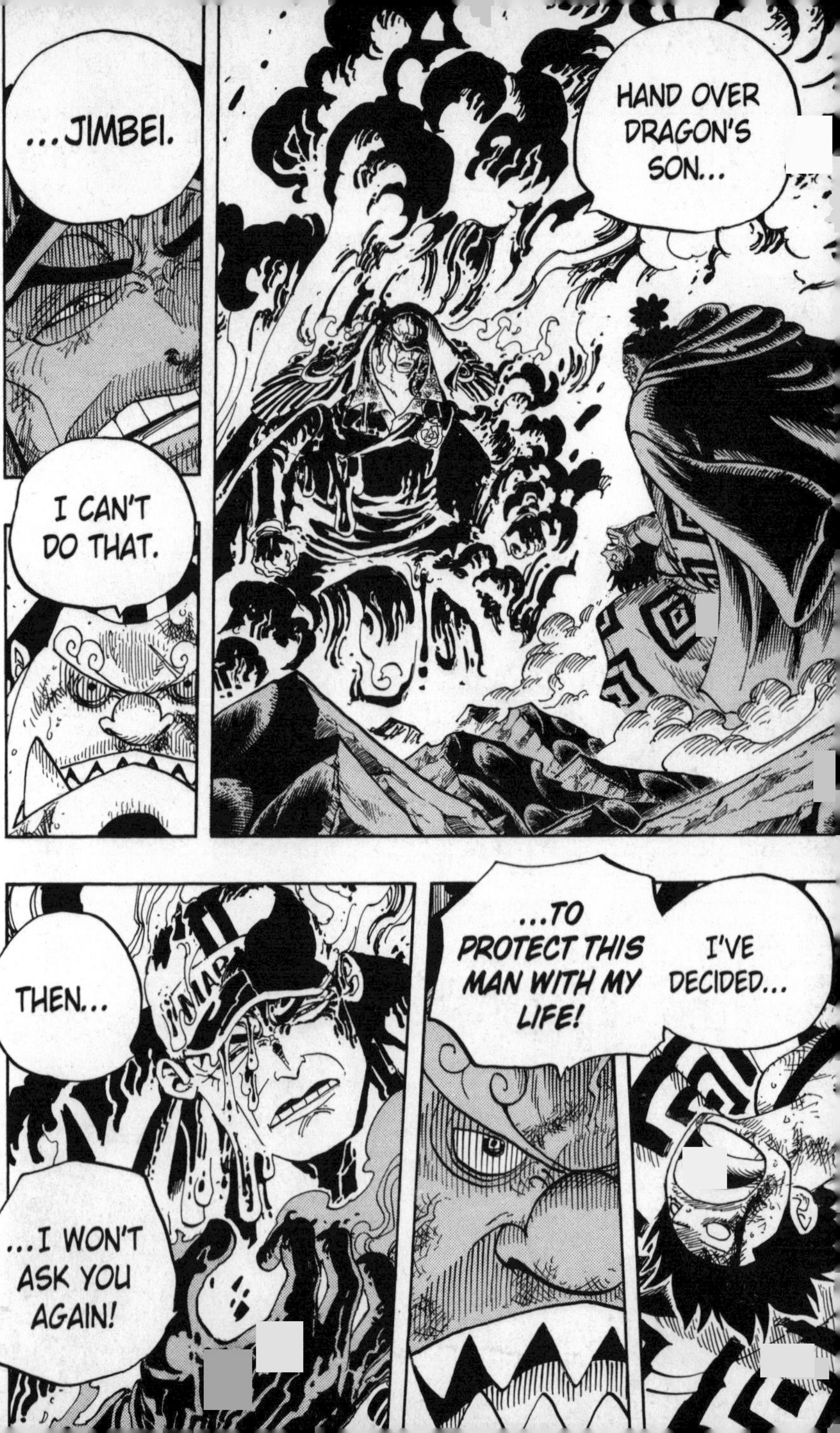
HAND OVER DRAGON'S SON...
...JIMBEI.
I CAN'T DO THAT.
I'VE DECIDED...
...TO PROTECT THIS MAN WITH MY LIFE!
THEN...
...I WON'T ASK YOU AGAIN!

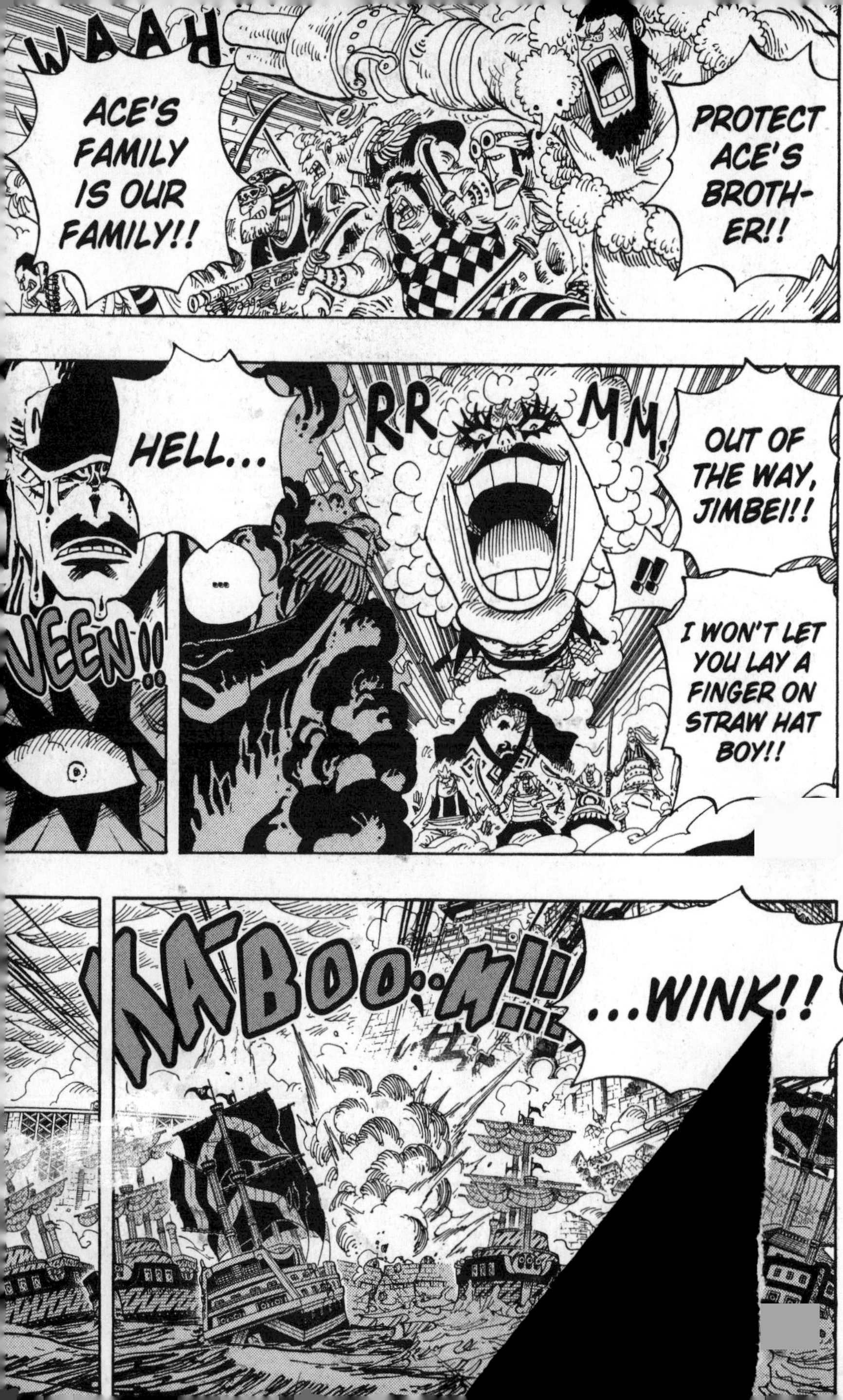
WAAH
PROTECT ACE'S BROTH-ER!!
ACE'S FAMILY IS OUR FAMILY!!
RR MM
OUT OF THE WAY, JIMBEI!!
!!
I WON'T LET YOU LAY A FINGER ON STRAW HAT BOY!!
...
HELL...
VEEN!!
...WINK!!
KABOO..M!!

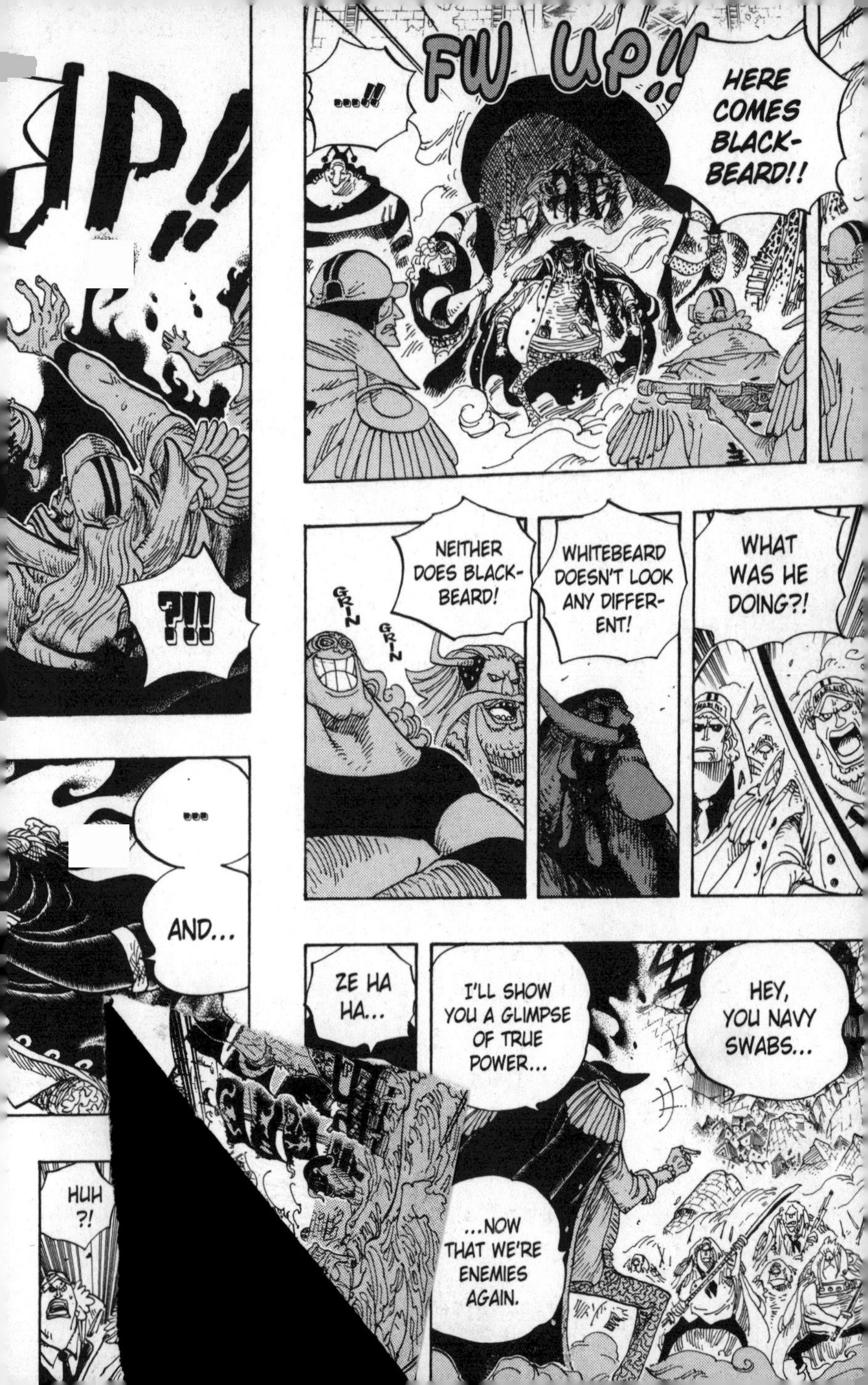
FW UP!!
HERE COMES BLACK-BEARD!!
...!!
WHAT WAS HE DOING?!
WHITEBEARD DOESN'T LOOK ANY DIFFERENT!
NEITHER DOES BLACK-BEARD!
GRIN
GRIN
HEY, YOU NAVY SWABS...
I'LL SHOW YOU A GLIMPSE OF TRUE POWER...
...NOW THAT WE'RE ENEMIES AGAIN.
ZE HA HA...
P!!
?!!
...
AND...
HUH ?!

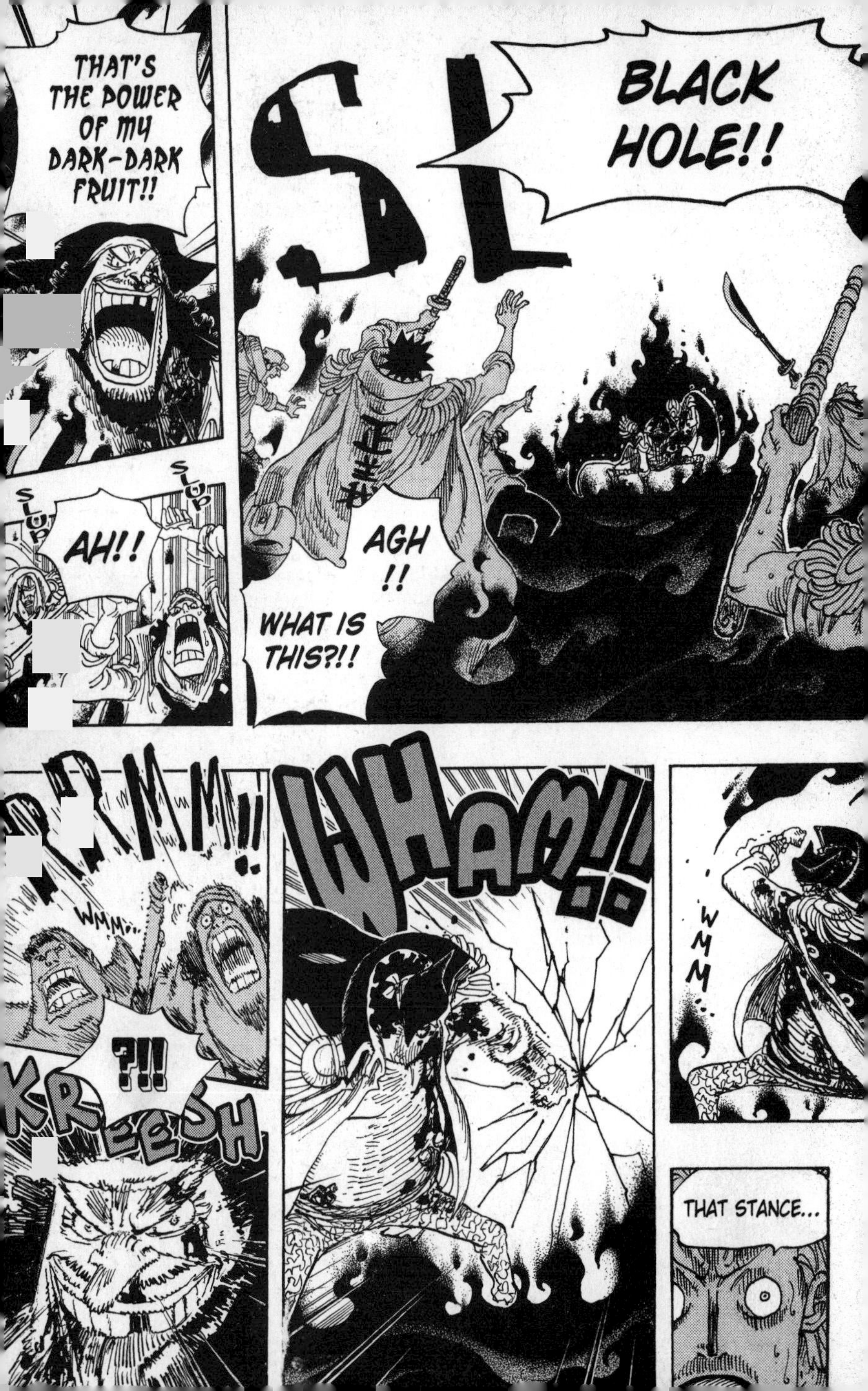
SHI
BLACK HOLE!!
AGH !!
WHAT IS THIS?!!
THAT'S THE POWER OF MY DARK-DARK FRUIT!!
SLUP
SLUP
AH!!
WMM...
THAT STANCE...
WHAM!!
RMMM!!
WMM...
?!!
KREESH

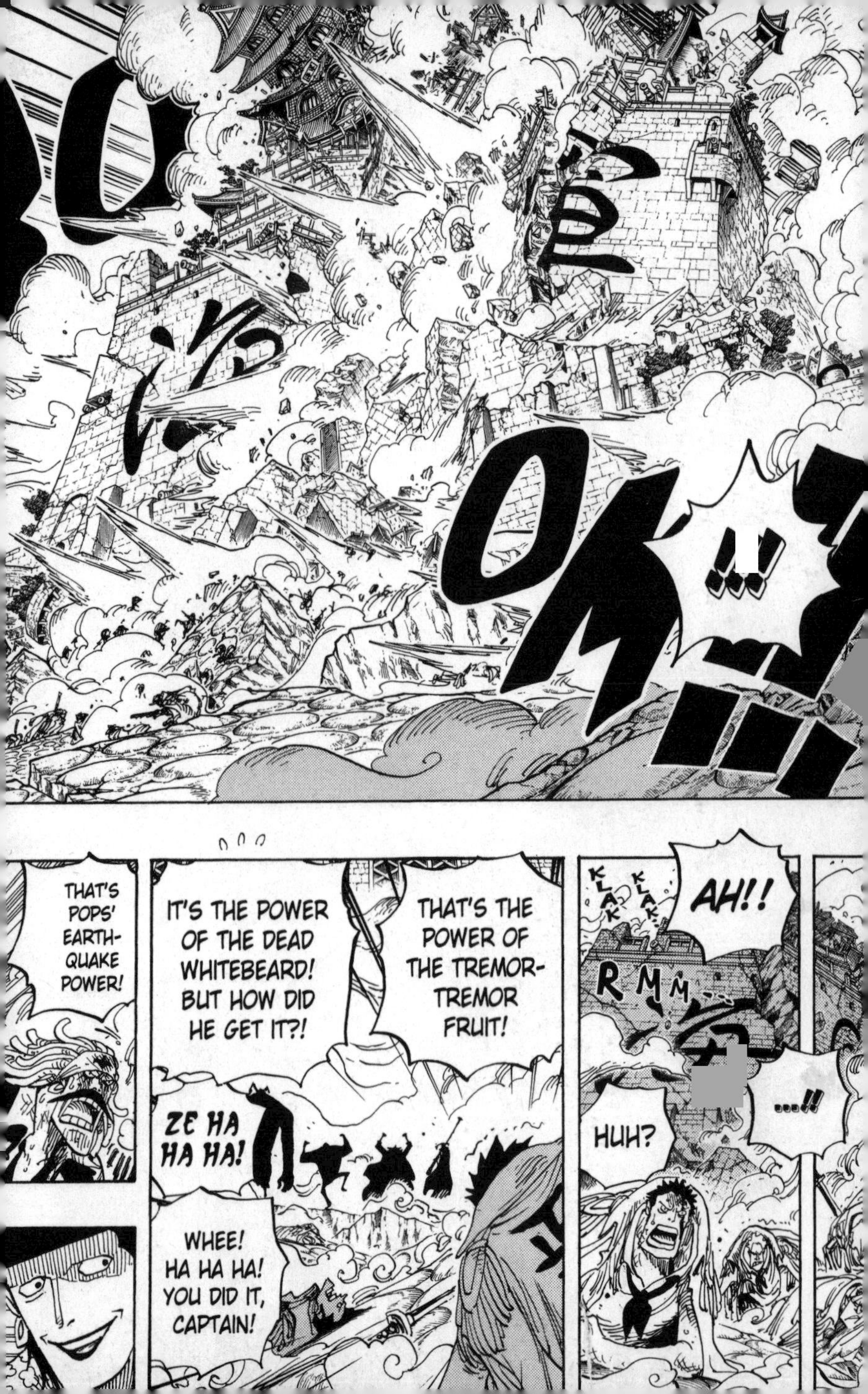
OM!!
AH!!
KLAK KLAK
RMMM
...!!
HUH?
THAT'S THE POWER OF THE TREMOR-TREMOR FRUIT!
IT'S THE POWER OF THE DEAD WHITEBEARD! BUT HOW DID HE GET IT?!
ZE HA HA HA!
WHEE! HA HA HA! YOU DID IT, CAPTAIN!
THAT'S POPS' EARTHQUAKE POWER!

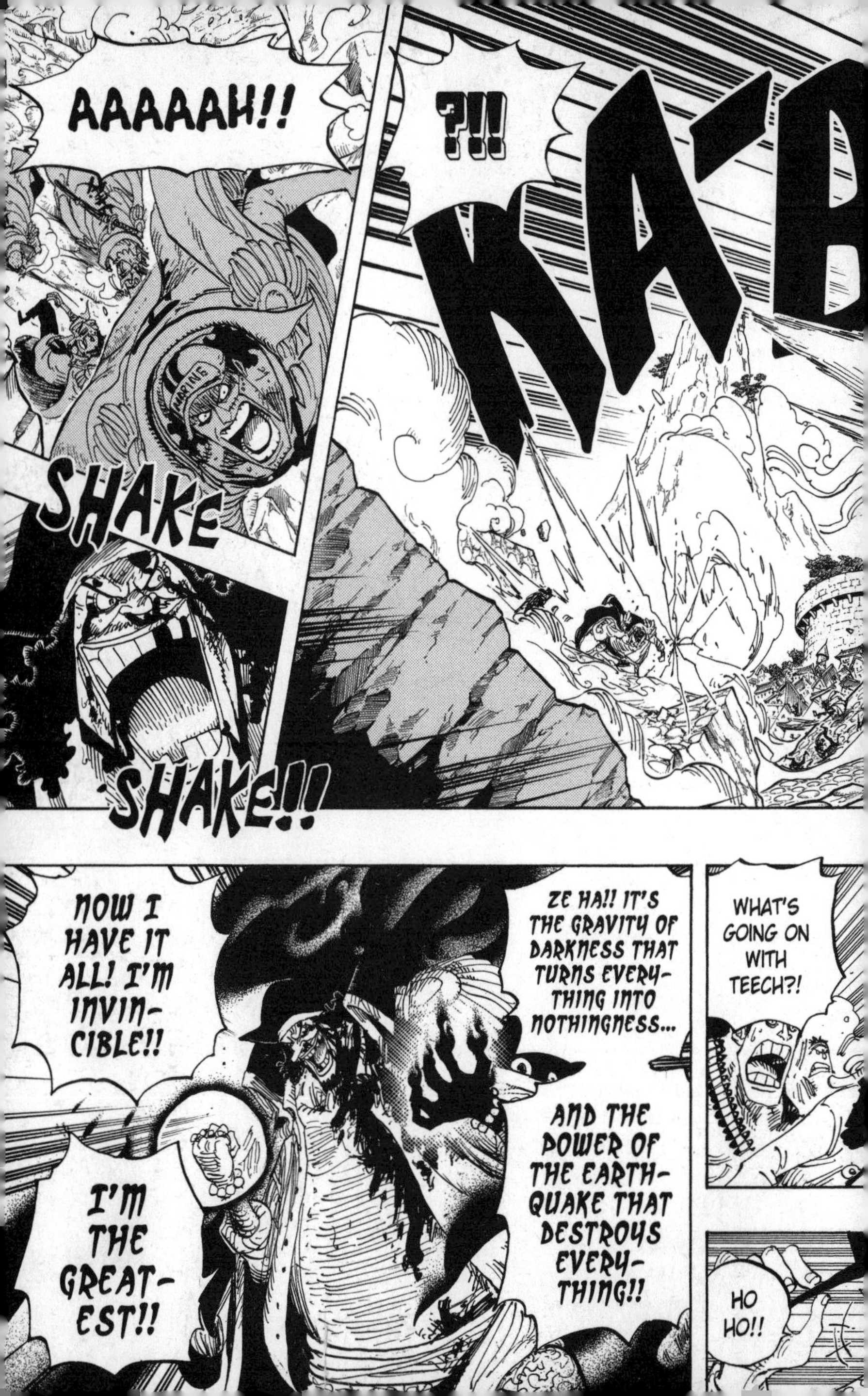
?!!
KA'B
AAAAAH!!
SHAKE
SHAKE!!
WHAT'S GOING ON WITH TEECH?!
HO HO!!
ZE HA!! IT'S THE GRAVITY OF DARKNESS THAT TURNS EVERY-THING INTO NOTHINGNESS...
AND THE POWER OF THE EARTH-QUAKE THAT DESTROYS EVERY-THING!!
NOW I HAVE IT ALL! I'M INVIN-CIBLE!!
I'M THE GREAT-EST!!

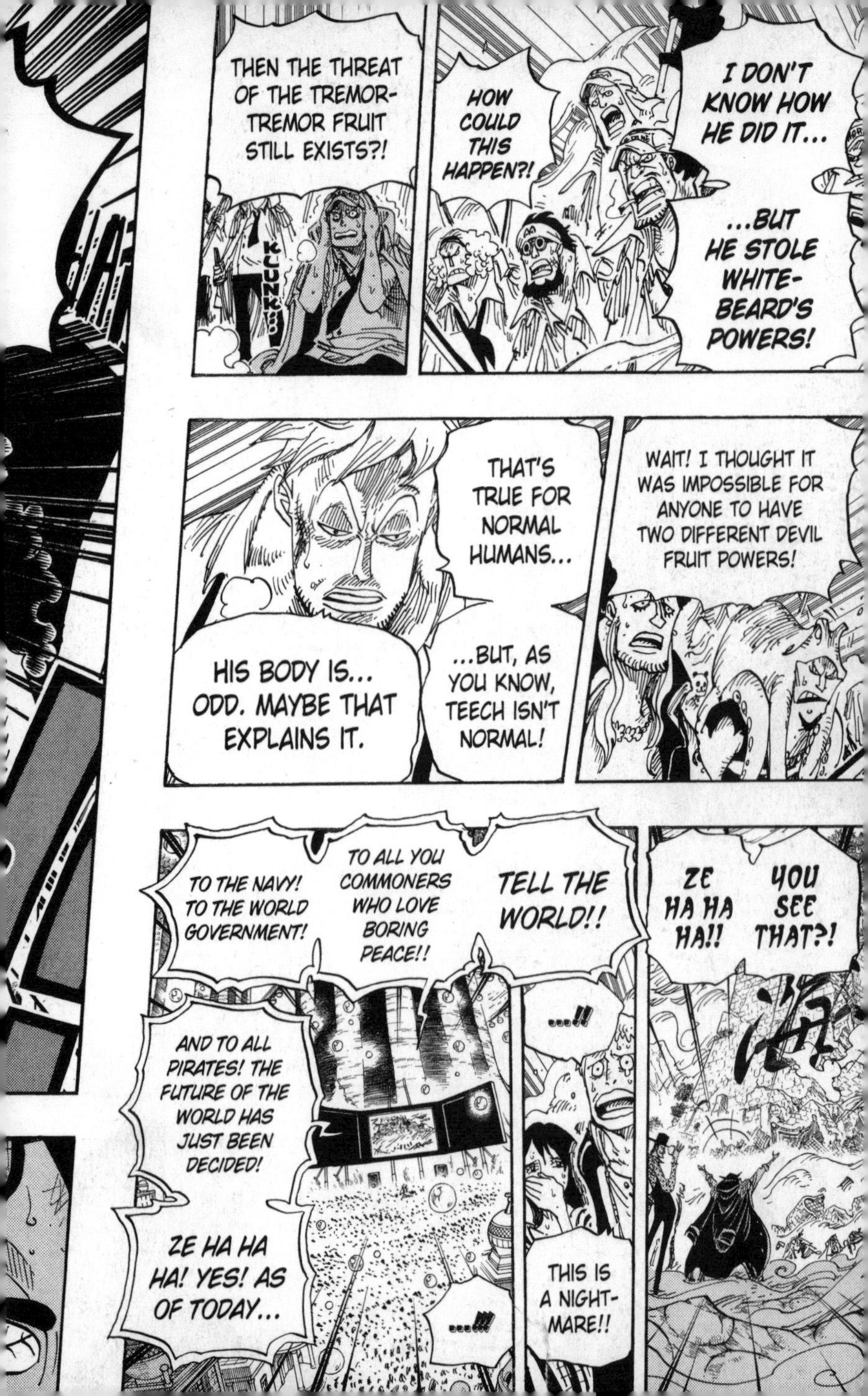
I DON'T KNOW HOW HE DID IT…
HOW COULD THIS HAPPEN?!
…BUT HE STOLE WHITE-BEARD'S POWERS!
THEN THE THREAT OF THE TREMOR-TREMOR FRUIT STILL EXISTS?!
KLUNK
WAIT! I THOUGHT IT WAS IMPOSSIBLE FOR ANYONE TO HAVE TWO DIFFERENT DEVIL FRUIT POWERS!
THAT'S TRUE FOR NORMAL HUMANS…
…BUT, AS YOU KNOW, TEECH ISN'T NORMAL!
HIS BODY IS… ODD. MAYBE THAT EXPLAINS IT.
YOU SEE THAT?!
ZE HA HA HA!!
TELL THE WORLD!!
TO ALL YOU COMMONERS WHO LOVE BORING PEACE!!
TO THE NAVY! TO THE WORLD GOVERNMENT!
…!!
THIS IS A NIGHT-MARE!!
AND TO ALL PIRATES! THE FUTURE OF THE WORLD HAS JUST BEEN DECIDED!
ZE HA HA HA! YES! AS OF TODAY…
……!!!

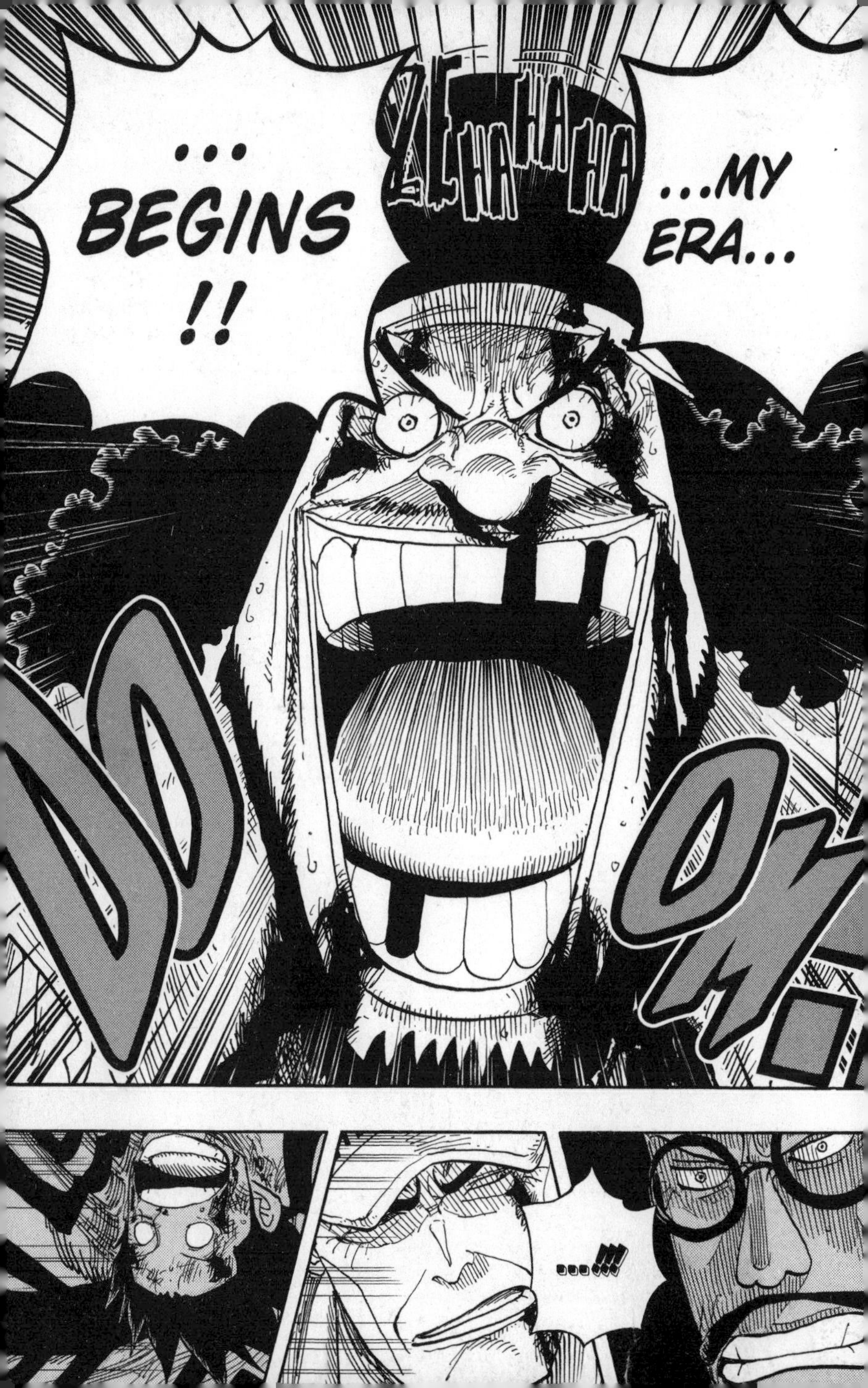
ZEHAHAHA
...MY ERA...
...BEGINS!!
...!!!

FOR THE NEW ERA

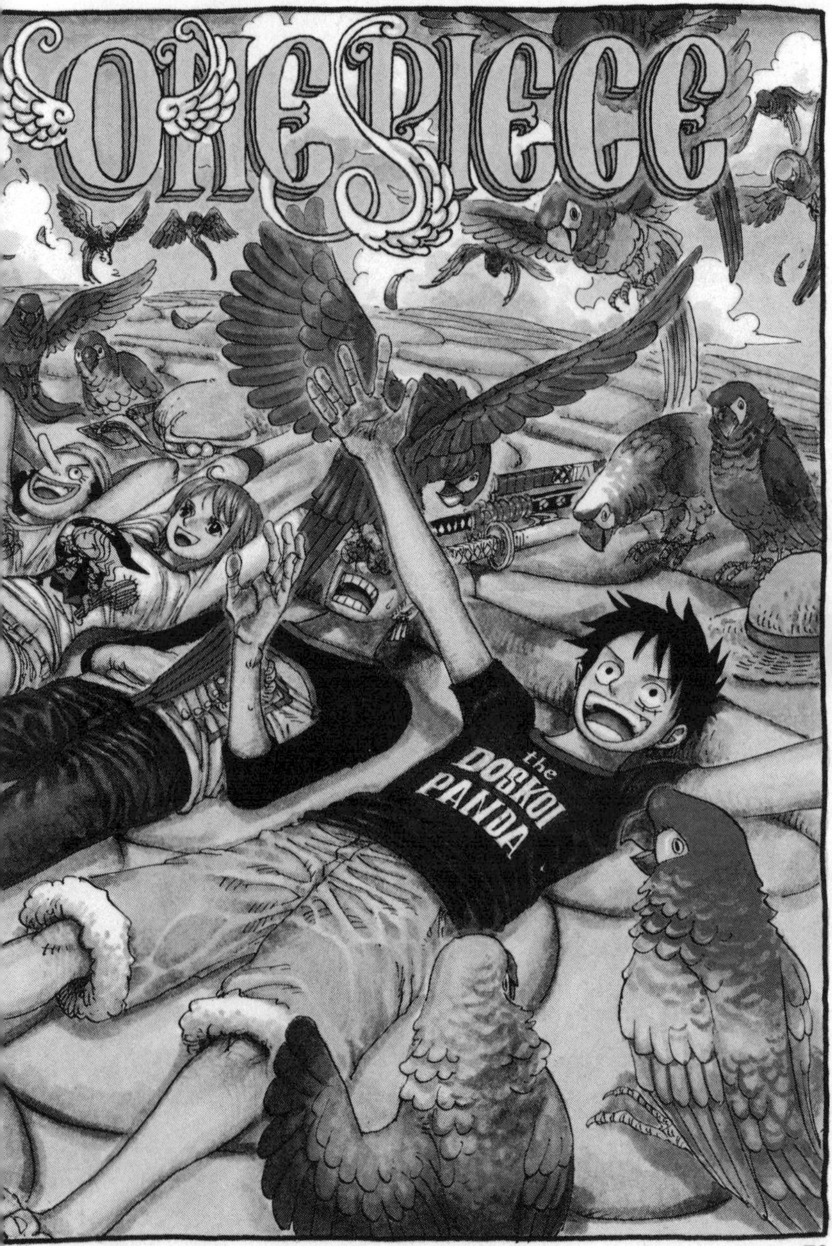
ONE PIECE
the
DOSKOI
PANDA

Chapter 578: A GIFT

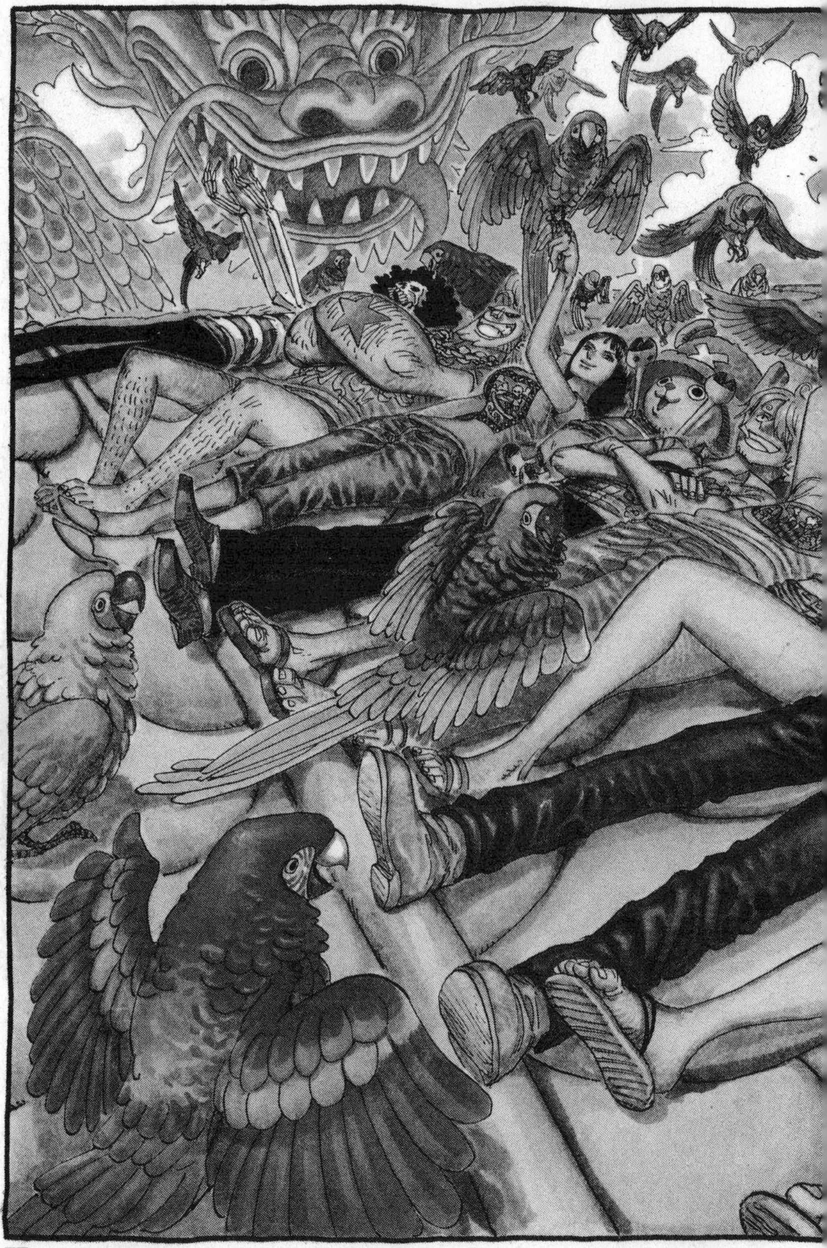

vol.59

ONE PIECE

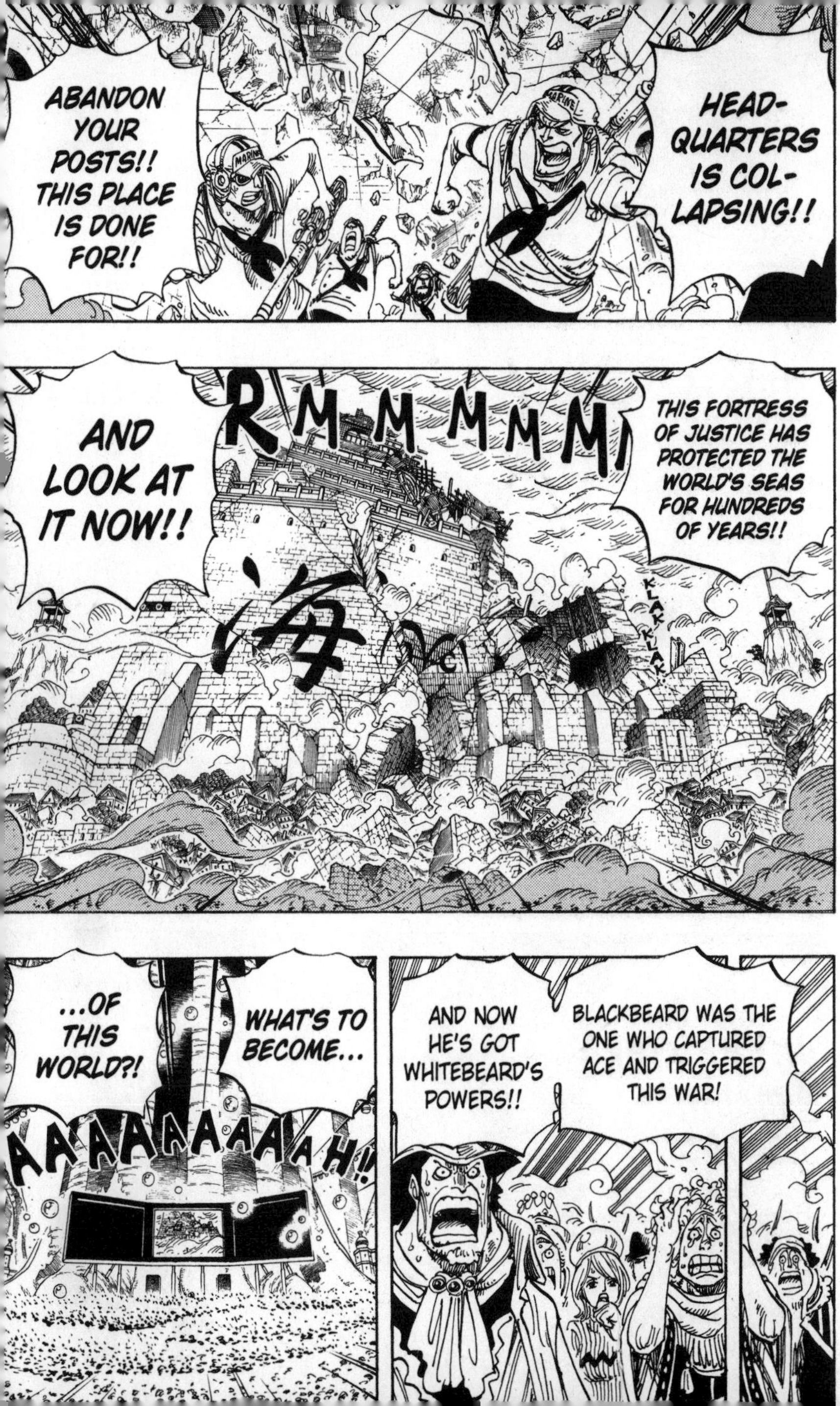
HEADQUARTERS IS COLLAPSING!!
ABANDON YOUR POSTS!! THIS PLACE IS DONE FOR!!
THIS FORTRESS OF JUSTICE HAS PROTECTED THE WORLD'S SEAS FOR HUNDREDS OF YEARS!!
RMMMMM
KLAK KLAK
AND LOOK AT IT NOW!!
BLACKBEARD WAS THE ONE WHO CAPTURED ACE AND TRIGGERED THIS WAR!
AND NOW HE'S GOT WHITEBEARD'S POWERS!!
WHAT'S TO BECOME...
...OF THIS WORLD?!
AAAAAAAAAAH!!

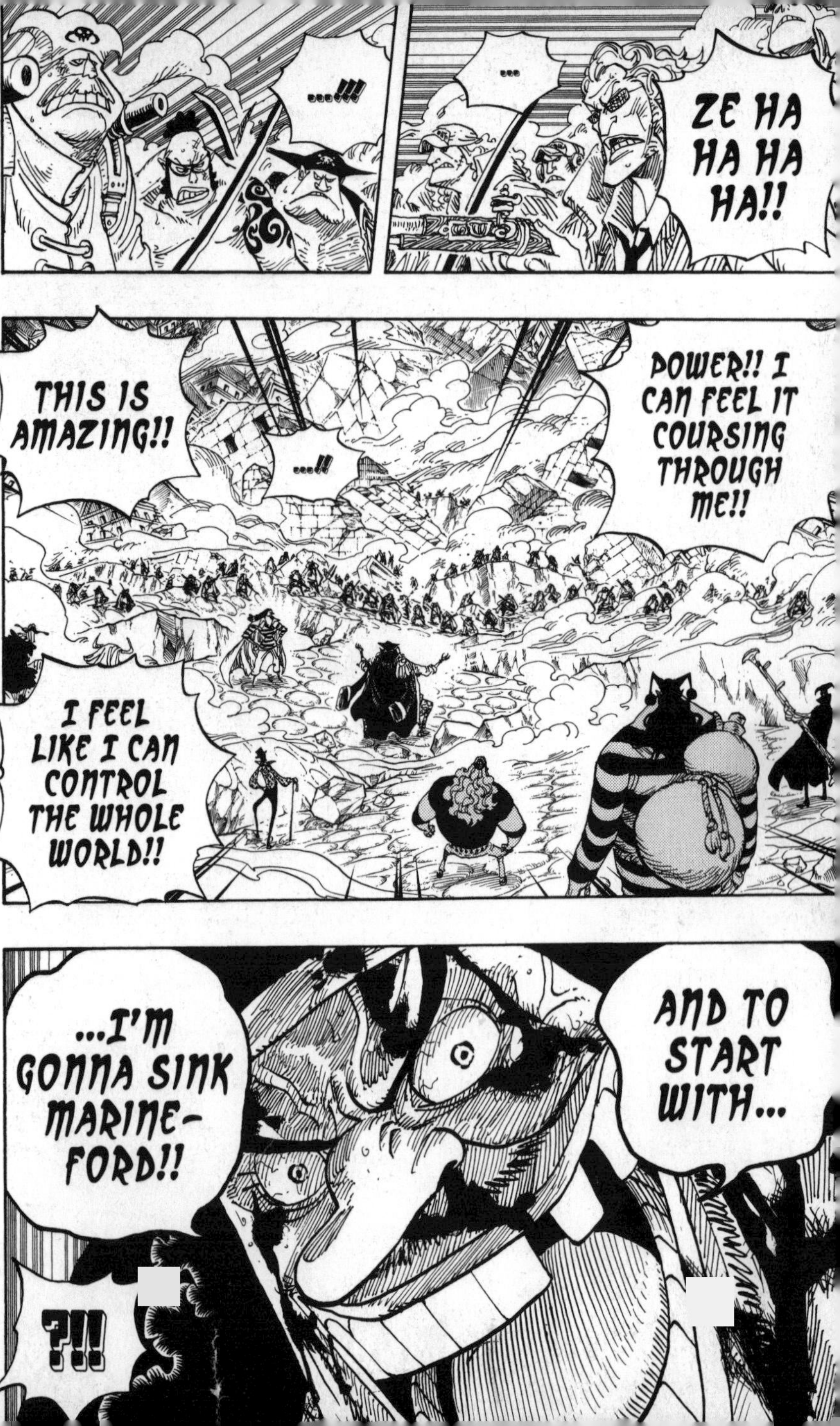
ZE HA HA HA HA!!
...
...!!!
POWER!! I CAN FEEL IT COURSING THROUGH ME!!
THIS IS AMAZING!!
...!!
I FEEL LIKE I CAN CONTROL THE WHOLE WORLD!!
AND TO START WITH...
...I'M GONNA SINK MARINE-FORD!!
?!!

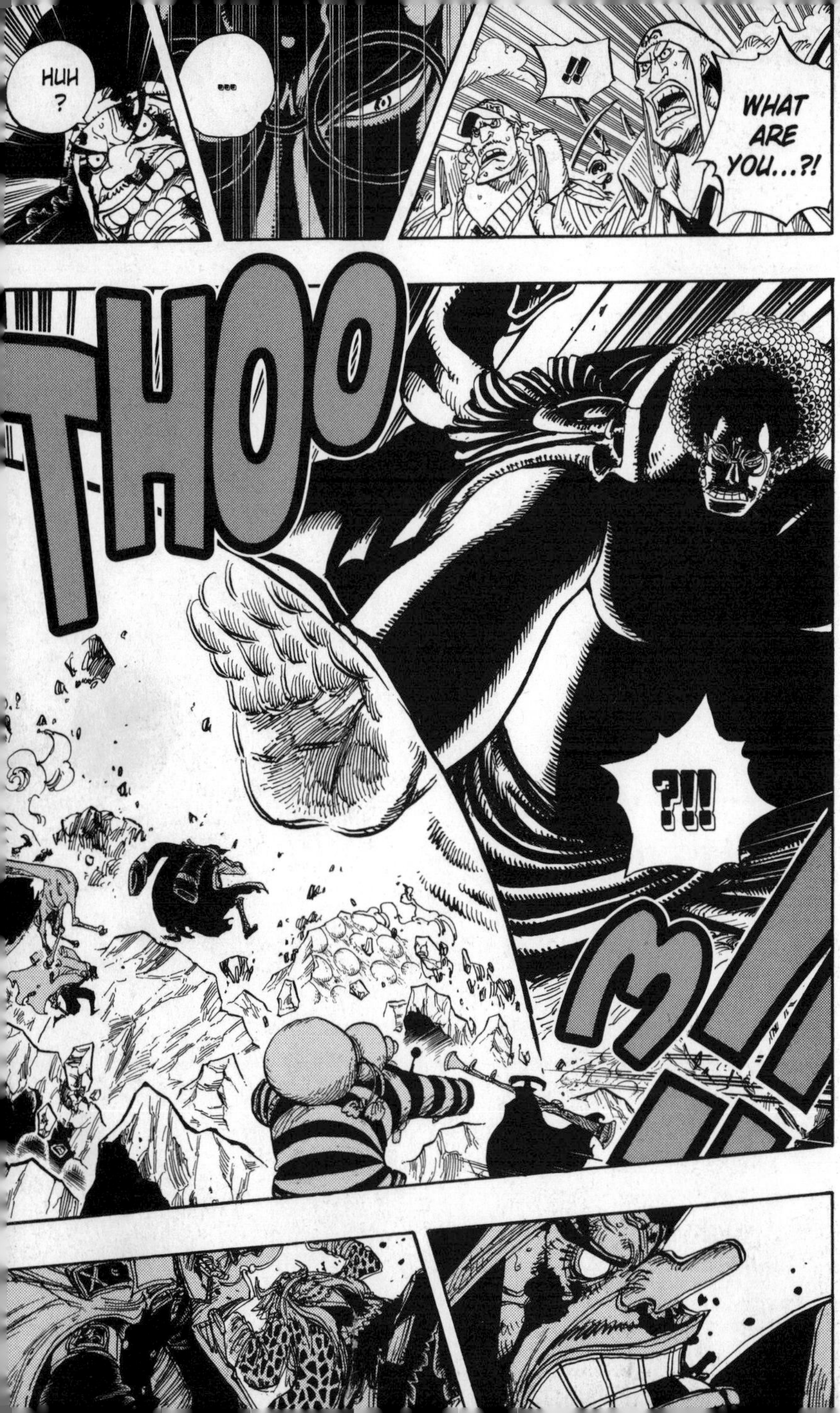
WHAT ARE YOU...?!
!!
...
HUH ?
?!!
THOO

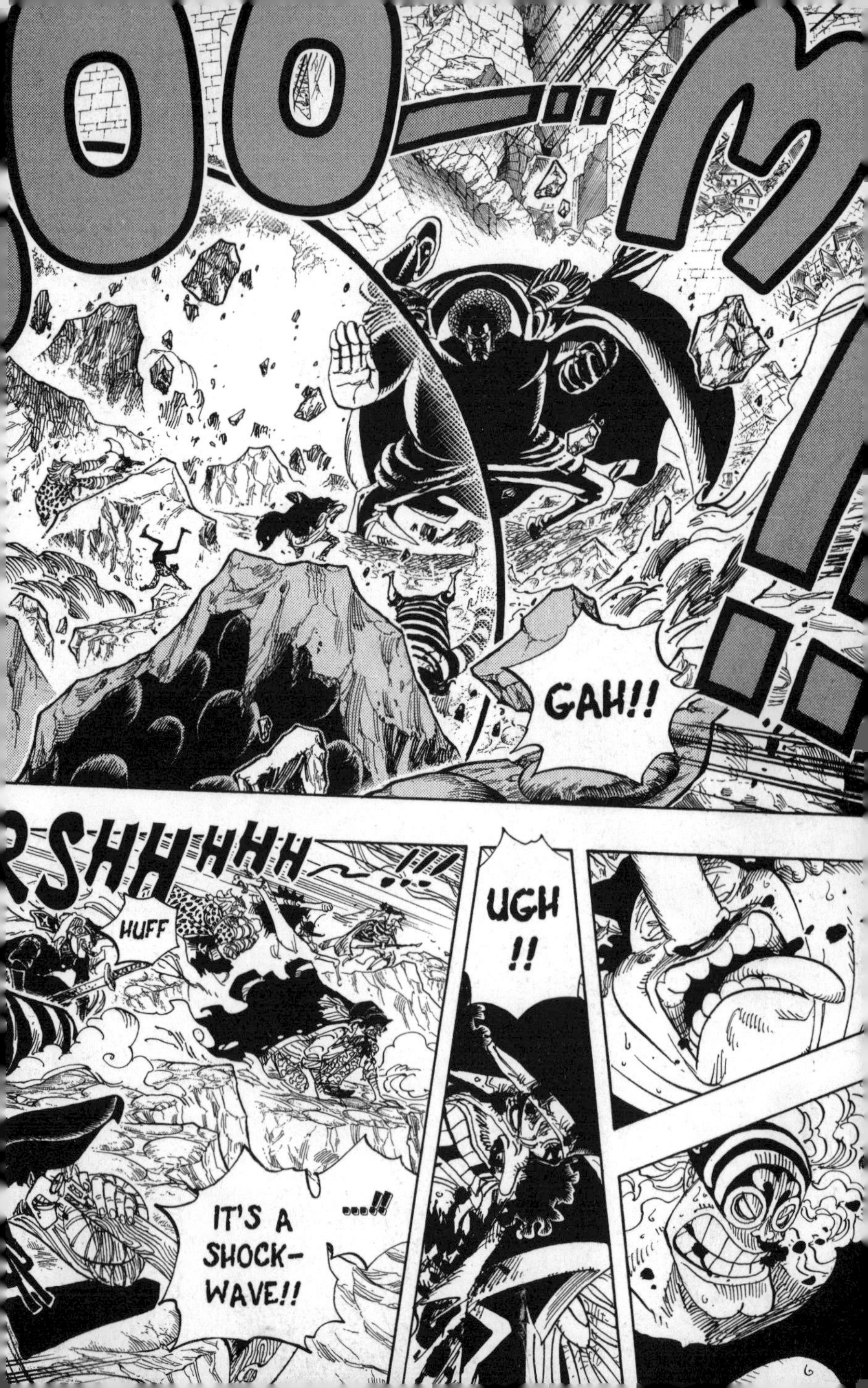
GAH!!
UGH !!
RSHHHHH~!!!
HUFF
...!!
IT'S A SHOCK-WAVE!!

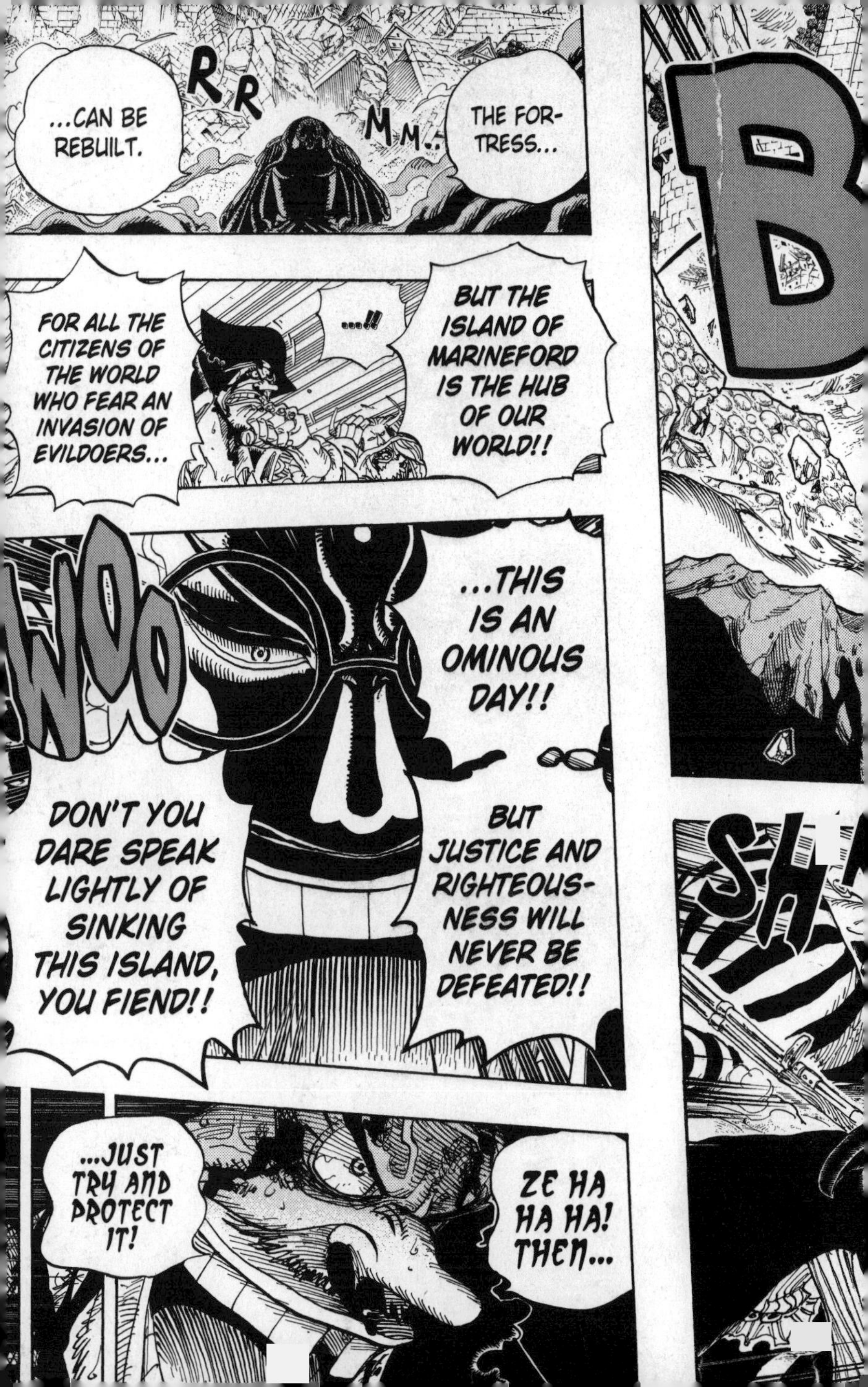
B
SH
THE FOR-TRESS...
RRMM..
...CAN BE REBUILT.
BUT THE ISLAND OF MARINEFORD IS THE HUB OF OUR WORLD!!
...!!
FOR ALL THE CITIZENS OF THE WORLD WHO FEAR AN INVASION OF EVILDOERS...
...THIS IS AN OMINOUS DAY!!
BUT JUSTICE AND RIGHTEOUS-NESS WILL NEVER BE DEFEATED!!
WOO
DON'T YOU DARE SPEAK LIGHTLY OF SINKING THIS ISLAND, YOU FIEND!!
ZE HA HA HA! THEN...
...JUST TRY AND PROTECT IT!

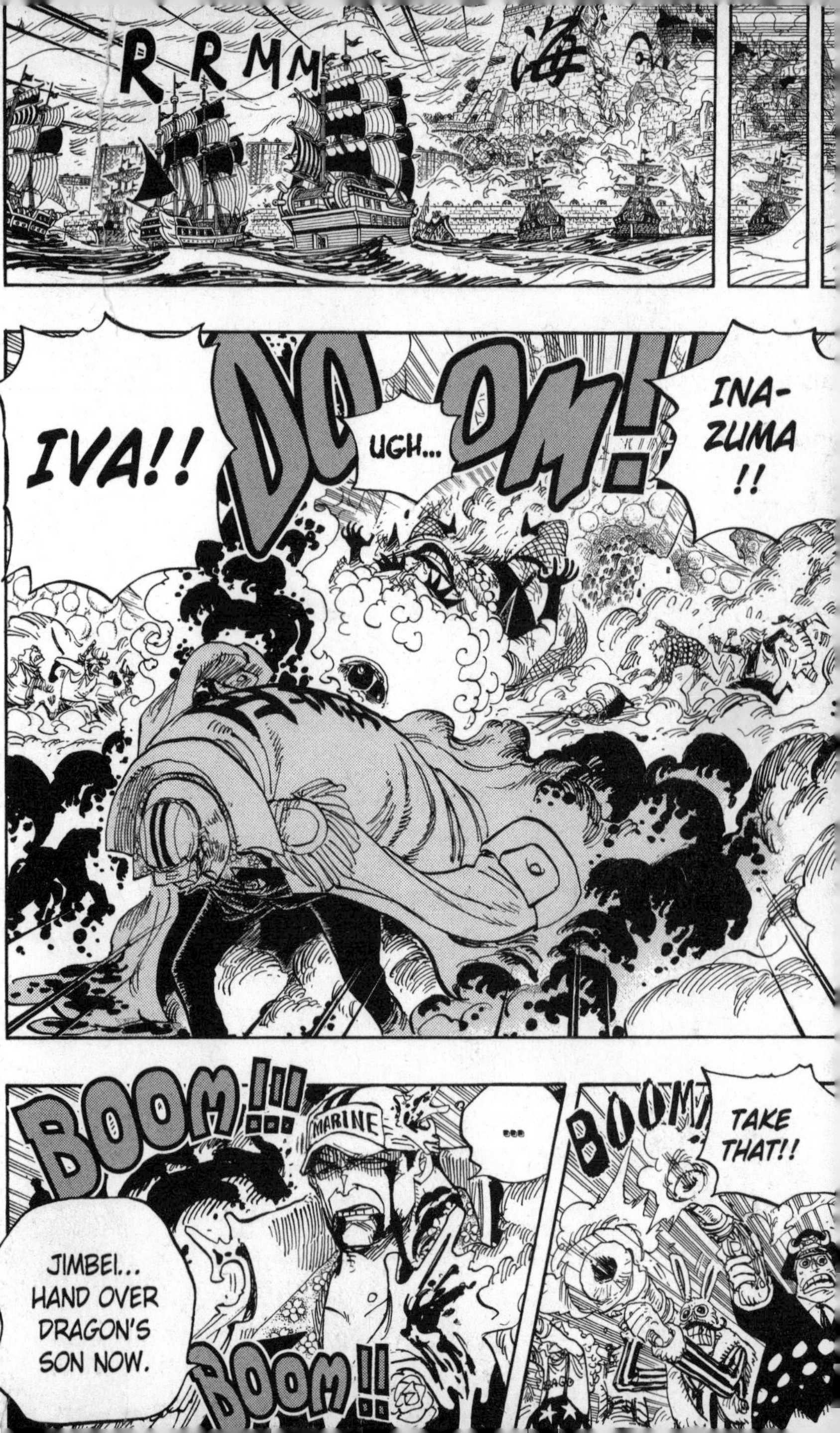
R R MM
海
INA-ZUMA!!
DO OM!
UGH...
IVA!!
TAKE THAT!!
BOOM
...
BOOM!!!
MARINE
JIMBEI... HAND OVER DRAGON'S SON NOW.
BOOM!!

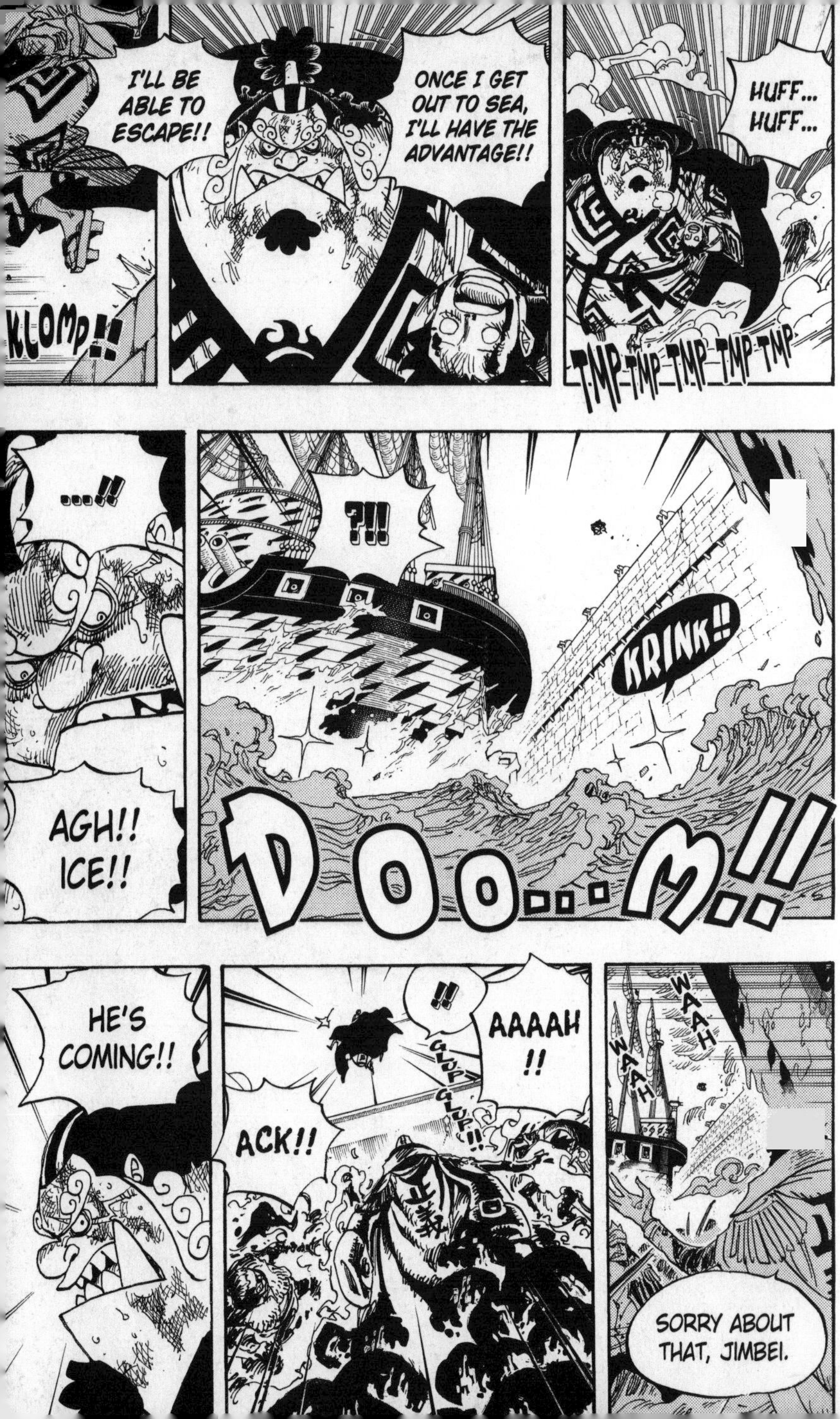
HUFF... HUFF...
TMP TMP TMP TMP TMP
ONCE I GET OUT TO SEA, I'LL HAVE THE ADVANTAGE!!
I'LL BE ABLE TO ESCAPE!!
KLOMP!!
?!!
KRINK!!
DOO...M!!
...!!
AGH!! ICE!!
WAAH
WAAH
SORRY ABOUT THAT, JIMBEI.
!!
AAAAH!!
GLUP
GLUP!!
ACK!!
HE'S COMING!!

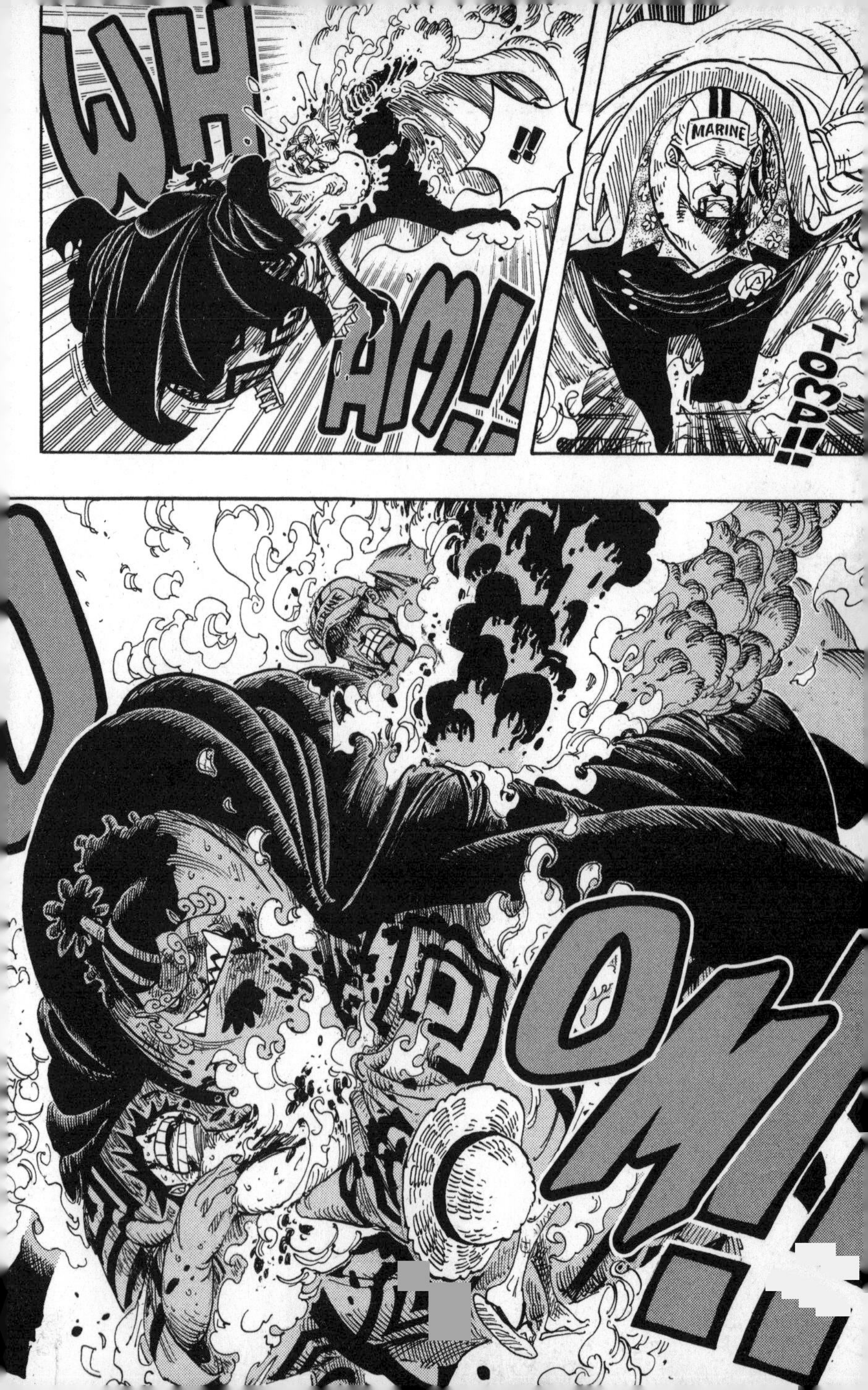
TOMP!!
WHAM!!
!!

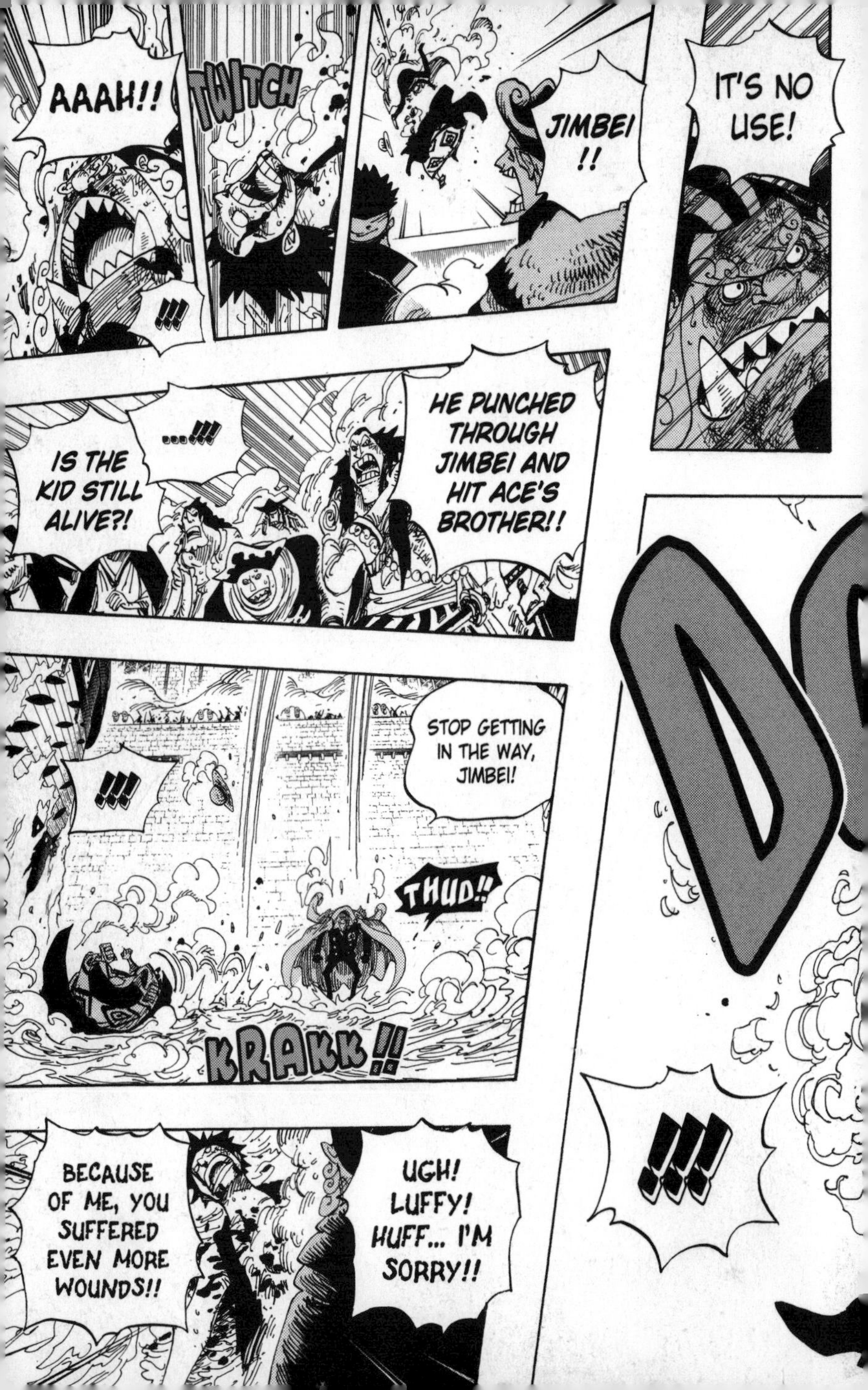
IT'S NO USE!
JIMBEI !!
TWITCH
AAAH!!
!!!
!!!
HE PUNCHED THROUGH JIMBEI AND HIT ACE'S BROTHER!!
...!!!
IS THE KID STILL ALIVE?!
STOP GETTING IN THE WAY, JIMBEI!
THUD!!
!!!
KRAKK!!
UGH! LUFFY! HUFF... I'M SORRY!!
BECAUSE OF ME, YOU SUFFERED EVEN MORE WOUNDS!!

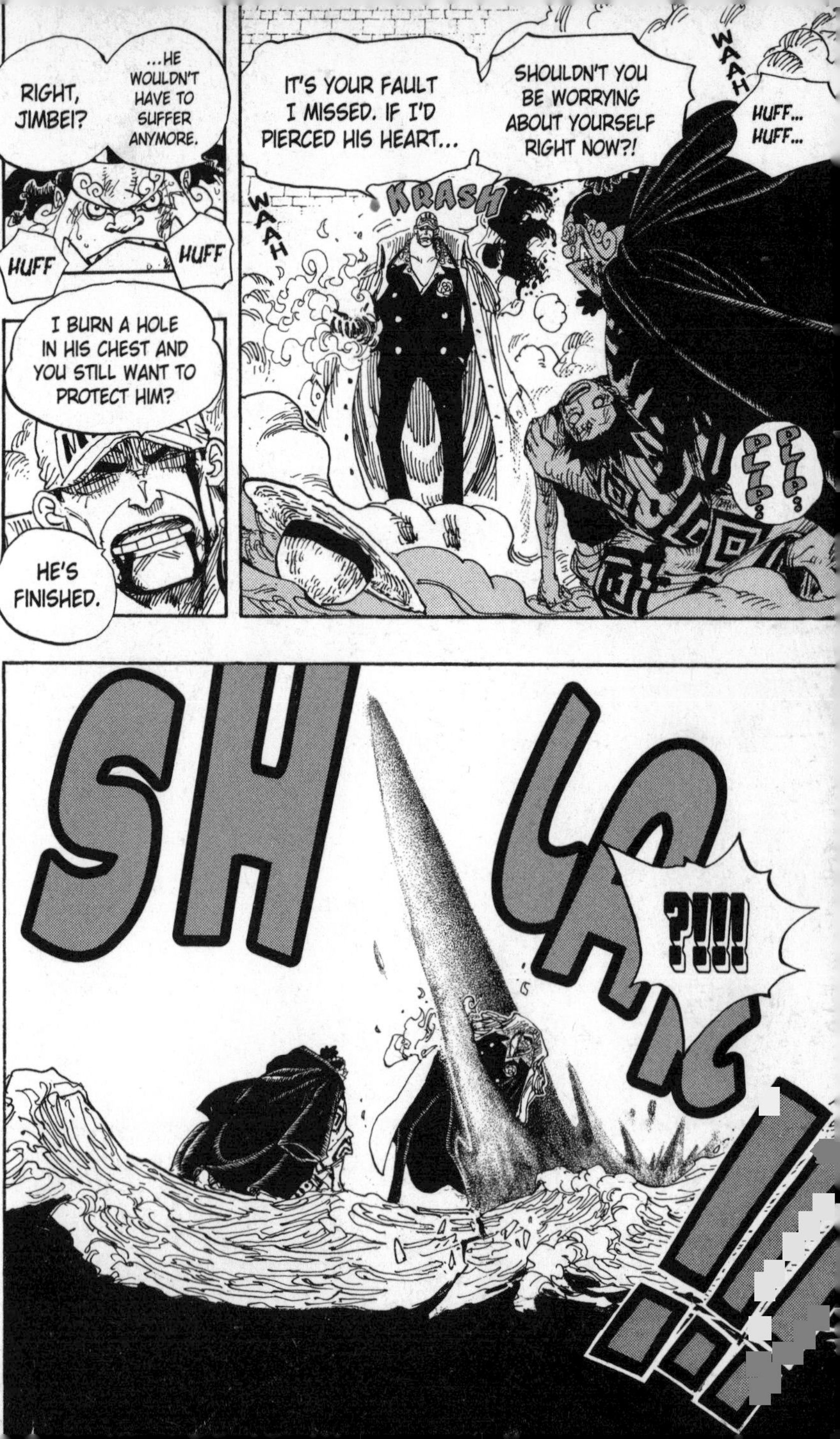
WAAH
HUFF... HUFF...
SHOULDN'T YOU BE WORRYING ABOUT YOURSELF RIGHT NOW?!
IT'S YOUR FAULT I MISSED. IF I'D PIERCED HIS HEART...
KRASH
WAAH
PLIP PLIP
...HE WOULDN'T HAVE TO SUFFER ANYMORE.
RIGHT, JIMBEI?
HUFF
HUFF
I BURN A HOLE IN HIS CHEST AND YOU STILL WANT TO PROTECT HIM?
HE'S FINISHED.
SH
?!!!

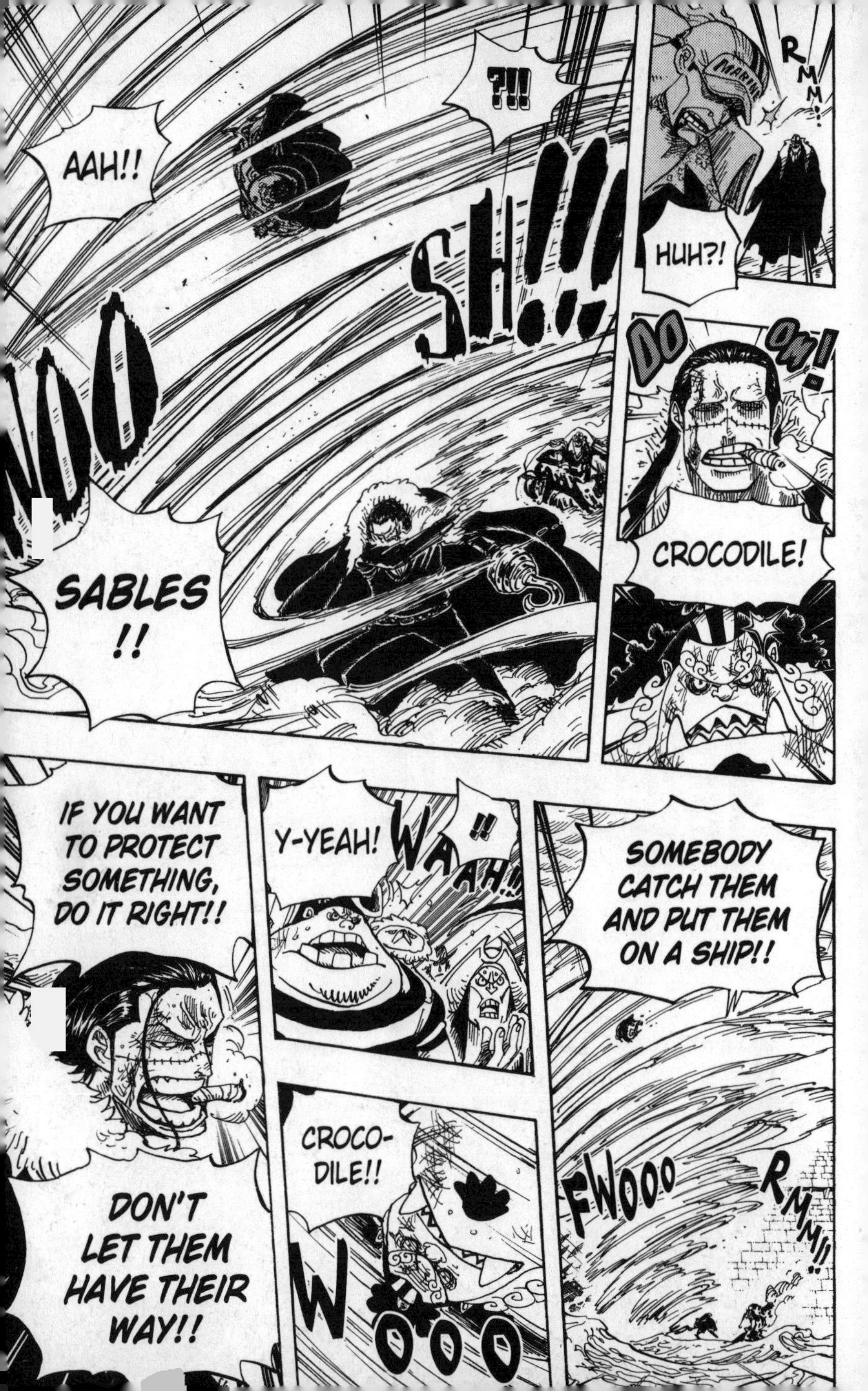
RMMM!!
HUH?!
DOOM!
CROCODILE!
?!!
AAH!!
SH!!!
WOOO
SABLES!!
SOMEBODY CATCH THEM AND PUT THEM ON A SHIP!!
FWOOORMMM!!
Y-YEAH!
WAAH!!
CROCO-DILE!!
WOOO
IF YOU WANT TO PROTECT SOMETHING, DO IT RIGHT!!
DON'T LET THEM HAVE THEIR WAY!!

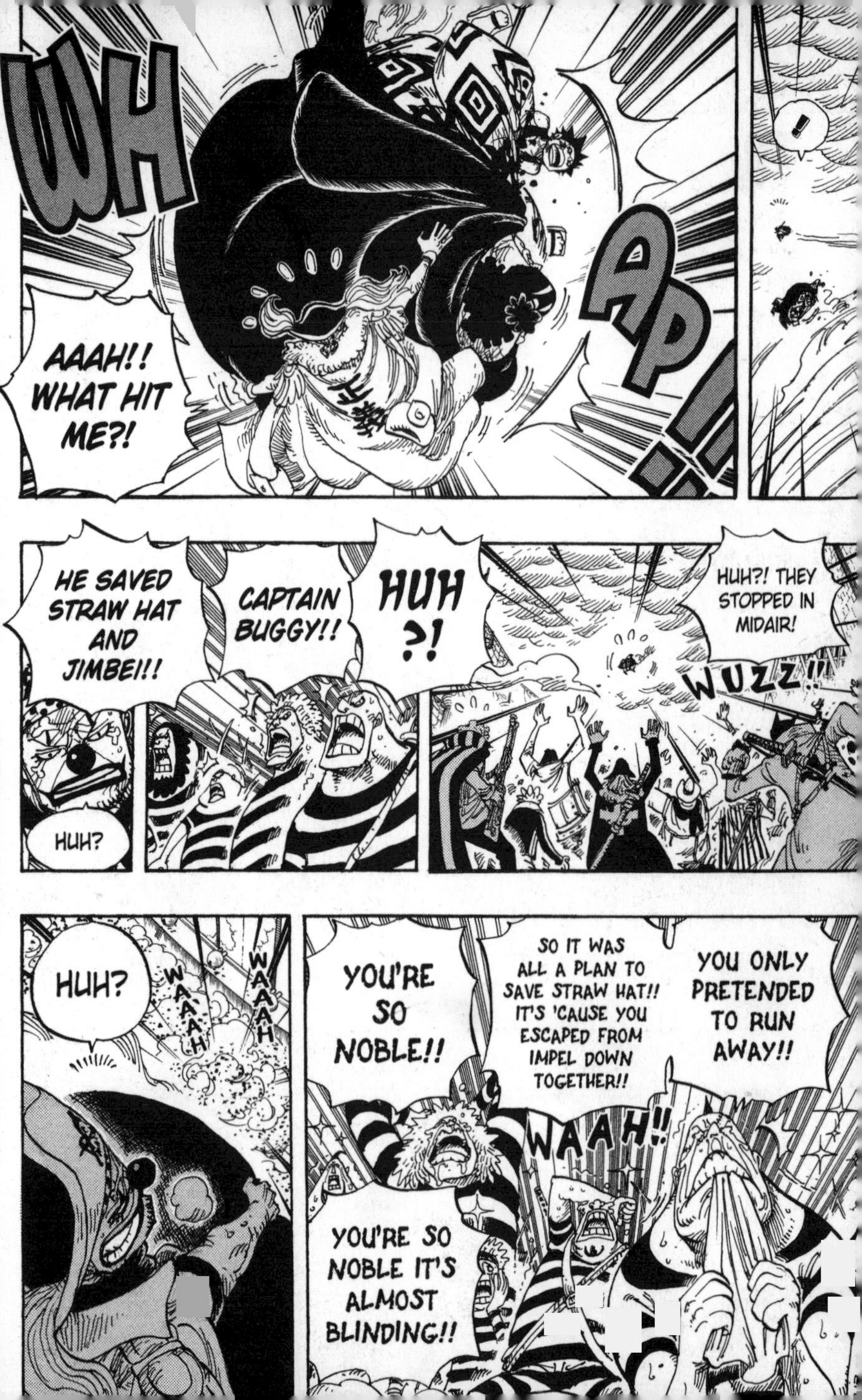

!
WH
AP!!
AAAH!! WHAT HIT ME?!
HUH?! THEY STOPPED IN MIDAIR!
WUZZ!!
HUH ?!
CAPTAIN BUGGY!!
HE SAVED STRAW HAT AND JIMBE!!
HUH?
YOU ONLY PRETENDED TO RUN AWAY!!
SO IT WAS ALL A PLAN TO SAVE STRAW HAT!! IT'S 'CAUSE YOU ESCAPED FROM IMPEL DOWN TOGETHER!!
YOU'RE SO NOBLE!!
WAAH!!
YOU'RE SO NOBLE IT'S ALMOST BLINDING!!
WAAAH
WAAAH
HUH?

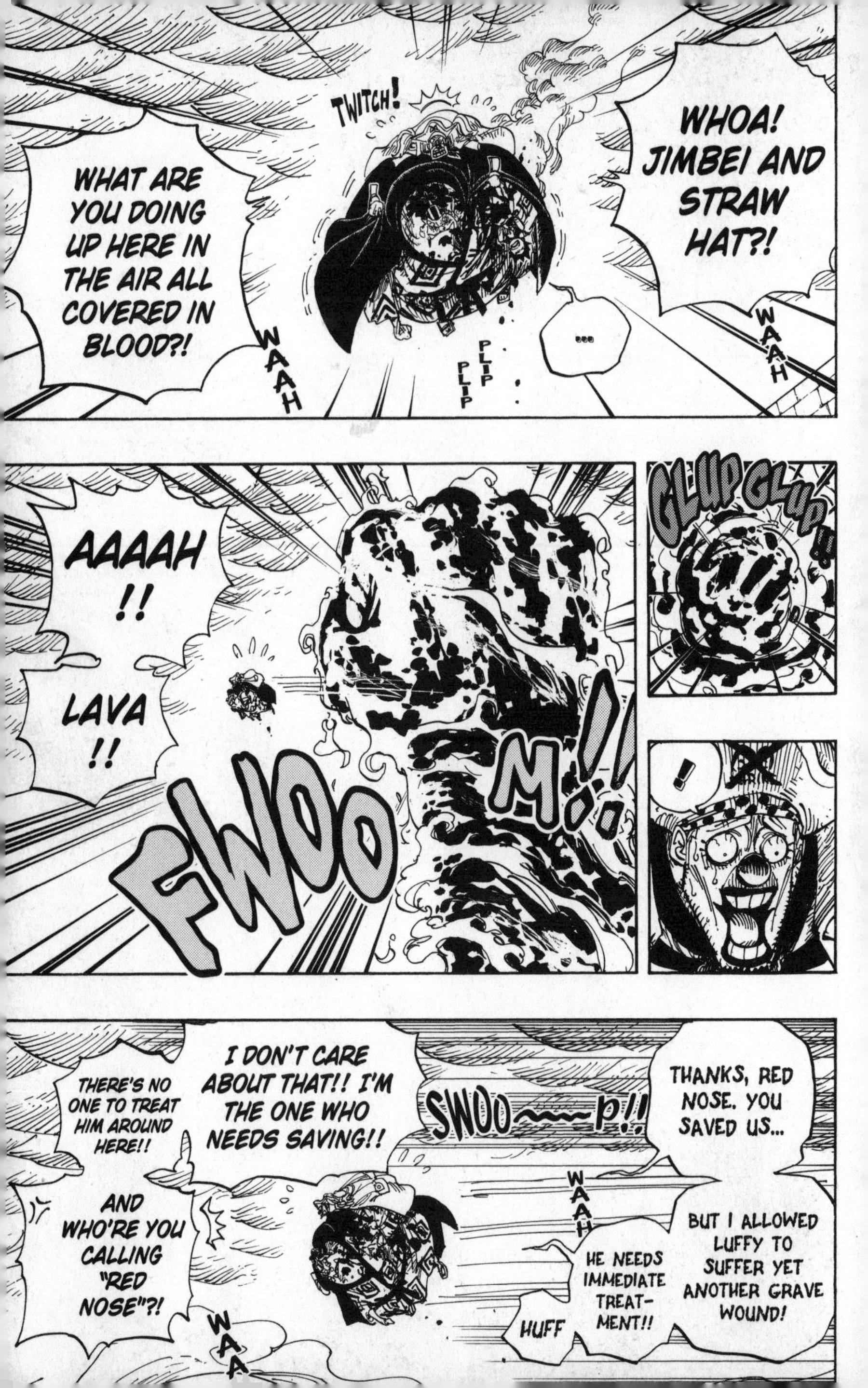
WHOA! JIMBEI AND STRAW HAT?!
WAAH
...
TWITCH!
PLIP PLIP
WHAT ARE YOU DOING UP HERE IN THE AIR ALL COVERED IN BLOOD?!
WAAH
GLUP GLUP!!
!
FWOOM!!
AAAAH!! LAVA!!
THANKS, RED NOSE. YOU SAVED US...
BUT I ALLOWED LUFFY TO SUFFER YET ANOTHER GRAVE WOUND!
HE NEEDS IMMEDIATE TREAT-MENT!!
WAAH
HUFF
SWOO~~P!!
I DON'T CARE ABOUT THAT!! I'M THE ONE WHO NEEDS SAVING!!
THERE'S NO ONE TO TREAT HIM AROUND HERE!!
AND WHO'RE YOU CALLING "RED NOSE"?!
WAA

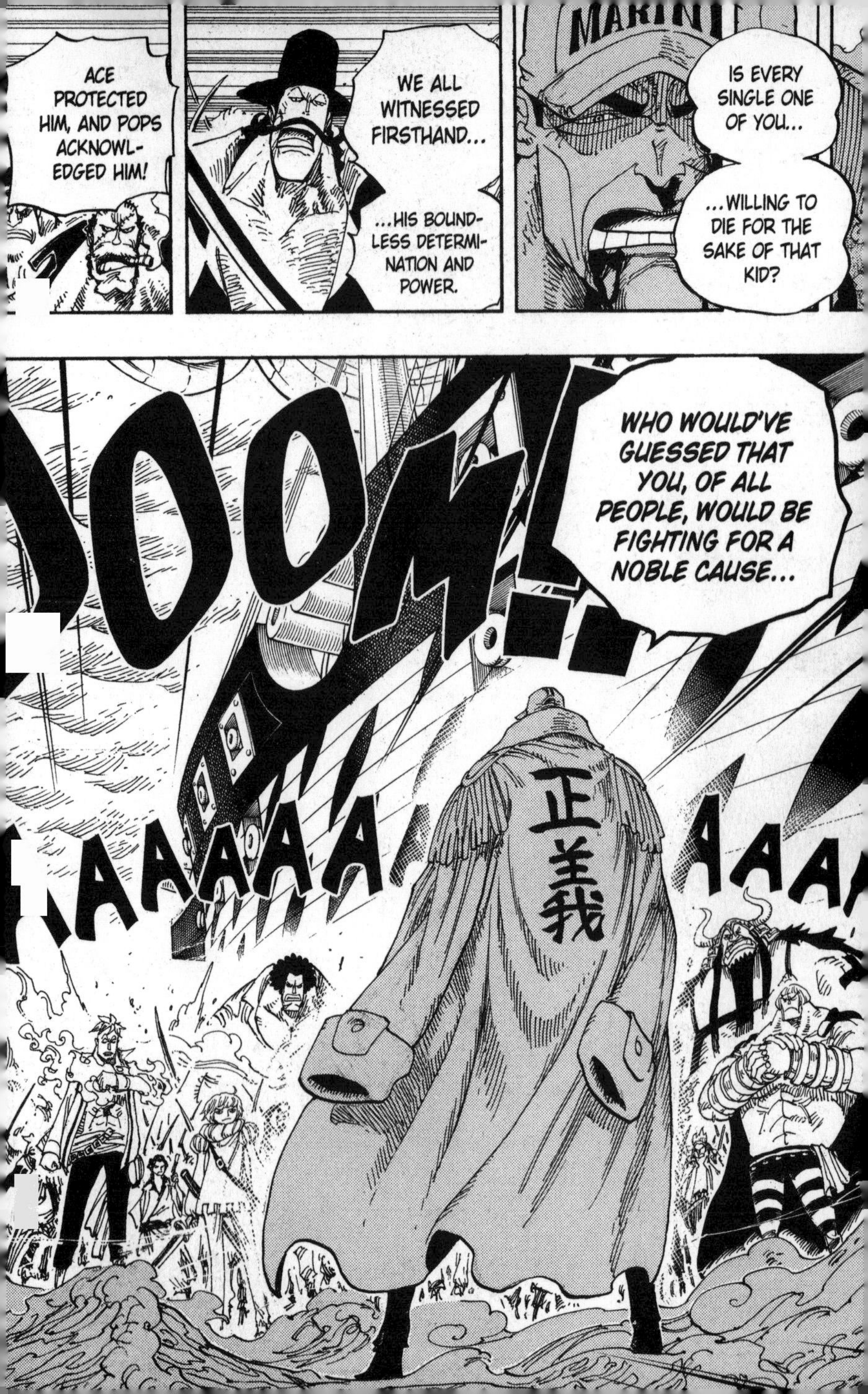
IS EVERY SINGLE ONE OF YOU...
...WILLING TO DIE FOR THE SAKE OF THAT KID?
WE ALL WITNESSED FIRSTHAND...
...HIS BOUNDLESS DETERMINATION AND POWER.
ACE PROTECTED HIM, AND POPS ACKNOWLEDGED HIM!
WHO WOULD'VE GUESSED THAT YOU, OF ALL PEOPLE, WOULD BE FIGHTING FOR A NOBLE CAUSE...
DOOM!!
AAAAAA AAA
正義

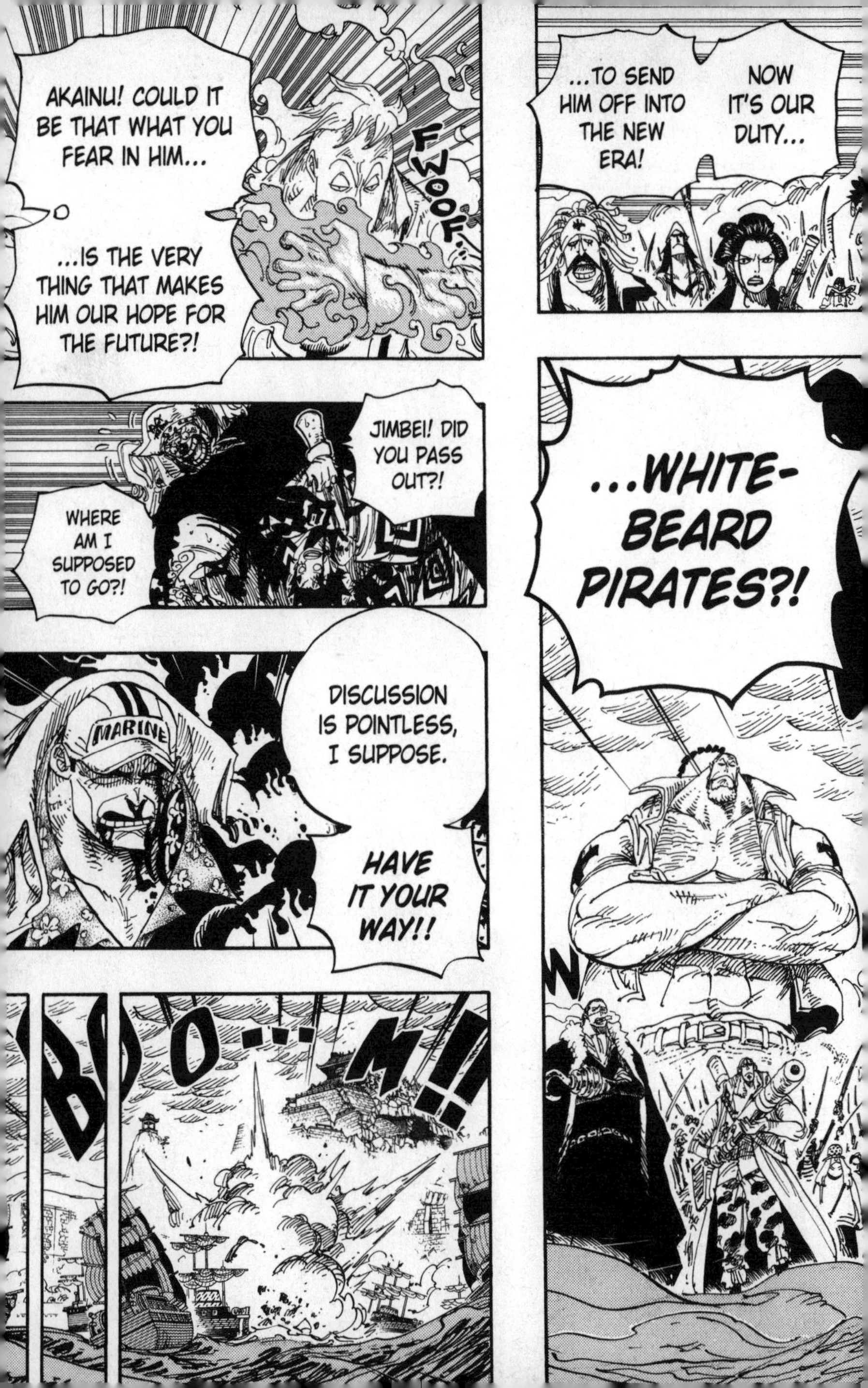
NOW IT'S OUR DUTY...
...TO SEND HIM OFF INTO THE NEW ERA!
...WHITE-BEARD PIRATES?!
AKAINU! COULD IT BE THAT WHAT YOU FEAR IN HIM...
FWOOF...
...IS THE VERY THING THAT MAKES HIM OUR HOPE FOR THE FUTURE?!
JIMBEI! DID YOU PASS OUT?!
WHERE AM I SUPPOSED TO GO?!
MARINE
DISCUSSION IS POINTLESS, I SUPPOSE.
HAVE IT YOUR WAY!!
BOO...M!!

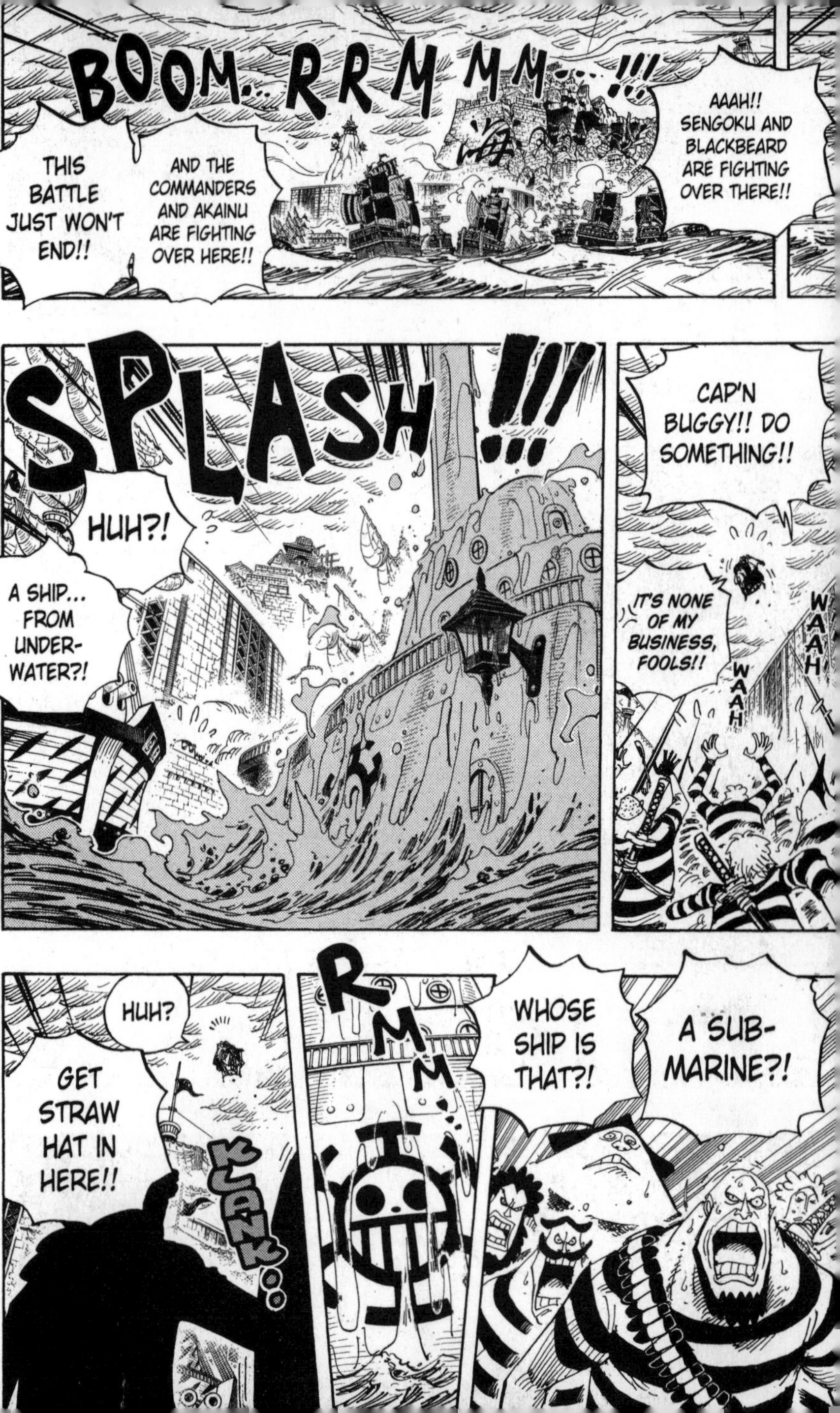
BOOM... RRMMMM...!!!
AAAH!! SENGOKU AND BLACKBEARD ARE FIGHTING OVER THERE!!
AND THE COMMANDERS AND AKAINU ARE FIGHTING OVER HERE!!
THIS BATTLE JUST WON'T END!!
CAP'N BUGGY!! DO SOMETHING!!
IT'S NONE OF MY BUSINESS, FOOLS!!
WAAH
WAAH
SPLASH!!!
HUH?!
A SHIP... FROM UNDER-WATER?!
A SUB-MARINE?!
WHOSE SHIP IS THAT?!
RMMM
HUH?
GET STRAW HAT IN HERE!!
KLANK...

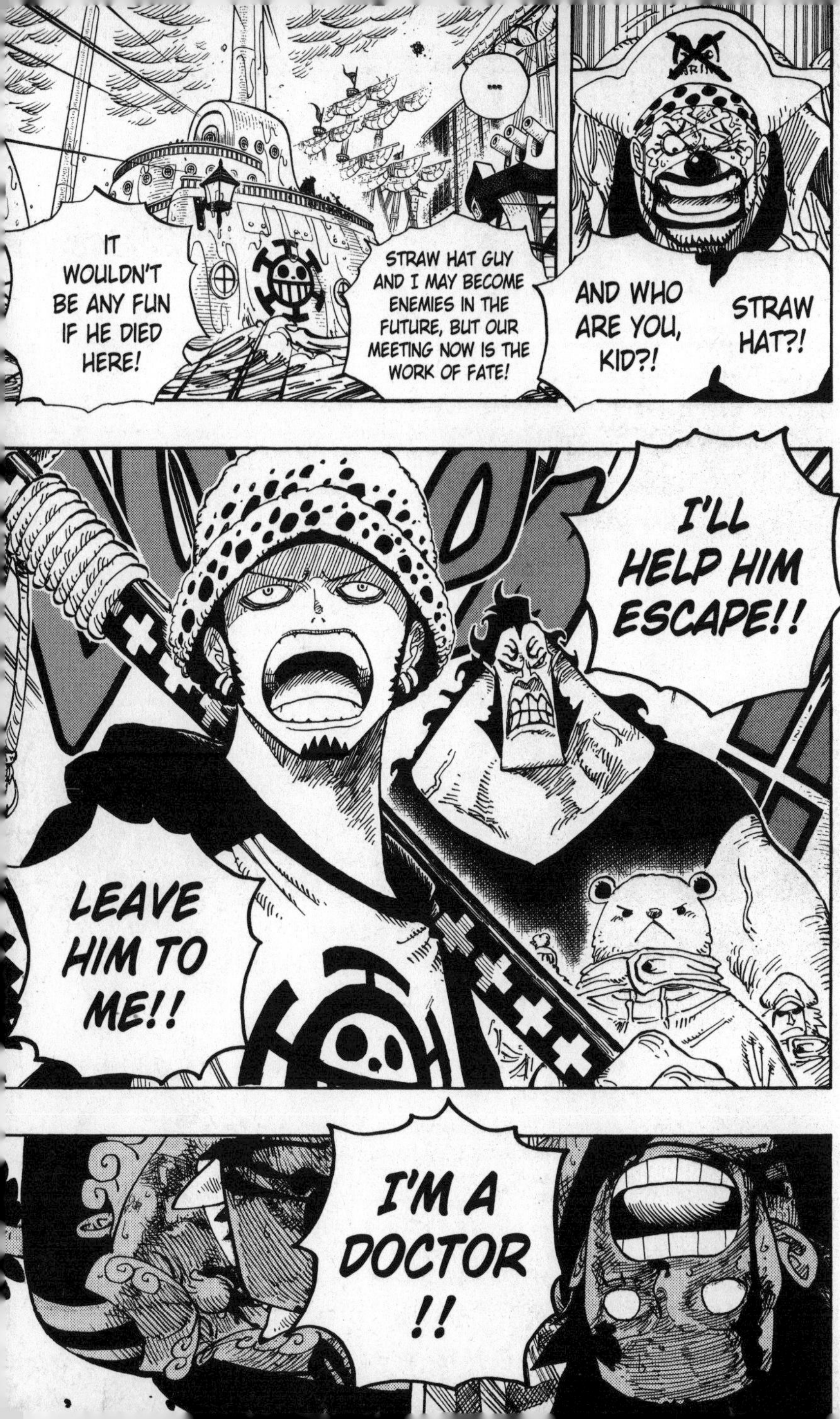
STRAW HAT?!
AND WHO ARE YOU, KID?!
STRAW HAT GUY AND I MAY BECOME ENEMIES IN THE FUTURE, BUT OUR MEETING NOW IS THE WORK OF FATE!
IT WOULDN'T BE ANY FUN IF HE DIED HERE!
I'LL HELP HIM ESCAPE!!
LEAVE HIM TO ME!!
I'M A DOCTOR!!

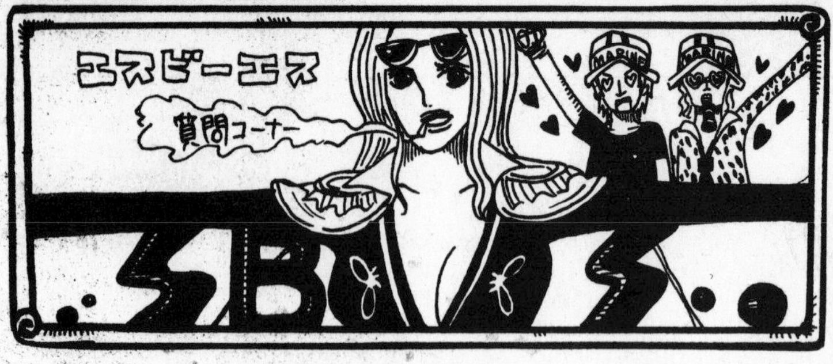
エスビーエス
質問コーナー
SBS

(Takeuchi Aika, Aichi)

Q: Who're you calling Four Eyes?

--Hidaruman

A: Okay. I'll pretend I didn't see that. Moving on to the next letter.

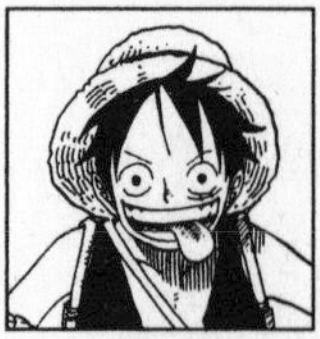

Q: Hello, Mr. Oda! This might be sudden, but can you show what's inside Luffy's head?! I want to know what's going inside your head too. Half of what's inside my friend's head is smut and the other half is games.

--Is it true that Mr. Oda's head is full of smut?!

A: You want to know what's inside his head? Can I just use that Brain Maker thing that was popular a few years ago on the web? Let's try taking a look at some other characters, too.

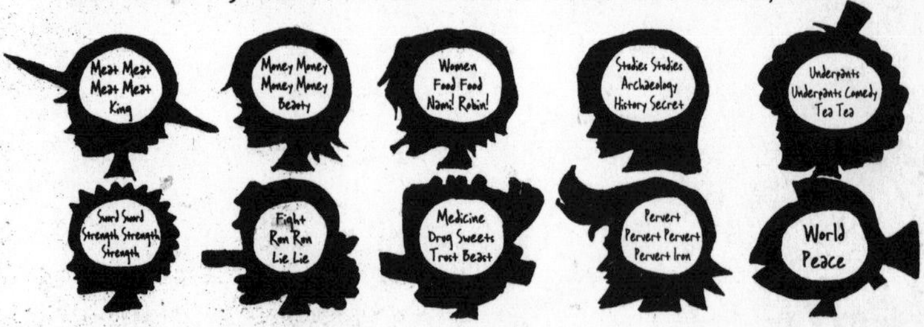
Meat Meat Meat Meat King
Money Money Money Money Beauty
Women Food Food Nami! Robin!
Studies Studies Archaeology History Secret
Underpants Underpants Comedy Tea Tea
Sword Sword Strength Strength Strength
Fight Ron Ron Lie Lie
Medicine Drug Sweets Trust Beast
Pervert Pervert Pervert Pervert Iron
World Peace

Also know that everyone's heart is filled with "friendship."

Q: Can the affiliate pirates of the Whitebeard Pirates (I'll call them the main force from here on) actually become an official division of the main force? Or is that reserved for the people that had always been with the main force?

--Amanatsuu

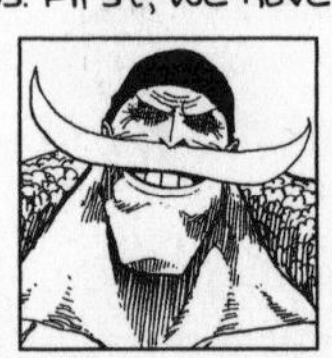

A: The structure of the Whitebeard Pirates is as follows. First, we have Whitebeard as the captain. Then we have the 16 division commanders. All 16 of the division leaders are on equal standing. Just because they have different numbers doesn't mean one has authority over another. The entire Whitebeard Pirates are built around these 16 teams. Now we have the 43 affiliate pirates of Whitebeard. They are not actually a part of Whitebeard's crew and they act completely independently. But because they have so much respect for Whitebeard, they will come to his aid at the drop of a hat. That's what they are. In Ace's case, after the Spade Pirates were disbanded, all of his crew joined the Whitebeard Pirates, so he became a division commander through that...

Chapter 579:
A FEW SECONDS OF COURAGE

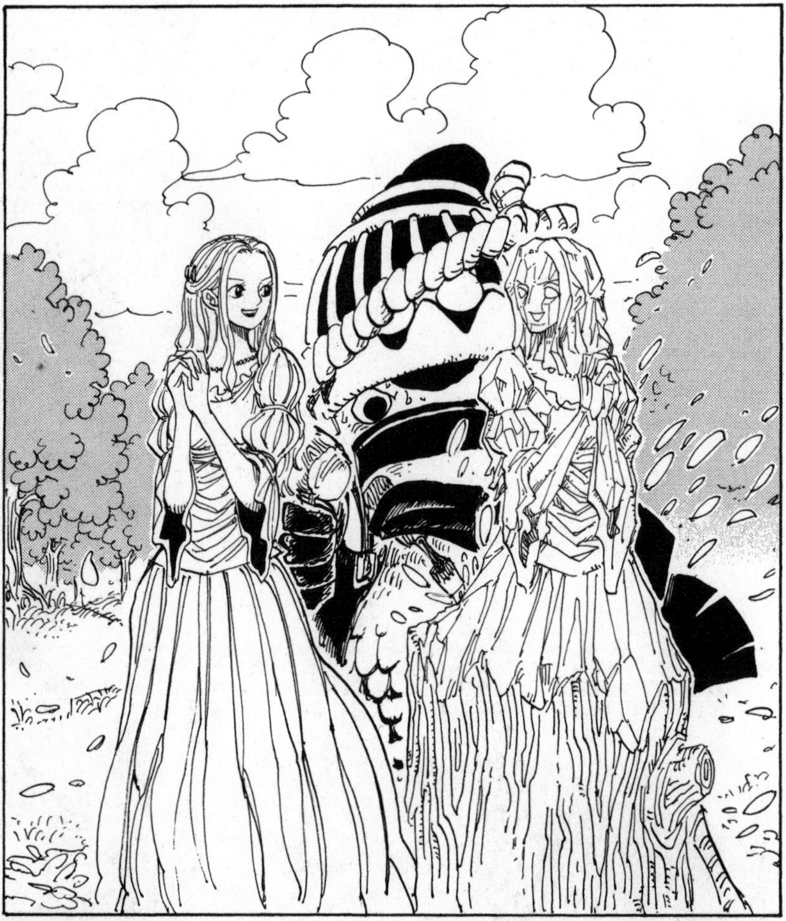

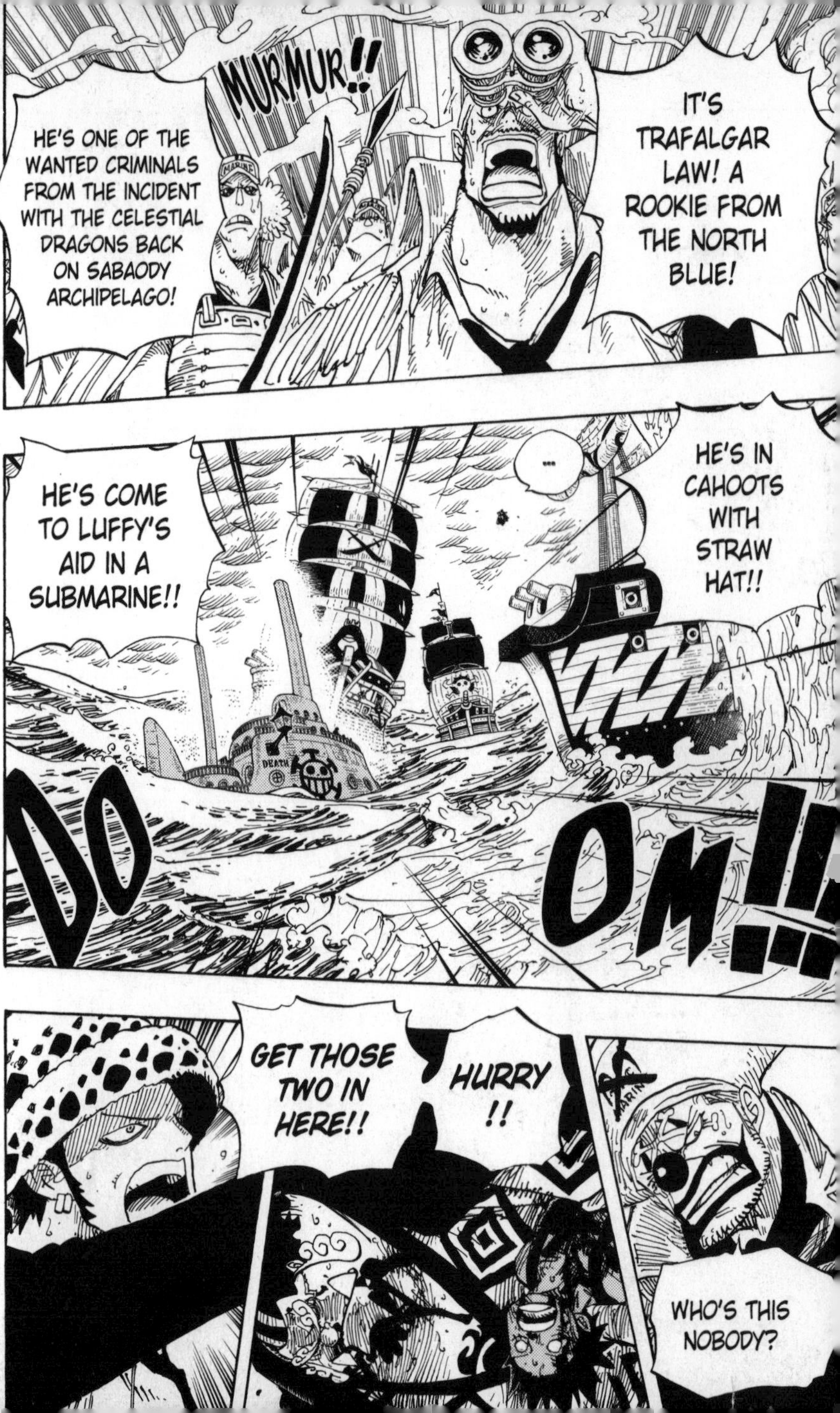
IT'S TRAFALGAR LAW! A ROOKIE FROM THE NORTH BLUE!
MURMUR!!
HE'S ONE OF THE WANTED CRIMINALS FROM THE INCIDENT WITH THE CELESTIAL DRAGONS BACK ON SABAODY ARCHIPELAGO!
HE'S IN CAHOOTS WITH STRAW HAT!!
...
HE'S COME TO LUFFY'S AID IN A SUBMARINE!!
DEATH
DO
OM!!!
WHO'S THIS NOBODY?
HURRY !!
GET THOSE TWO IN HERE!!

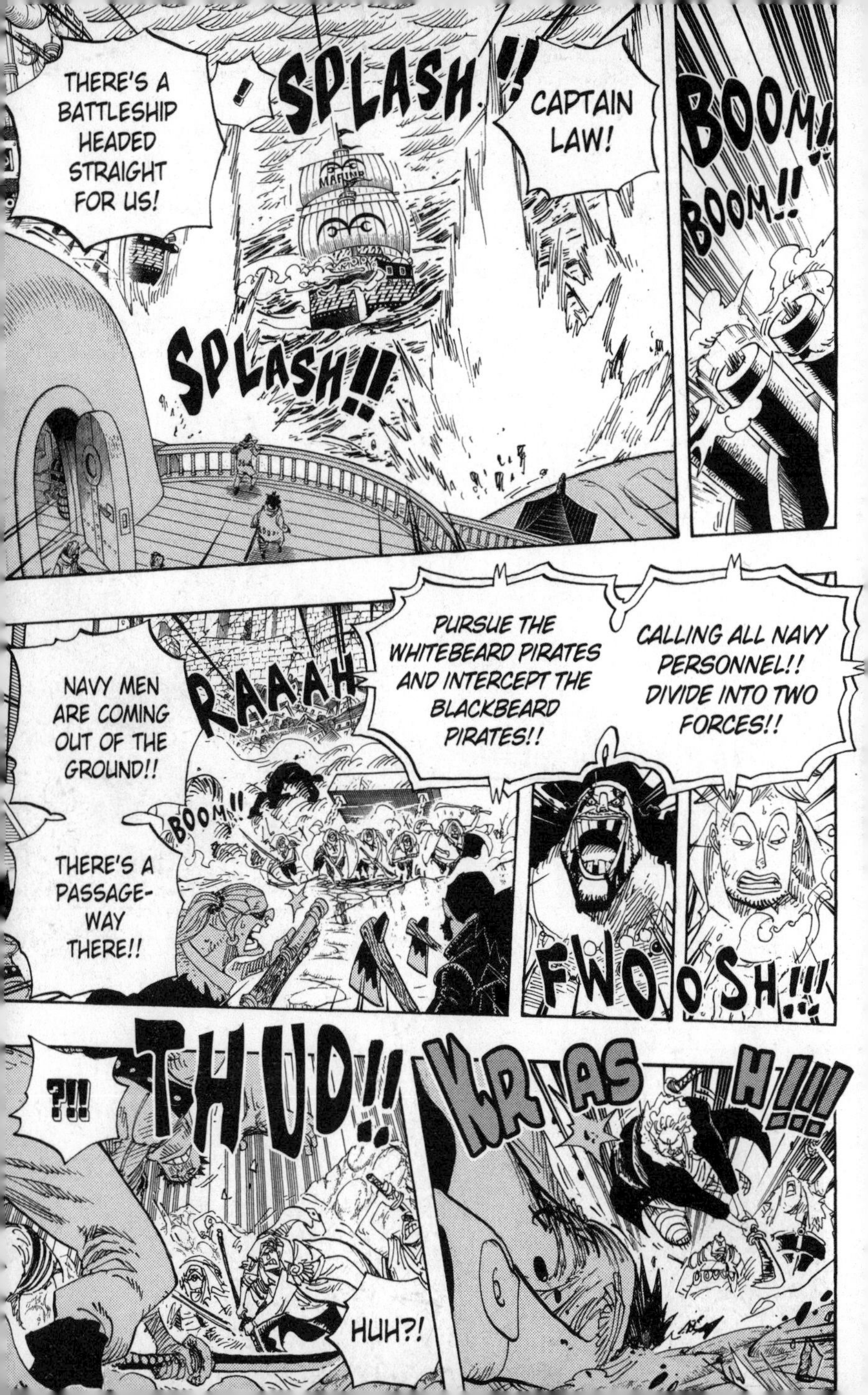

BOOM!!
BOOM!!
CAPTAIN LAW!
SPLASH!!
!
THERE'S A BATTLESHIP HEADED STRAIGHT FOR US!
SPLASH!!
CALLING ALL NAVY PERSONNEL!! DIVIDE INTO TWO FORCES!!
PURSUE THE WHITEBEARD PIRATES AND INTERCEPT THE BLACKBEARD PIRATES!!
FWOOSH!!!
RAAAH
NAVY MEN ARE COMING OUT OF THE GROUND!!
BOOM!!
THERE'S A PASSAGE-WAY THERE!!
KRASH!!!
THUD!!
?!!
HUH?!

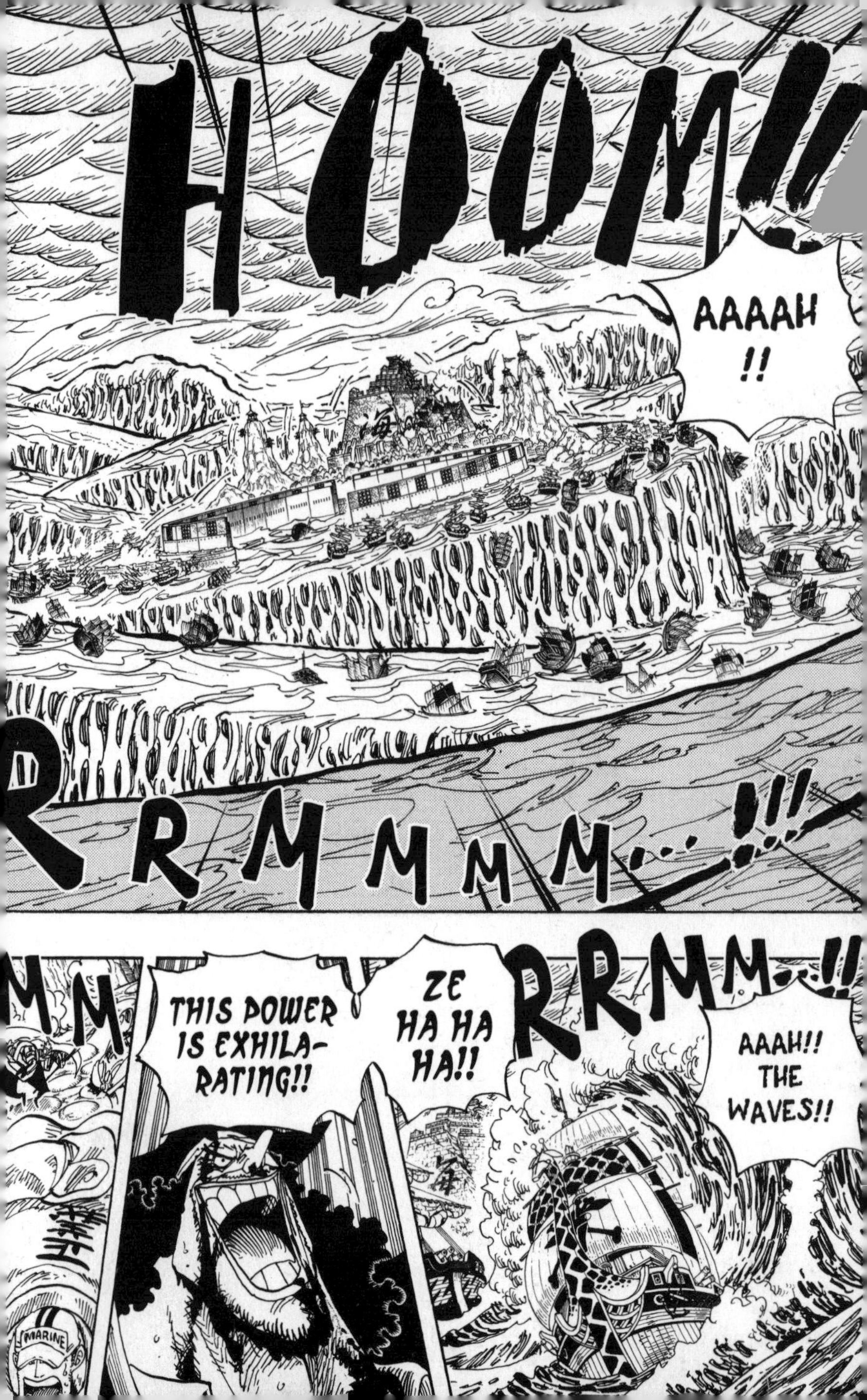
HOOM!!
AAAAH!!
RRMMMM...!!!
RRMM..!!
AAAH!! THE WAVES!!
ZE HA HA HA!!
THIS POWER IS EXHILA-RATING!!
MM
MARINE

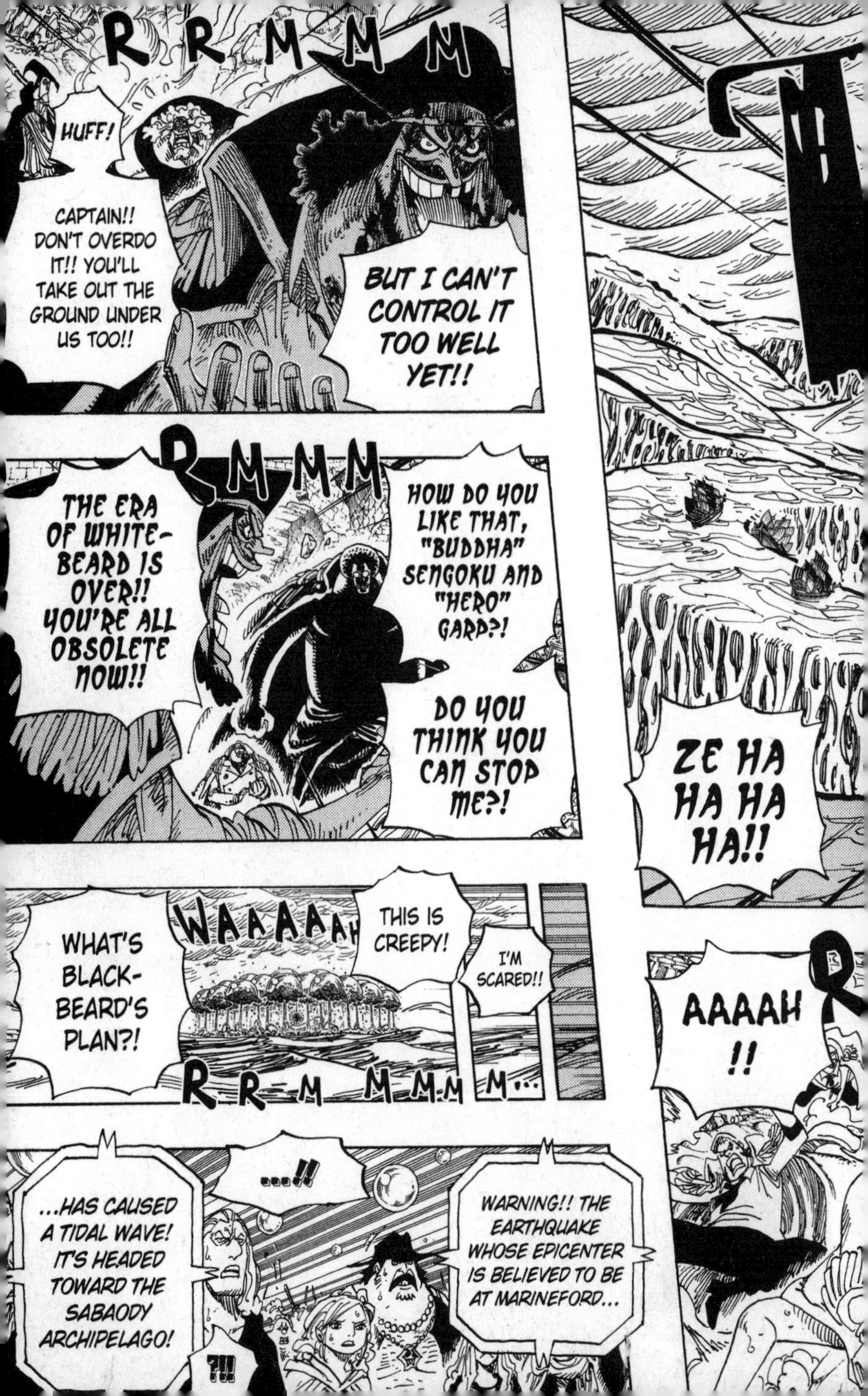
ZE HA HA HA HA!!
RRMMM
HUFF!
CAPTAIN!! DON'T OVERDO IT!! YOU'LL TAKE OUT THE GROUND UNDER US TOO!!
BUT I CAN'T CONTROL IT TOO WELL YET!!
RMMM
HOW DO YOU LIKE THAT, "BUDDHA" SENGOKU AND "HERO" GARP?!
DO YOU THINK YOU CAN STOP ME?!
THE ERA OF WHITE-BEARD IS OVER!! YOU'RE ALL OBSOLETE NOW!!
R
AAAAH !!
THIS IS CREEPY!
I'M SCARED!!
WAAAAAH
WHAT'S BLACK-BEARD'S PLAN?!
RRMMMMM...
WARNING!! THE EARTHQUAKE WHOSE EPICENTER IS BELIEVED TO BE AT MARINEFORD...
...!!
...HAS CAUSED A TIDAL WAVE! IT'S HEADED TOWARD THE SABAODY ARCHIPELAGO!
?!!

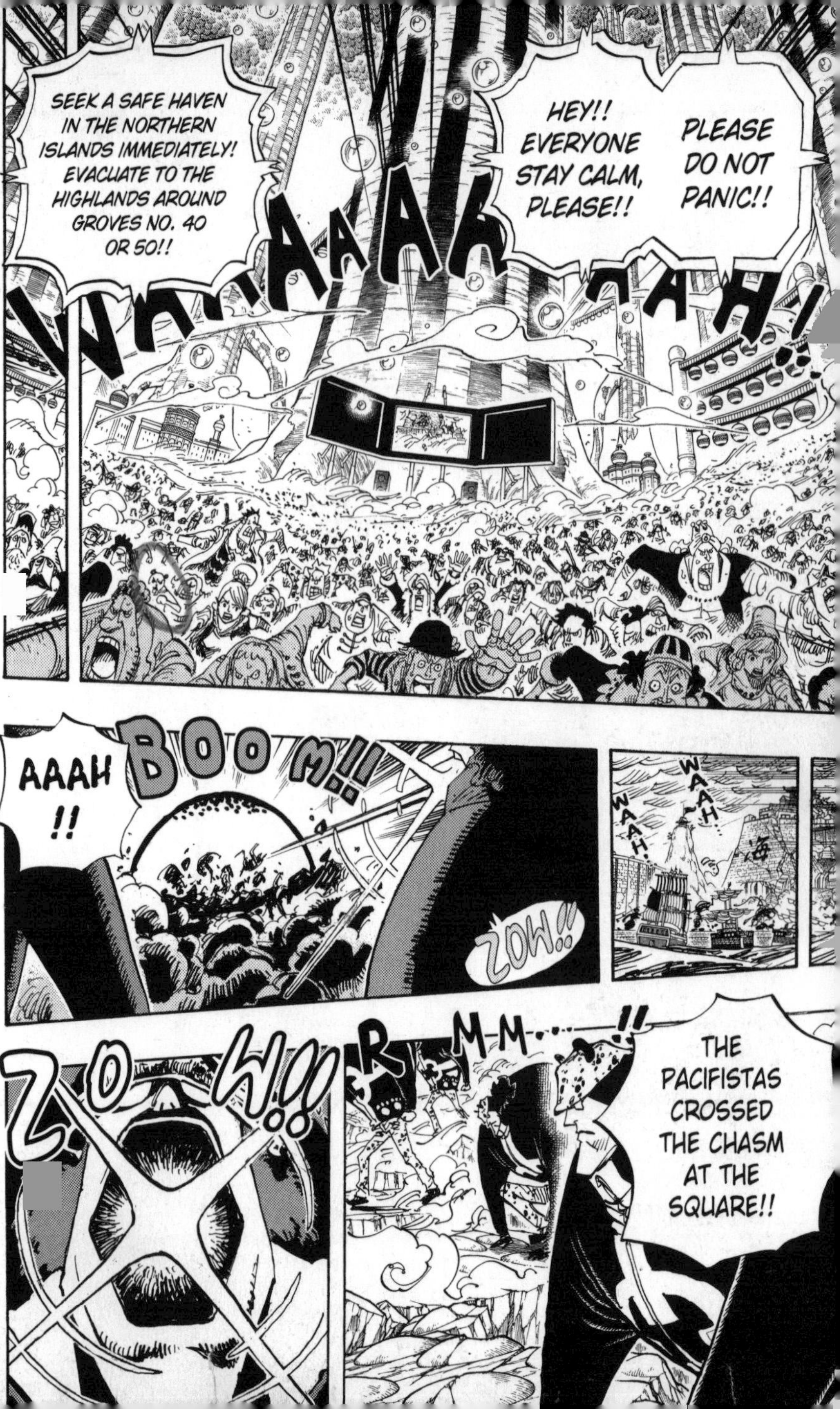
PLEASE DO NOT PANIC!!
HEY!! EVERYONE STAY CALM, PLEASE!!
SEEK A SAFE HAVEN IN THE NORTHERN ISLANDS IMMEDIATELY! EVACUATE TO THE HIGHLANDS AROUND GROVES NO. 40 OR 50!!
AAAH !!
BOOM!!
ZOW!!
THE PACIFISTAS CROSSED THE CHASM AT THE SQUARE!!

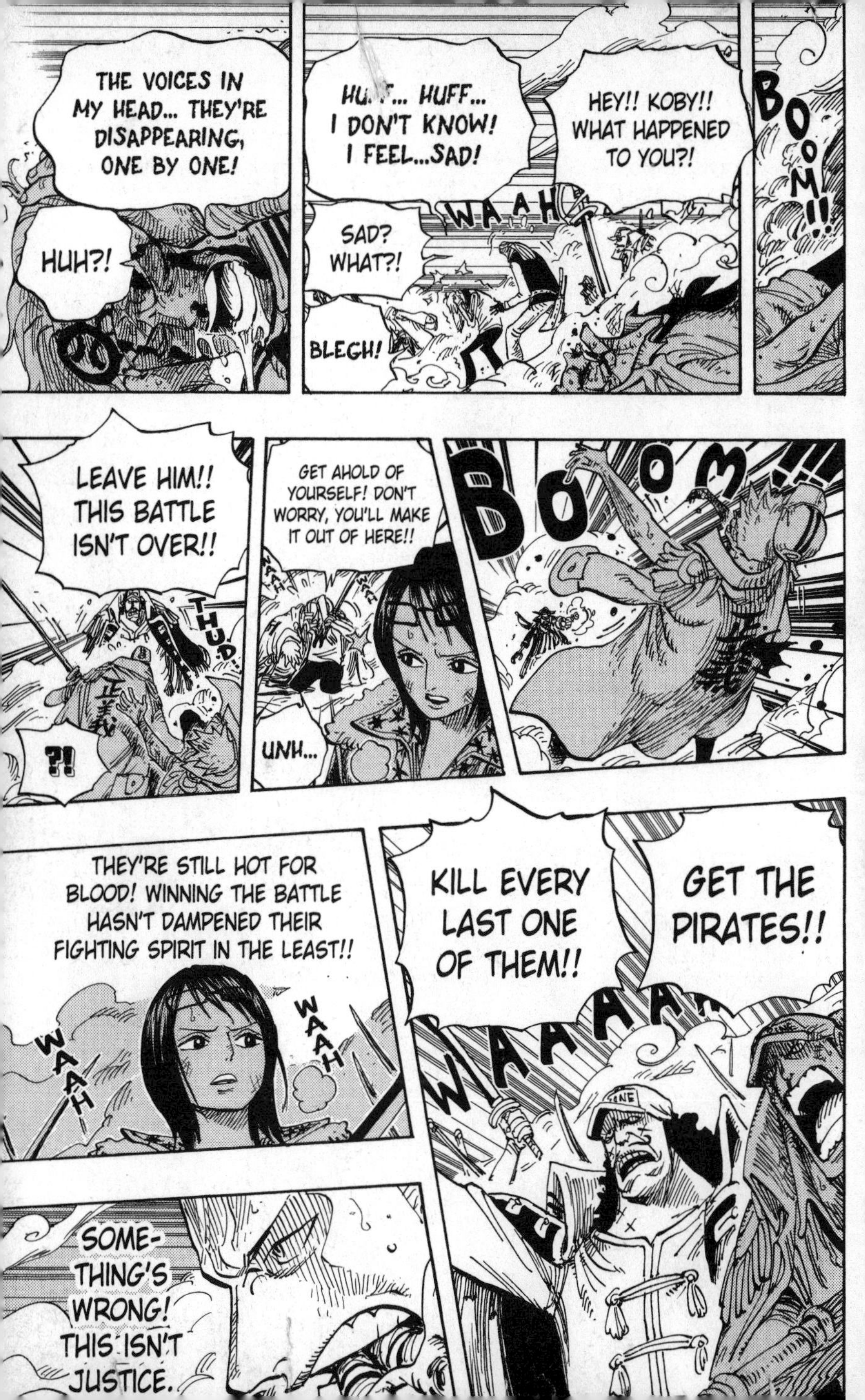
BOOM!!
HEY!! KOBY!! WHAT HAPPENED TO YOU?!
HUFF... HUFF... I DON'T KNOW! I FEEL...SAD!
WAAH
SAD? WHAT?!
BLEGH!
THE VOICES IN MY HEAD... THEY'RE DISAPPEARING, ONE BY ONE!
HUH?!
BOOM!!
GET AHOLD OF YOURSELF! DON'T WORRY, YOU'LL MAKE IT OUT OF HERE!!
UNH...
LEAVE HIM!! THIS BATTLE ISN'T OVER!!
THUD
?!
GET THE PIRATES!!
KILL EVERY LAST ONE OF THEM!!
WAAAAA
THEY'RE STILL HOT FOR BLOOD! WINNING THE BATTLE HASN'T DAMPENED THEIR FIGHTING SPIRIT IN THE LEAST!!
WAAH
WAAH
SOME-THING'S WRONG! THIS ISN'T JUSTICE.

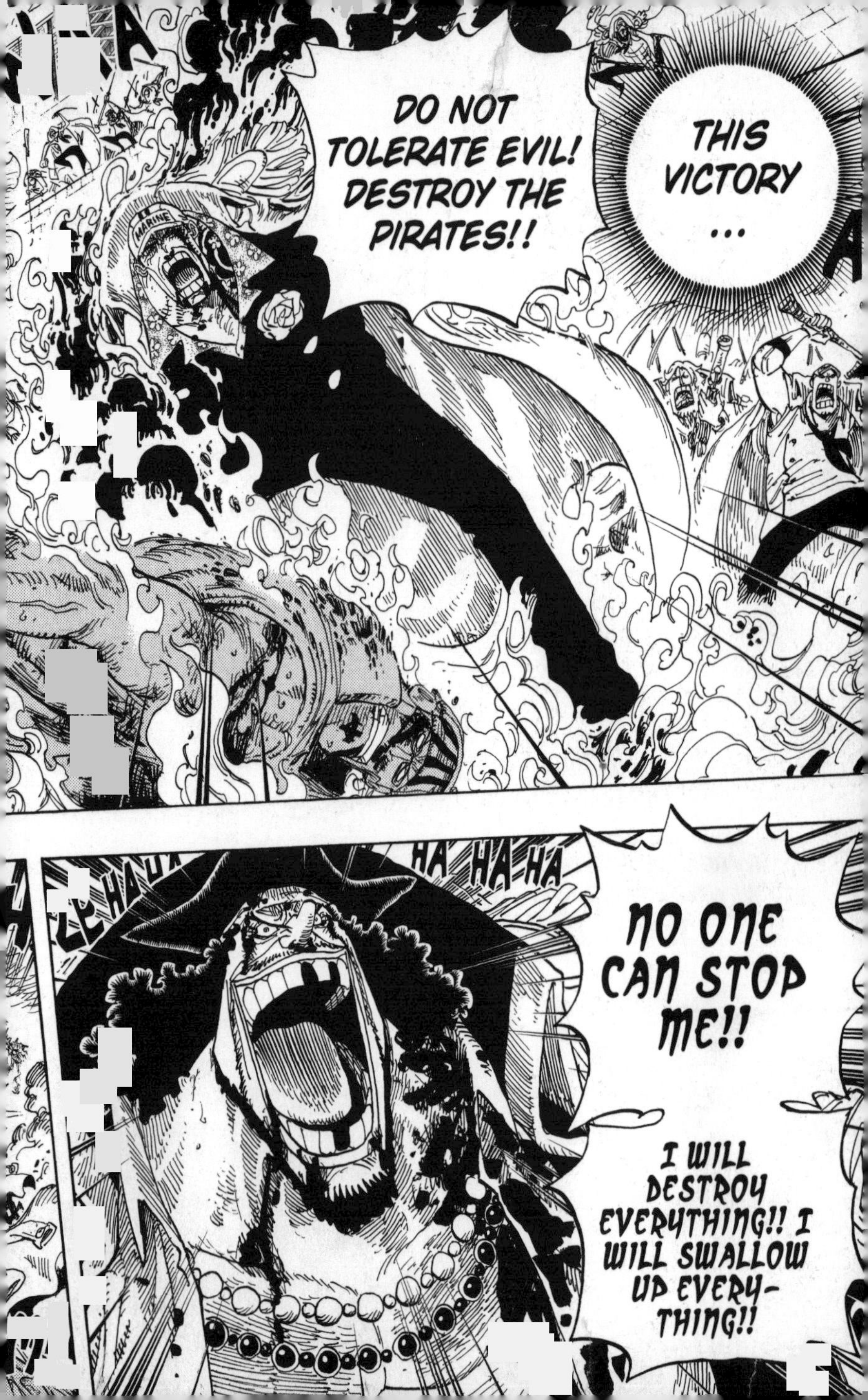
THIS VICTORY ...
DO NOT TOLERATE EVIL! DESTROY THE PIRATES!!
HA HA HA
NO ONE CAN STOP ME!!
I WILL DESTROY EVERYTHING!! I WILL SWALLOW UP EVERY-THING!!

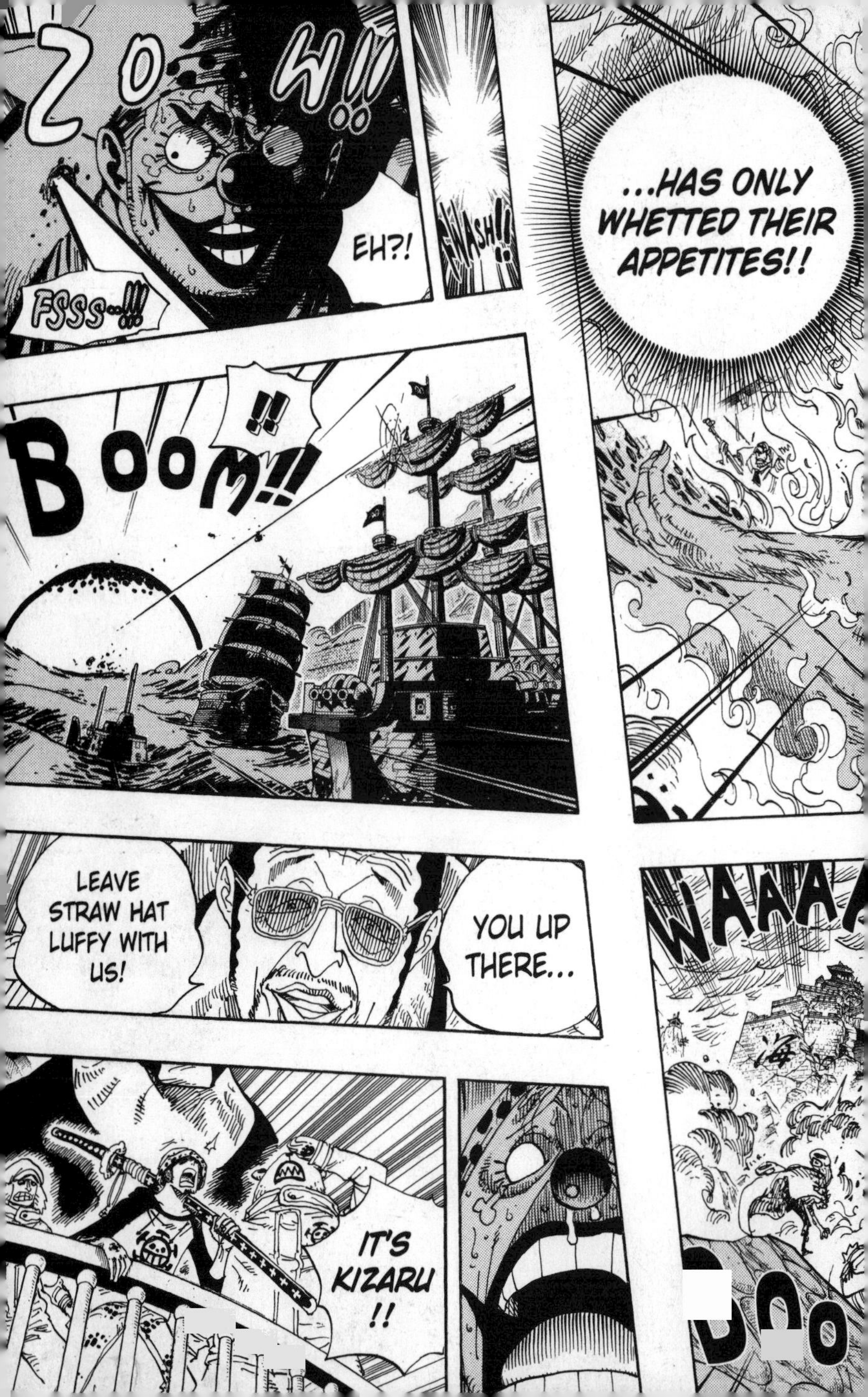
...HAS ONLY WHETTED THEIR APPETITES!!
WASH!!
ZO..W!!
EH?!
FSSS..!!!
!!
BOOM!!
WAAAA
DOO
YOU UP THERE...
LEAVE STRAW HAT LUFFY WITH US!
IT'S KIZARU!!

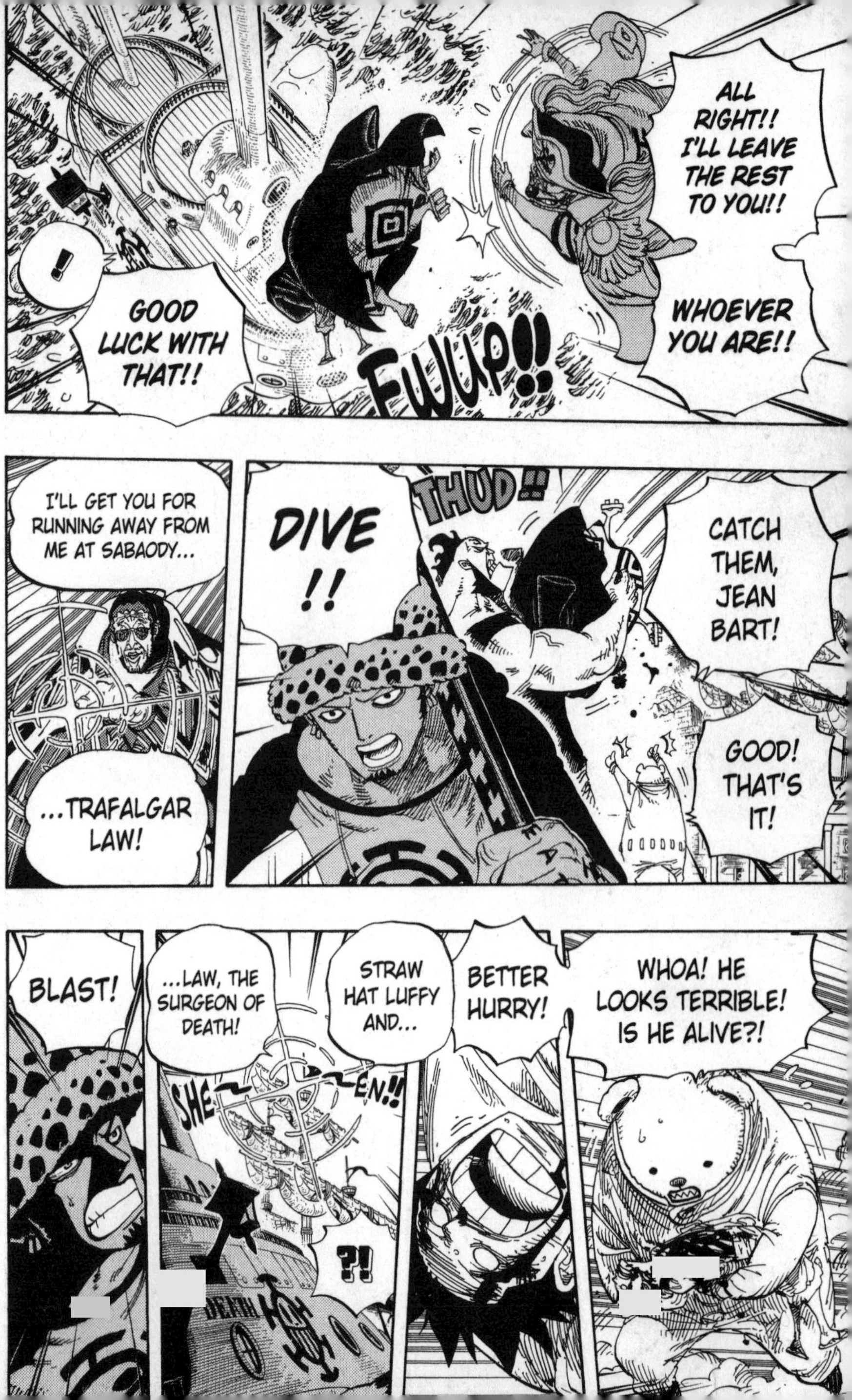
ALL RIGHT!! I'LL LEAVE THE REST TO YOU!!
WHOEVER YOU ARE!!
FWUP!!
!
GOOD LUCK WITH THAT!!
CATCH THEM, JEAN BART!
THUD!!
DIVE!!
GOOD! THAT'S IT!
I'LL GET YOU FOR RUNNING AWAY FROM ME AT SABAODY...
...TRAFALGAR LAW!
WHOA! HE LOOKS TERRIBLE! IS HE ALIVE?!
BETTER HURRY!
?!
STRAW HAT LUFFY AND...
...LAW, THE SURGEON OF DEATH!
BLAST!

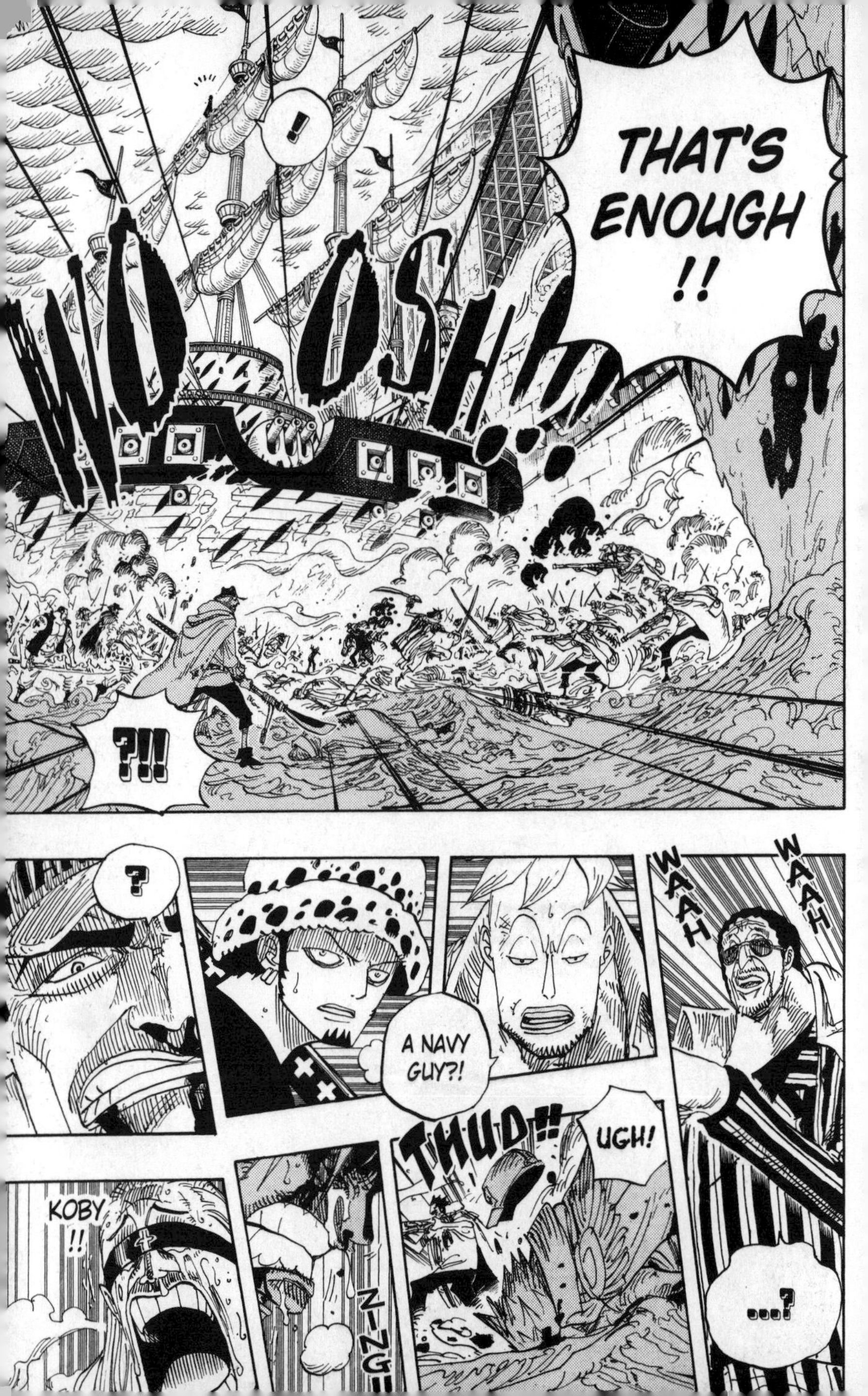
THAT'S ENOUGH!!
!
WHOOSH!!
?!!
WAAH WAAH
A NAVY GUY?!
?
...?
UGH!
THUD!!
ZING!!
KOBY!!

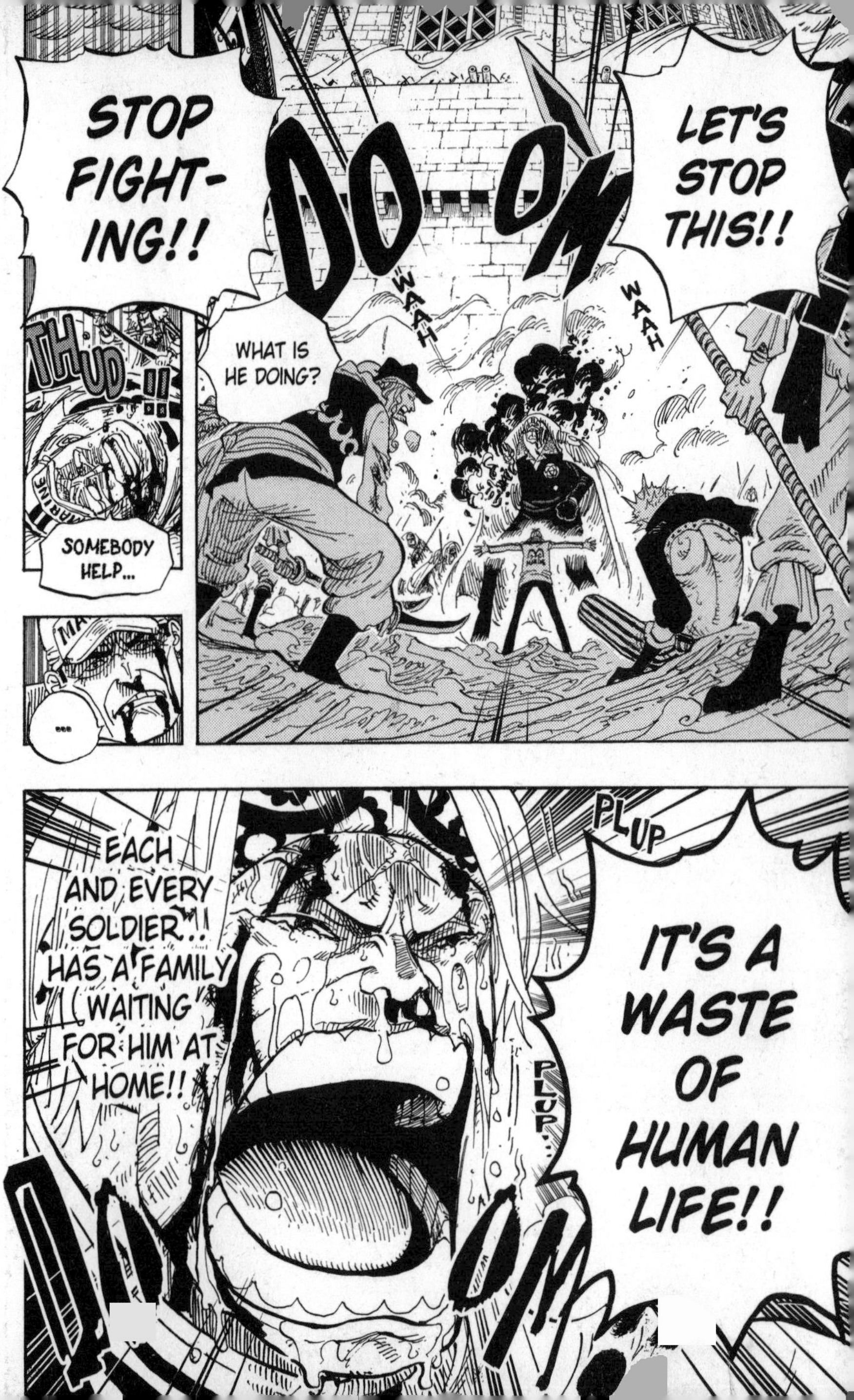
LET'S STOP THIS!!
DO-ON
STOP FIGHTING!!
WAAH
WAAH
WHAT IS HE DOING?
THUD!!
SOMEBODY HELP...
...
PLUP
IT'S A WASTE OF HUMAN LIFE!!
PLUP...
EACH AND EVERY SOLDIER... HAS A FAMILY WAITING FOR HIM AT HOME!!

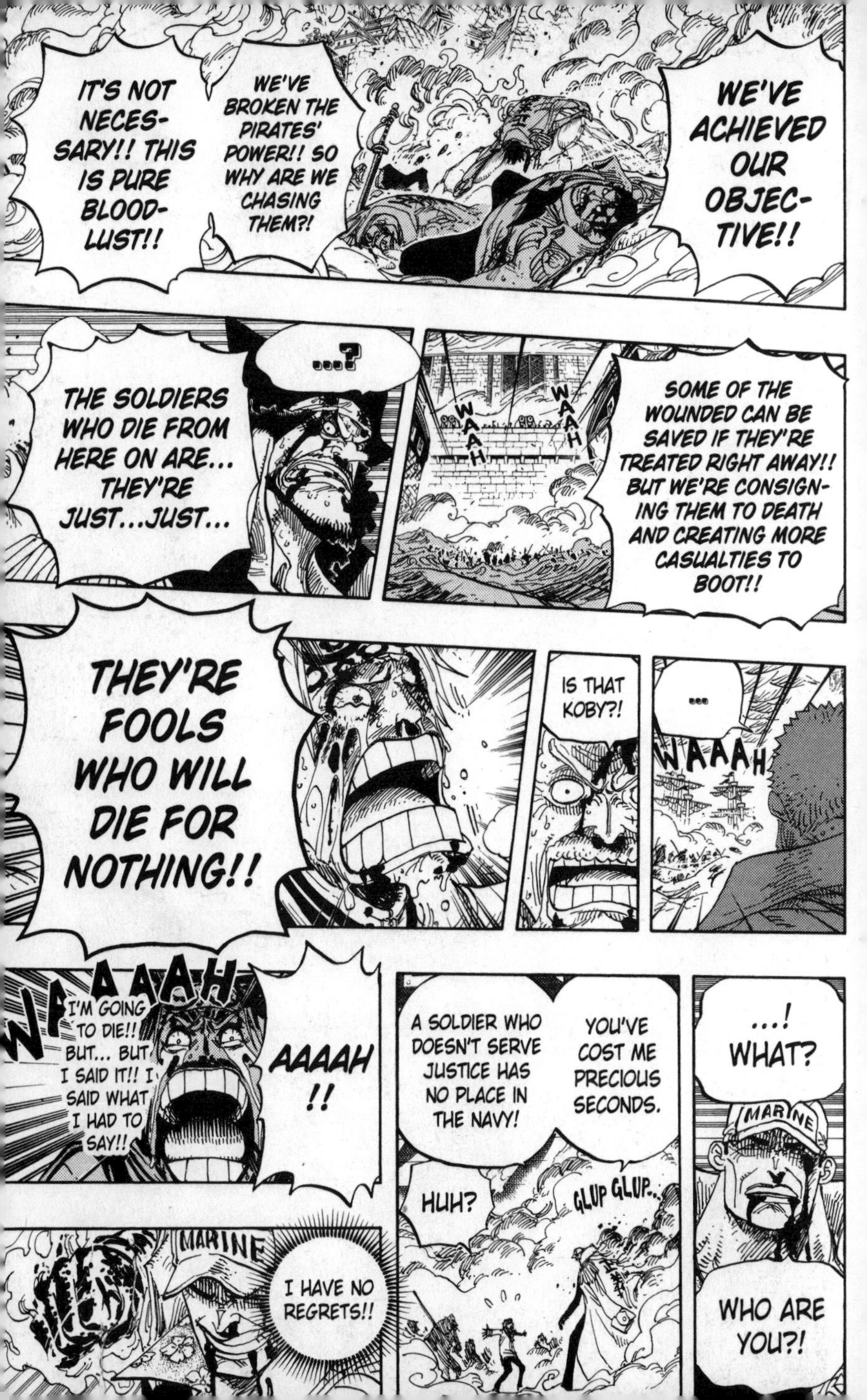
WE'VE ACHIEVED OUR OBJECTIVE!!
WE'VE BROKEN THE PIRATES' POWER!! SO WHY ARE WE CHASING THEM?!
IT'S NOT NECES-SARY!! THIS IS PURE BLOOD-LUST!!
WAAH
WAAH
SOME OF THE WOUNDED CAN BE SAVED IF THEY'RE TREATED RIGHT AWAY!! BUT WE'RE CONSIGN-ING THEM TO DEATH AND CREATING MORE CASUALTIES TO BOOT!!
...?
THE SOLDIERS WHO DIE FROM HERE ON ARE... THEY'RE JUST...JUST...
...
WAAAH
IS THAT KOBY?!
THEY'RE FOOLS WHO WILL DIE FOR NOTHING!!
...! WHAT?
WHO ARE YOU?!
YOU'VE COST ME PRECIOUS SECONDS.
A SOLDIER WHO DOESN'T SERVE JUSTICE HAS NO PLACE IN THE NAVY!
HUH?
GLUP GLUP...
AAAAH!!
WAAAAH
I'M GOING TO DIE!! BUT... BUT I SAID IT!! I SAID WHAT I HAD TO SAY!!
I HAVE NO REGRETS!!

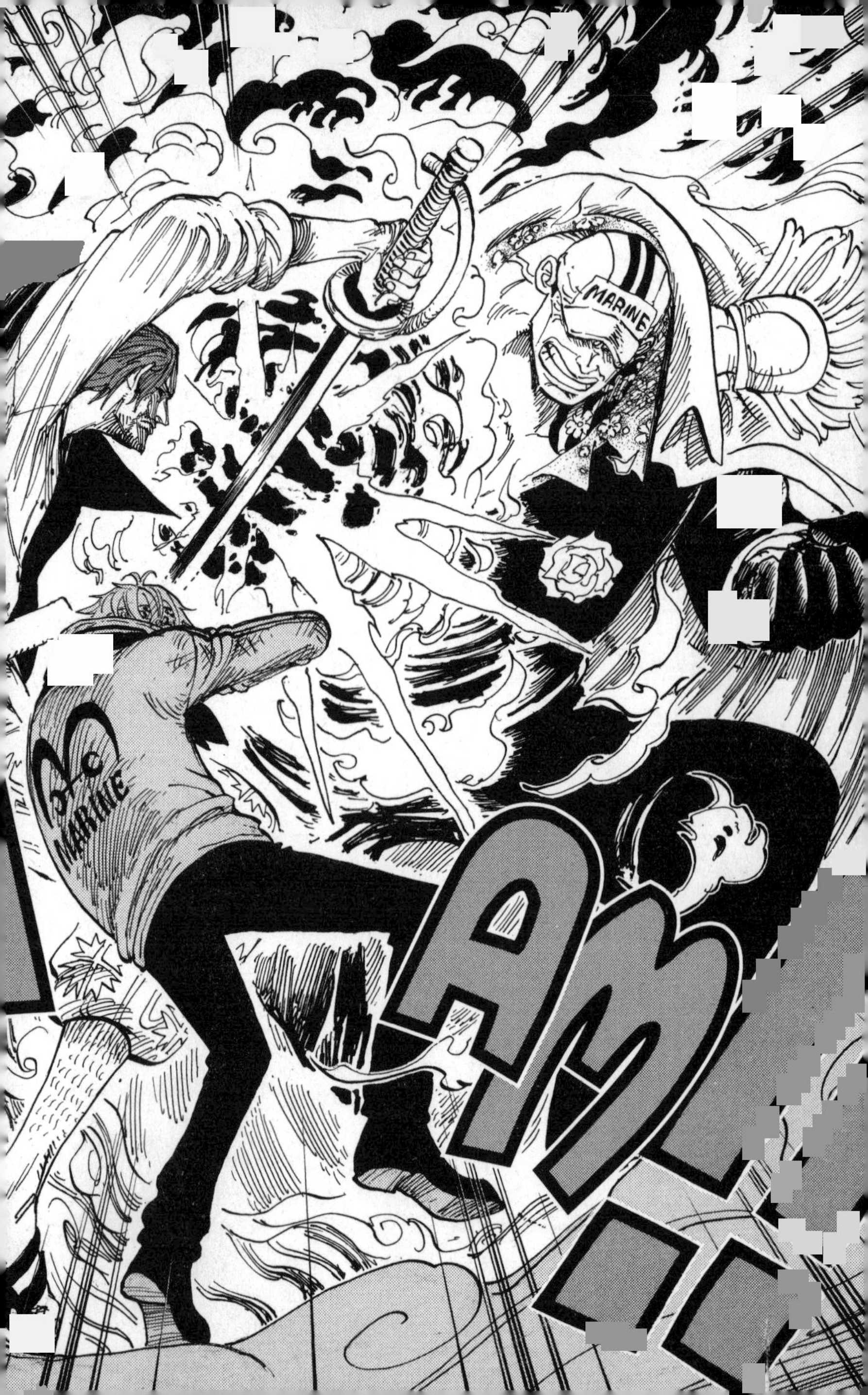
MARINE
MARINE

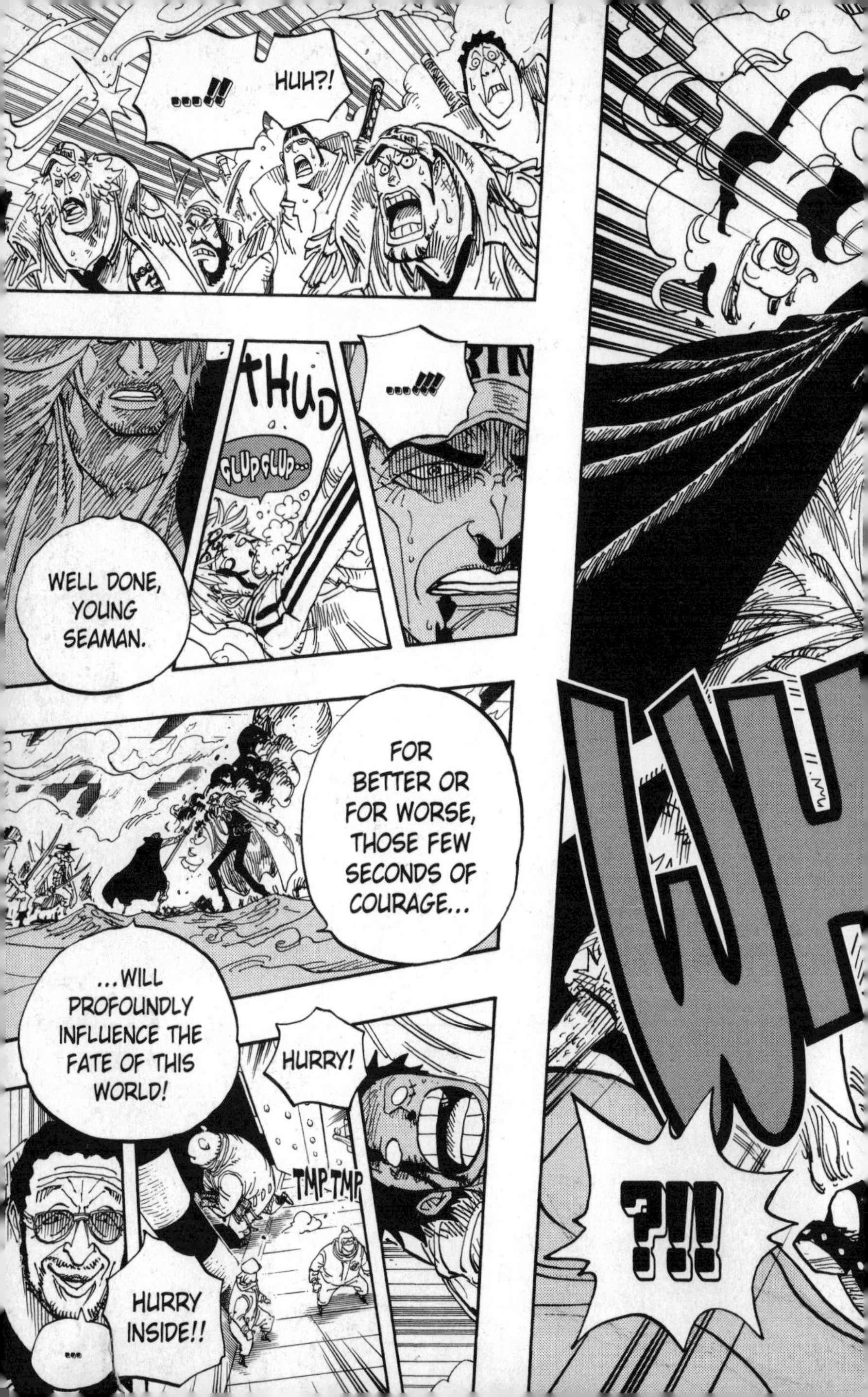
?!!
HUH?!
...!!
...!!!
GLUPGLUP...
THUD
WELL DONE, YOUNG SEAMAN.
FOR BETTER OR FOR WORSE, THOSE FEW SECONDS OF COURAGE...
...WILL PROFOUNDLY INFLUENCE THE FATE OF THIS WORLD!
HURRY!
TMP TMP
HURRY INSIDE!!
...

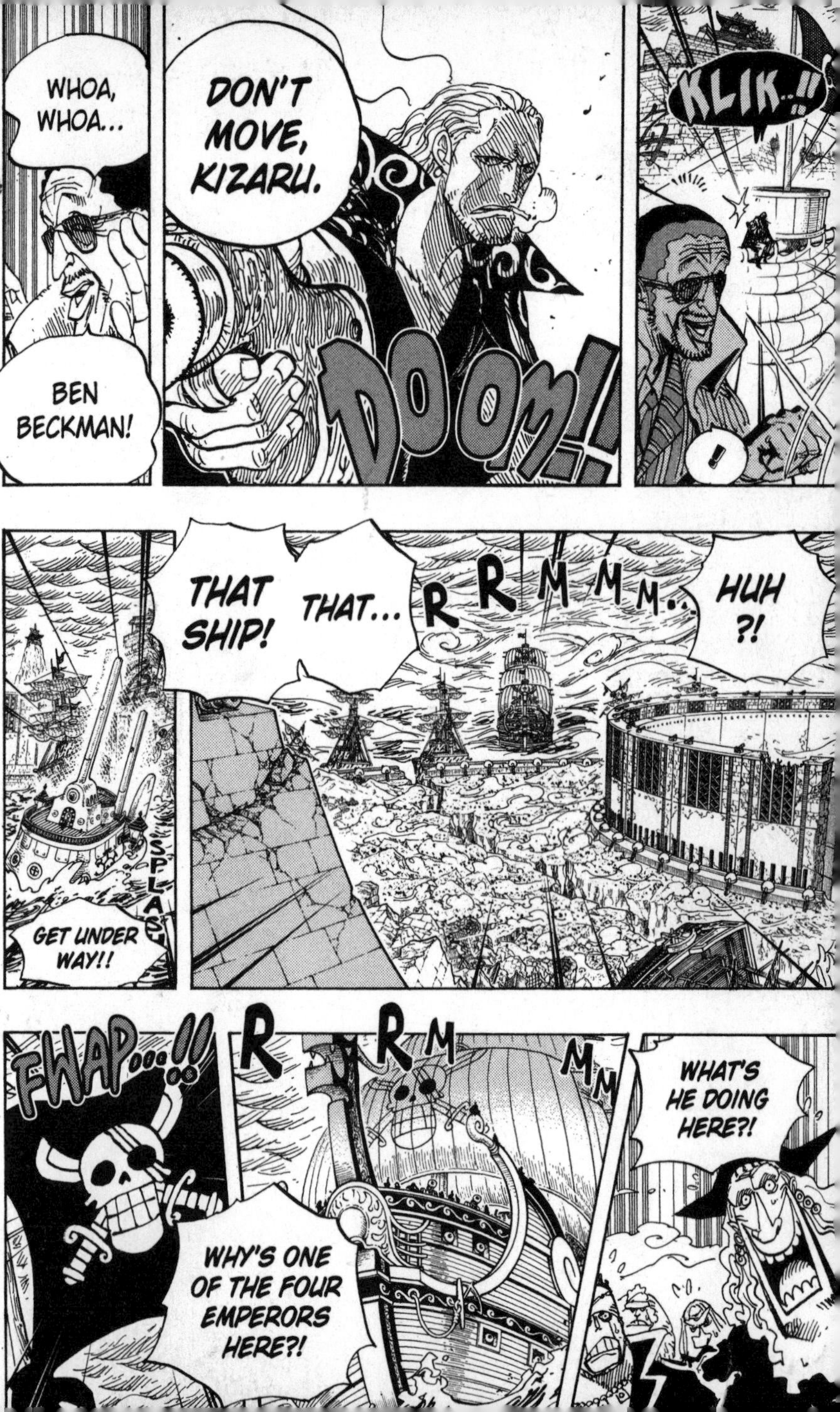
KLIK..!!
!
DON'T MOVE, KIZARU.
DOOM!!
WHOA, WHOA...
BEN BECKMAN!
HUH?!
RRMMM..
THAT...
THAT SHIP!
GET UNDER WAY!!
SPLASH
WHAT'S HE DOING HERE?!
RRMMM
WHY'S ONE OF THE FOUR EMPERORS HERE?!
FWAP...!!

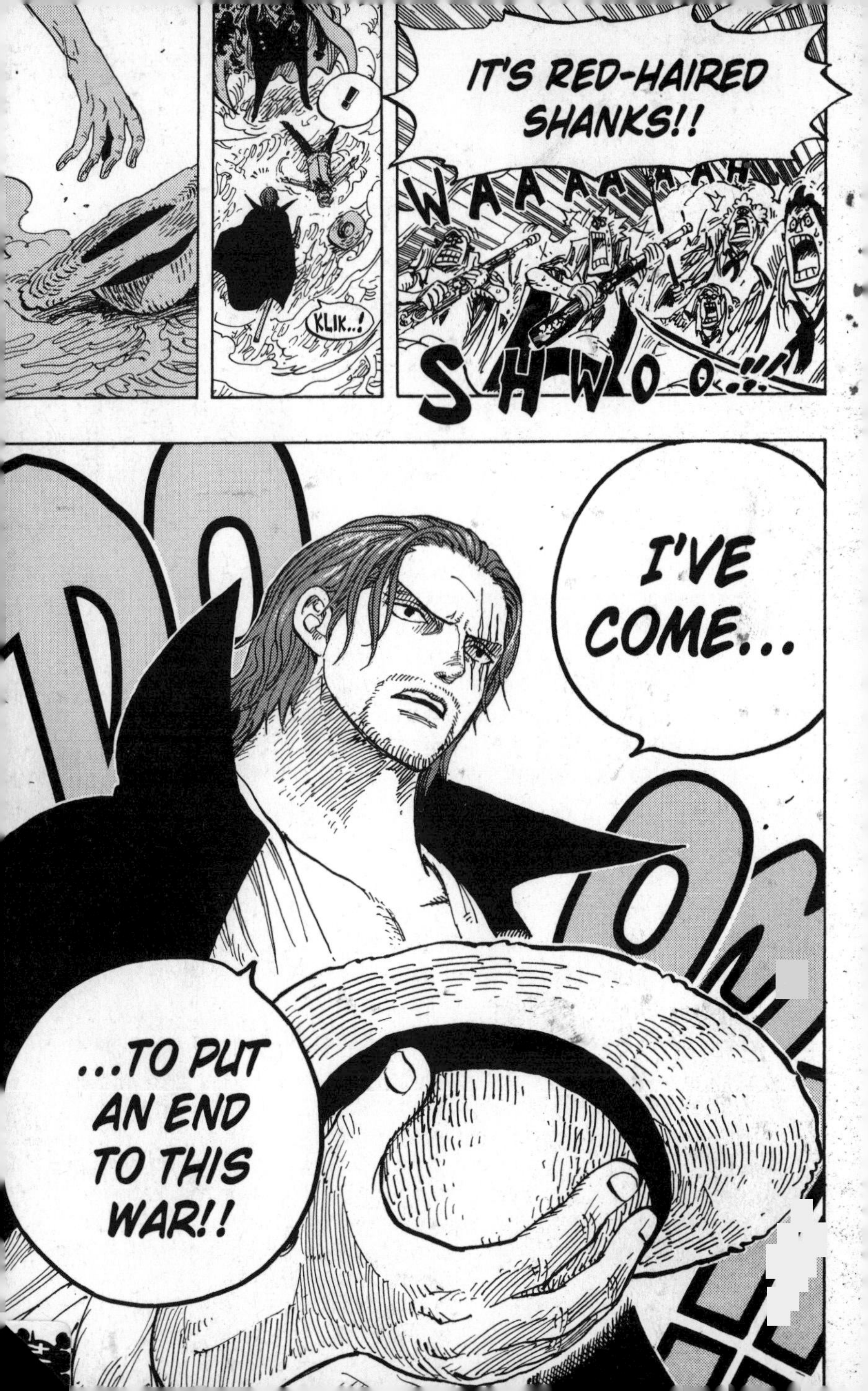
IT'S RED-HAIRED SHANKS!!
WAAAAAAH
SHWOO..!!
!
KLIK..!
I'VE COME...
...TO PUT AN END TO THIS WAR!!

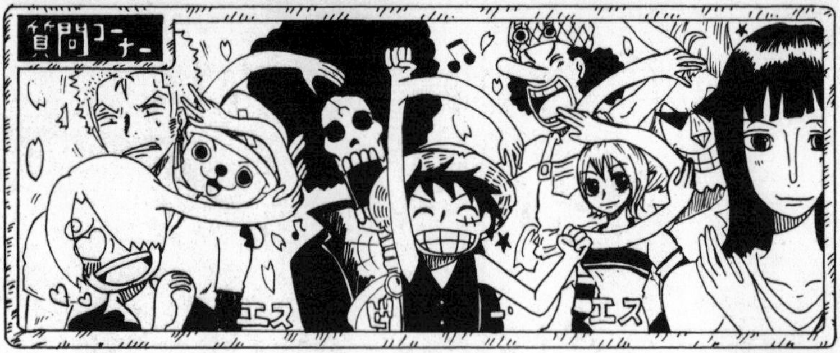
質問コーナー

(Aoki Shunsuke, Wakayama)

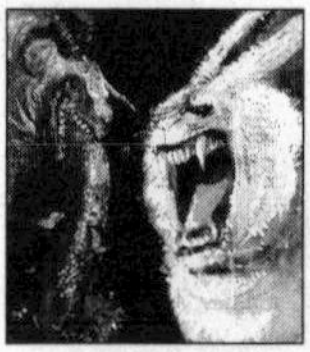

Q: What's up! Your careless statement in volume 58 made me into a "Man-eating Giant Rabbit Year" and "Anaconda Swallowing Devil Capricorn." What do you have to say for yourself?!

--Herbivore

A: Oh, is that so? So you're also one of those people who was told that you were born in Rabbit Year and that you're Capricorn since birth? But you still don't like the ones I thought of? Fine, I will think of something else for your zodiac and sign. I hope you'll like it. You are now an "Underpants Hat Pervert Rabbit Year" and "Getting Weird Ideas from Looking at the Assembly Line Pervert Capricorn."

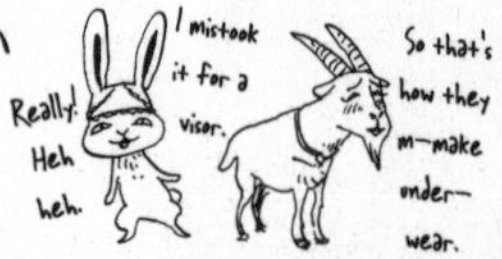
Really! Heh heh.
I mistook it for a visor.
So that's how they m-make under-wear.

Q: Hello! (·∀·) I'm an 18-year-old who loves Bob Dylan. When I saw chapter 572 and saw the title, it's that famous tune by Bob Dylan! "The Times They Are A-Changin'"! I was so surprised when I saw it. Are you also a fan of Bob Dylan, Odacchi? It's really great to see how the title and what happened in the chapter matched so well! (LOL)

--I Listen to Bob Dylan to Cheer Up

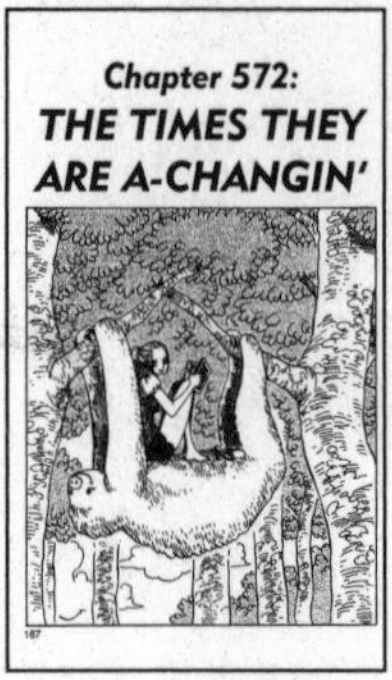
Chapter 572:
THE TIMES THEY ARE A-CHANGIN'

A: Yes, you're right. It's something that only people who know it would understand. I did it again. Bob Dylan is this huge American singer. I don't really know that much about him, but I figured that this title was perfect, so I used it. When the chapter was being serialized in Jump, it was just the English title. But thinking that some people might not understand, I added a Japanese translation of it in volume 58.

Chapter 580: THE WAR'S CONCLUSION

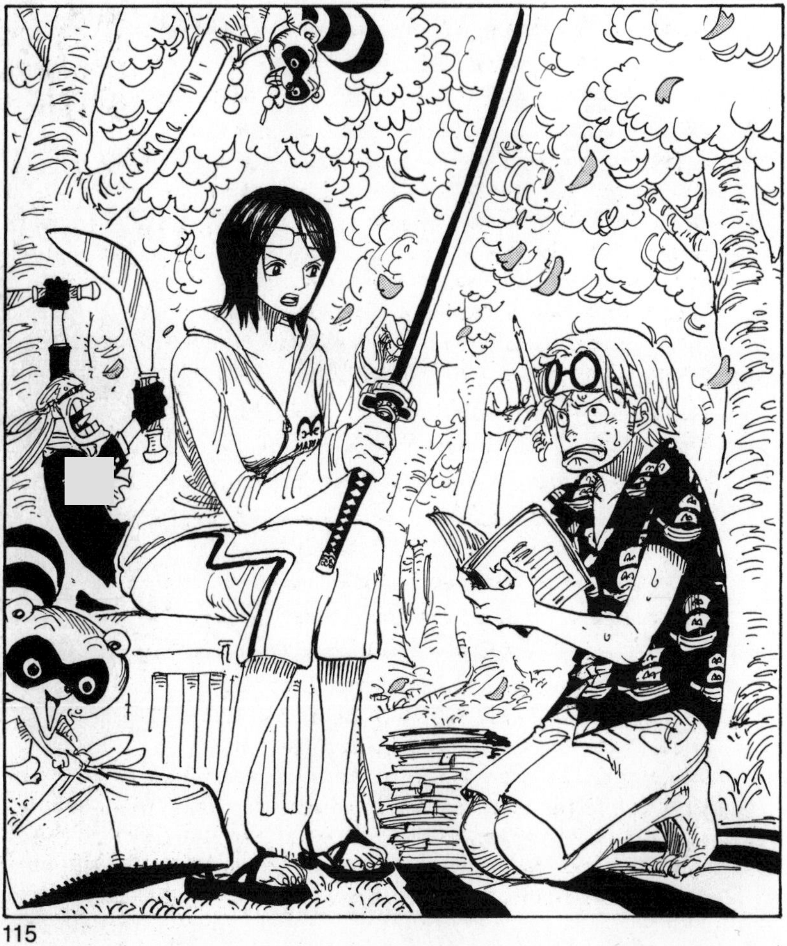

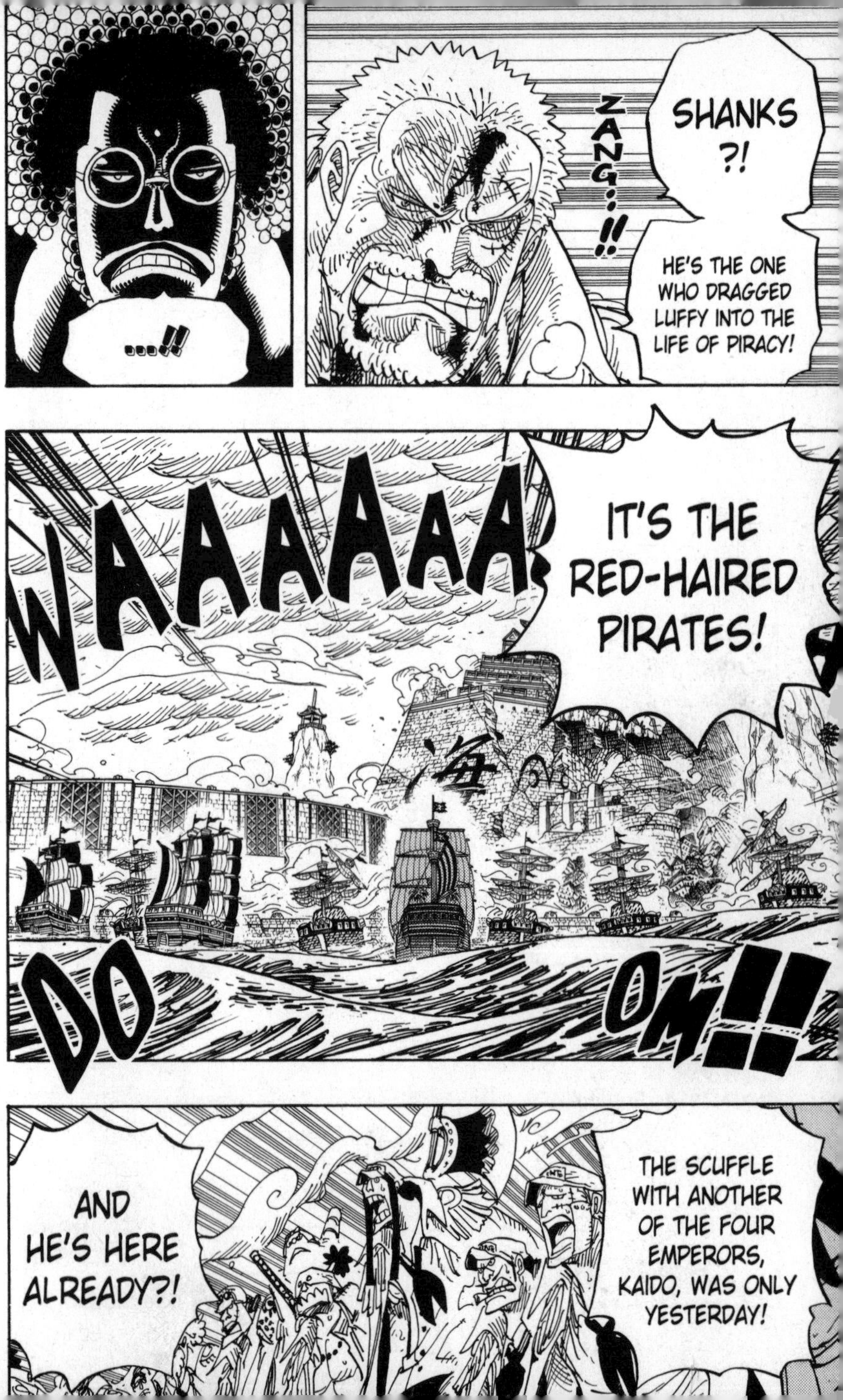
SHANKS ?!
ZANG...!!
HE'S THE ONE WHO DRAGGED LUFFY INTO THE LIFE OF PIRACY!
...!!
IT'S THE RED-HAIRED PIRATES!
WAAAAAA
DO OM!!
THE SCUFFLE WITH ANOTHER OF THE FOUR EMPERORS, KAIDO, WAS ONLY YESTERDAY!
AND HE'S HERE ALREADY?!

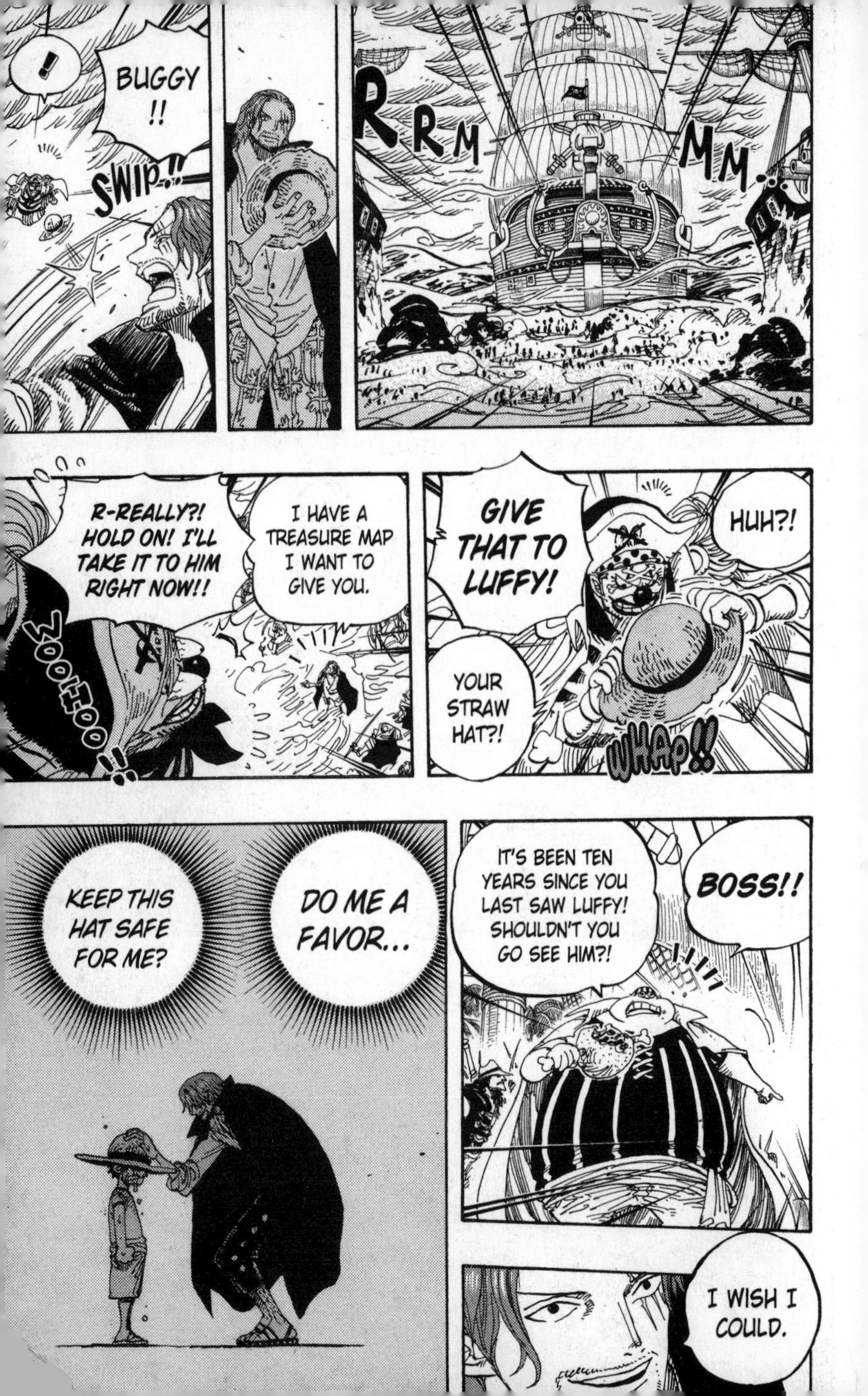
RRRMMM..
!
BUGGY !!
SWIP.!!
GIVE THAT TO LUFFY!
HUH?!
YOUR STRAW HAT?!
WHAP!!
I HAVE A TREASURE MAP I WANT TO GIVE YOU.
R-REALLY?! HOLD ON! I'LL TAKE IT TO HIM RIGHT NOW!!
WOOHOO!!
BOSS!!
IT'S BEEN TEN YEARS SINCE YOU LAST SAW LUFFY! SHOULDN'T YOU GO SEE HIM?!
I WISH I COULD.
DO ME A FAVOR...
KEEP THIS HAT SAFE FOR ME?

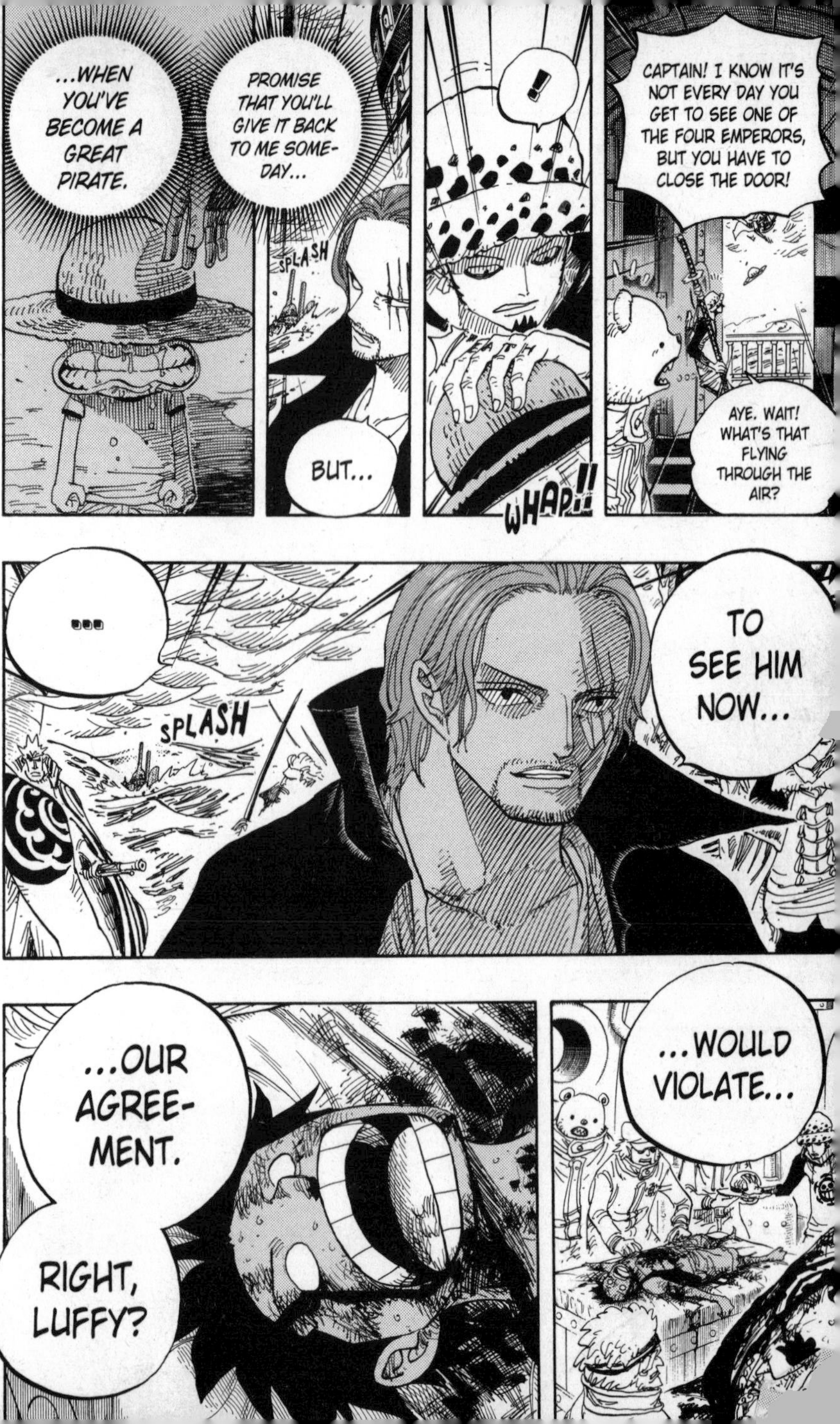
CAPTAIN! I KNOW IT'S NOT EVERY DAY YOU GET TO SEE ONE OF THE FOUR EMPERORS, BUT YOU HAVE TO CLOSE THE DOOR!
AYE. WAIT! WHAT'S THAT FLYING THROUGH THE AIR?
!
WHAP!!
PROMISE THAT YOU'LL GIVE IT BACK TO ME SOME-DAY...
SPLASH
BUT...
...WHEN YOU'VE BECOME A GREAT PIRATE.
TO SEE HIM NOW...
SPLASH
...
...WOULD VIOLATE...
...OUR AGREE-MENT.
RIGHT, LUFFY?

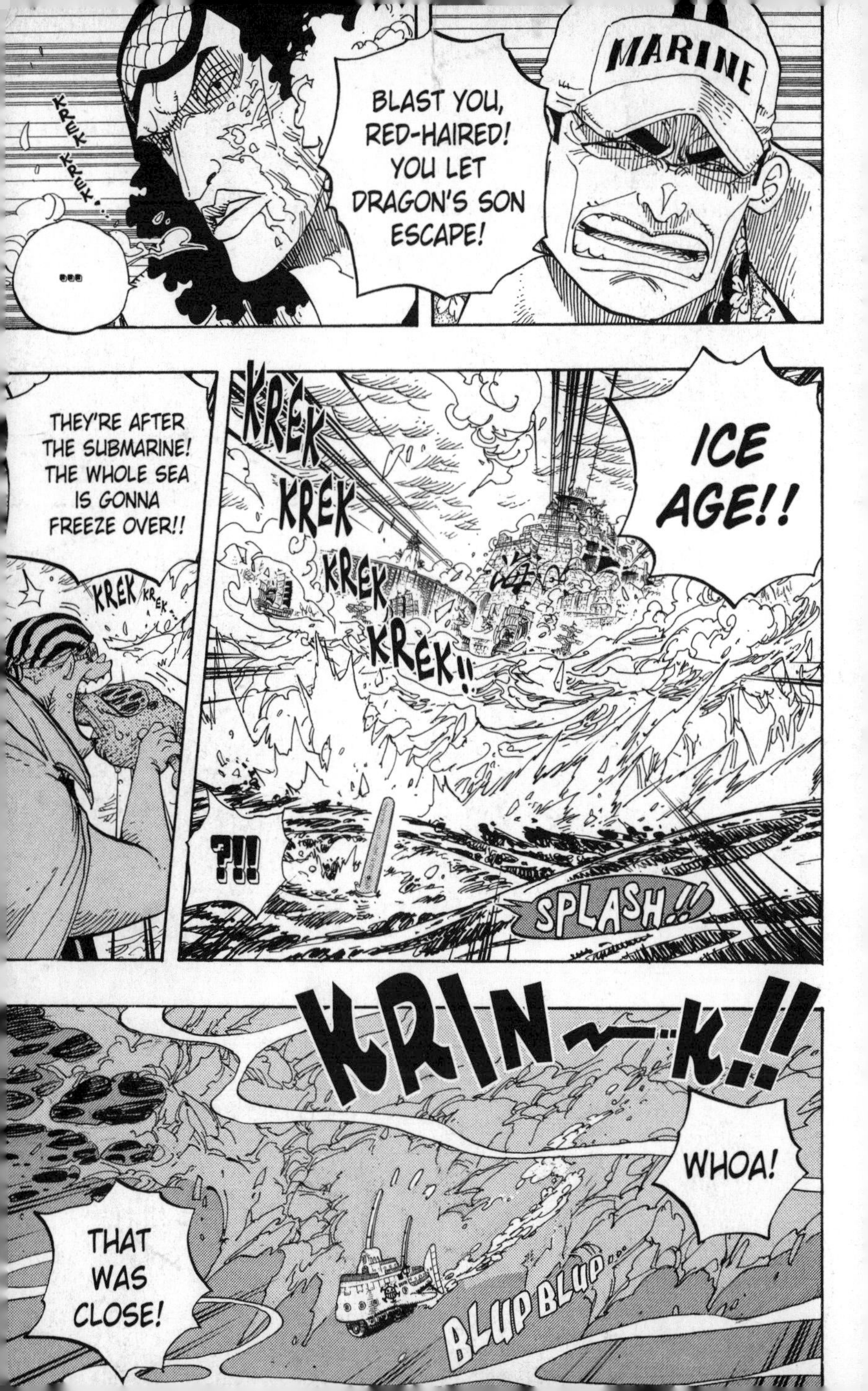
BLAST YOU, RED-HAIRED! YOU LET DRAGON'S SON ESCAPE!
...
KREK KREK...
ICE AGE!!
KREK KREK KREK KREK!!
THEY'RE AFTER THE SUBMARINE! THE WHOLE SEA IS GONNA FREEZE OVER!!
KREK KREK...
SPLASH!!
?!!
KRIN~~K!!
WHOA!
THAT WAS CLOSE!
BLUP BLUP...

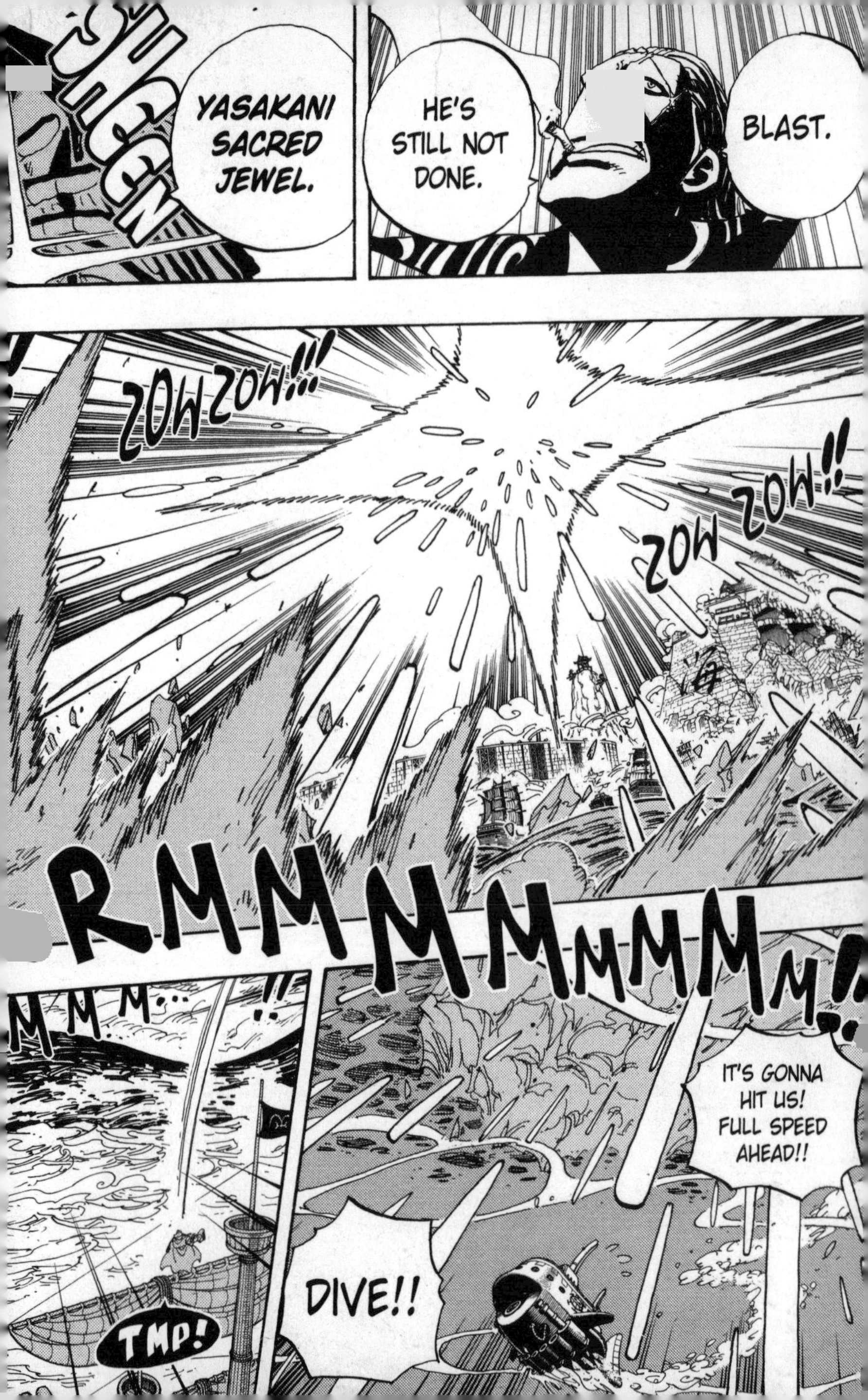
BLAST.
HE'S STILL NOT DONE.
SHGGN
YASAKANI SACRED JEWEL.
ZOW ZOW!!
ZOW ZOW!!
RMMMMMMMMMM!!
IT'S GONNA HIT US! FULL SPEED AHEAD!!
DIVE!!
MMM...!!
TMP!

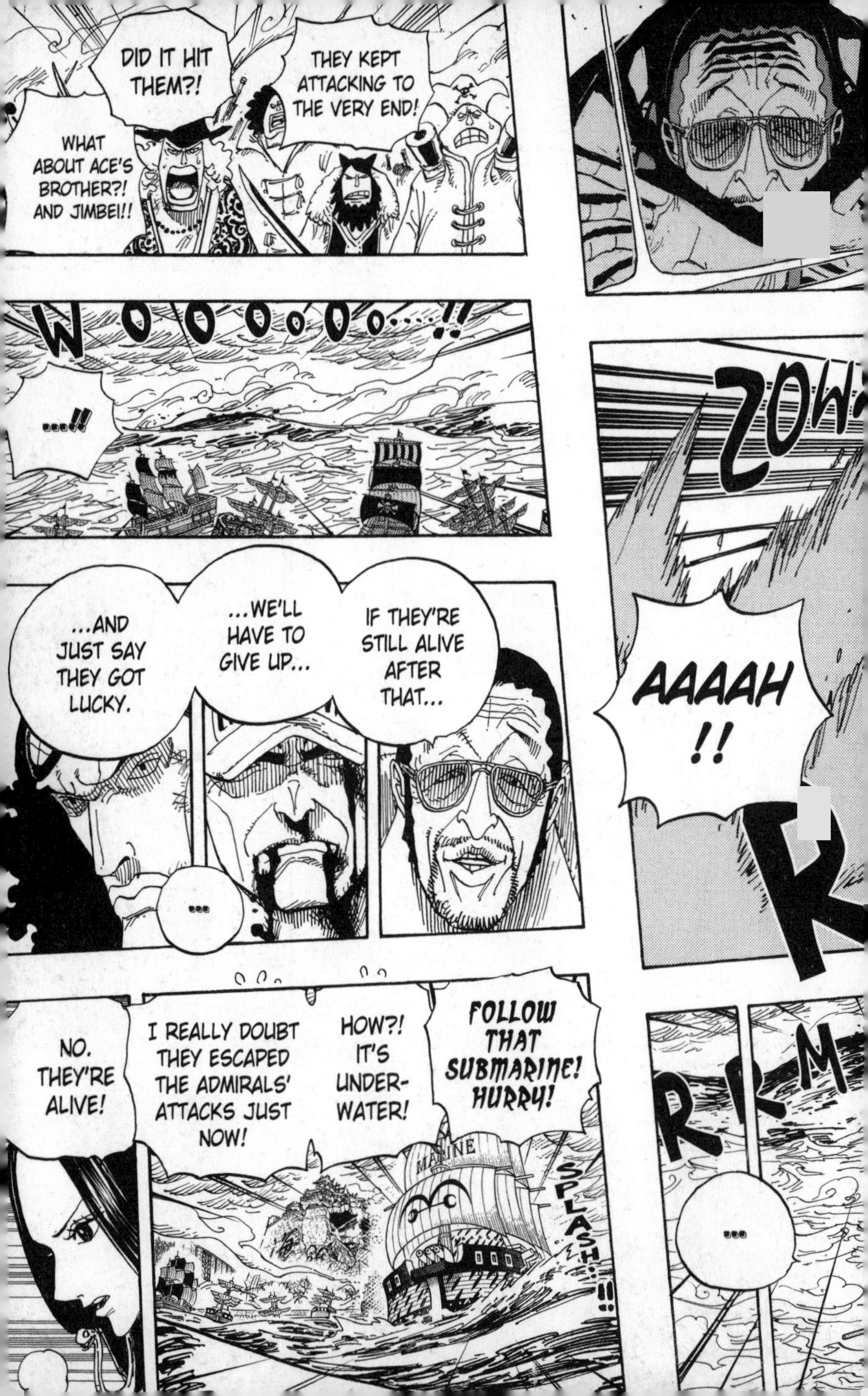
ZOW
AAAAH!!
R
RRM
...
THEY KEPT ATTACKING TO THE VERY END!
DID IT HIT THEM?!
WHAT ABOUT ACE'S BROTHER?! AND JIMBEI!!
WOOOOOO...!!
...!!
IF THEY'RE STILL ALIVE AFTER THAT...
...WE'LL HAVE TO GIVE UP...
...AND JUST SAY THEY GOT LUCKY.
...
FOLLOW THAT SUBMARINE! HURRY!
SPLASH!!
HOW?! IT'S UNDERWATER!
I REALLY DOUBT THEY ESCAPED THE ADMIRALS' ATTACKS JUST NOW!
NO. THEY'RE ALIVE!

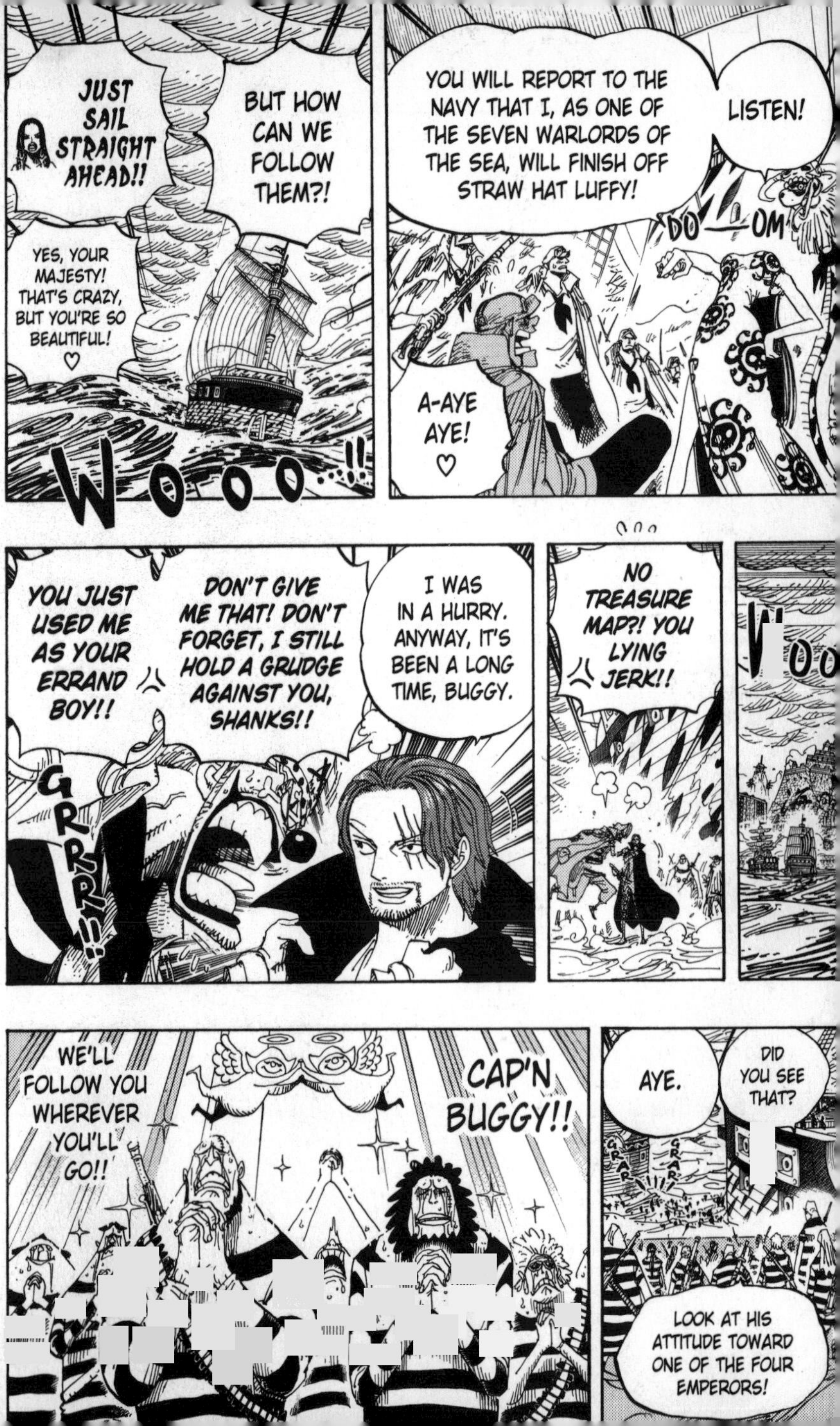
LISTEN!
YOU WILL REPORT TO THE NAVY THAT I, AS ONE OF THE SEVEN WARLORDS OF THE SEA, WILL FINISH OFF STRAW HAT LUFFY!
DO—OM
A-AYE AYE! ♡
BUT HOW CAN WE FOLLOW THEM?!
JUST SAIL STRAIGHT AHEAD!!
YES, YOUR MAJESTY! THAT'S CRAZY, BUT YOU'RE SO BEAUTIFUL! ♡
WOOO...!!
NO TREASURE MAP?! YOU LYING JERK!!
I WAS IN A HURRY. ANYWAY, IT'S BEEN A LONG TIME, BUGGY.
DON'T GIVE ME THAT! DON'T FORGET, I STILL HOLD A GRUDGE AGAINST YOU, SHANKS!!
YOU JUST USED ME AS YOUR ERRAND BOY!!
GRRRR!!
DID YOU SEE THAT?
AYE.
GRAR
GRAR
LOOK AT HIS ATTITUDE TOWARD ONE OF THE FOUR EMPERORS!
CAP'N BUGGY!!
WE'LL FOLLOW YOU WHEREVER YOU'LL GO!!

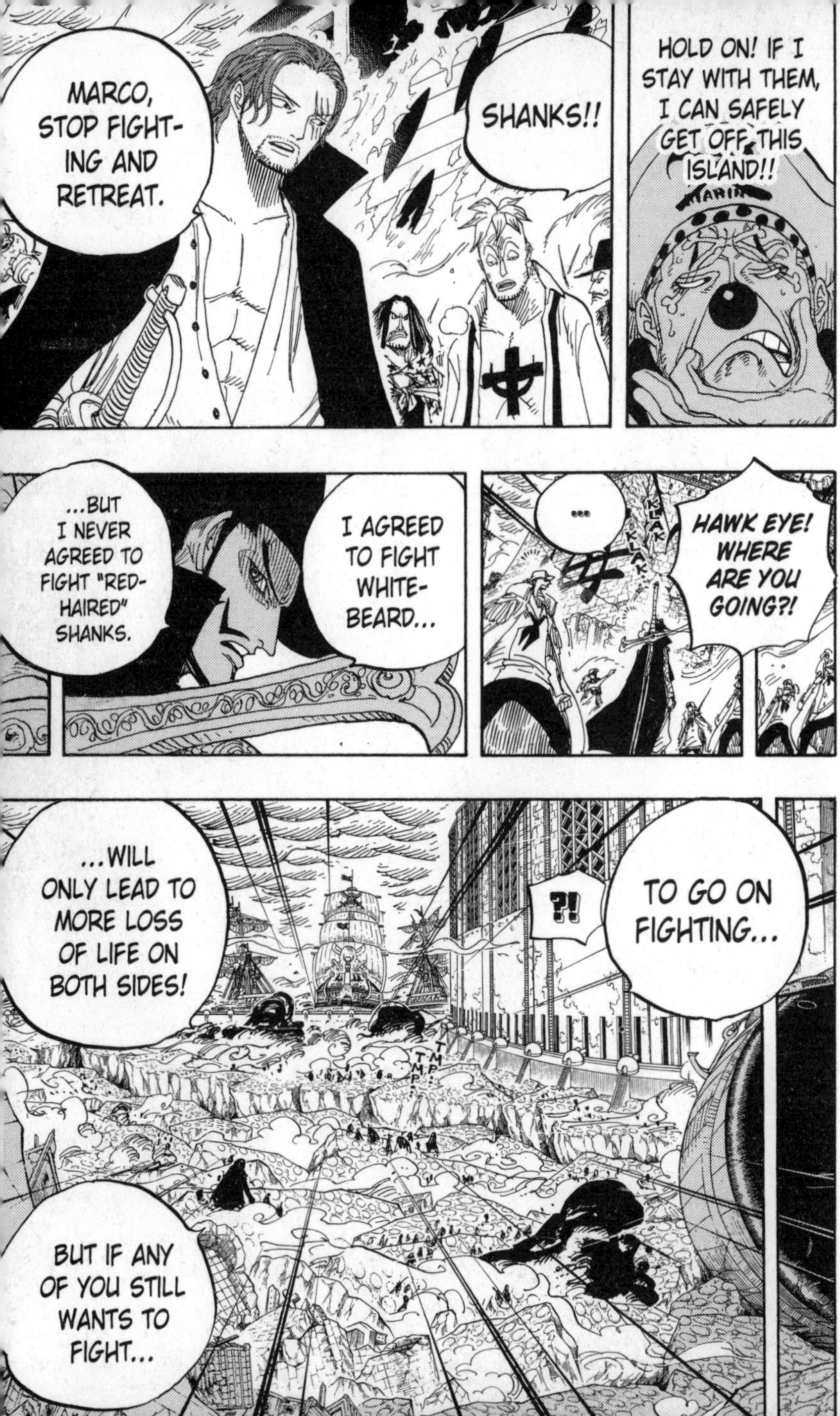
HOLD ON! IF I STAY WITH THEM, I CAN SAFELY GET OFF THIS ISLAND!!
SHANKS!!
MARCO, STOP FIGHTING AND RETREAT.
HAWK EYE! WHERE ARE YOU GOING?!
KLAK KLAK
...
I AGREED TO FIGHT WHITEBEARD...
...BUT I NEVER AGREED TO FIGHT "RED-HAIRED" SHANKS.
TO GO ON FIGHTING...
?!
...WILL ONLY LEAD TO MORE LOSS OF LIFE ON BOTH SIDES!
TMP TMP
BUT IF ANY OF YOU STILL WANTS TO FIGHT...

COME ON!!

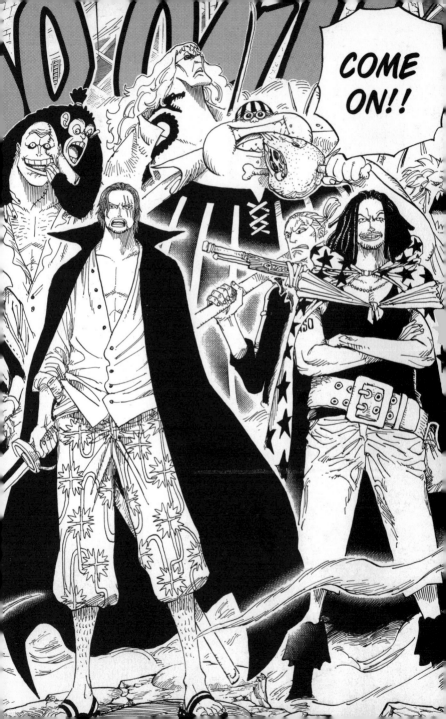

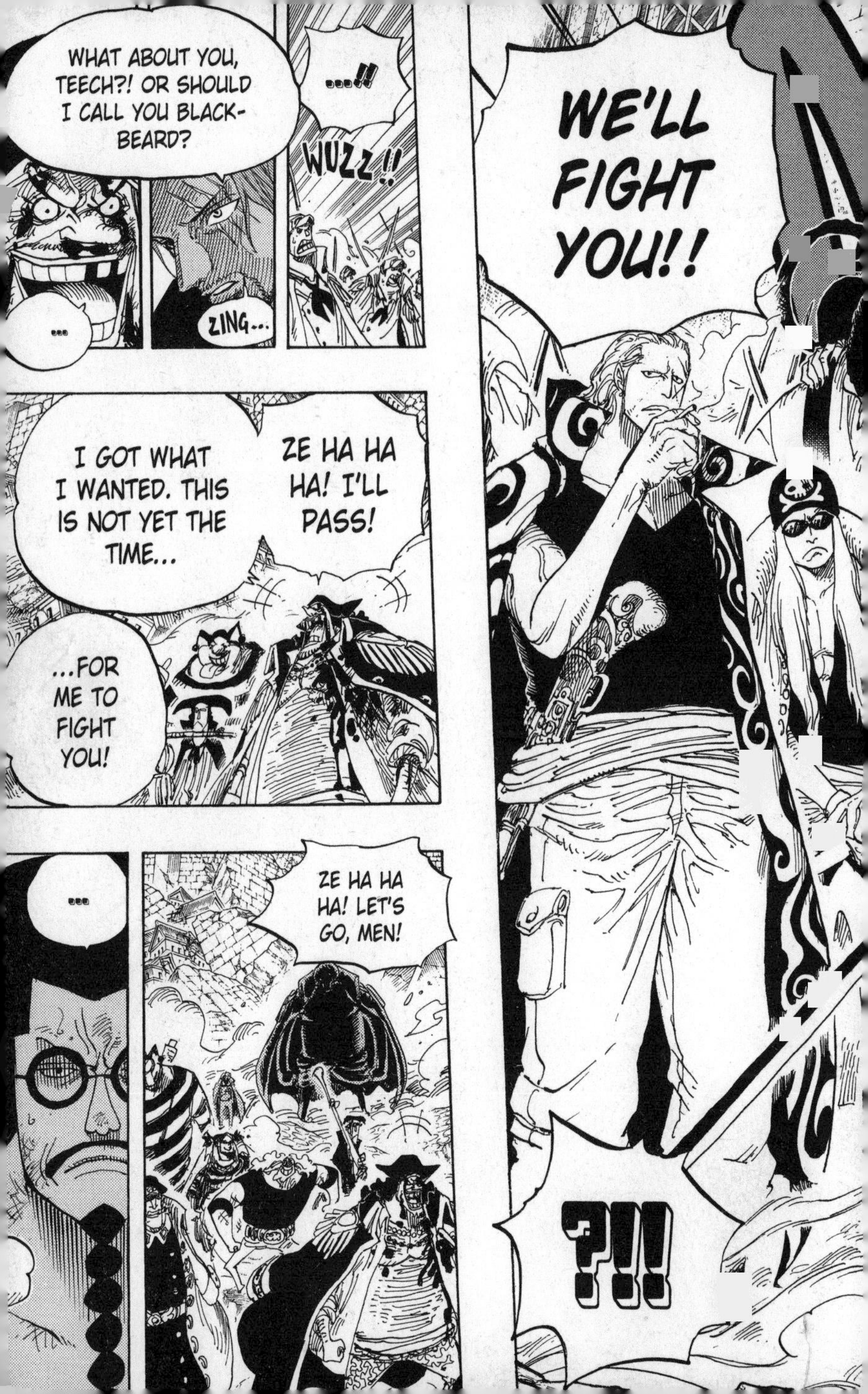
WE'LL FIGHT YOU!!
?!!
...!!
WUZZ!!
ZING...
WHAT ABOUT YOU, TEECH?! OR SHOULD I CALL YOU BLACK-BEARD?
...
ZE HA HA HA! I'LL PASS!
I GOT WHAT I WANTED. THIS IS NOT YET THE TIME...
...FOR ME TO FIGHT YOU!
ZE HA HA HA! LET'S GO, MEN!
...

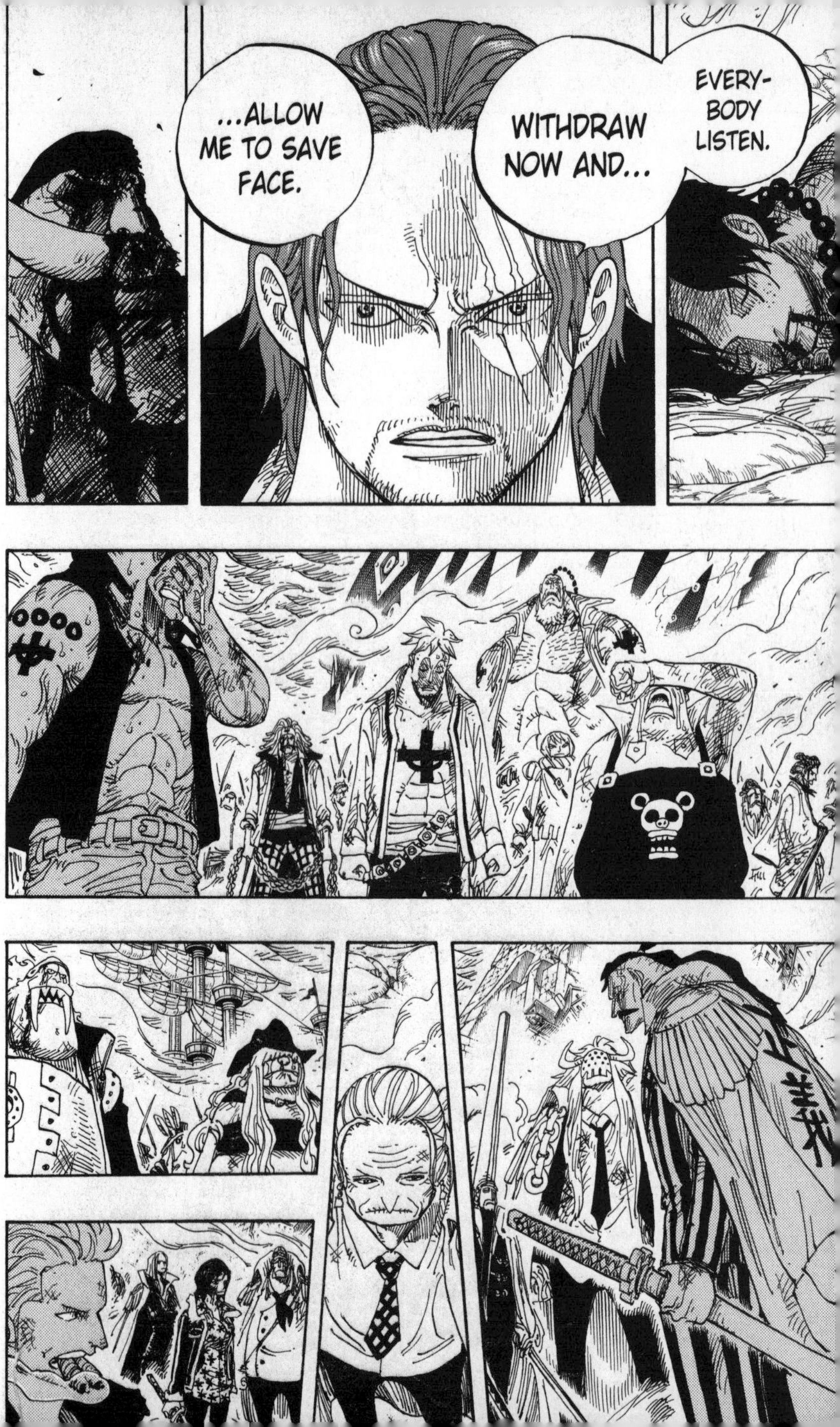
EVERY-BODY LISTEN.
WITHDRAW NOW AND...
...ALLOW ME TO SAVE FACE.

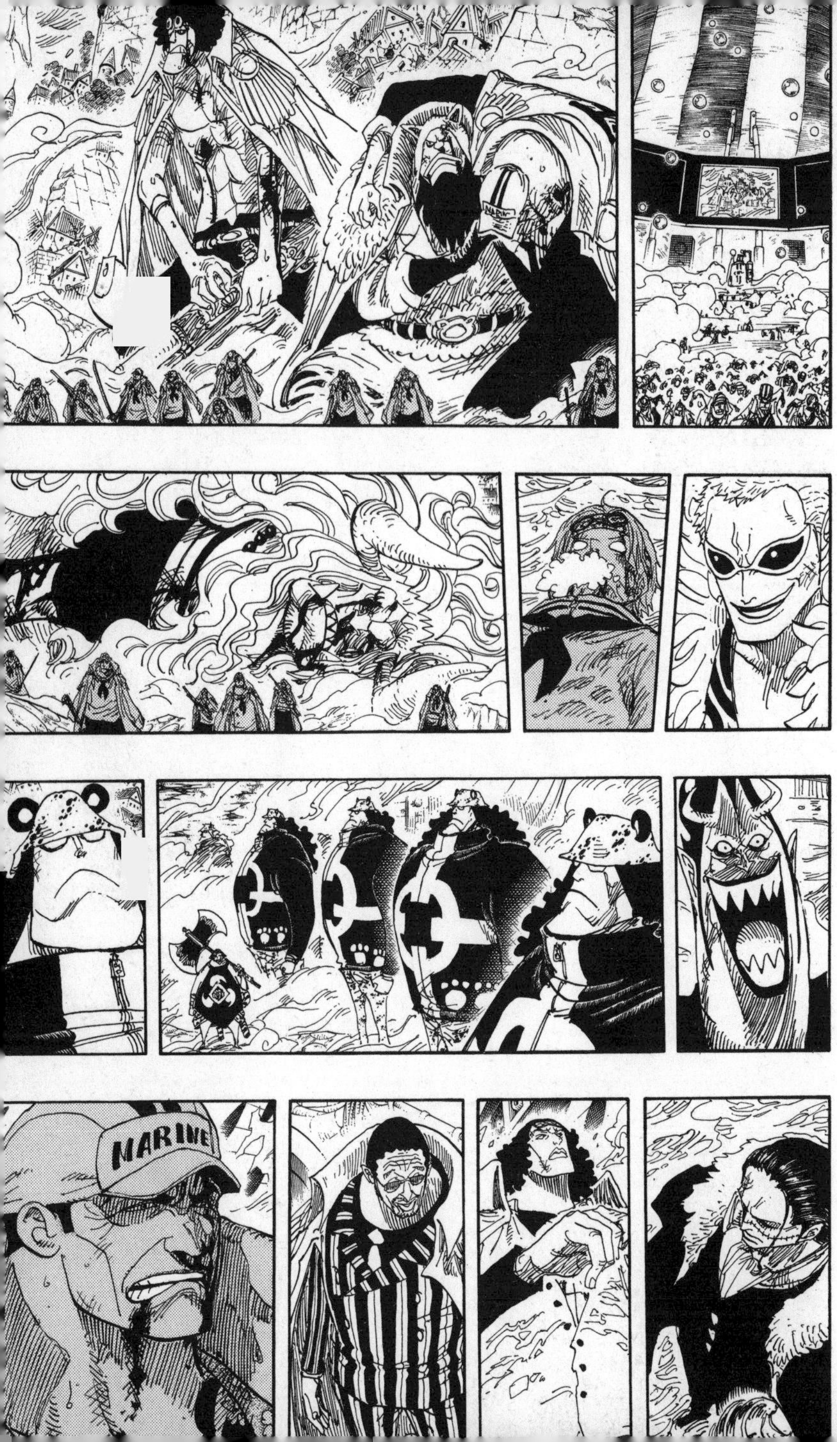
MARINE

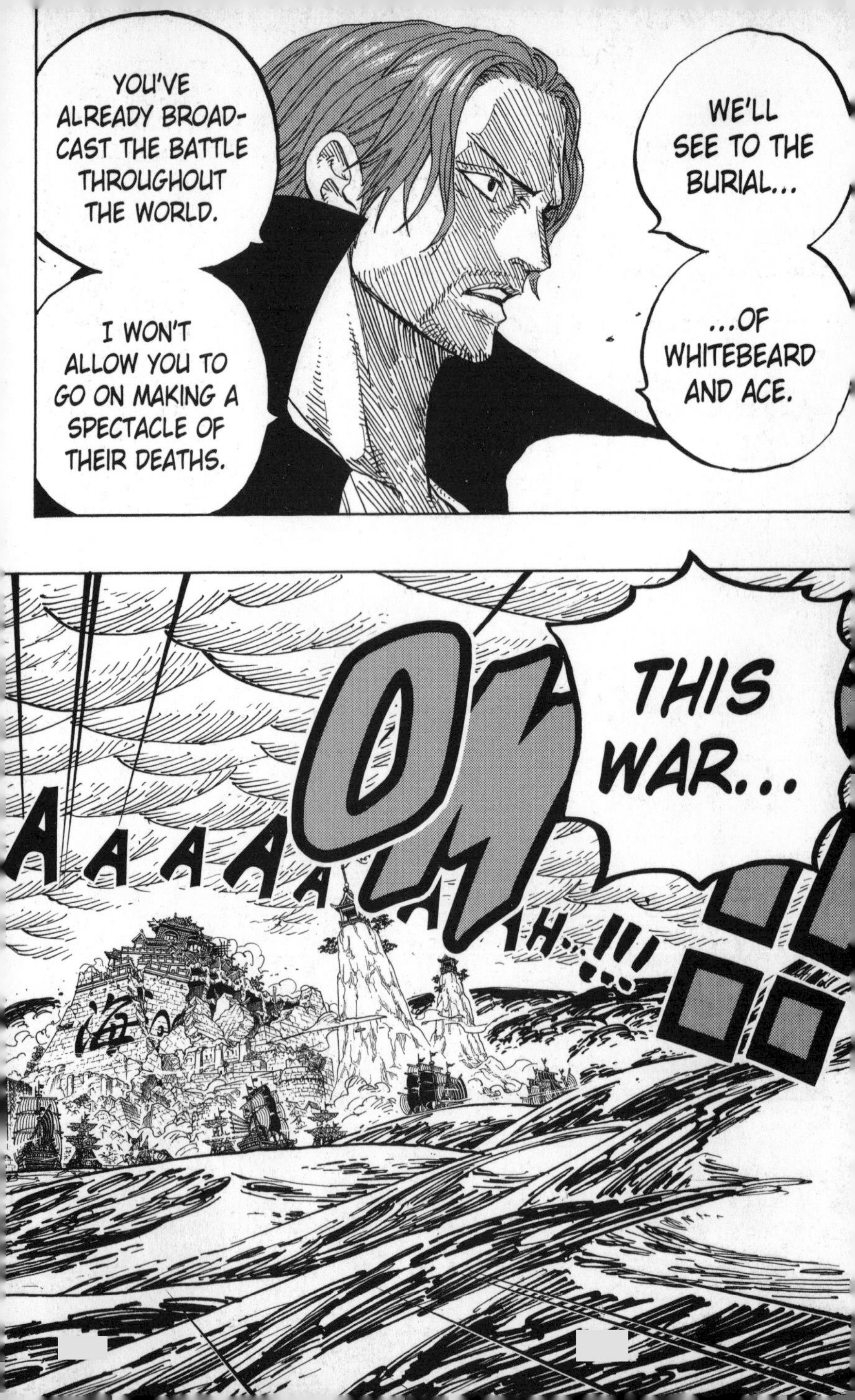
WE'LL SEE TO THE BURIAL...
...OF WHITEBEARD AND ACE.
YOU'VE ALREADY BROAD-CAST THE BATTLE THROUGHOUT THE WORLD.
I WON'T ALLOW YOU TO GO ON MAKING A SPECTACLE OF THEIR DEATHS.
THIS WAR...
AAAAAAAH...!!!

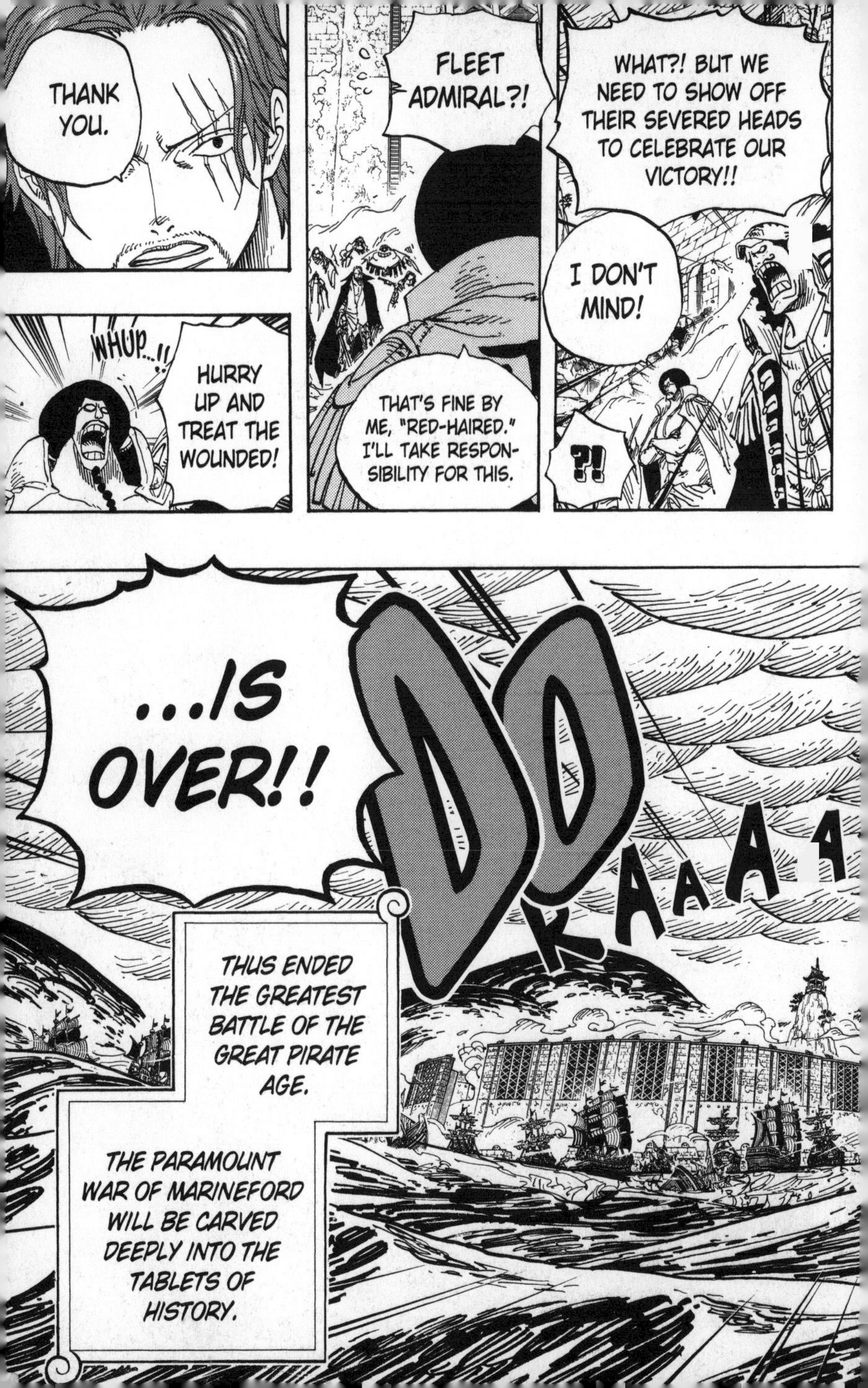
WHAT?! BUT WE NEED TO SHOW OFF THEIR SEVERED HEADS TO CELEBRATE OUR VICTORY!!
I DON'T MIND!
?!
FLEET ADMIRAL?!
THAT'S FINE BY ME, "RED-HAIRED." I'LL TAKE RESPONSIBILITY FOR THIS.
THANK YOU.
WHUP...!!
HURRY UP AND TREAT THE WOUNDED!
...IS OVER!!
DOKAAAA
THUS ENDED THE GREATEST BATTLE OF THE GREAT PIRATE AGE.
THE PARAMOUNT WAR OF MARINEFORD WILL BE CARVED DEEPLY INTO THE TABLETS OF HISTORY.

SBS Question Corner (Skull Yukichi, Iwate)

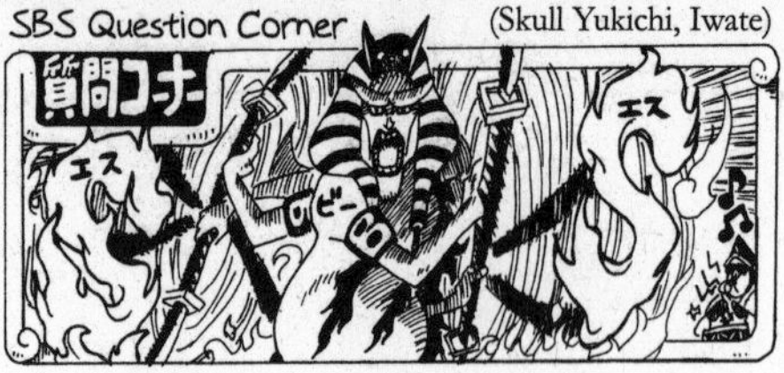
質問コーナー
エス
エス

A: It's time for BIO! (Bring it on!) Now let's start! Yep. Hey, you guys! Why are you picking all the character birthdays on your own?! Anyway, I put a lot of my love into the characters too! I won't let you decide all of them! Bring it on!

Q: About Law's birthday, how about making it October 6, since that sounds similar to the first symbols of his name in Japanese?

--Hamuchi

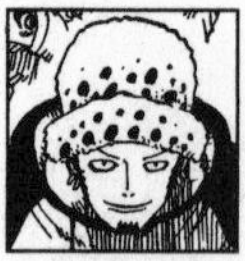

A: Sure.

Q: I have a request. My favorite pirate in all of *One Piece* is Blackbeard, Marshall D. Teech. How about making his birthday August 3, since 8 and 3 can be read in Japanese to sound like the name of his power?

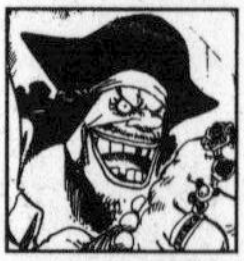

A: Sure.

Q: Listen to this! A new guy at my workplace said that he didn't know Marco's birthday! His birthday is October 5! It's so easy to remember since he's the leader of Division 1 and Marco could be read as 0 and 5! Don't you think so, Mr. Oda?!♡

--Whitebeard Nurse Team Medical Chart Writer, Marunyamu

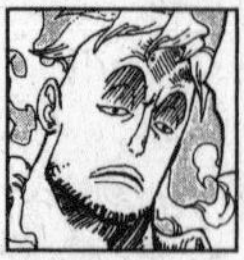

A: Uh...sure. I guess so. Yeah... That's correct.

Q: Let's make Crocodile's birthday September 5. Since the first part of his name could sound like 9 and 5. When we're picking birthdays, you never seem excited. Why don't you get Iva to get you some Emporio Energy Hormone before you answer me?

--Akimasa Ultimate

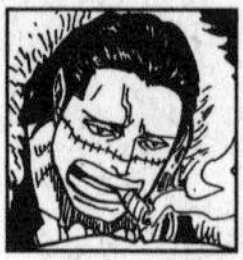

A: Woohaa! Sure thing! Wooohaaaa!!

Q: This might be sudden, but let's make Iva's birthday January 8. What do you think?

--First-gen Kitetsu

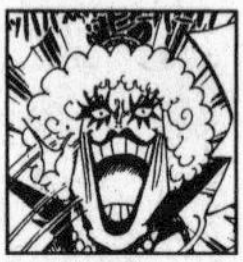

A: Sure thing! Woohaa!

Q: So about the Marine Admirals... How about making their birthdays the same as the people they're based on?

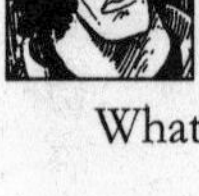

Aokiji-September 21 (Yusaku Matsuda)

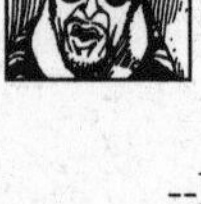

Kizaru-November 23 (Kunie Tanaka)

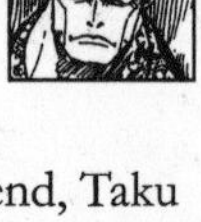
MARINE

Akainu-August 16 (Bunta Sugawara)

What do you think?

--Nishimura's Friend, Taku

A: Whatever! Do what you want! Woohaa!!

Chapter 581: CREEPING FUTURE

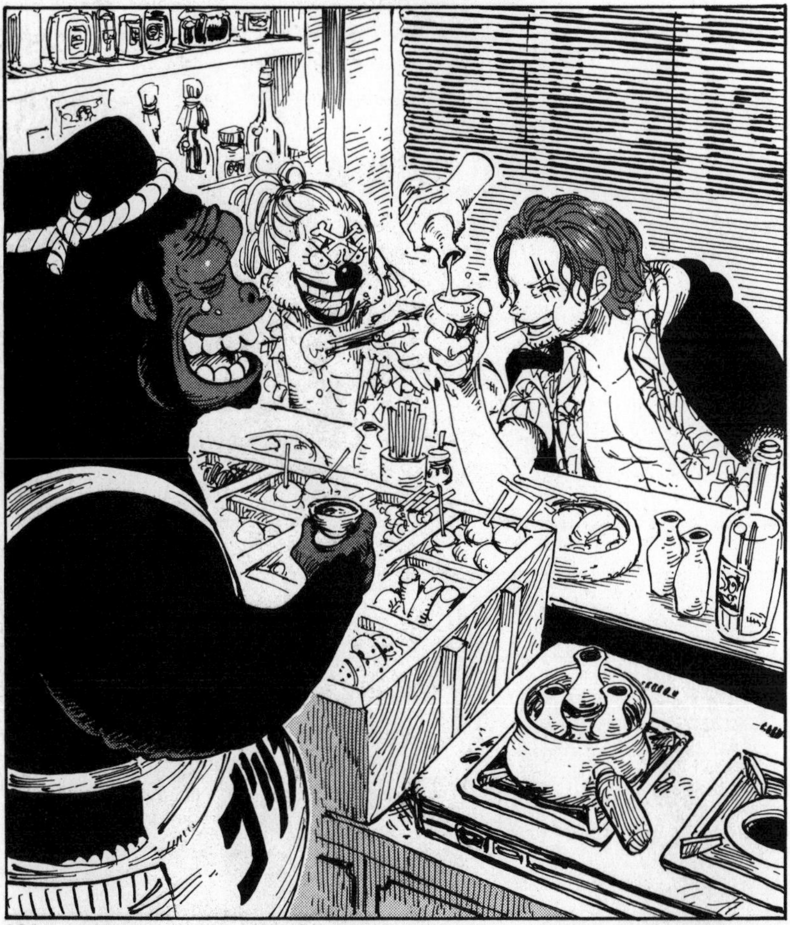

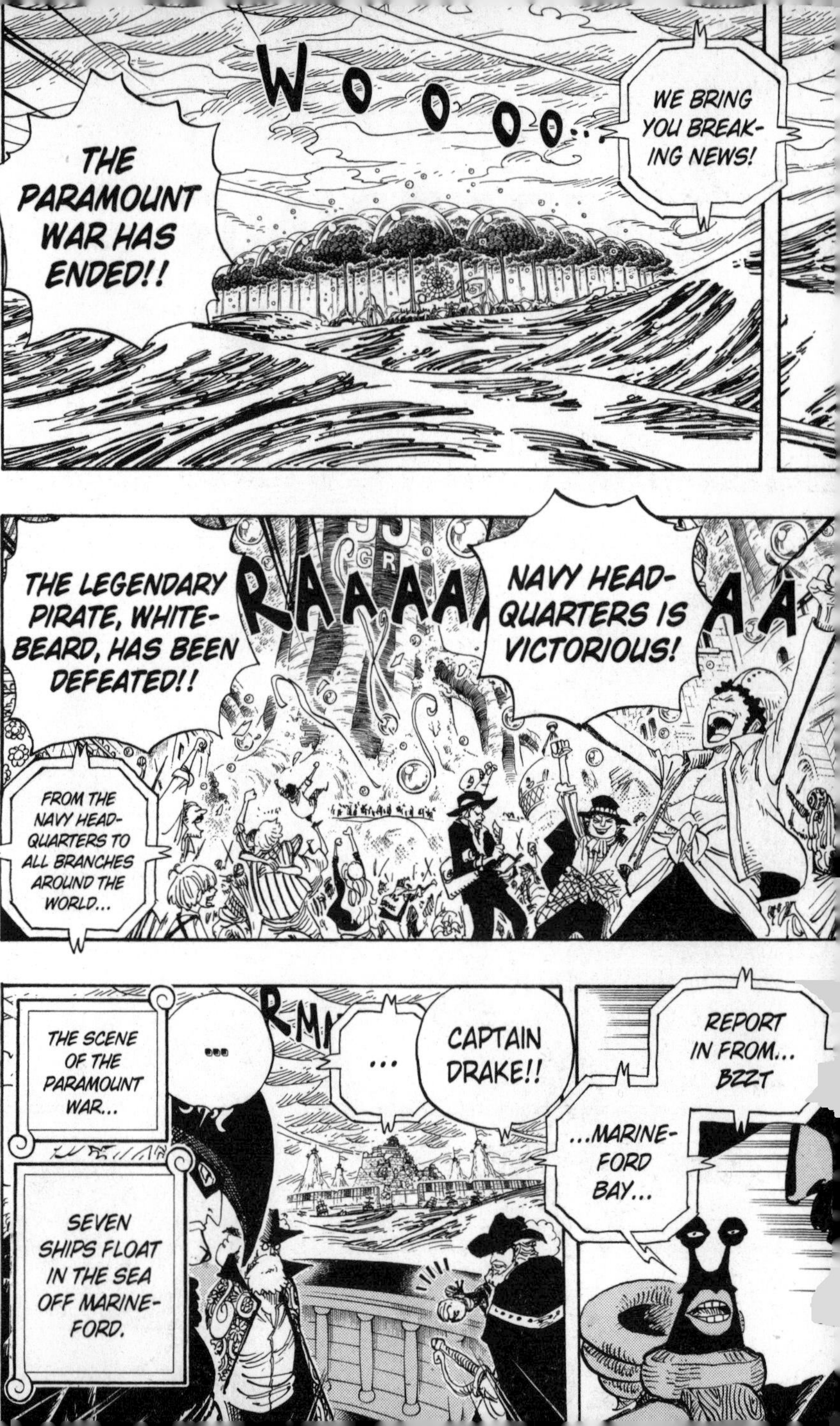
WE BRING YOU BREAKING NEWS!
WOOOO...
THE PARAMOUNT WAR HAS ENDED!!
AA
NAVY HEADQUARTERS IS VICTORIOUS!
RAAAA
THE LEGENDARY PIRATE, WHITEBEARD, HAS BEEN DEFEATED!!
FROM THE NAVY HEADQUARTERS TO ALL BRANCHES AROUND THE WORLD...
REPORT IN FROM... BZZT
...MARINEFORD BAY...
CAPTAIN DRAKE!!
...
...
THE SCENE OF THE PARAMOUNT WAR...
SEVEN SHIPS FLOAT IN THE SEA OFF MARINEFORD.

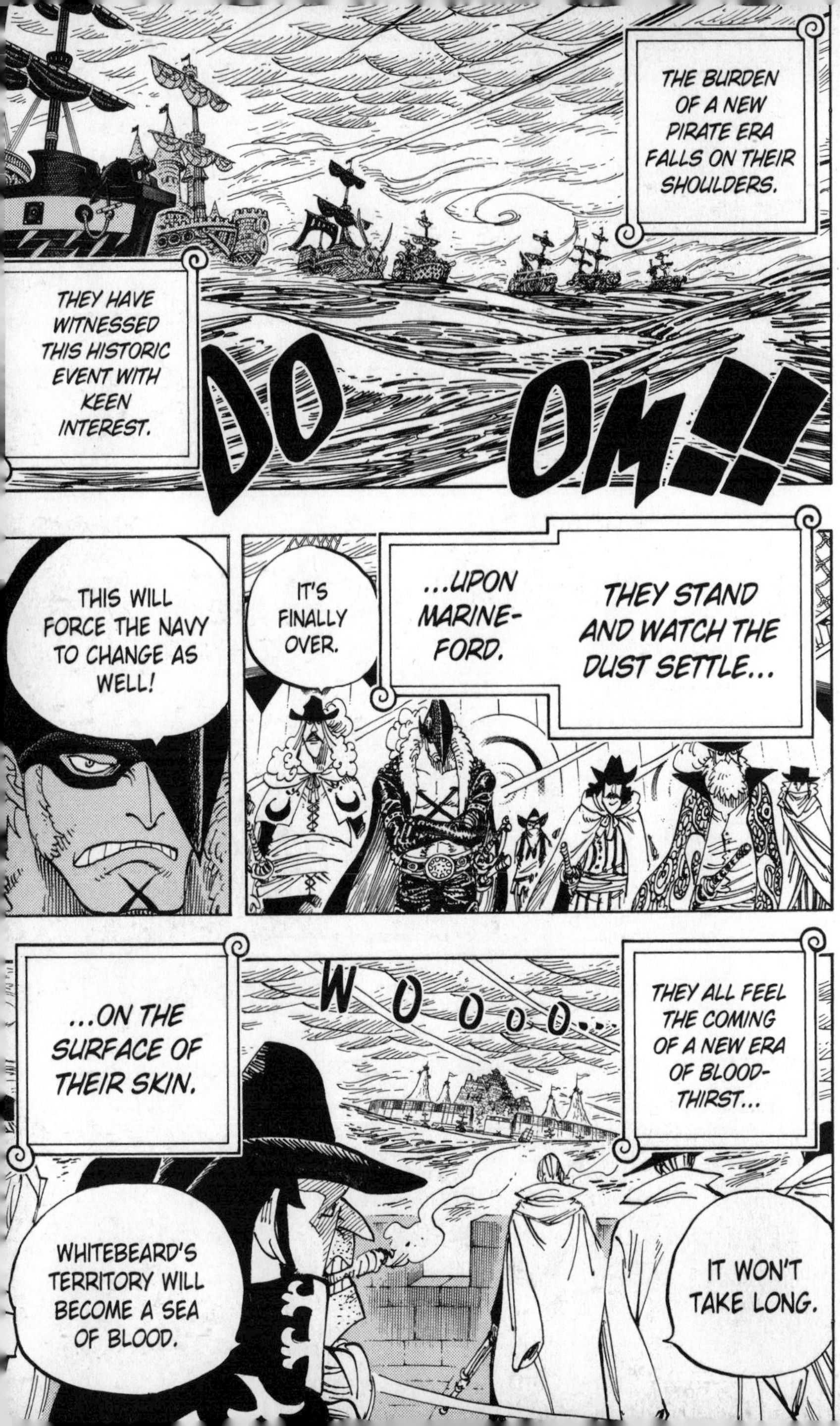
THE BURDEN OF A NEW PIRATE ERA FALLS ON THEIR SHOULDERS.
THEY HAVE WITNESSED THIS HISTORIC EVENT WITH KEEN INTEREST.
DOOM!!
THEY STAND AND WATCH THE DUST SETTLE...
...UPON MARINE-FORD.
IT'S FINALLY OVER.
THIS WILL FORCE THE NAVY TO CHANGE AS WELL!
THEY ALL FEEL THE COMING OF A NEW ERA OF BLOOD-THIRST...
WOOOO...
...ON THE SURFACE OF THEIR SKIN.
IT WON'T TAKE LONG.
WHITEBEARD'S TERRITORY WILL BECOME A SEA OF BLOOD.

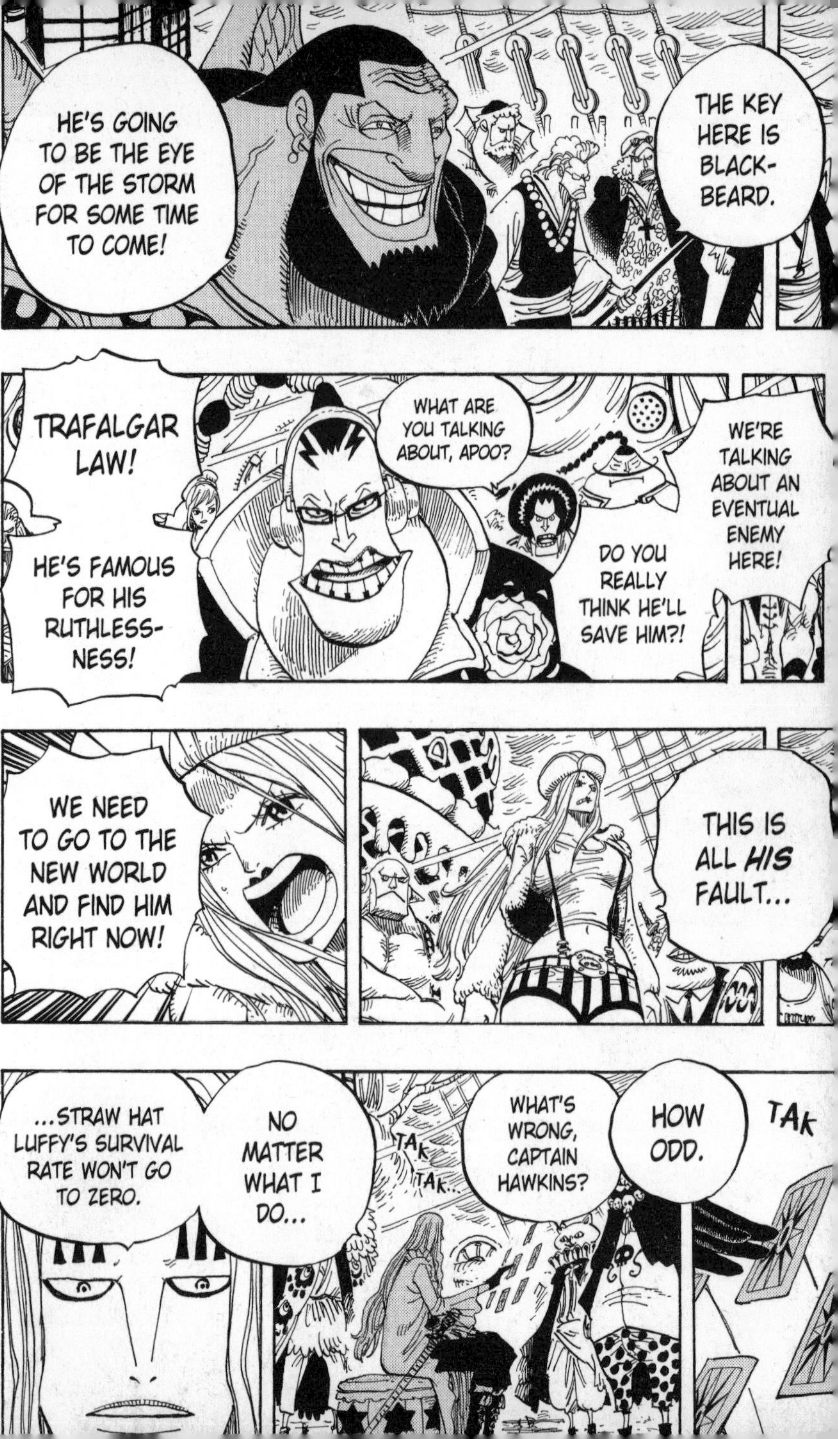
THE KEY HERE IS BLACK-BEARD.
HE'S GOING TO BE THE EYE OF THE STORM FOR SOME TIME TO COME!
WE'RE TALKING ABOUT AN EVENTUAL ENEMY HERE!
DO YOU REALLY THINK HE'LL SAVE HIM?!
WHAT ARE YOU TALKING ABOUT, APOO?
TRAFALGAR LAW!
HE'S FAMOUS FOR HIS RUTHLESS-NESS!
THIS IS ALL *HIS* FAULT...
WE NEED TO GO TO THE NEW WORLD AND FIND HIM RIGHT NOW!
TAK
HOW ODD.
WHAT'S WRONG, CAPTAIN HAWKINS?
TAK TAK...
NO MATTER WHAT I DO...
...STRAW HAT LUFFY'S SURVIVAL RATE WON'T GO TO ZERO.

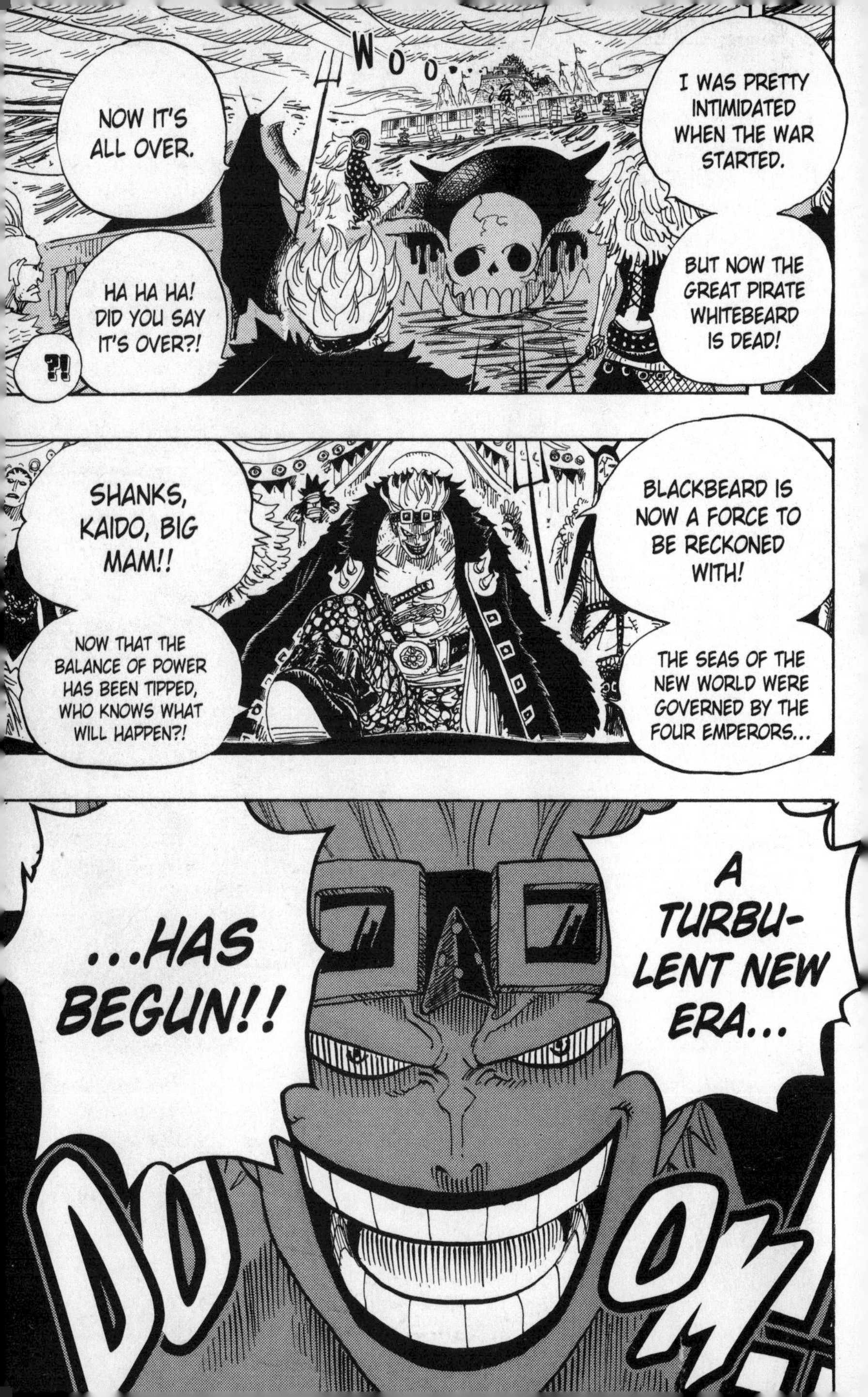
I WAS PRETTY INTIMIDATED WHEN THE WAR STARTED.
BUT NOW THE GREAT PIRATE WHITEBEARD IS DEAD!
WOO...
NOW IT'S ALL OVER.
HA HA HA! DID YOU SAY IT'S OVER?!
?!
BLACKBEARD IS NOW A FORCE TO BE RECKONED WITH!
THE SEAS OF THE NEW WORLD WERE GOVERNED BY THE FOUR EMPERORS...
SHANKS, KAIDO, BIG MAM!!
NOW THAT THE BALANCE OF POWER HAS BEEN TIPPED, WHO KNOWS WHAT WILL HAPPEN?!
A TURBU-LENT NEW ERA...
...HAS BEGUN!!
DOOM

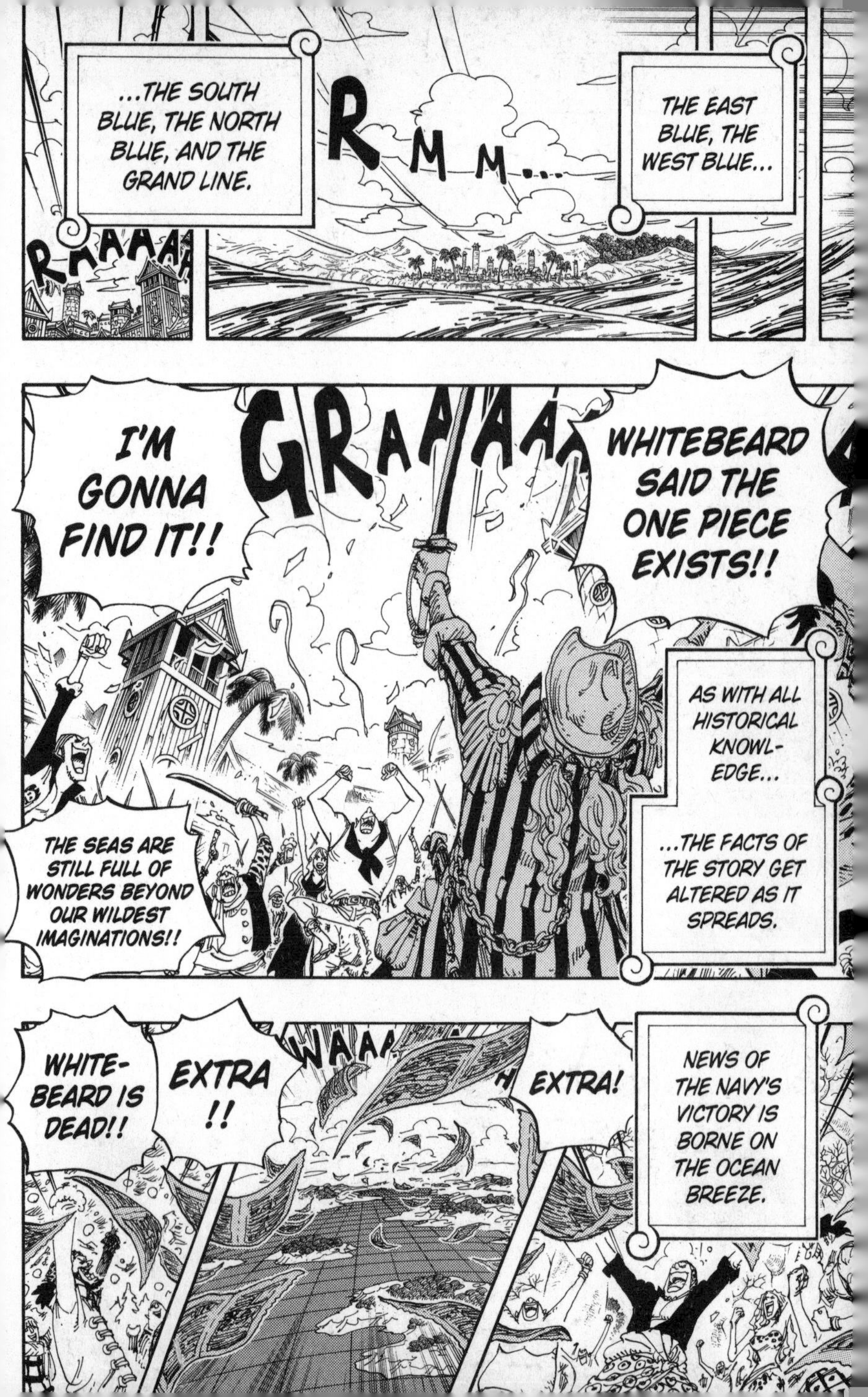
THE EAST BLUE, THE WEST BLUE...
RMM...
...THE SOUTH BLUE, THE NORTH BLUE, AND THE GRAND LINE.
RAAAAA
WHITEBEARD SAID THE ONE PIECE EXISTS!!
GRAAAA
I'M GONNA FIND IT!!
AS WITH ALL HISTORICAL KNOWL-EDGE...
...THE FACTS OF THE STORY GET ALTERED AS IT SPREADS.
THE SEAS ARE STILL FULL OF WONDERS BEYOND OUR WILDEST IMAGINATIONS!!
NEWS OF THE NAVY'S VICTORY IS BORNE ON THE OCEAN BREEZE.
EXTRA!
WAAA
EXTRA!!
WHITE-BEARD IS DEAD!!

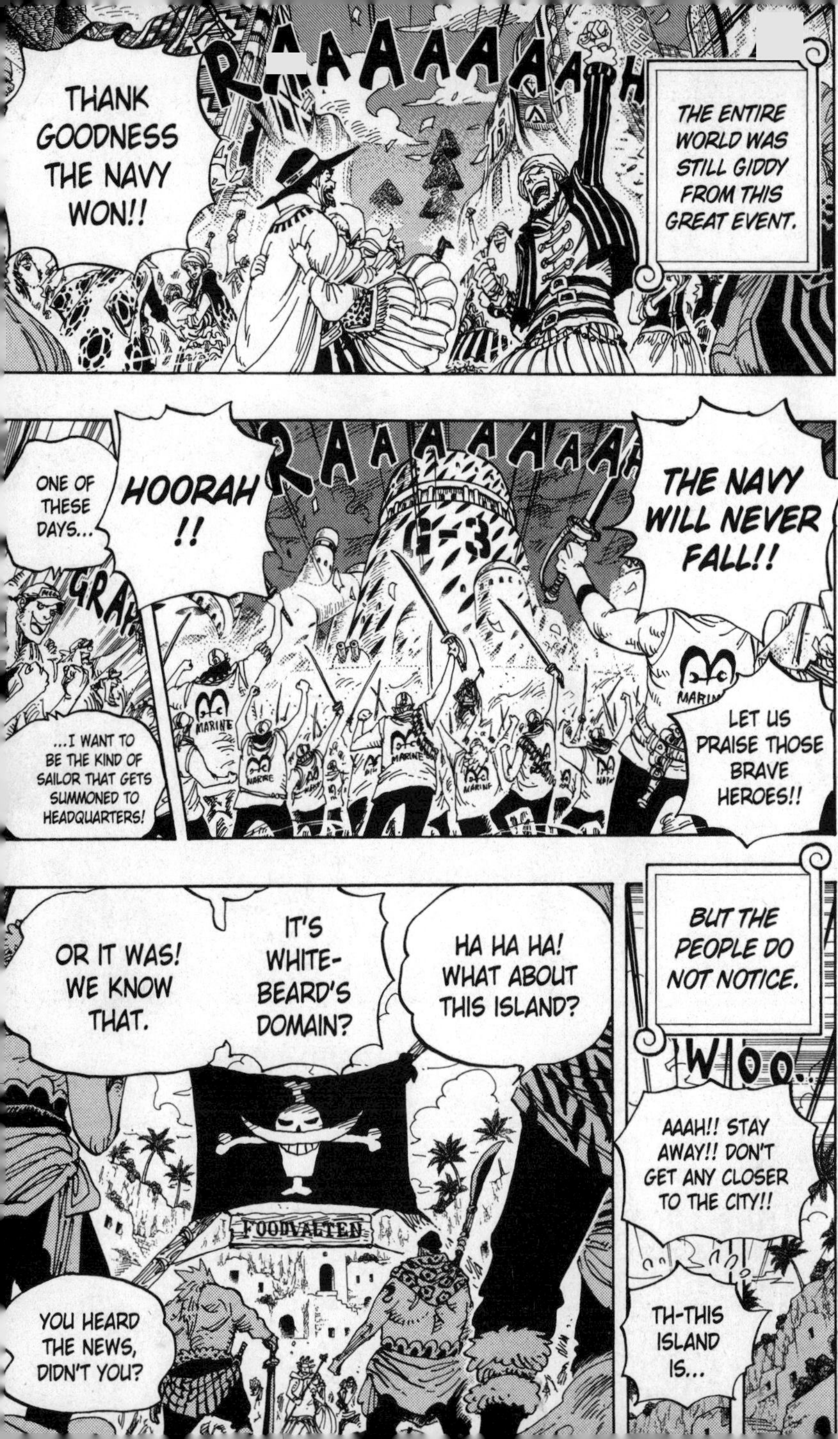
THE ENTIRE WORLD WAS STILL GIDDY FROM THIS GREAT EVENT.
RAAAAAAAH
THANK GOODNESS THE NAVY WON!!
THE NAVY WILL NEVER FALL!!
LET US PRAISE THOSE BRAVE HEROES!!
RAAAAAAAAAH
G-3
HOORAH!!
ONE OF THESE DAYS...
GRAH
...I WANT TO BE THE KIND OF SAILOR THAT GETS SUMMONED TO HEADQUARTERS!
BUT THE PEOPLE DO NOT NOTICE.
WOO..
AAAH!! STAY AWAY!! DON'T GET ANY CLOSER TO THE CITY!!
TH-THIS ISLAND IS...
HA HA HA! WHAT ABOUT THIS ISLAND?
IT'S WHITE-BEARD'S DOMAIN?
OR IT WAS! WE KNOW THAT.
FOODVALTEN
YOU HEARD THE NEWS, DIDN'T YOU?

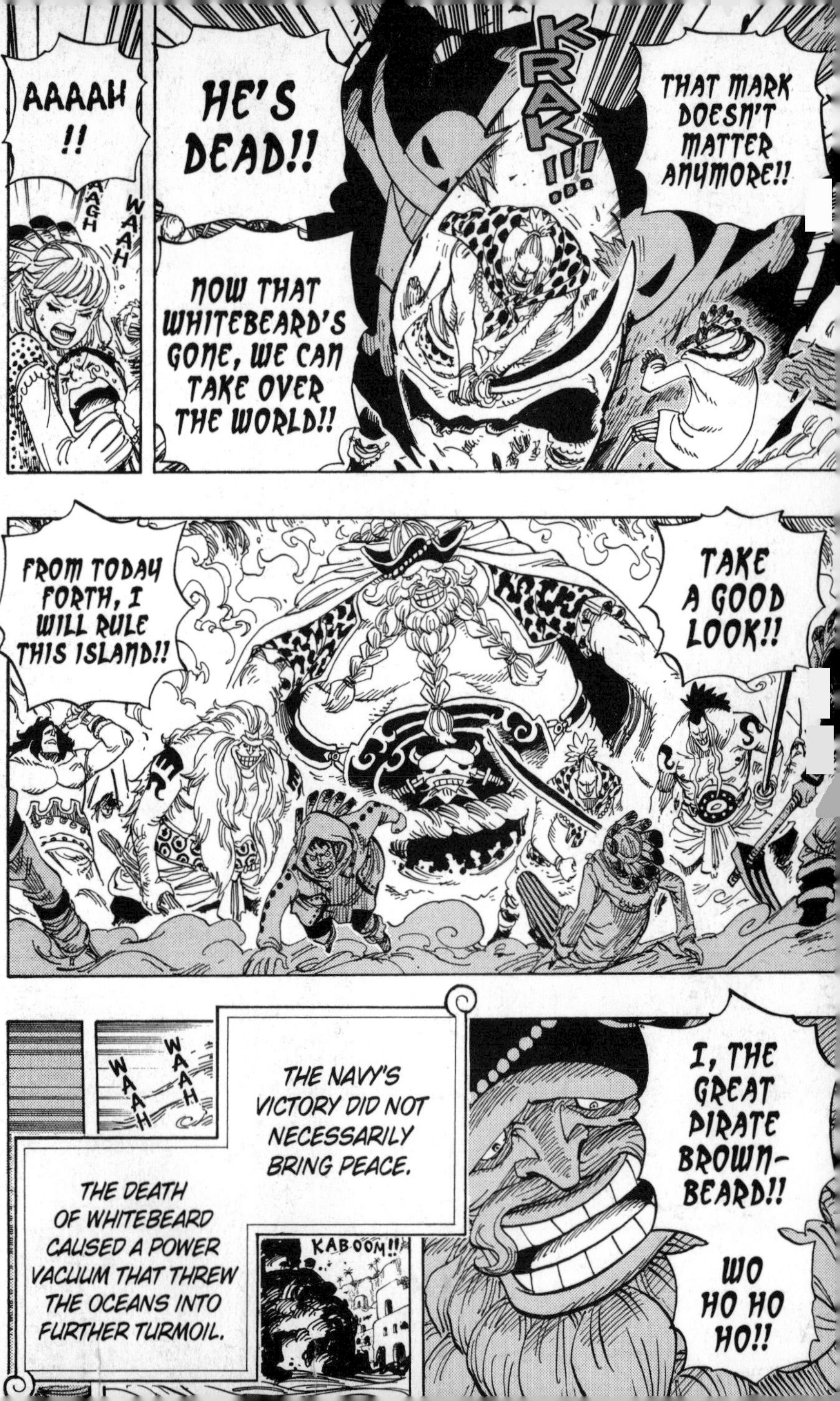
THAT MARK DOESN'T MATTER ANYMORE!!
KRAK!!!...
HE'S DEAD!!
NOW THAT WHITEBEARD'S GONE, WE CAN TAKE OVER THE WORLD!!
AAAAH!!
AAGH
WAAAH
TAKE A GOOD LOOK!!
FROM TODAY FORTH, I WILL RULE THIS ISLAND!!
I, THE GREAT PIRATE BROWN-BEARD!!
WO HO HO HO!!
THE NAVY'S VICTORY DID NOT NECESSARILY BRING PEACE.
WAAAH
WAAAH
THE DEATH OF WHITEBEARD CAUSED A POWER VACUUM THAT THREW THE OCEANS INTO FURTHER TURMOIL.
KABOOM!!

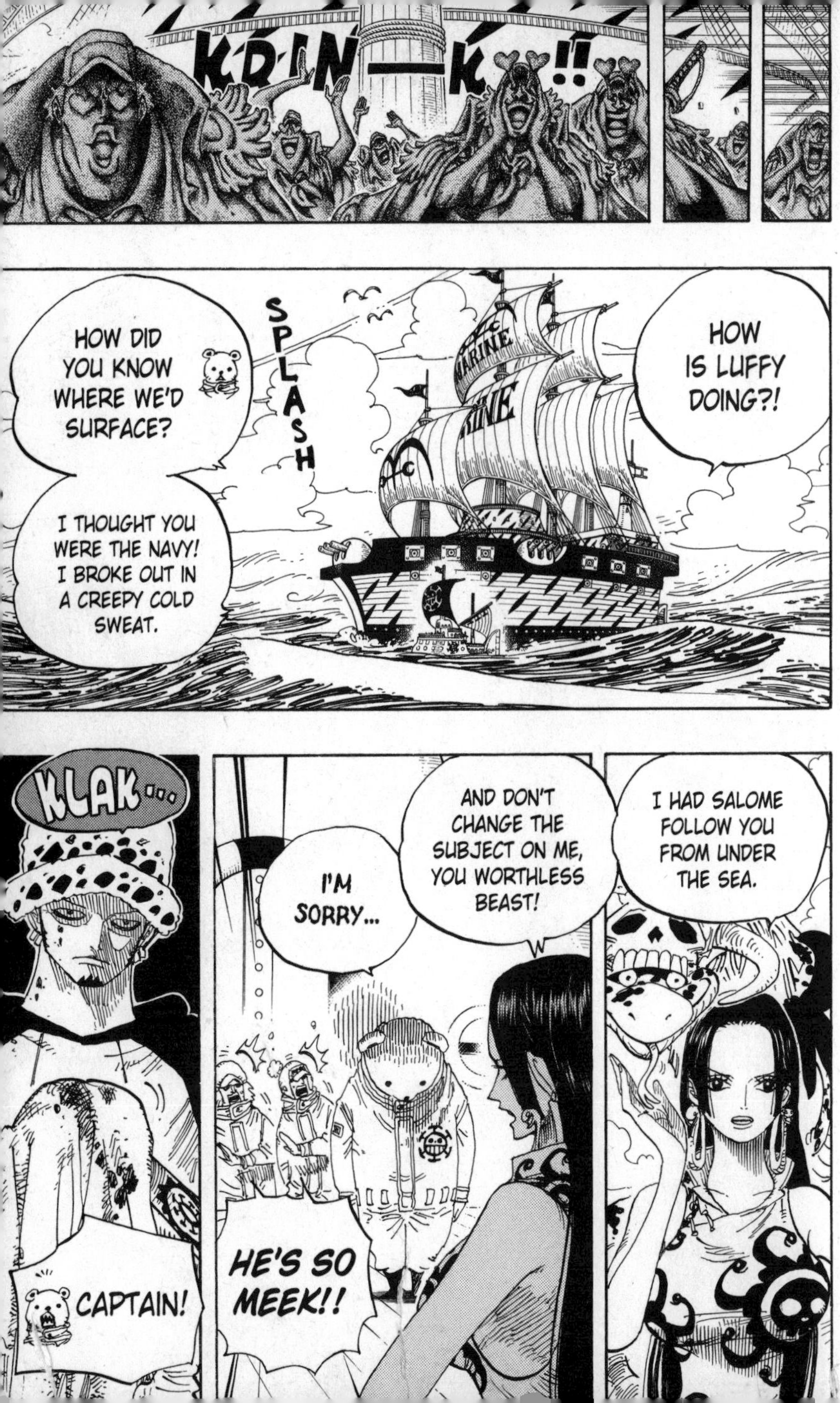
KRIN—K!!
HOW IS LUFFY DOING?!
SPLASH
HOW DID YOU KNOW WHERE WE'D SURFACE?
I THOUGHT YOU WERE THE NAVY! I BROKE OUT IN A CREEPY COLD SWEAT.
I HAD SALOME FOLLOW YOU FROM UNDER THE SEA.
AND DON'T CHANGE THE SUBJECT ON ME, YOU WORTHLESS BEAST!
I'M SORRY...
HE'S SO MEEK!!
KLAK...
CAPTAIN!

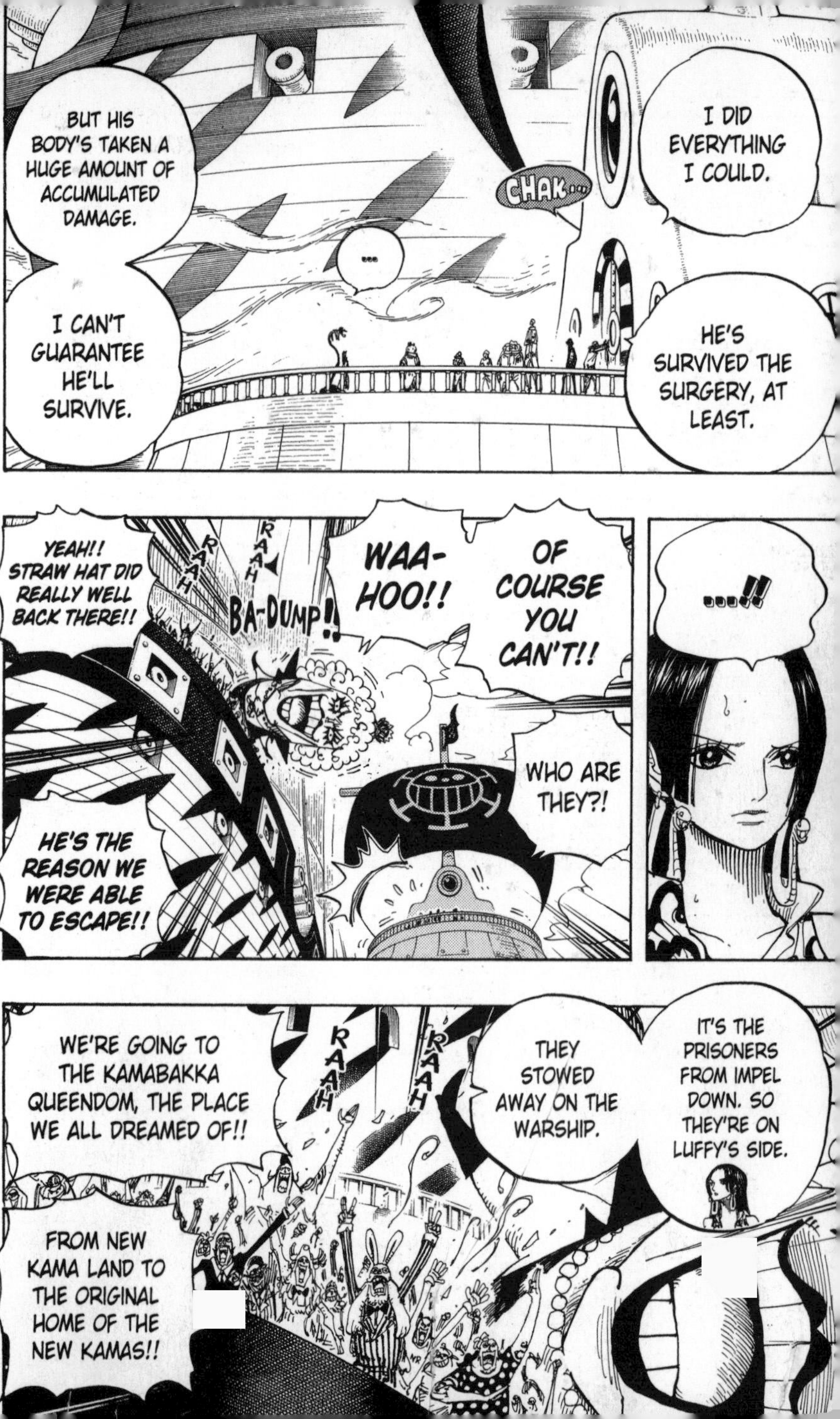
I DID EVERYTHING I COULD.
CHAK...
HE'S SURVIVED THE SURGERY, AT LEAST.
...
BUT HIS BODY'S TAKEN A HUGE AMOUNT OF ACCUMULATED DAMAGE.
I CAN'T GUARANTEE HE'LL SURVIVE.
...!!
OF COURSE YOU CAN'T!!
WAA-HOO!!
WHO ARE THEY?!
BA-DUMP!!
RAAH
RAAH
YEAH!! STRAW HAT DID REALLY WELL BACK THERE!!
HE'S THE REASON WE WERE ABLE TO ESCAPE!!
IT'S THE PRISONERS FROM IMPEL DOWN. SO THEY'RE ON LUFFY'S SIDE.
THEY STOWED AWAY ON THE WARSHIP.
RAAH
RAAH
WE'RE GOING TO THE KAMABAKKA QUEENDOM, THE PLACE WE ALL DREAMED OF!!
FROM NEW KAMA LAND TO THE ORIGINAL HOME OF THE NEW KAMAS!!

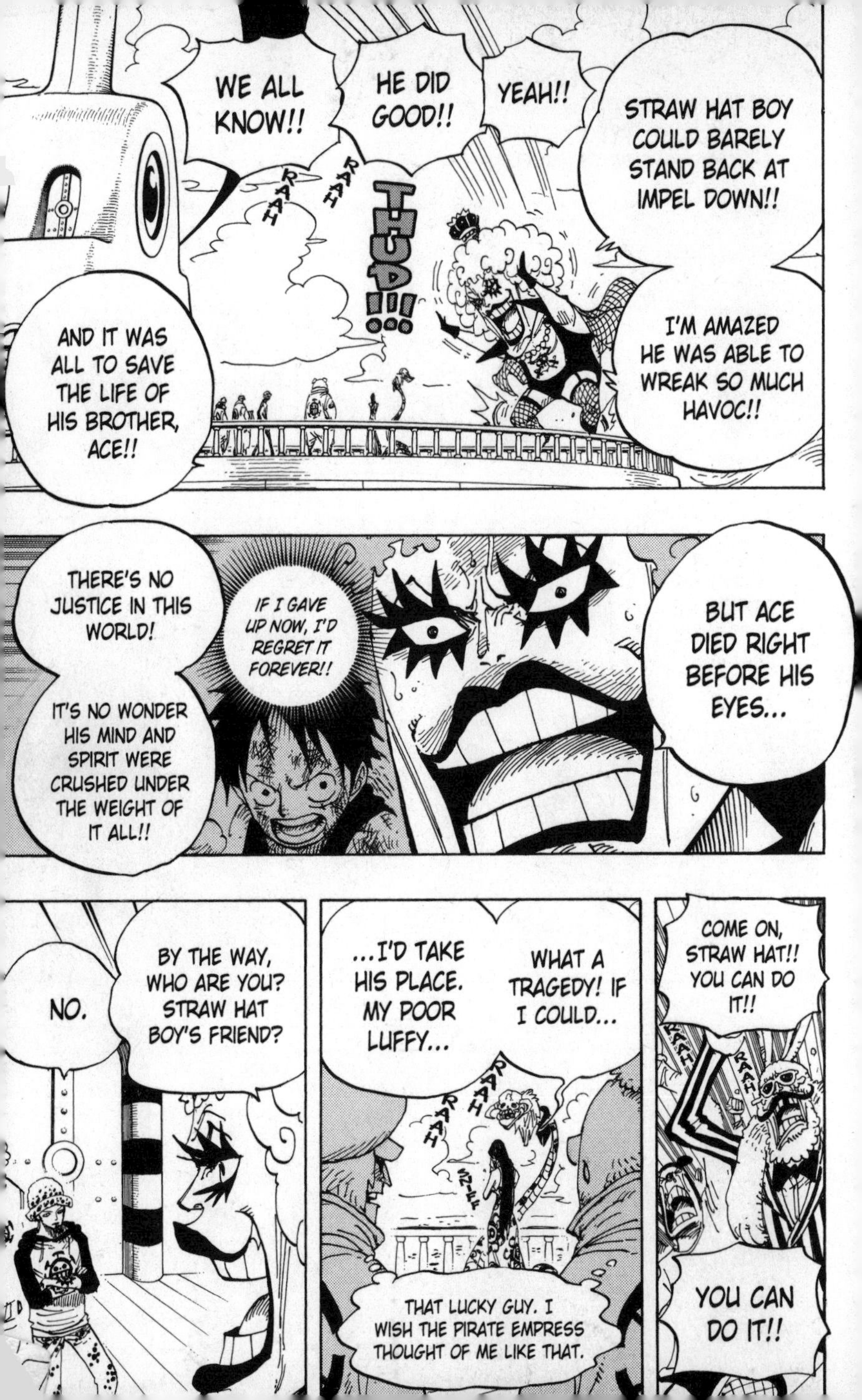
STRAW HAT BOY COULD BARELY STAND BACK AT IMPEL DOWN!!
I'M AMAZED HE WAS ABLE TO WREAK SO MUCH HAVOC!!
YEAH!!
HE DID GOOD!!
WE ALL KNOW!!
RAAH
RAAH
THUD!!!
AND IT WAS ALL TO SAVE THE LIFE OF HIS BROTHER, ACE!!
BUT ACE DIED RIGHT BEFORE HIS EYES...
IF I GAVE UP NOW, I'D REGRET IT FOREVER!!
THERE'S NO JUSTICE IN THIS WORLD!
IT'S NO WONDER HIS MIND AND SPIRIT WERE CRUSHED UNDER THE WEIGHT OF IT ALL!!
COME ON, STRAW HAT!! YOU CAN DO IT!!
RAAH
RAAH
YOU CAN DO IT!!
WHAT A TRAGEDY! IF I COULD...
...I'D TAKE HIS PLACE. MY POOR LUFFY...
RAAH
RAAH
SNIFF
THAT LUCKY GUY. I WISH THE PIRATE EMPRESS THOUGHT OF ME LIKE THAT.
BY THE WAY, WHO ARE YOU? STRAW HAT BOY'S FRIEND?
NO.

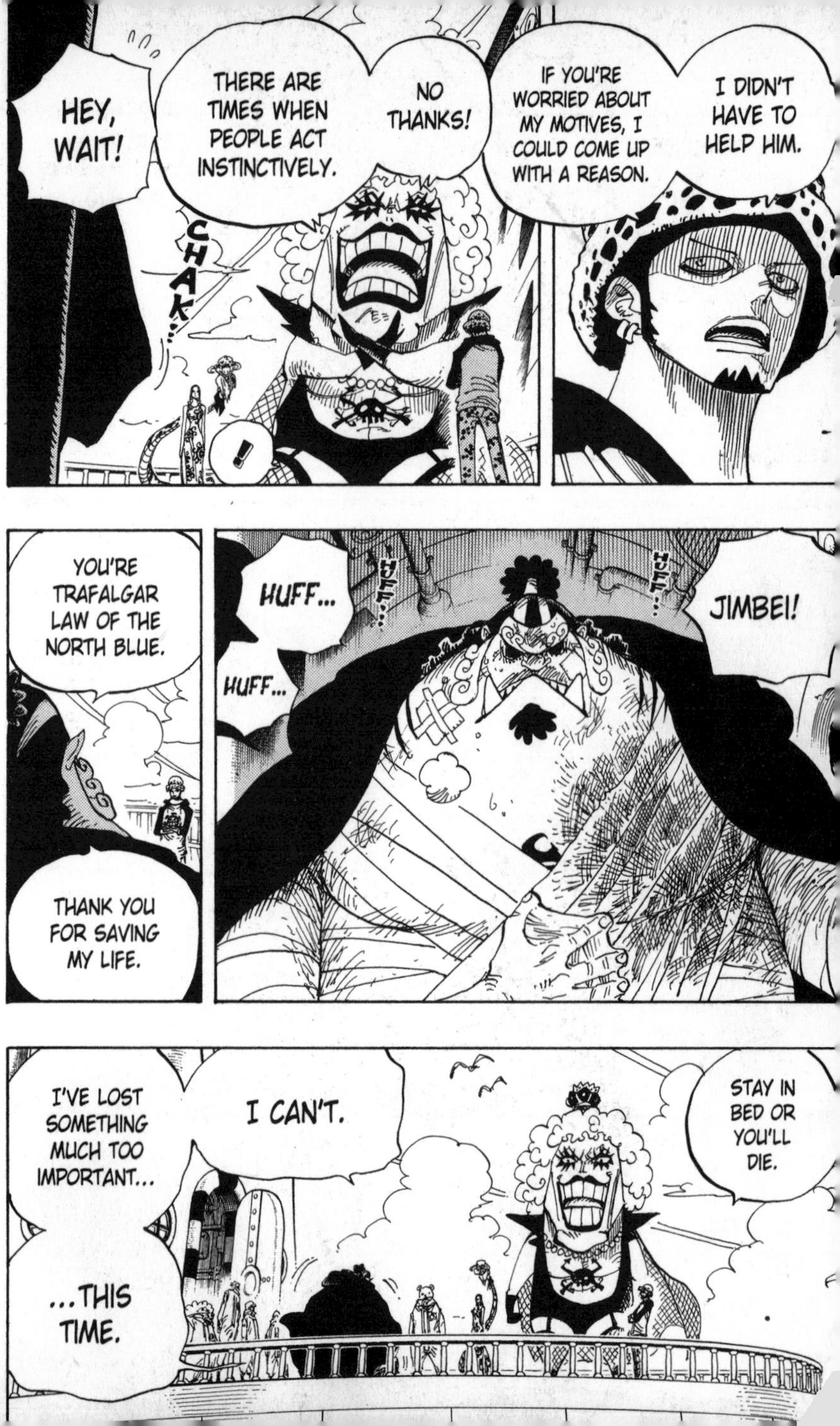
I DIDN'T HAVE TO HELP HIM.
IF YOU'RE WORRIED ABOUT MY MOTIVES, I COULD COME UP WITH A REASON.
NO THANKS!
THERE ARE TIMES WHEN PEOPLE ACT INSTINCTIVELY.
HEY, WAIT!
CHAK...
!
HUFF...
JIMBEI!
HUFF...
HUFF...
HUFF...
YOU'RE TRAFALGAR LAW OF THE NORTH BLUE.
THANK YOU FOR SAVING MY LIFE.
STAY IN BED OR YOU'LL DIE.
I CAN'T.
I'VE LOST SOMETHING MUCH TOO IMPORTANT...
...THIS TIME.

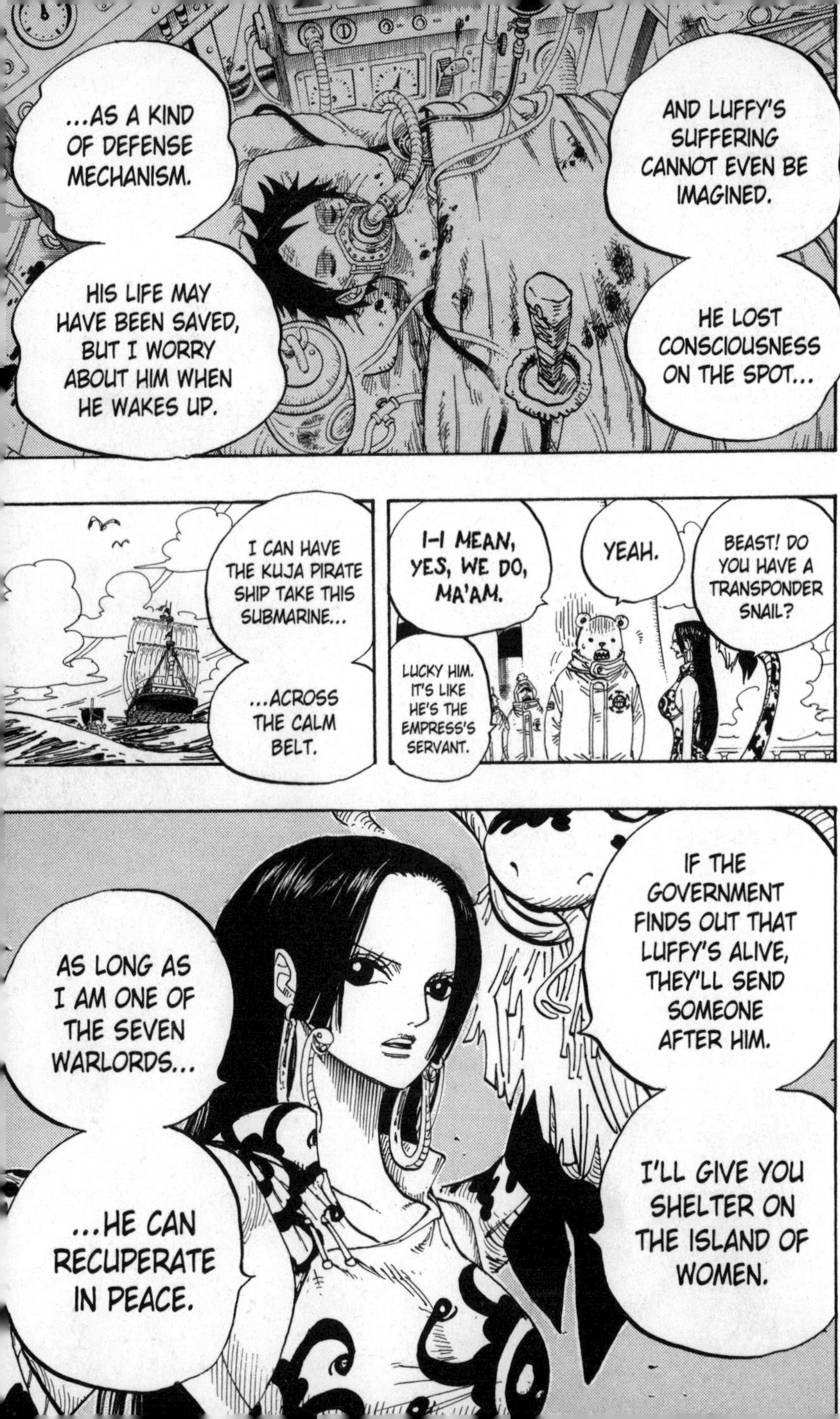
AND LUFFY'S SUFFERING CANNOT EVEN BE IMAGINED.
HE LOST CONSCIOUSNESS ON THE SPOT...
...AS A KIND OF DEFENSE MECHANISM.
HIS LIFE MAY HAVE BEEN SAVED, BUT I WORRY ABOUT HIM WHEN HE WAKES UP.
BEAST! DO YOU HAVE A TRANSPONDER SNAIL?
YEAH.
I-I MEAN, YES, WE DO, MA'AM.
LUCKY HIM. IT'S LIKE HE'S THE EMPRESS'S SERVANT.
I CAN HAVE THE KUJA PIRATE SHIP TAKE THIS SUBMARINE...
...ACROSS THE CALM BELT.
IF THE GOVERNMENT FINDS OUT THAT LUFFY'S ALIVE, THEY'LL SEND SOMEONE AFTER HIM.
I'LL GIVE YOU SHELTER ON THE ISLAND OF WOMEN.
AS LONG AS I AM ONE OF THE SEVEN WARLORDS...
...HE CAN RECUPERATE IN PEACE.

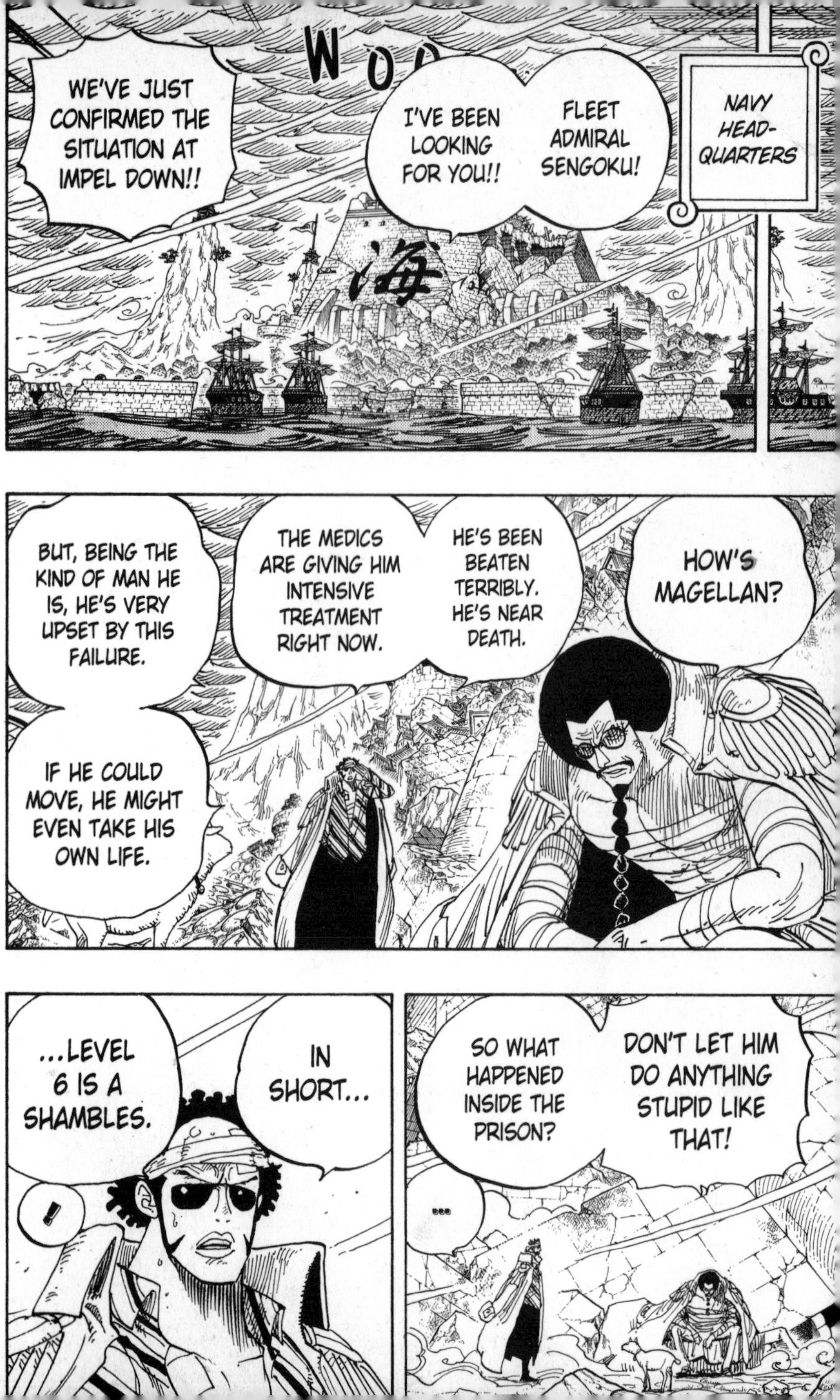
NAVY HEADQUARTERS
WO
FLEET ADMIRAL SENGOKU!
I'VE BEEN LOOKING FOR YOU!!
WE'VE JUST CONFIRMED THE SITUATION AT IMPEL DOWN!!
HOW'S MAGELLAN?
HE'S BEEN BEATEN TERRIBLY. HE'S NEAR DEATH.
THE MEDICS ARE GIVING HIM INTENSIVE TREATMENT RIGHT NOW.
BUT, BEING THE KIND OF MAN HE IS, HE'S VERY UPSET BY THIS FAILURE.
IF HE COULD MOVE, HE MIGHT EVEN TAKE HIS OWN LIFE.
DON'T LET HIM DO ANYTHING STUPID LIKE THAT!
SO WHAT HAPPENED INSIDE THE PRISON?
...
IN SHORT...
...LEVEL 6 IS A SHAMBLES.
!

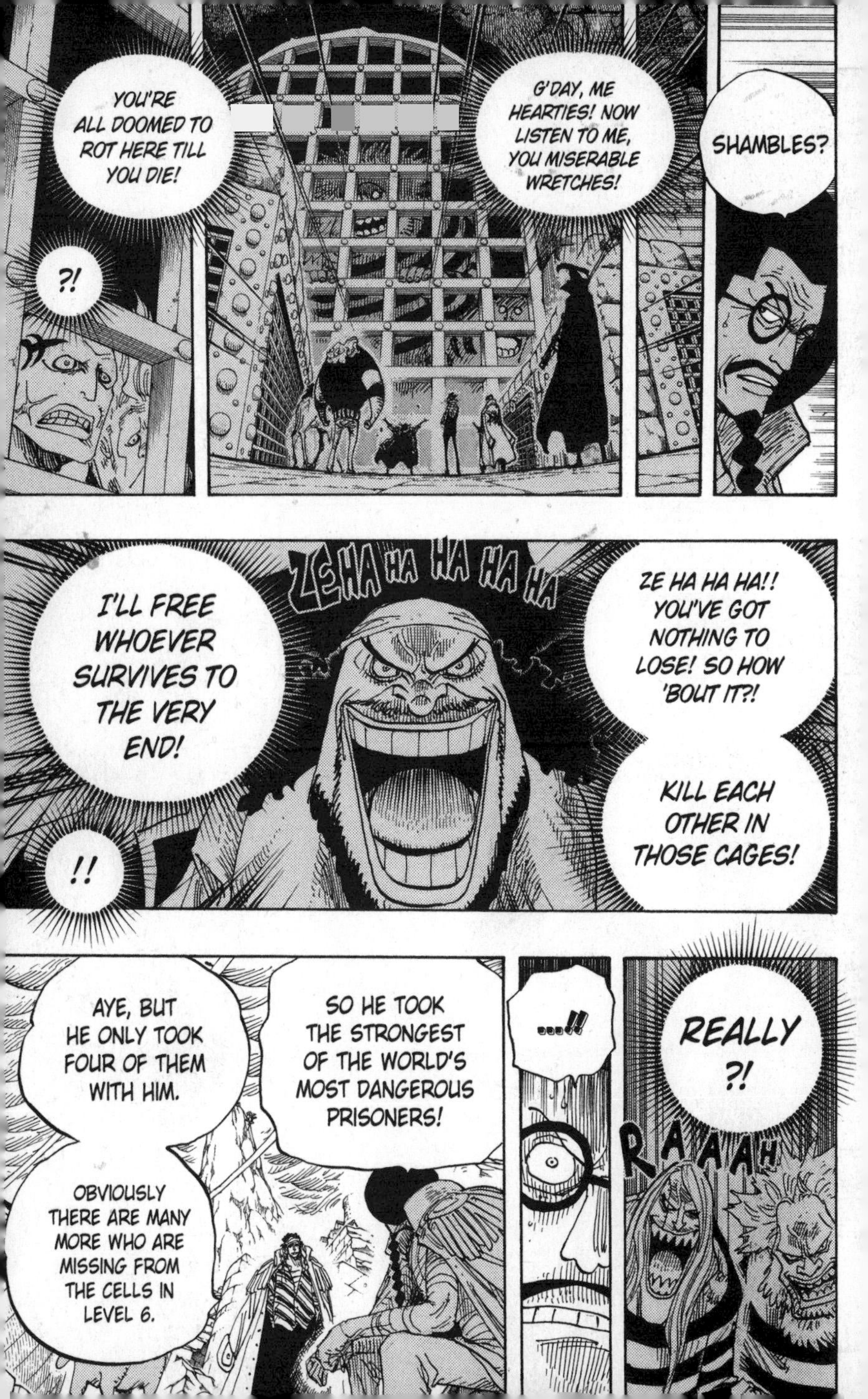
SHAMBLES?
G'DAY, ME HEARTIES! NOW LISTEN TO ME, YOU MISERABLE WRETCHES!
YOU'RE ALL DOOMED TO ROT HERE TILL YOU DIE!
?!
ZE HA HA HA!! YOU'VE GOT NOTHING TO LOSE! SO HOW 'BOUT IT?!
KILL EACH OTHER IN THOSE CAGES!
ZEHA HA HA HA HA
I'LL FREE WHOEVER SURVIVES TO THE VERY END!
!!
REALLY ?!
RAAAH
...!!
SO HE TOOK THE STRONGEST OF THE WORLD'S MOST DANGEROUS PRISONERS!
AYE, BUT HE ONLY TOOK FOUR OF THEM WITH HIM.
OBVIOUSLY THERE ARE MANY MORE WHO ARE MISSING FROM THE CELLS IN LEVEL 6.

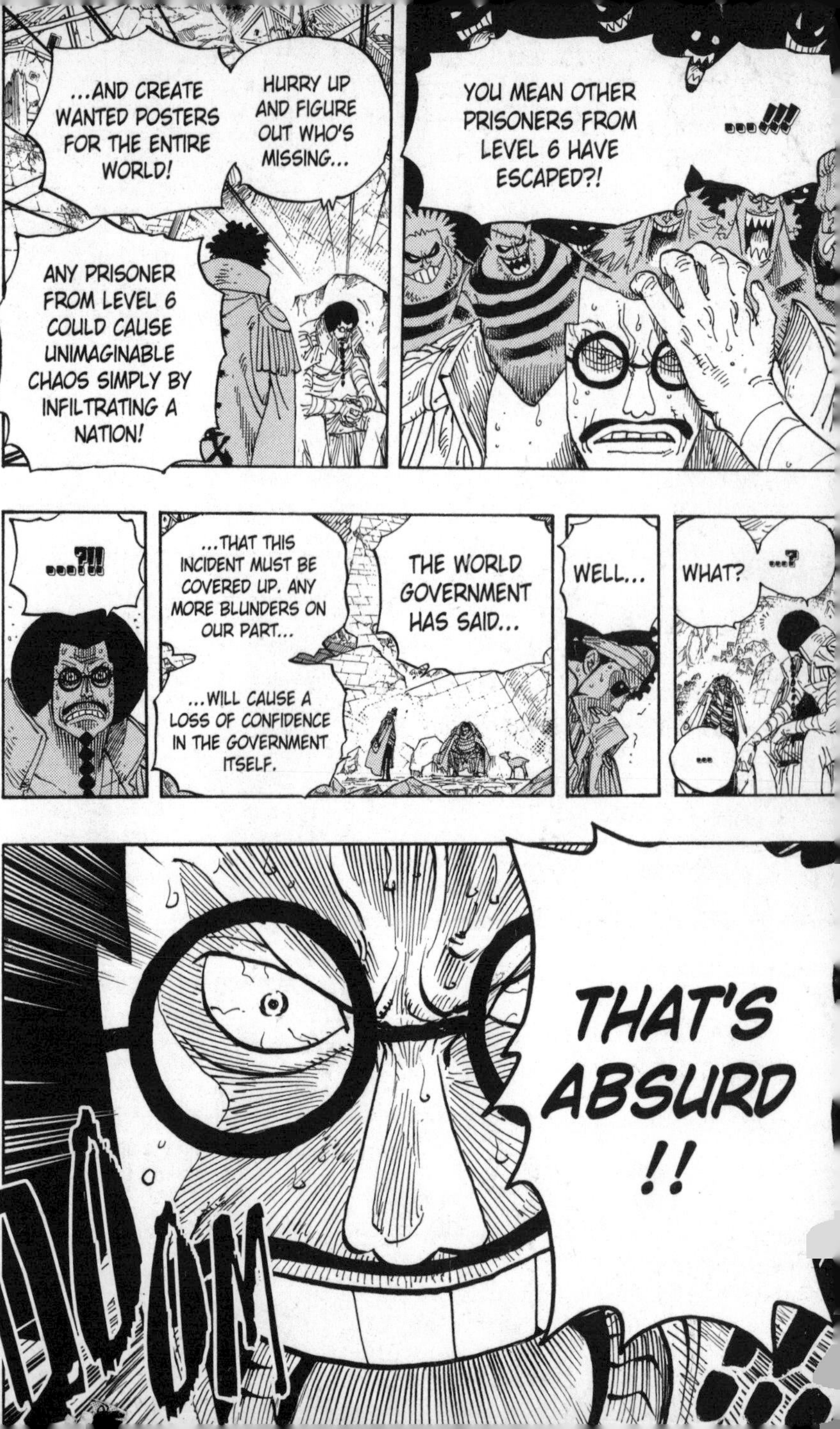
YOU MEAN OTHER PRISONERS FROM LEVEL 6 HAVE ESCAPED?!
...!!!
HURRY UP AND FIGURE OUT WHO'S MISSING...
...AND CREATE WANTED POSTERS FOR THE ENTIRE WORLD!
ANY PRISONER FROM LEVEL 6 COULD CAUSE UNIMAGINABLE CHAOS SIMPLY BY INFILTRATING A NATION!
...?
WHAT?
...
WELL...
THE WORLD GOVERNMENT HAS SAID...
...THAT THIS INCIDENT MUST BE COVERED UP. ANY MORE BLUNDERS ON OUR PART...
...WILL CAUSE A LOSS OF CONFIDENCE IN THE GOVERNMENT ITSELF.
...?!!
THAT'S ABSURD !!
DOOM

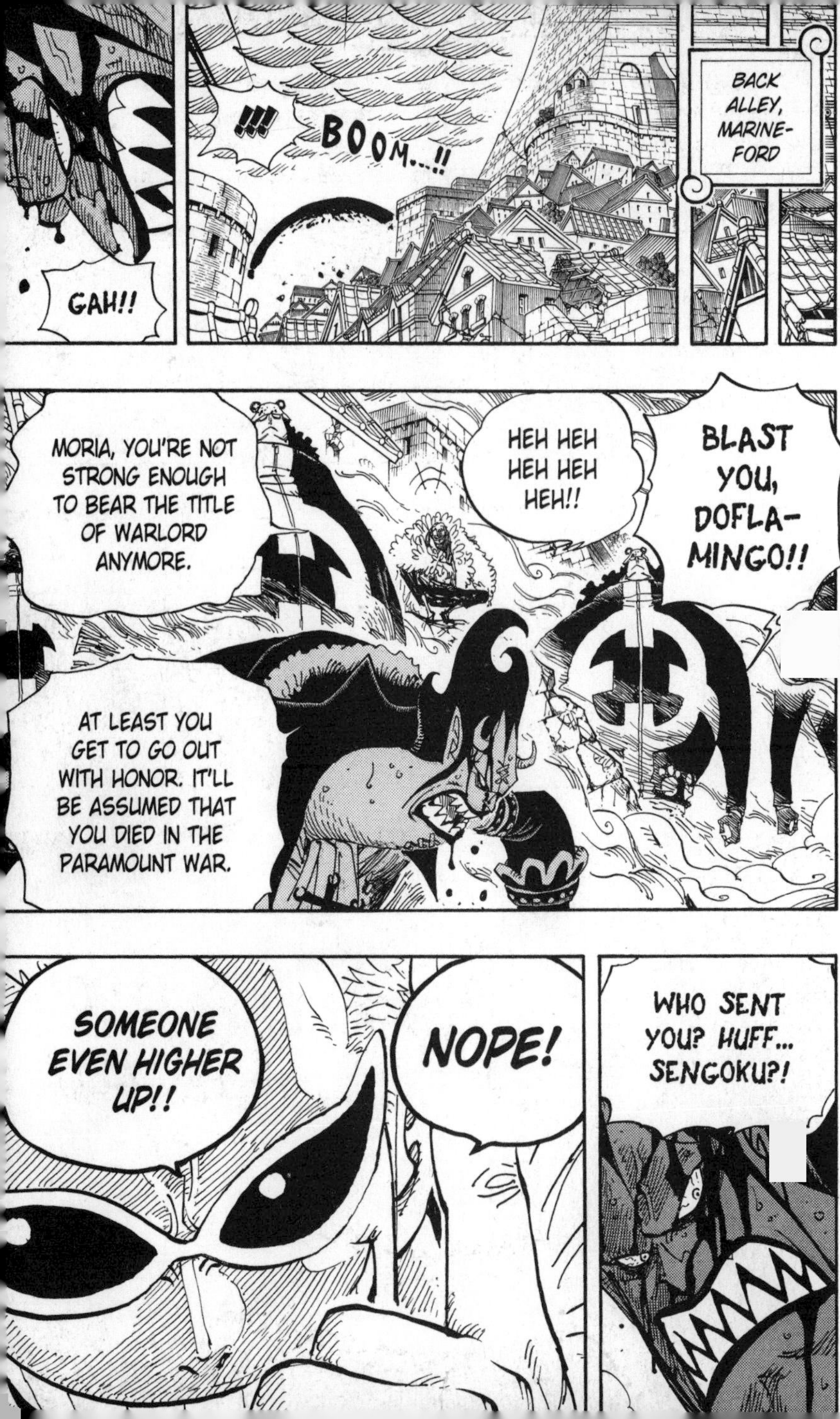
BACK ALLEY, MARINEFORD
BOOM...!!
!!!
GAH!!
BLAST YOU, DOFLAMINGO!!
HEH HEH HEH HEH HEH!!
MORIA, YOU'RE NOT STRONG ENOUGH TO BEAR THE TITLE OF WARLORD ANYMORE.
AT LEAST YOU GET TO GO OUT WITH HONOR. IT'LL BE ASSUMED THAT YOU DIED IN THE PARAMOUNT WAR.
WHO SENT YOU? HUFF... SENGOKU?!
NOPE!
SOMEONE EVEN HIGHER UP!!

LUFFY AND ACE

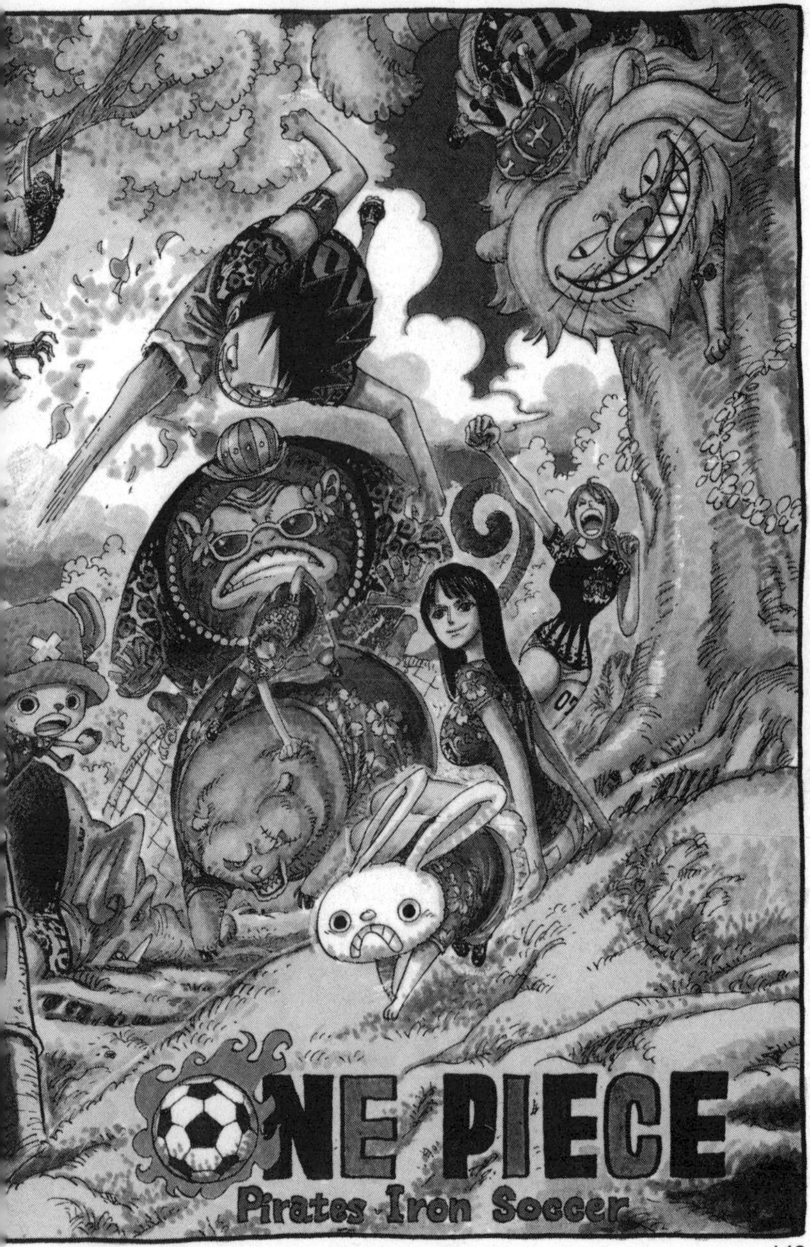
ONE PIECE
Pirates Iron Soccer

Chapter 582:

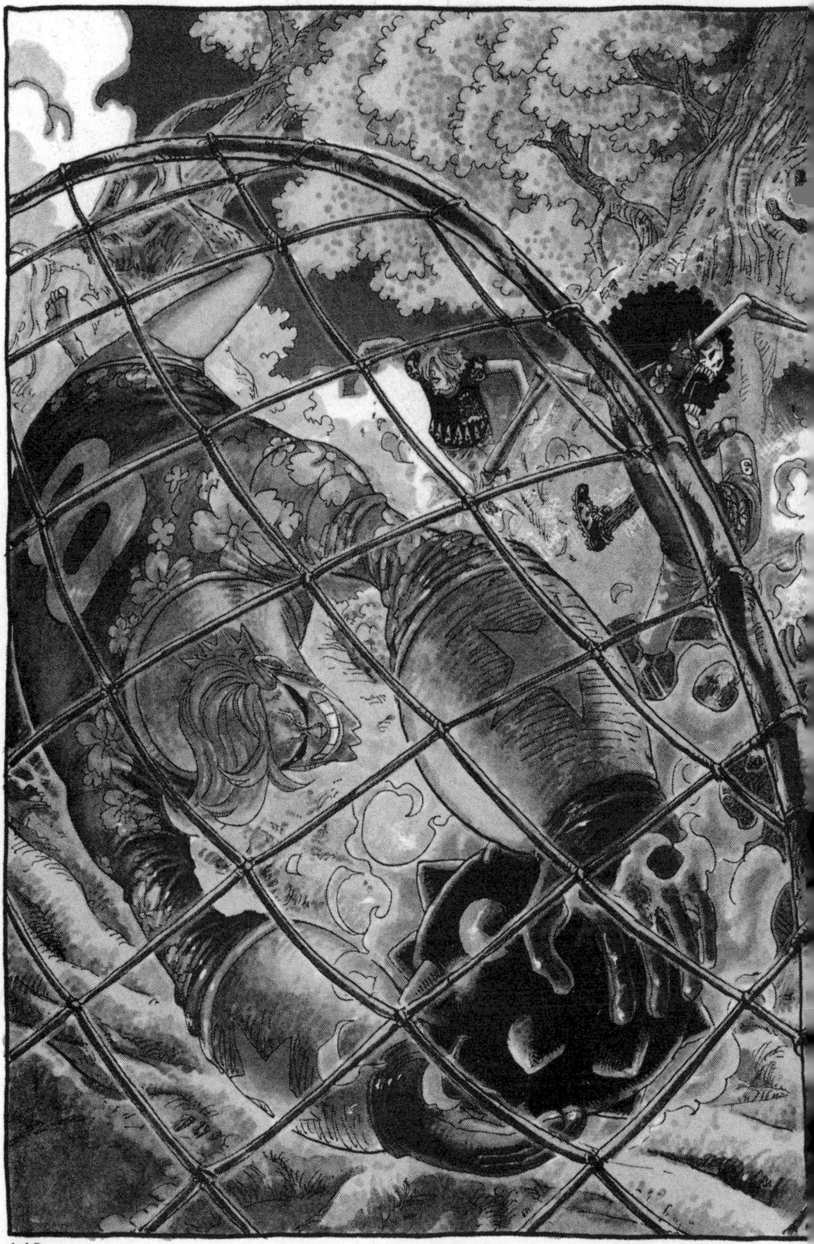

vol.59
ONE PIECE

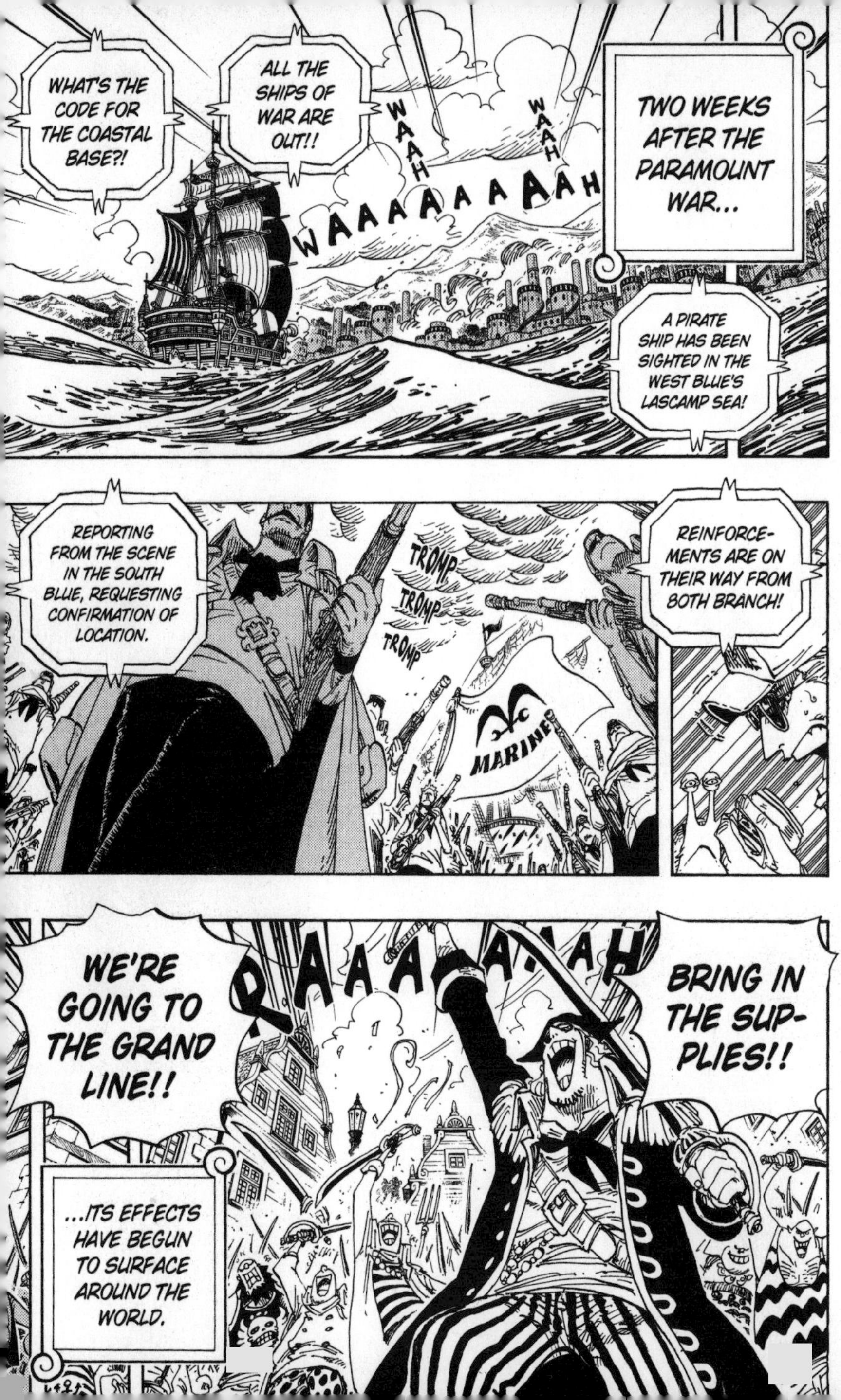
TWO WEEKS AFTER THE PARAMOUNT WAR...
A PIRATE SHIP HAS BEEN SIGHTED IN THE WEST BLUE'S LASCAMP SEA!
WAAH
WAAH
WAAAAAAAAAH
ALL THE SHIPS OF WAR ARE OUT!!
WHAT'S THE CODE FOR THE COASTAL BASE?!
REINFORCE-MENTS ARE ON THEIR WAY FROM 80TH BRANCH!
MARINE
TROMP
TROMP
TROMP
REPORTING FROM THE SCENE IN THE SOUTH BLUE, REQUESTING CONFIRMATION OF LOCATION.
BRING IN THE SUP-PLIES!!
RAAAAAAH
WE'RE GOING TO THE GRAND LINE!!
...ITS EFFECTS HAVE BEGUN TO SURFACE AROUND THE WORLD.

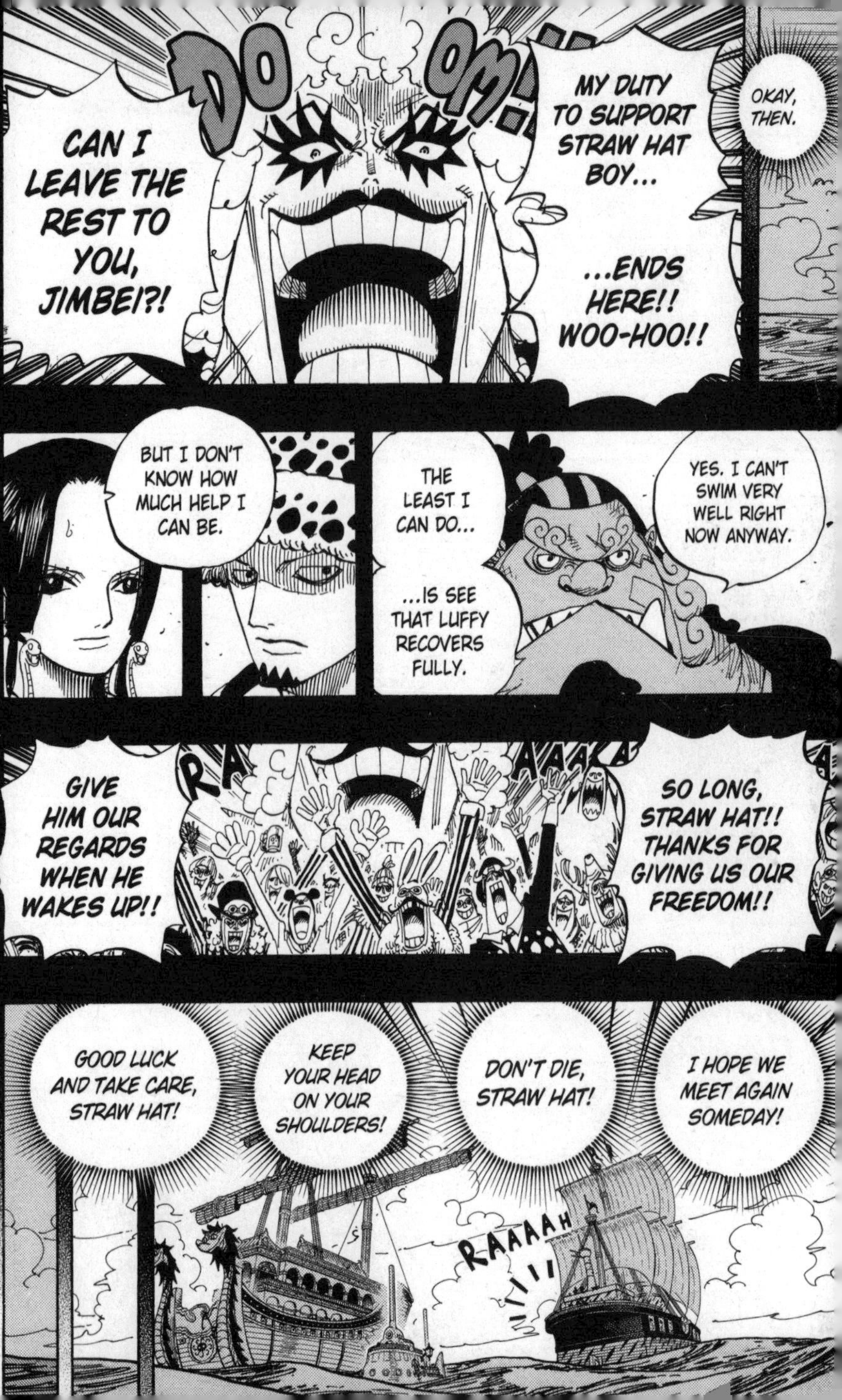
OKAY, THEN.
DOOM!
MY DUTY TO SUPPORT STRAW HAT BOY...
...ENDS HERE!! WOO-HOO!!
CAN I LEAVE THE REST TO YOU, JIMBEI?!
YES. I CAN'T SWIM VERY WELL RIGHT NOW ANYWAY.
THE LEAST I CAN DO...
...IS SEE THAT LUFFY RECOVERS FULLY.
BUT I DON'T KNOW HOW MUCH HELP I CAN BE.
SO LONG, STRAW HAT!! THANKS FOR GIVING US OUR FREEDOM!!
RAAAA
GIVE HIM OUR REGARDS WHEN HE WAKES UP!!
I HOPE WE MEET AGAIN SOMEDAY!
DON'T DIE, STRAW HAT!
KEEP YOUR HEAD ON YOUR SHOULDERS!
GOOD LUCK AND TAKE CARE, STRAW HAT!
RAAAAH

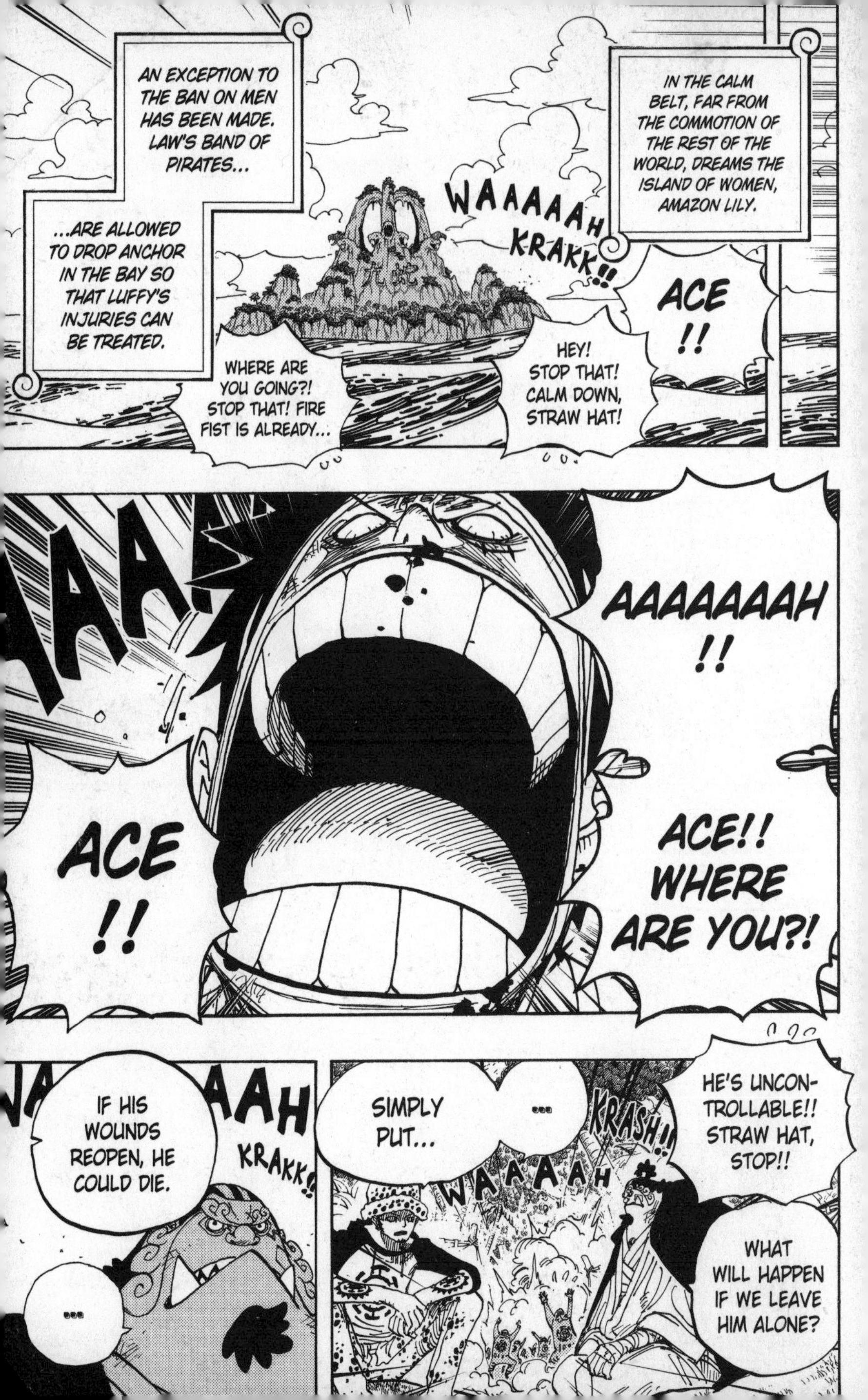
IN THE CALM BELT, FAR FROM THE COMMOTION OF THE REST OF THE WORLD, DREAMS THE ISLAND OF WOMEN, AMAZON LILY.
AN EXCEPTION TO THE BAN ON MEN HAS BEEN MADE. LAW'S BAND OF PIRATES...
...ARE ALLOWED TO DROP ANCHOR IN THE BAY SO THAT LUFFY'S INJURIES CAN BE TREATED.
WAAAAAH KRAKK!!
ACE !!
HEY! STOP THAT! CALM DOWN, STRAW HAT!
WHERE ARE YOU GOING?! STOP THAT! FIRE FIST IS ALREADY...
AAAAAAAH !!
ACE!! WHERE ARE YOU?!
ACE !!
HE'S UNCON-TROLLABLE!! STRAW HAT, STOP!!
KRASH!!
WAAAAAH
WHAT WILL HAPPEN IF WE LEAVE HIM ALONE?
...
SIMPLY PUT...
AAH KRAKK!!
IF HIS WOUNDS REOPEN, HE COULD DIE.
...

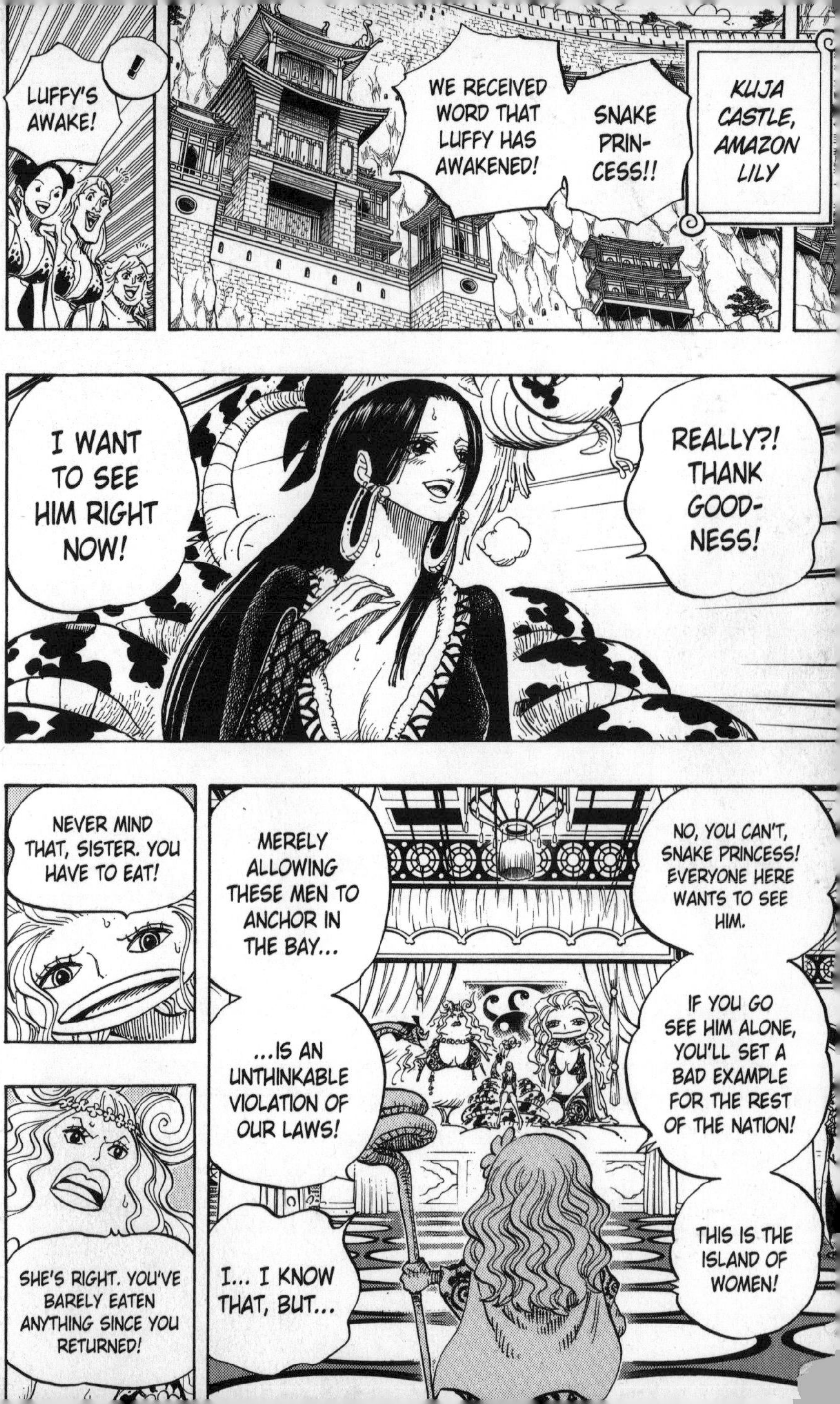
KUJA CASTLE, AMAZON LILY
SNAKE PRIN- CESS!!
WE RECEIVED WORD THAT LUFFY HAS AWAKENED!
!
LUFFY'S AWAKE!
REALLY?! THANK GOOD- NESS!
I WANT TO SEE HIM RIGHT NOW!
NO, YOU CAN'T, SNAKE PRINCESS! EVERYONE HERE WANTS TO SEE HIM.
IF YOU GO SEE HIM ALONE, YOU'LL SET A BAD EXAMPLE FOR THE REST OF THE NATION!
THIS IS THE ISLAND OF WOMEN!
MERELY ALLOWING THESE MEN TO ANCHOR IN THE BAY...
...IS AN UNTHINKABLE VIOLATION OF OUR LAWS!
I... I KNOW THAT, BUT...
NEVER MIND THAT, SISTER. YOU HAVE TO EAT!
SHE'S RIGHT. YOU'VE BARELY EATEN ANYTHING SINCE YOU RETURNED!

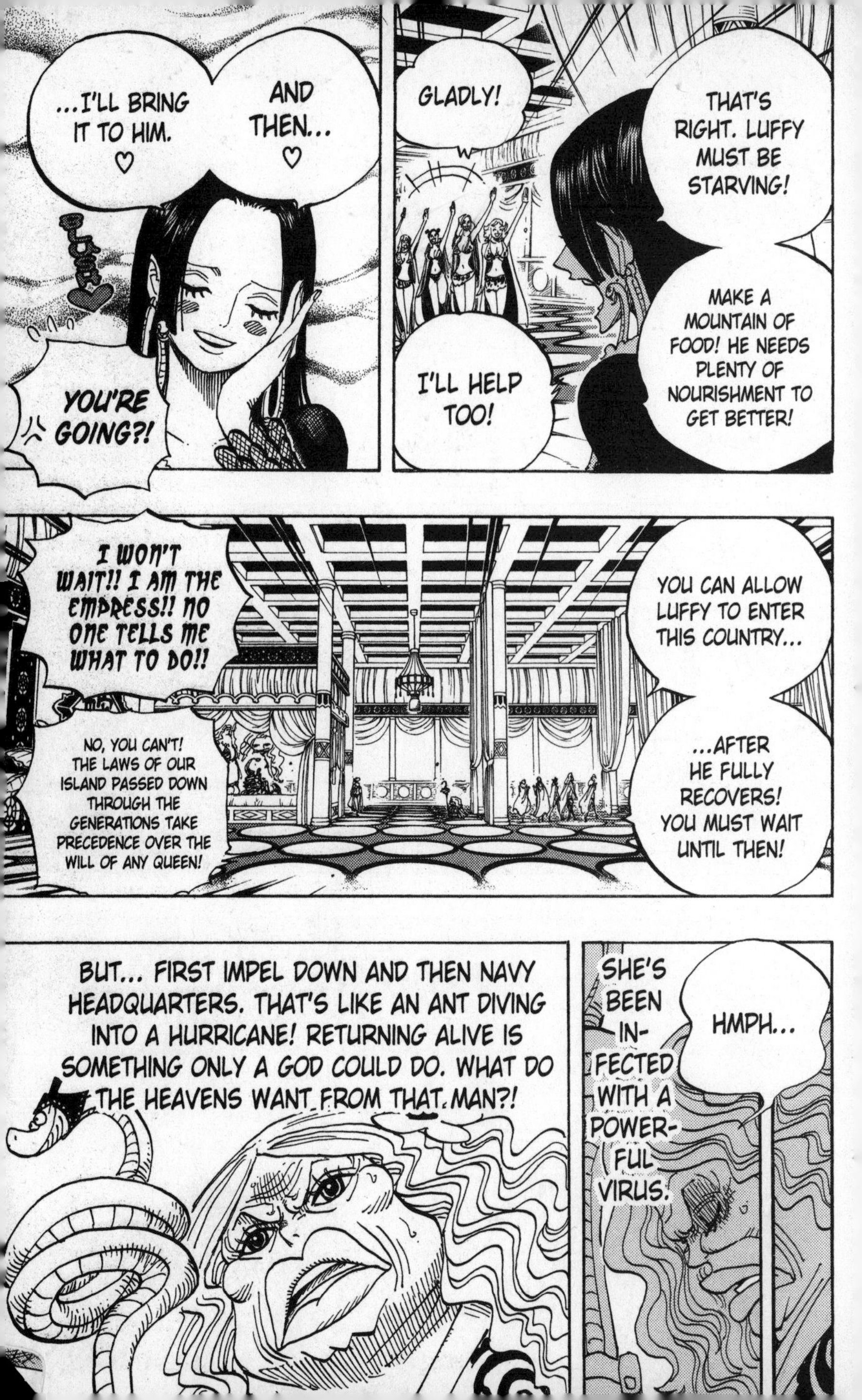
THAT'S RIGHT. LUFFY MUST BE STARVING!
MAKE A MOUNTAIN OF FOOD! HE NEEDS PLENTY OF NOURISHMENT TO GET BETTER!
GLADLY!
I'LL HELP TOO!
AND THEN... ♡
...I'LL BRING IT TO HIM. ♡
YOU'RE GOING?!
YOU CAN ALLOW LUFFY TO ENTER THIS COUNTRY...
...AFTER HE FULLY RECOVERS! YOU MUST WAIT UNTIL THEN!
I WON'T WAIT!! I AM THE EMPRESS!! NO ONE TELLS ME WHAT TO DO!!
NO, YOU CAN'T! THE LAWS OF OUR ISLAND PASSED DOWN THROUGH THE GENERATIONS TAKE PRECEDENCE OVER THE WILL OF ANY QUEEN!
HMPH...
SHE'S BEEN IN-FECTED WITH A POWER-FUL VIRUS.
BUT... FIRST IMPEL DOWN AND THEN NAVY HEADQUARTERS. THAT'S LIKE AN ANT DIVING INTO A HURRICANE! RETURNING ALIVE IS SOMETHING ONLY A GOD COULD DO. WHAT DO THE HEAVENS WANT FROM THAT MAN?!

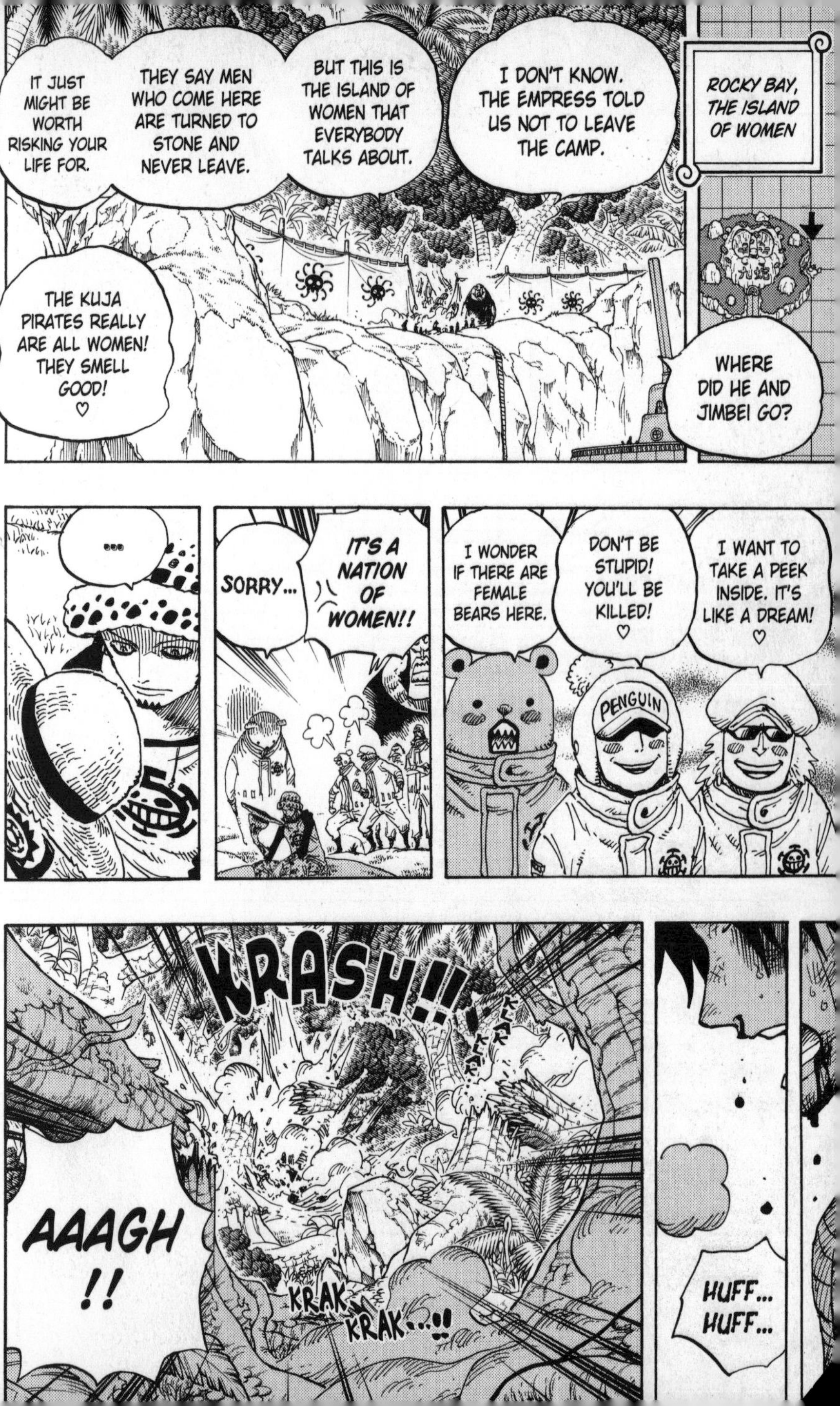
ROCKY BAY, THE ISLAND OF WOMEN
WHERE DID HE AND JIMBEI GO?
I DON'T KNOW. THE EMPRESS TOLD US NOT TO LEAVE THE CAMP.
BUT THIS IS THE ISLAND OF WOMEN THAT EVERYBODY TALKS ABOUT.
THEY SAY MEN WHO COME HERE ARE TURNED TO STONE AND NEVER LEAVE.
IT JUST MIGHT BE WORTH RISKING YOUR LIFE FOR.
THE KUJA PIRATES REALLY ARE ALL WOMEN! THEY SMELL GOOD! ♡
I WANT TO TAKE A PEEK INSIDE. IT'S LIKE A DREAM! ♡
DON'T BE STUPID! YOU'LL BE KILLED! ♡
I WONDER IF THERE ARE FEMALE BEARS HERE.
PENGUIN
IT'S A NATION OF WOMEN!!
SORRY...
...
HUFF... HUFF...
KRASH!!
KLAK KLAK
KRAK KRAK...!!
AAAGH !!

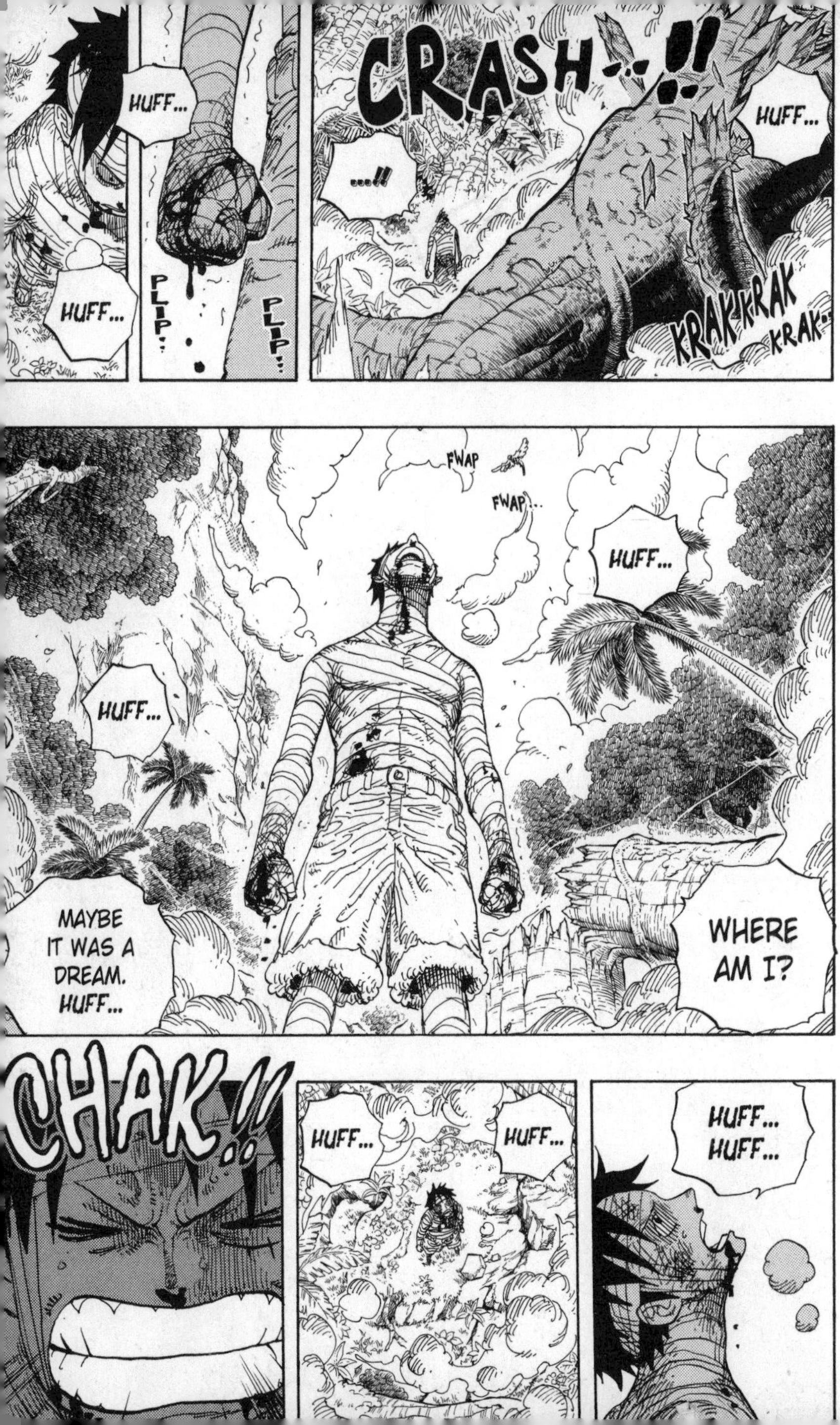
HUFF...
CRASH...!!
...!!
KRAK KRAK KRAK...
PLIP...
PLIP...
HUFF...
HUFF...
FWAP
FWAP...
HUFF...
HUFF...
WHERE AM I?
MAYBE IT WAS A DREAM. HUFF...
HUFF... HUFF...
HUFF...
HUFF...
CHAK!!

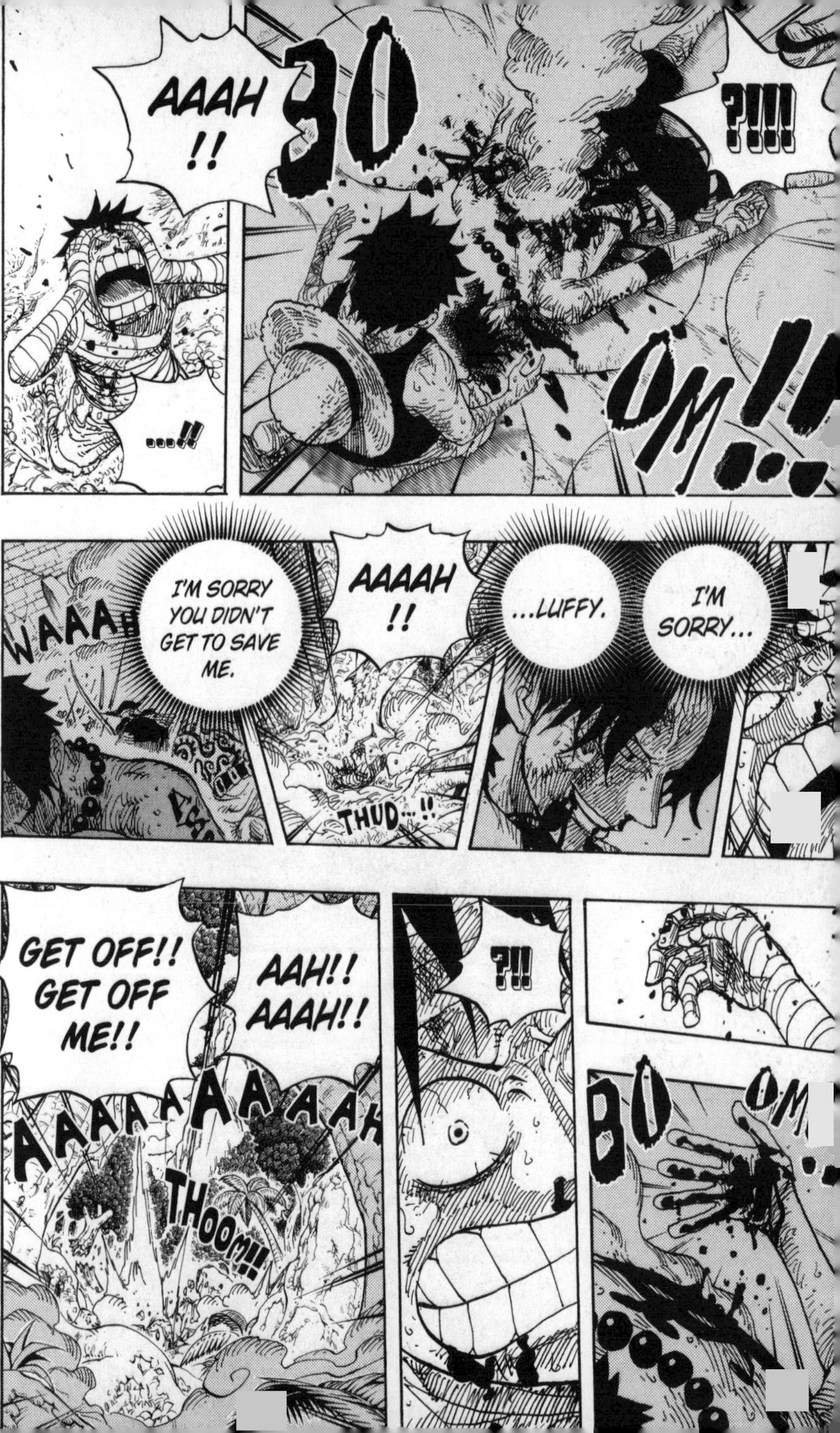
?!!!
BO
OM!!...
AAAH !!
...!!
I'M SORRY...
...LUFFY.
AAAAH !!
THUD...!!
I'M SORRY YOU DIDN'T GET TO SAVE ME.
WAAAH
BO
OM...
?!!
GET OFF!! GET OFF ME!!
AAH!! AAAH!!
AAAAAAAAAAAH
THOOM!!

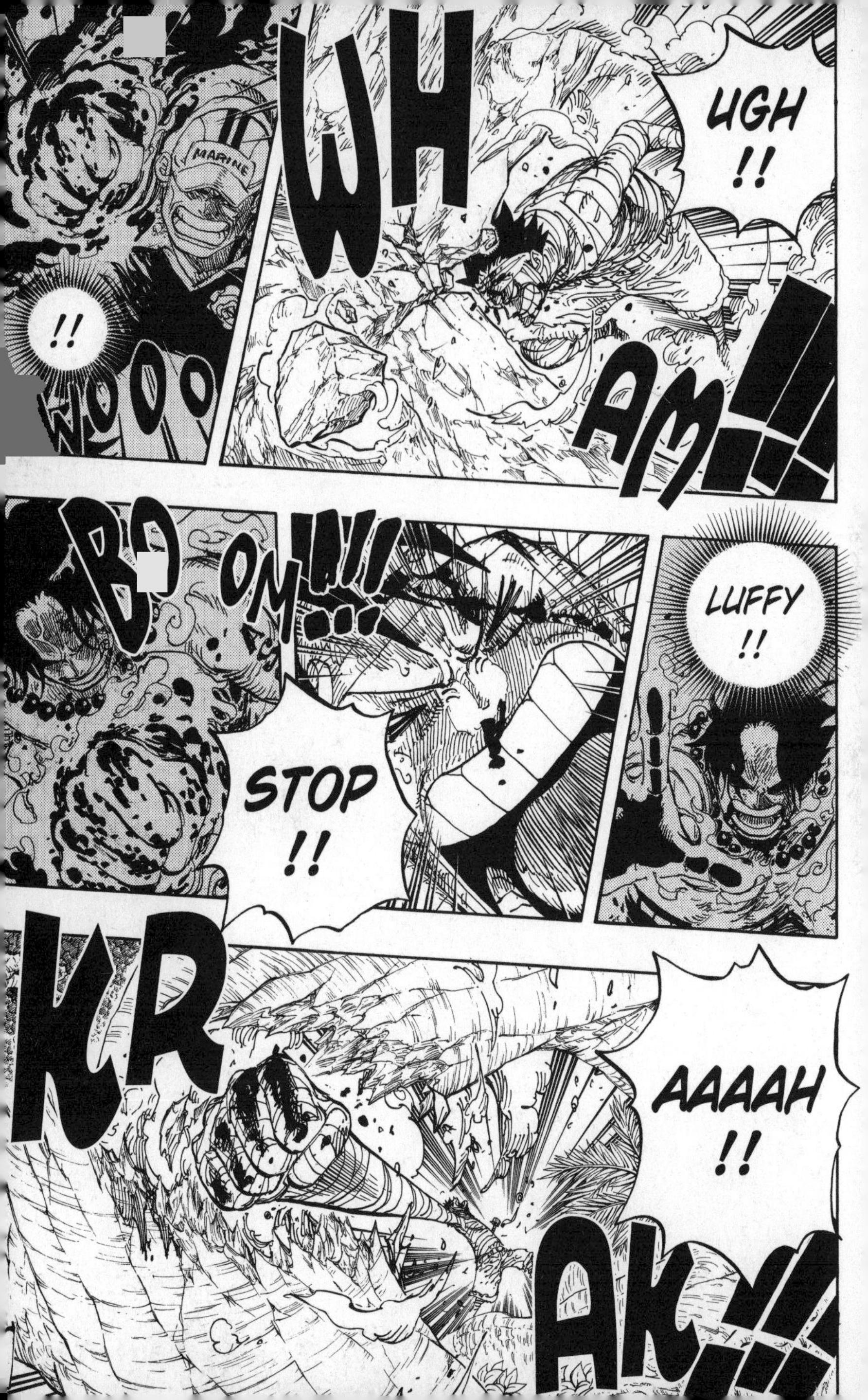
UGH !!
WH
AM!!!
!!
WOOO
LUFFY !!
STOP !!
BO
OM!!!!
AAAAH !!
KR
AK!!!

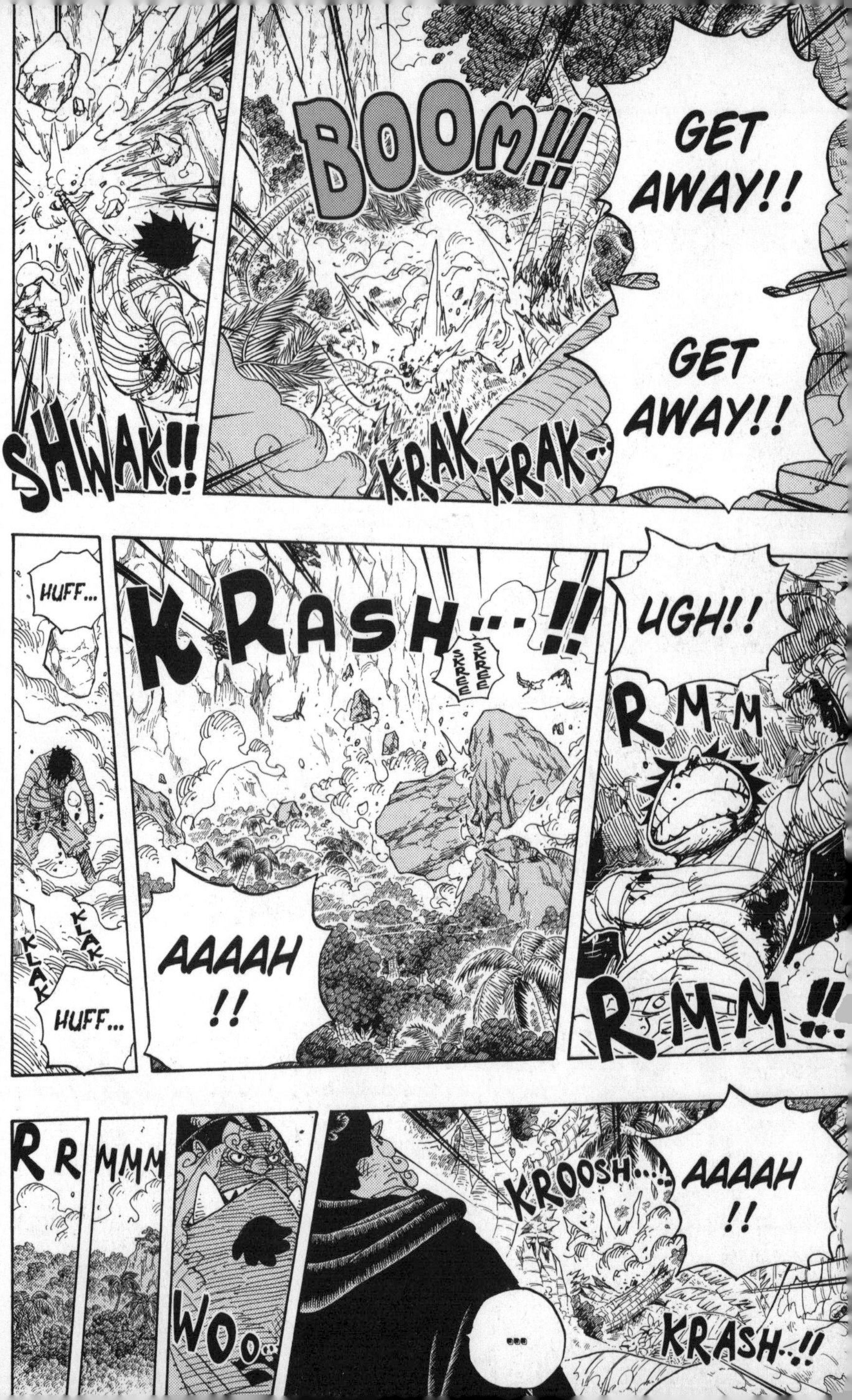
GET AWAY!!
GET AWAY!!
BOOM!!
KRAK KRAK...
SHWAK!!
UGH!!
RMM
RMM!!
KRASH...!!
SKREE SKREE
AAAAH!!
HUFF...
KLAK KLAK
HUFF...
AAAAH!!
KROOSH...
KRASH..!!
...
WOO...
RR MMM

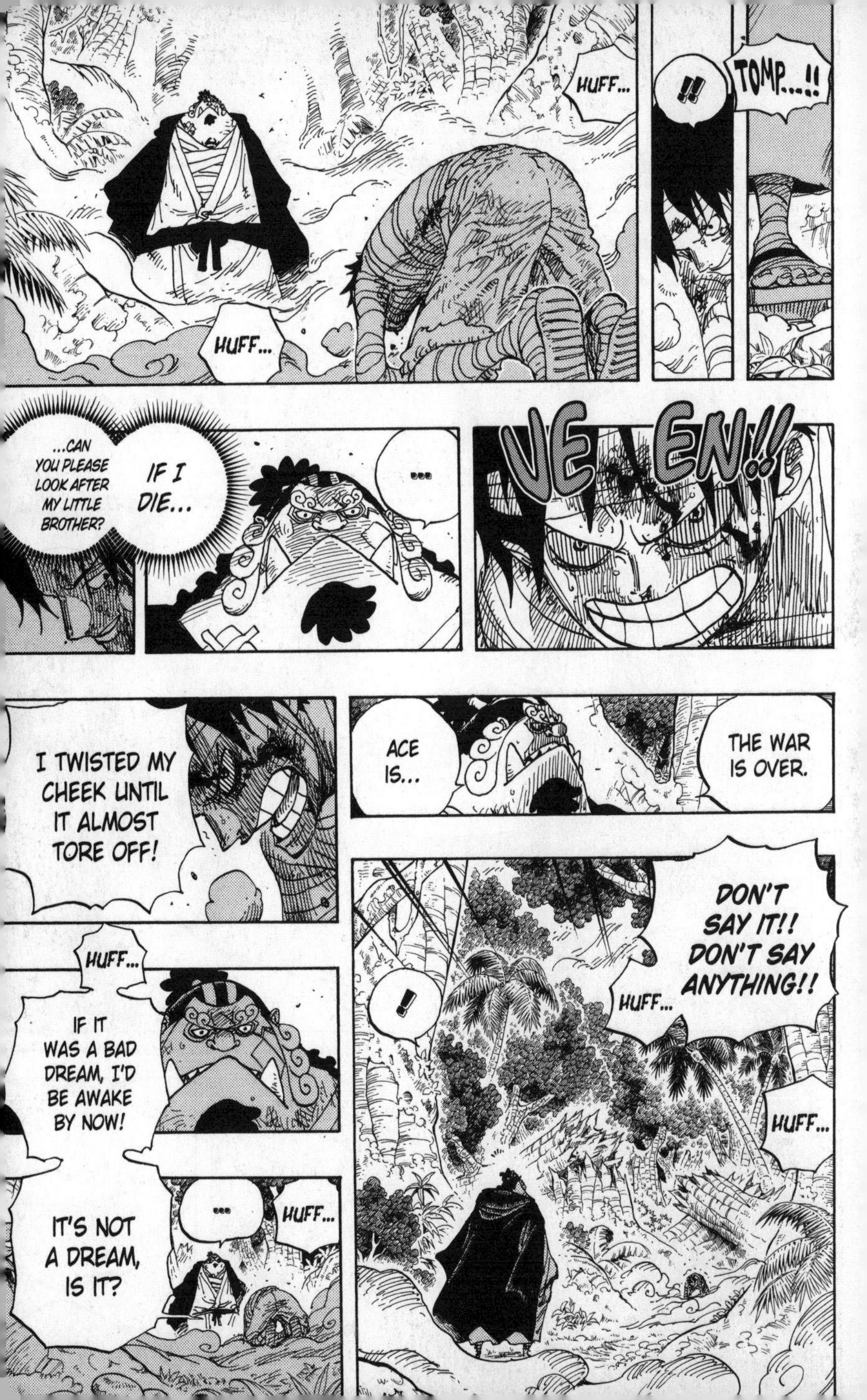
TOMP...!!
!!
HUFF...
HUFF...
VE EN!!
...
IF I DIE...
...CAN YOU PLEASE LOOK AFTER MY LITTLE BROTHER?
THE WAR IS OVER.
ACE IS...
DON'T SAY IT!! DON'T SAY ANYTHING!!
HUFF...
!
HUFF...
I TWISTED MY CHEEK UNTIL IT ALMOST TORE OFF!
HUFF...
IF IT WAS A BAD DREAM, I'D BE AWAKE BY NOW!
HUFF...
...
IT'S NOT A DREAM, IS IT?

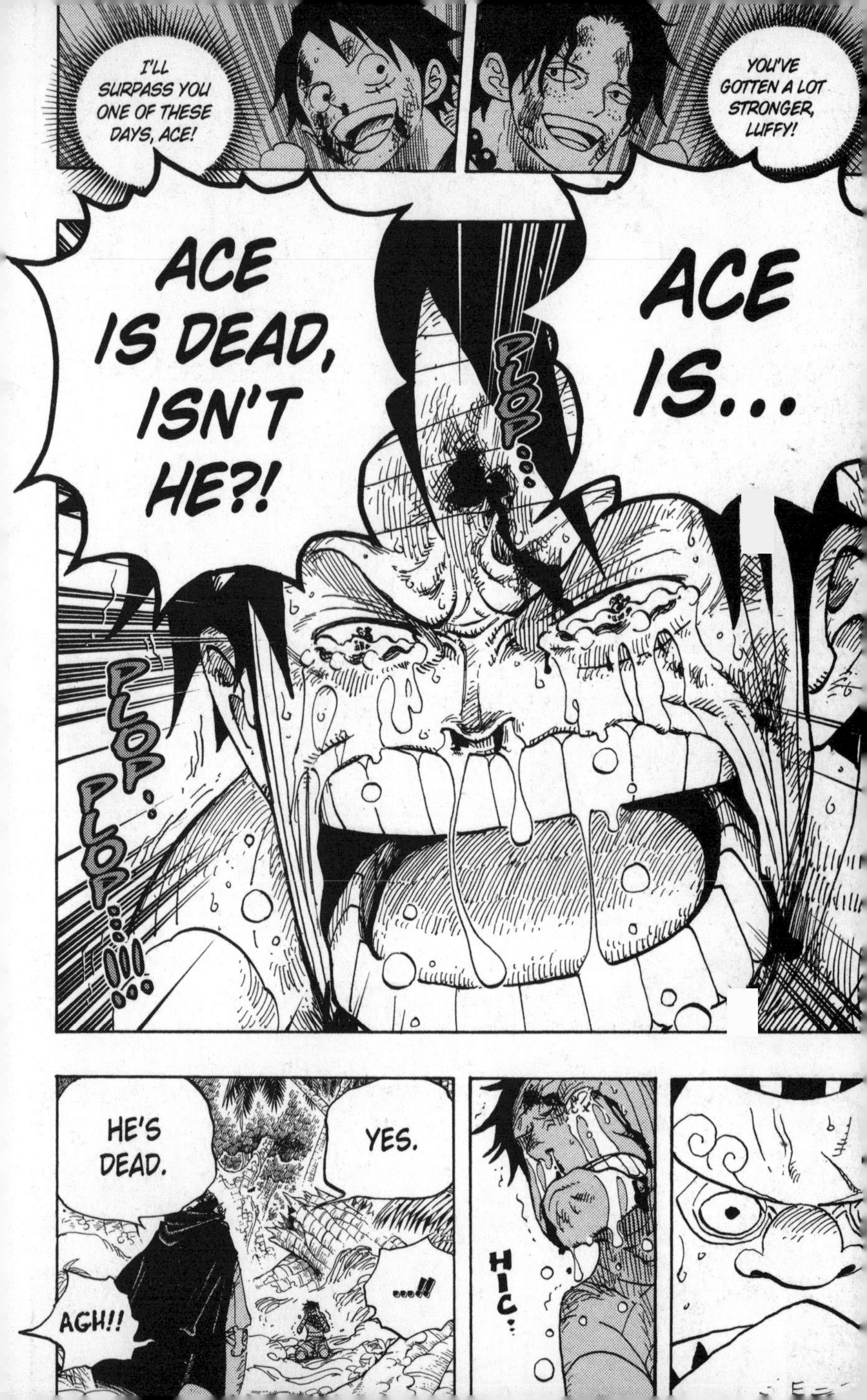
YOU'VE GOTTEN A LOT STRONGER, LUFFY!
I'LL SURPASS YOU ONE OF THESE DAYS, ACE!
ACE IS...
PLOP...
ACE IS DEAD, ISN'T HE?!
PLOP! PLOP...!!!
HIC...
YES.
HE'S DEAD.
...!!
AGH!!

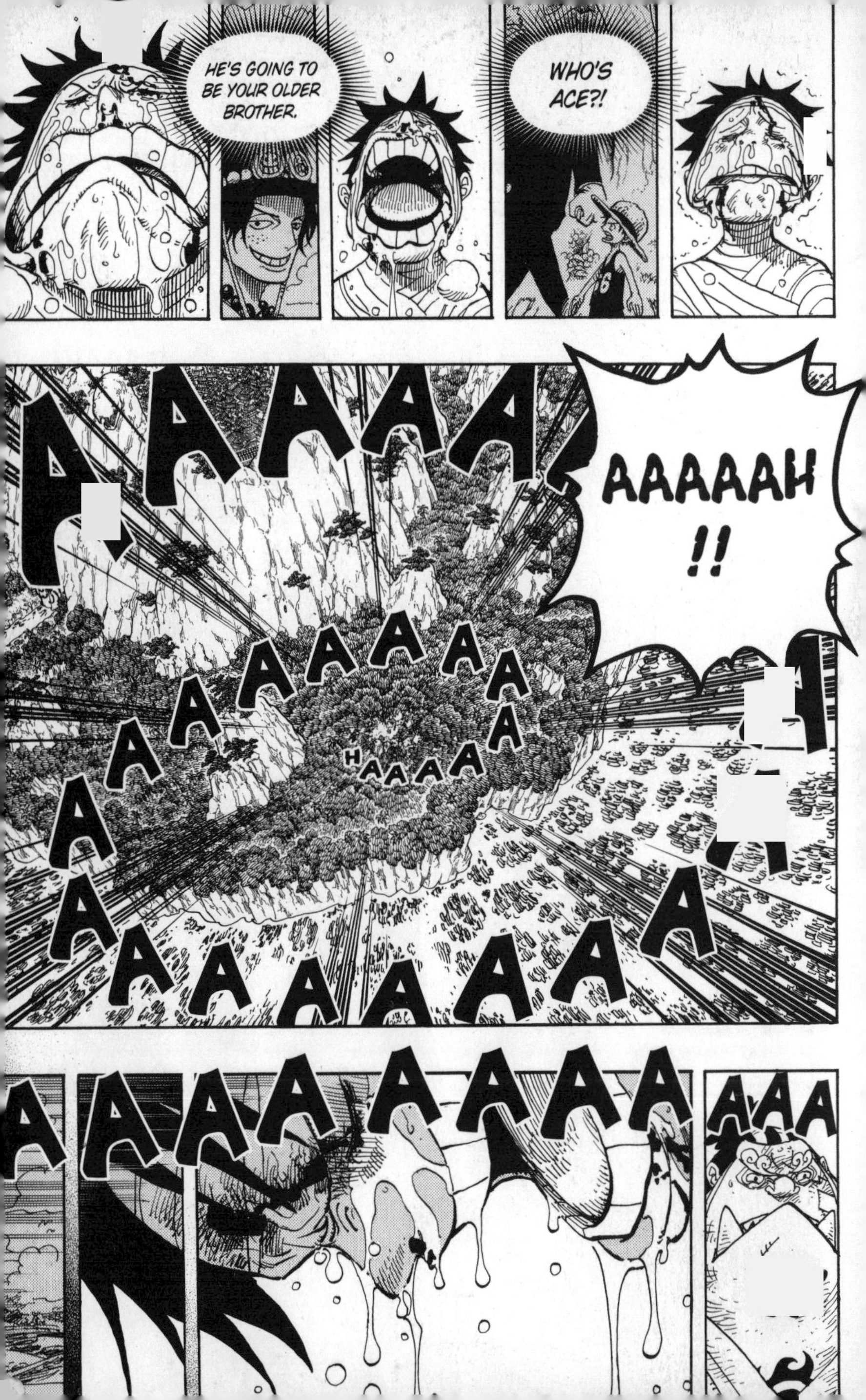

WHO'S ACE?!
HE'S GOING TO BE YOUR OLDER BROTHER.
AAAAAH !!
HAAAA

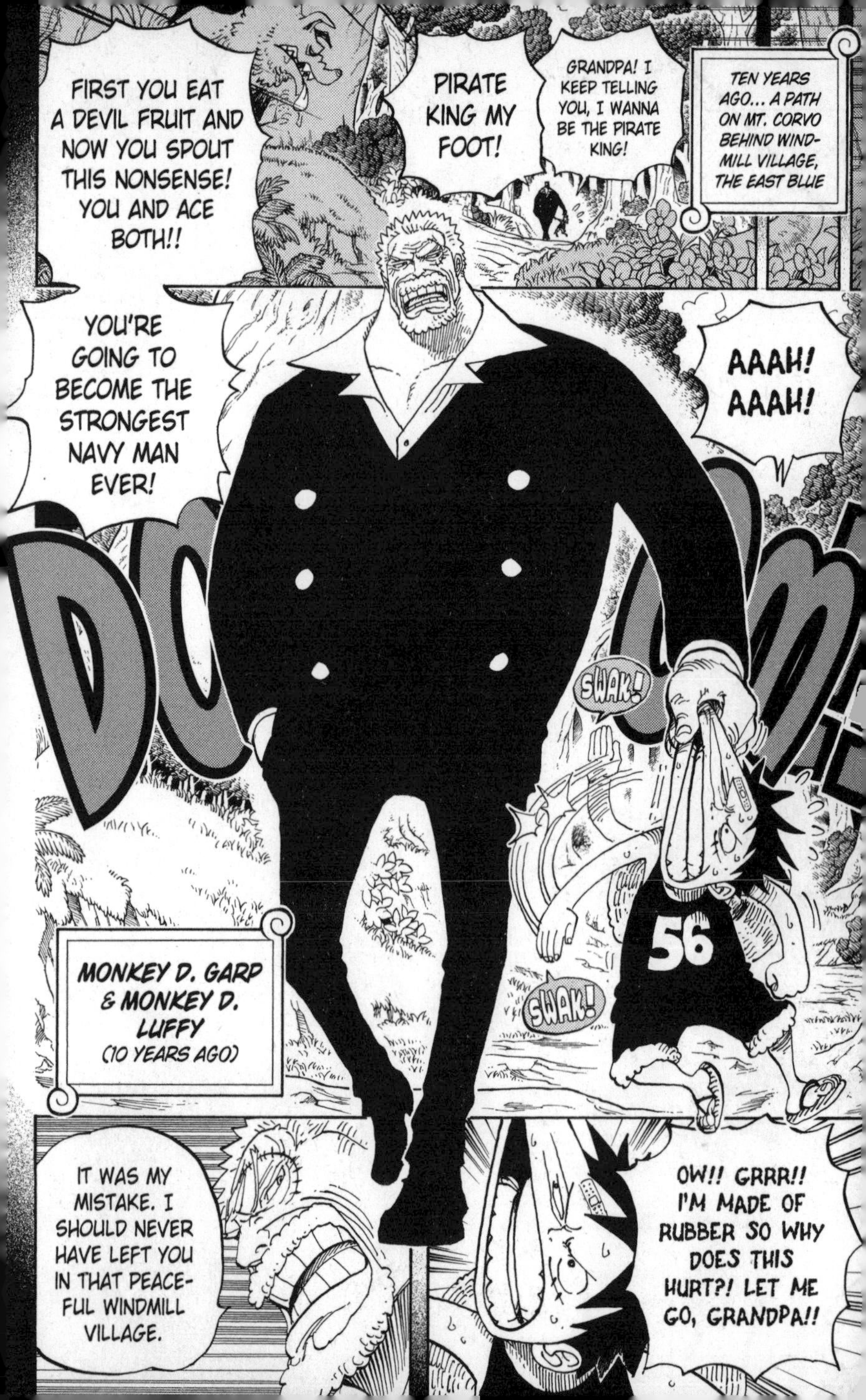
TEN YEARS AGO... A PATH ON MT. CORVO BEHIND WINDMILL VILLAGE, THE EAST BLUE
GRANDPA! I KEEP TELLING YOU, I WANNA BE THE PIRATE KING!
PIRATE KING MY FOOT!
FIRST YOU EAT A DEVIL FRUIT AND NOW YOU SPOUT THIS NONSENSE! YOU AND ACE BOTH!!
AAAH! AAAH!
YOU'RE GOING TO BECOME THE STRONGEST NAVY MAN EVER!
SWAK!
SWAK!
MONKEY D. GARP & MONKEY D. LUFFY
(10 YEARS AGO)
OW!! GRRR!! I'M MADE OF RUBBER SO WHY DOES THIS HURT?! LET ME GO, GRANDPA!!
IT WAS MY MISTAKE. I SHOULD NEVER HAVE LEFT YOU IN THAT PEACEFUL WINDMILL VILLAGE.

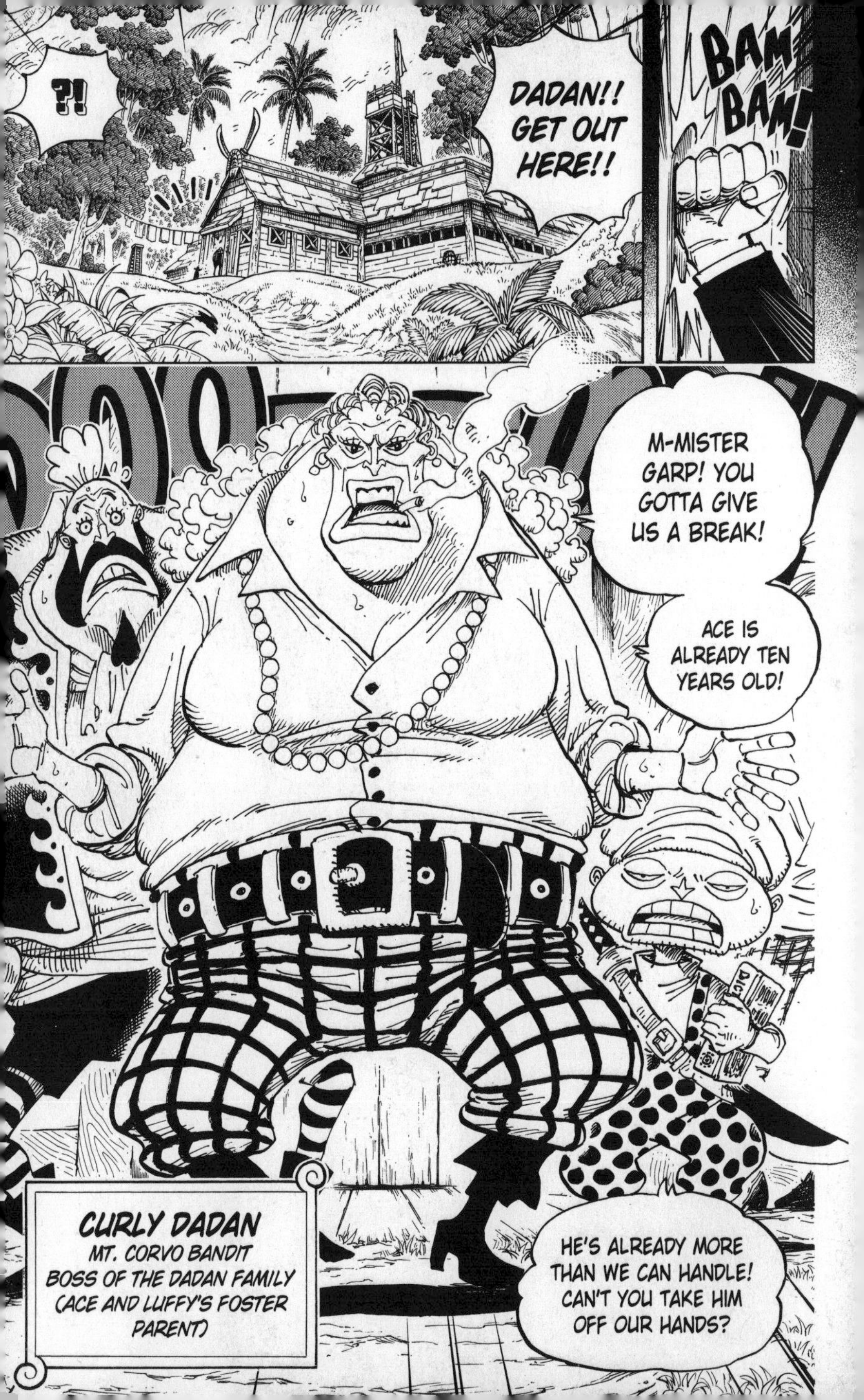
BAM BAM!
DADAN!! GET OUT HERE!!
?!
M-MISTER GARP! YOU GOTTA GIVE US A BREAK!
ACE IS ALREADY TEN YEARS OLD!
HE'S ALREADY MORE THAN WE CAN HANDLE! CAN'T YOU TAKE HIM OFF OUR HANDS?
CURLY DADAN
MT. CORVO BANDIT
BOSS OF THE DADAN FAMILY
(ACE AND LUFFY'S FOSTER PARENT)

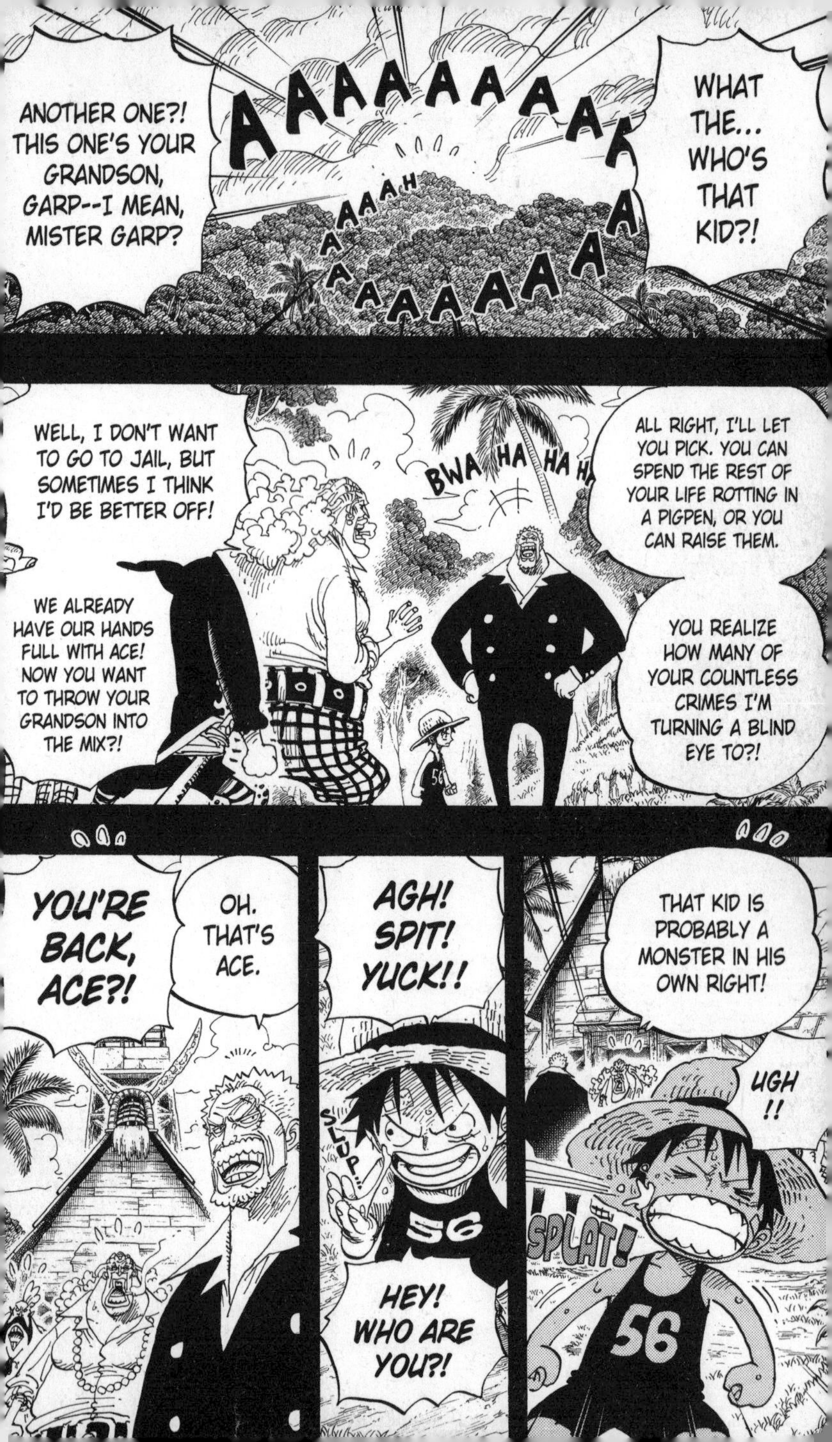
WHAT THE... WHO'S THAT KID?!
AAAAAAAAAAAAAAAAAAAAAAAAAH
ANOTHER ONE?! THIS ONE'S YOUR GRANDSON, GARP--I MEAN, MISTER GARP?
ALL RIGHT, I'LL LET YOU PICK. YOU CAN SPEND THE REST OF YOUR LIFE ROTTING IN A PIGPEN, OR YOU CAN RAISE THEM.
BWA HA HA HA
WELL, I DON'T WANT TO GO TO JAIL, BUT SOMETIMES I THINK I'D BE BETTER OFF!
YOU REALIZE HOW MANY OF YOUR COUNTLESS CRIMES I'M TURNING A BLIND EYE TO?!
WE ALREADY HAVE OUR HANDS FULL WITH ACE! NOW YOU WANT TO THROW YOUR GRANDSON INTO THE MIX?!
THAT KID IS PROBABLY A MONSTER IN HIS OWN RIGHT!
UGH !!
SPLAT!
AGH! SPIT! YUCK!!
SLUP...
HEY! WHO ARE YOU?!
OH. THAT'S ACE.
YOU'RE BACK, ACE?!

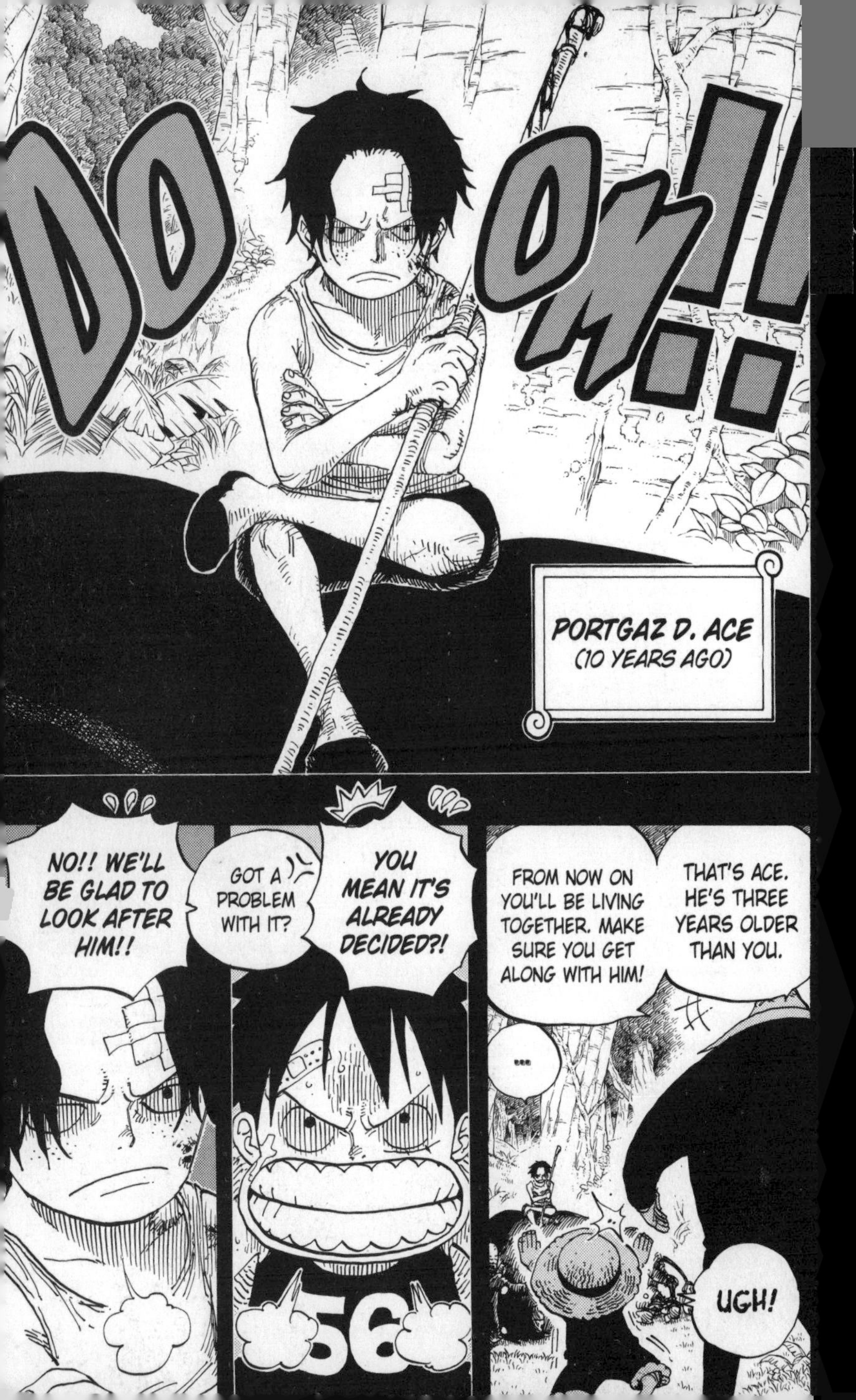
DOOM!!
PORTGAZ D. ACE (10 YEARS AGO)
THAT'S ACE. HE'S THREE YEARS OLDER THAN YOU.
FROM NOW ON YOU'LL BE LIVING TOGETHER. MAKE SURE YOU GET ALONG WITH HIM!
...
UGH!
YOU MEAN IT'S ALREADY DECIDED?!
GOT A PROBLEM WITH IT?
NO!! WE'LL BE GLAD TO LOOK AFTER HIM!!

(Kobayashi Mutsumi, Kanagawa)

Q: I was thinking of buying a Nami body pillow, so I wanted to ask you, Odacchi, on how to use it. --Nobuo

A: I see... How would I know?!⁉ It looks like those kinds of things are really being sold. I never saw the actual thing in person so I wouldn't know, but don't you just shove that thing between your legs and then go to sleep? Listen, everyone. You may think I know every single piece of One Piece merchandise that's out, but it's my media manager Onishi that deals with that. I just read the merchandise section in Jump and go, "Oh, I didn't know they had that." As long as the people who made it and the people who buy it get some fun out of it, I really don't mind. But I am always anticipating what's coming out next for the Portrait of Pirates figure series. Those are pretty expensive, but they're nice.

©Eiichiro Oda/Shueisha, Fuji TV, Toei Animation.

"One Piece Beauty Die-Cut Body Pillow" Sold by: Kowa, Inc.

Q: I have a serious question. How many kinds of tones does *One Piece* use? Just one kind? Do shonen manga tend to have very few types of tones? Also Mr. Oda, do you know how to use the "fading" technique by scraping off tones? Please answer me! --MangaLover MS

S-50

S-53

A: Just one?! How rude! I use up to three! I use the famous I-C screen tones. There are the light ones, the dark ones, and the so-called "sand graphic" ones. For people who don't know what screen tones are, think of them as transparent stickers that are used on the manga. When you go to the kind of stores that carry them, they usually have hundreds of different types available. But I use only three. I haven't done the "fading" technique in a while. I remember doing a lot of it back when I was working as an assistant. My own staff members do it too. In regards to how you're supposed to do it, first, you take a utility knife and...

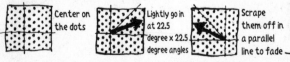

FWIP...!!

Center on the dots

Lightly go in at 22.5 degree x 22.5 degree angles

Scrape them off in a parallel line to fade

We use this "fade" and "overlap" method instead of gradation tones when trying to show the sunset effect. In recent times, people seem to be able to do a lot more with the computer. But as long as I'm working on One Piece, I want to work with my own hands.

Chapter 583:
GRAY TERMINAL

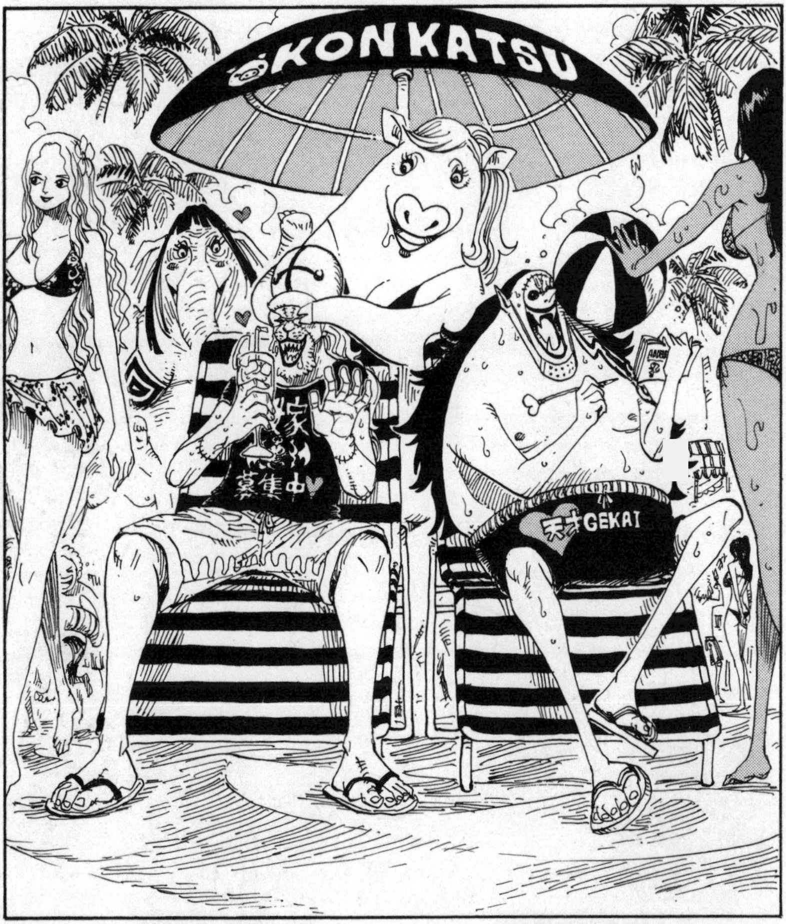
KONKATSU
募集中♥
天才GEKAI

*SEARCHING FOR A WIFE

*GENIUS SURGEON

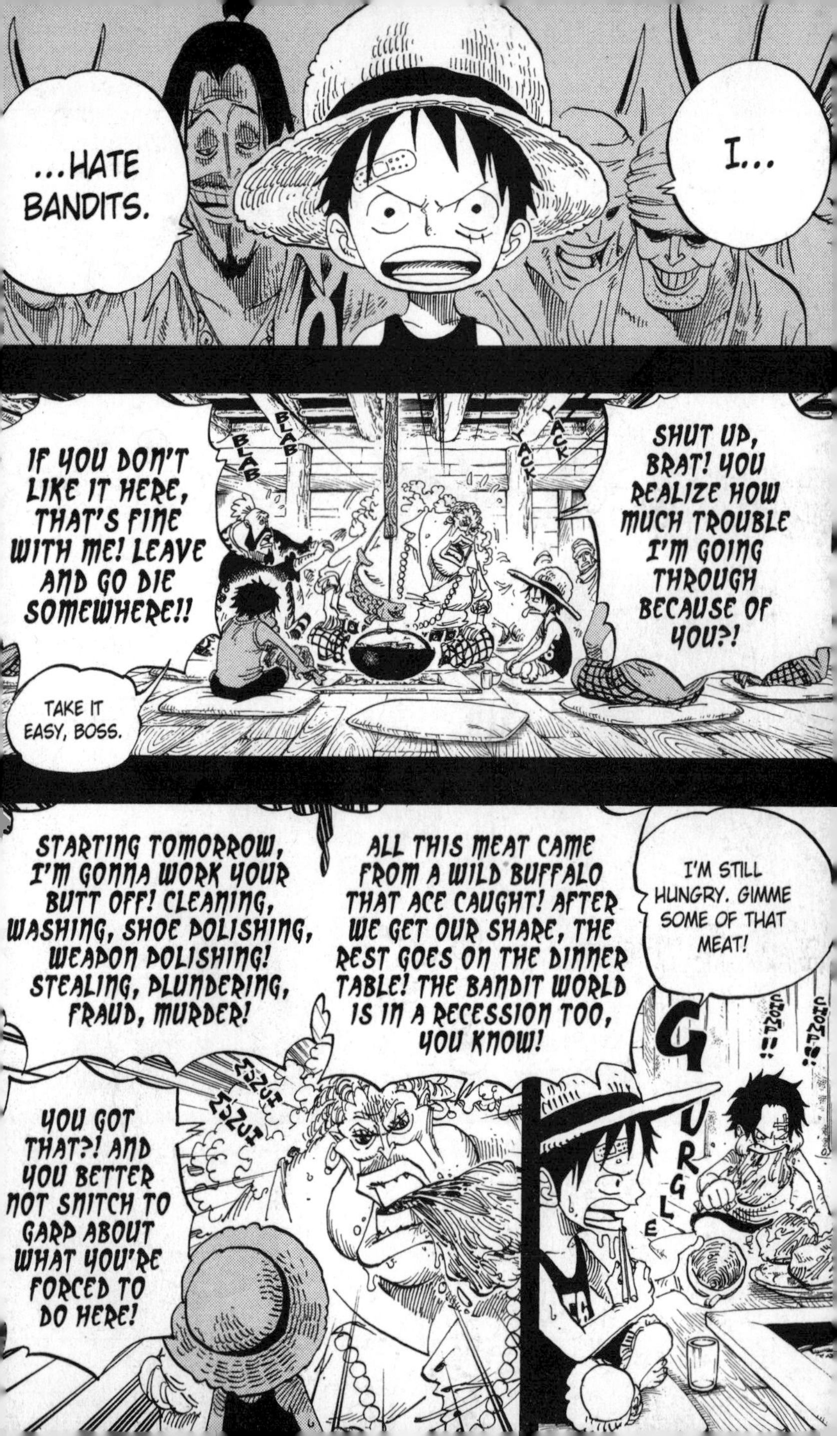
I...
...HATE BANDITS.
YACK YACK
SHUT UP, BRAT! YOU REALIZE HOW MUCH TROUBLE I'M GOING THROUGH BECAUSE OF YOU?!
BLAB BLAB
IF YOU DON'T LIKE IT HERE, THAT'S FINE WITH ME! LEAVE AND GO DIE SOMEWHERE!!
TAKE IT EASY, BOSS.
ALL THIS MEAT CAME FROM A WILD BUFFALO THAT ACE CAUGHT! AFTER WE GET OUR SHARE, THE REST GOES ON THE DINNER TABLE! THE BANDIT WORLD IS IN A RECESSION TOO, YOU KNOW!
STARTING TOMORROW, I'M GONNA WORK YOUR BUTT OFF! CLEANING, WASHING, SHOE POLISHING, WEAPON POLISHING! STEALING, PLUNDERING, FRAUD, MURDER!
ZUZU ZUZU
YOU GOT THAT?! AND YOU BETTER NOT SNITCH TO GARP ABOUT WHAT YOU'RE FORCED TO DO HERE!
I'M STILL HUNGRY. GIMME SOME OF THAT MEAT!
CHOMP!! CHOMP!!
GURGLE

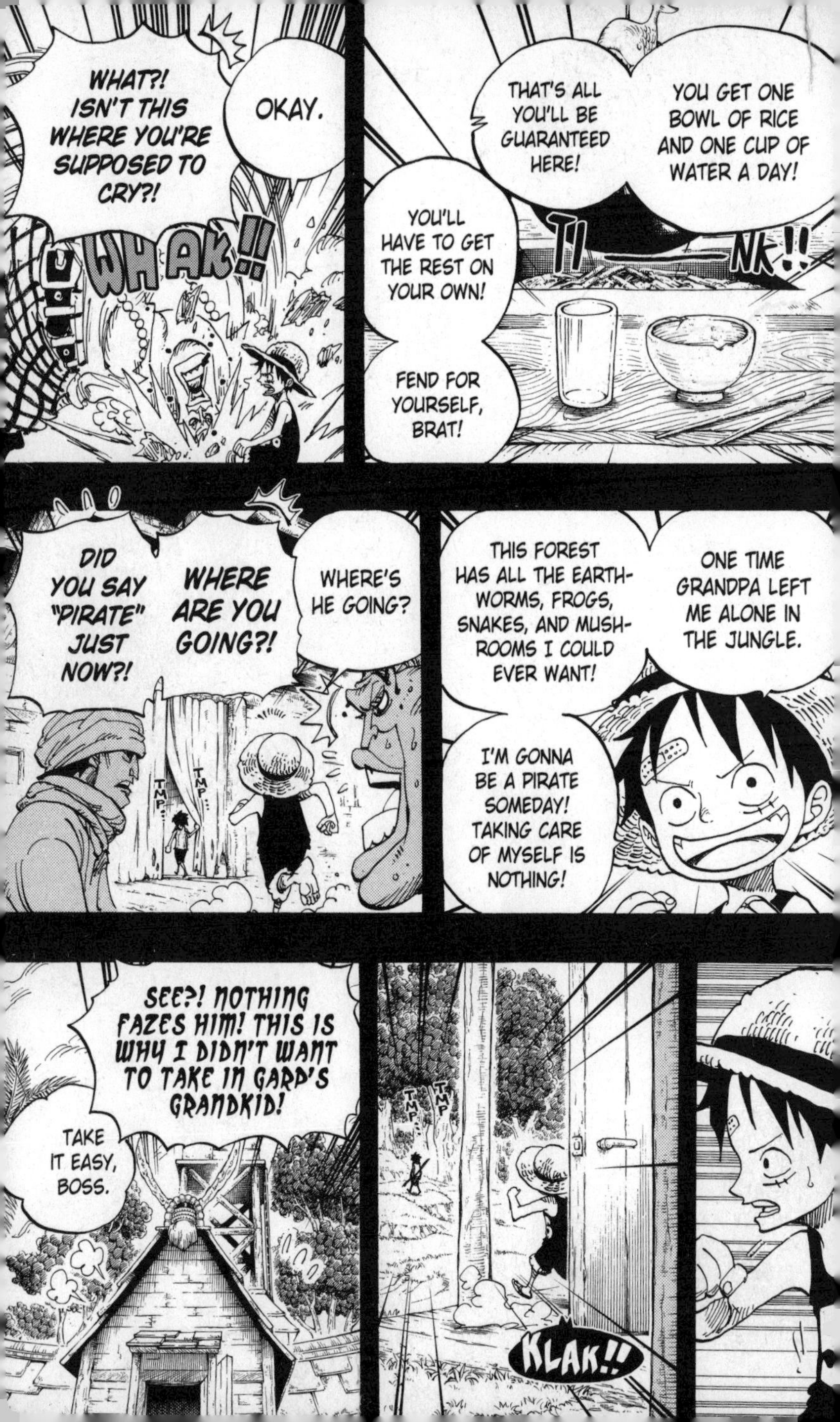
YOU GET ONE BOWL OF RICE AND ONE CUP OF WATER A DAY!
THAT'S ALL YOU'LL BE GUARANTEED HERE!
YOU'LL HAVE TO GET THE REST ON YOUR OWN!
FEND FOR YOURSELF, BRAT!
TI—NK!!
OKAY.
WHAT?! ISN'T THIS WHERE YOU'RE SUPPOSED TO CRY?!
WHAK!!
ONE TIME GRANDPA LEFT ME ALONE IN THE JUNGLE.
THIS FOREST HAS ALL THE EARTH-WORMS, FROGS, SNAKES, AND MUSH-ROOMS I COULD EVER WANT!
I'M GONNA BE A PIRATE SOMEDAY! TAKING CARE OF MYSELF IS NOTHING!
WHERE'S HE GOING?
WHERE ARE YOU GOING?!
DID YOU SAY "PIRATE" JUST NOW?!
TMP... TMP...
TMP... TMP
KLAK!!
SEE?! NOTHING FAZES HIM! THIS IS WHY I DIDN'T WANT TO TAKE IN GARP'S GRANDKID!
TAKE IT EASY, BOSS.

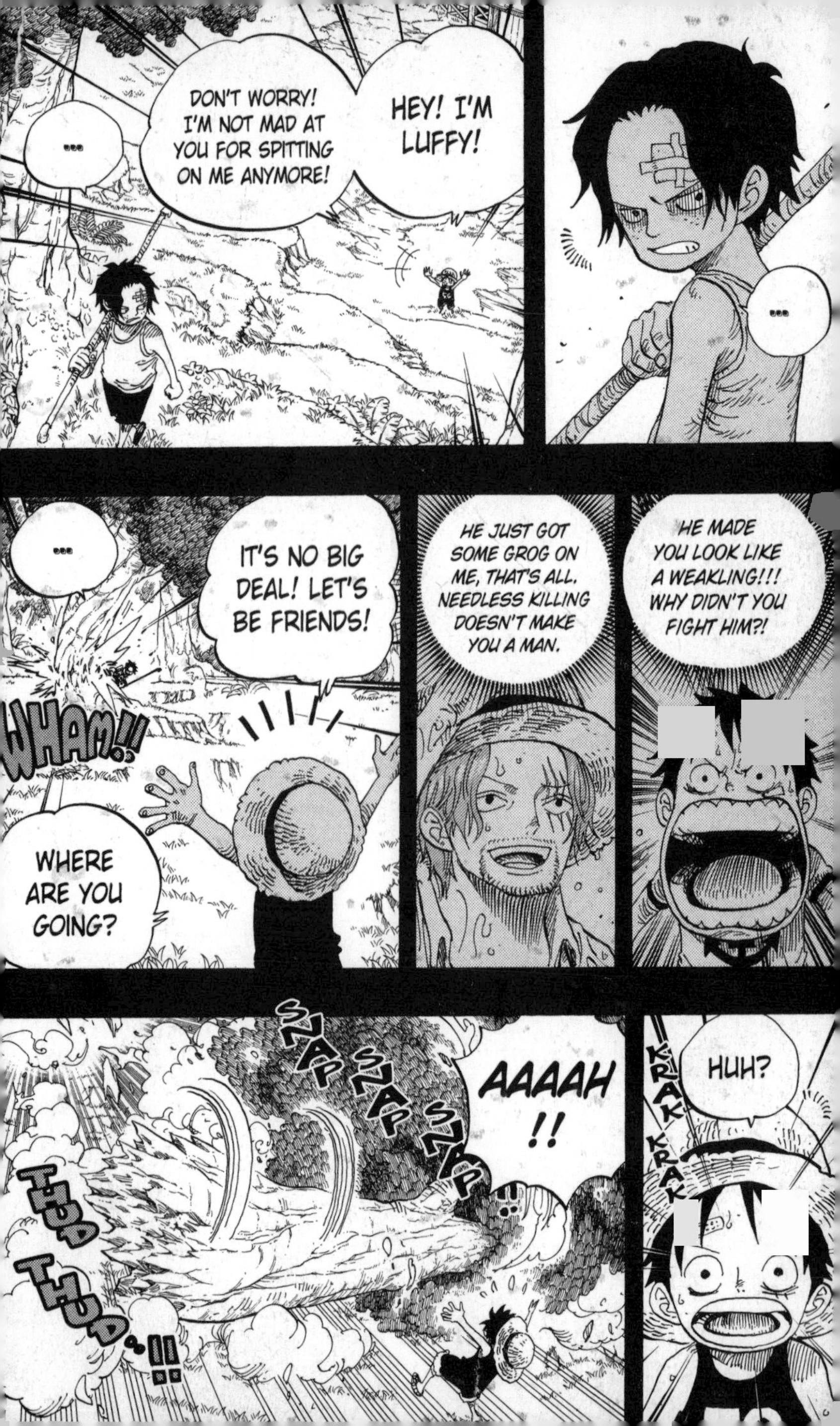
...
HEY! I'M LUFFY!
DON'T WORRY! I'M NOT MAD AT YOU FOR SPITTING ON ME ANYMORE!
...
HE MADE YOU LOOK LIKE A WEAKLING!!! WHY DIDN'T YOU FIGHT HIM?!
HE JUST GOT SOME GROG ON ME, THAT'S ALL. NEEDLESS KILLING DOESN'T MAKE YOU A MAN.
IT'S NO BIG DEAL! LET'S BE FRIENDS!
...
WHAM!!
WHERE ARE YOU GOING?
KRAK KRAK
HUH?
AAAAH!!
SNAP SNAP SNAP
THUD THUD!!

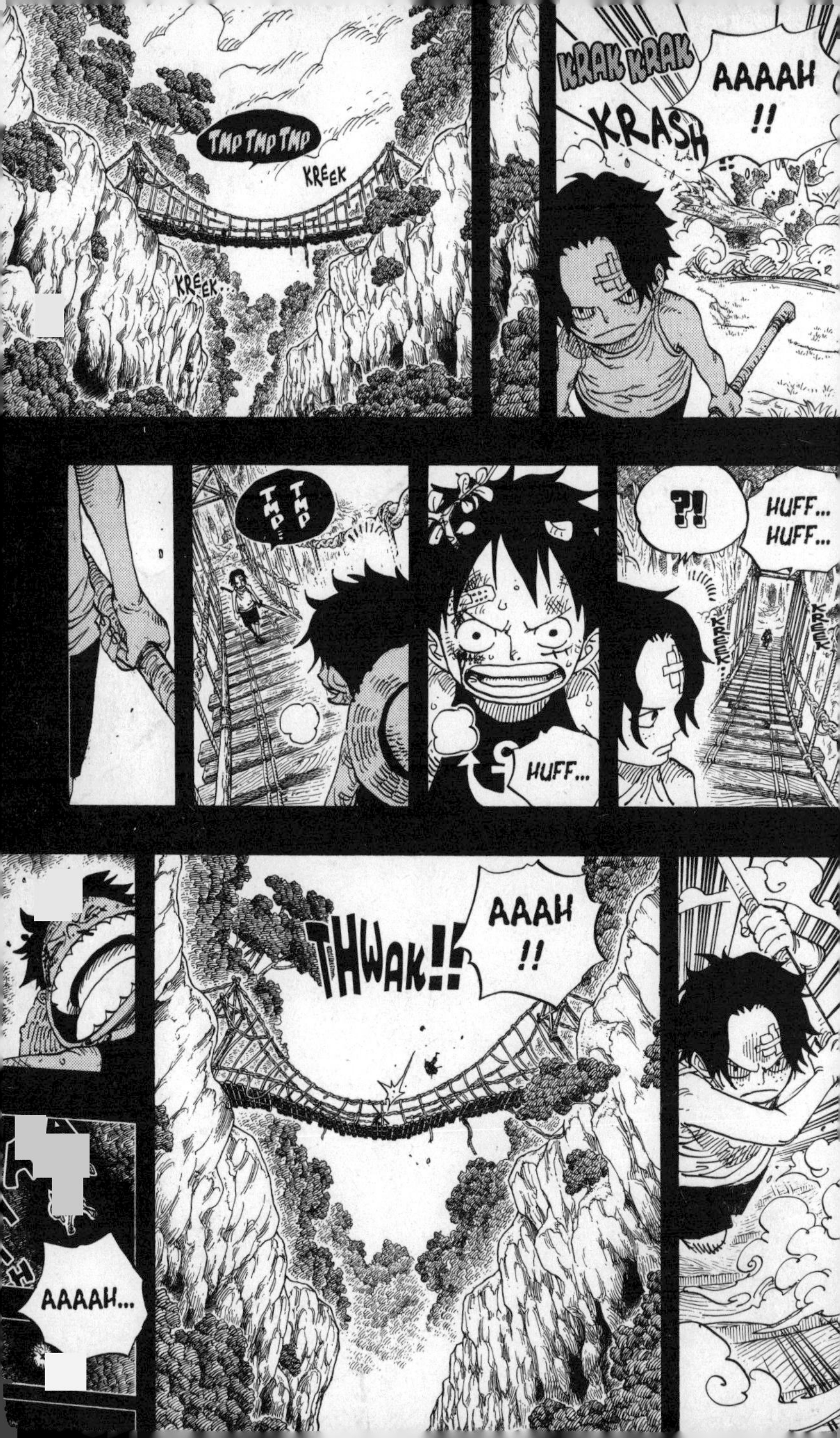
KRAK KRAK
AAAAH !!
KRASH
TMP TMP TMP
KREEK
KREEK
?!
HUFF... HUFF...
KREEK
KREEK
HUFF...
TMP... TMP
AAAH !!
THWAK!!
AAAAH...

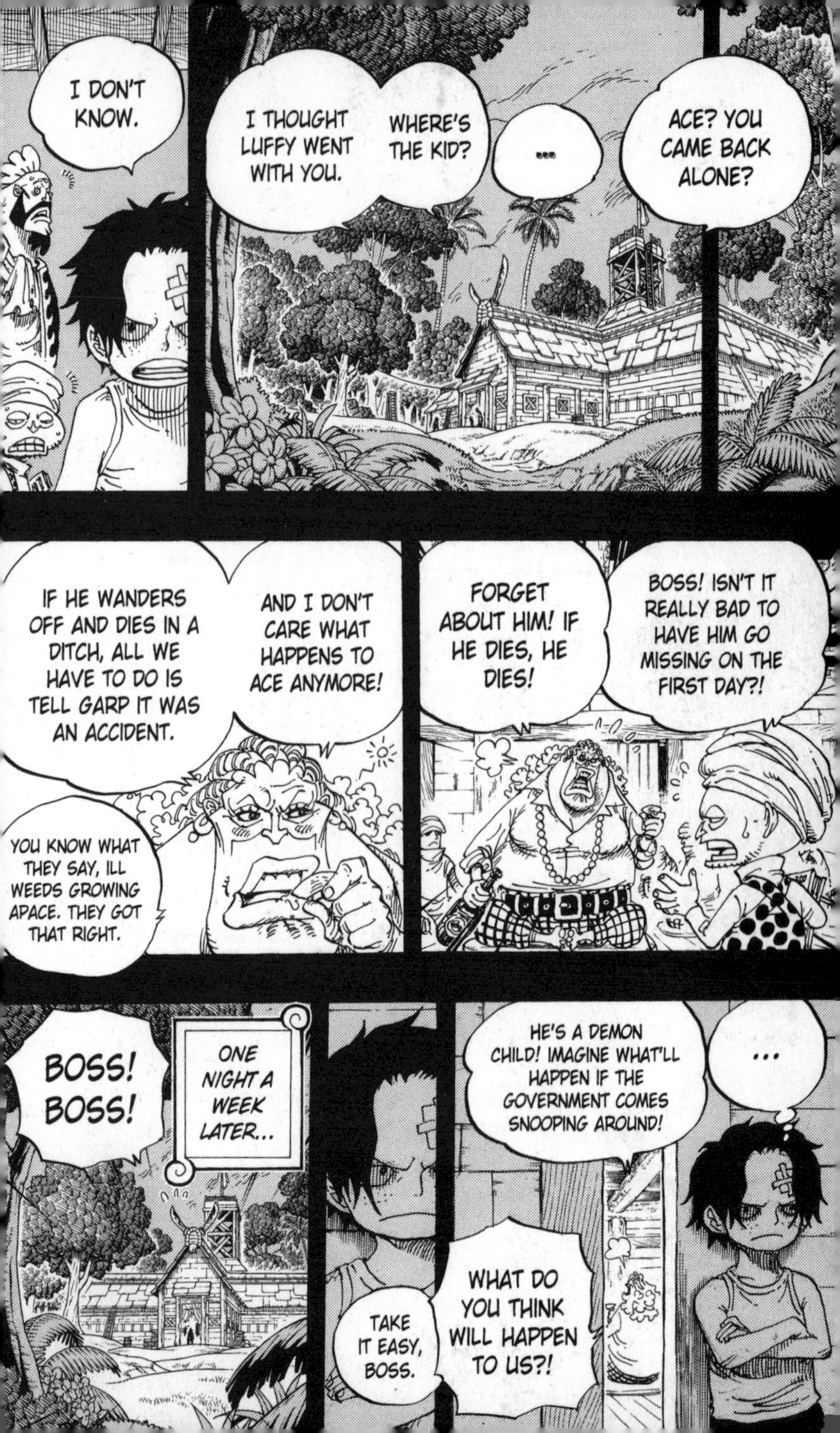
ACE? YOU CAME BACK ALONE?
...
WHERE'S THE KID?
I THOUGHT LUFFY WENT WITH YOU.
I DON'T KNOW.
BOSS! ISN'T IT REALLY BAD TO HAVE HIM GO MISSING ON THE FIRST DAY?!
FORGET ABOUT HIM! IF HE DIES, HE DIES!
AND I DON'T CARE WHAT HAPPENS TO ACE ANYMORE!
IF HE WANDERS OFF AND DIES IN A DITCH, ALL WE HAVE TO DO IS TELL GARP IT WAS AN ACCIDENT.
YOU KNOW WHAT THEY SAY, ILL WEEDS GROWING APACE. THEY GOT THAT RIGHT.
...
HE'S A DEMON CHILD! IMAGINE WHAT'LL HAPPEN IF THE GOVERNMENT COMES SNOOPING AROUND!
WHAT DO YOU THINK WILL HAPPEN TO US?!
TAKE IT EASY, BOSS.
ONE NIGHT A WEEK LATER...
BOSS! BOSS!

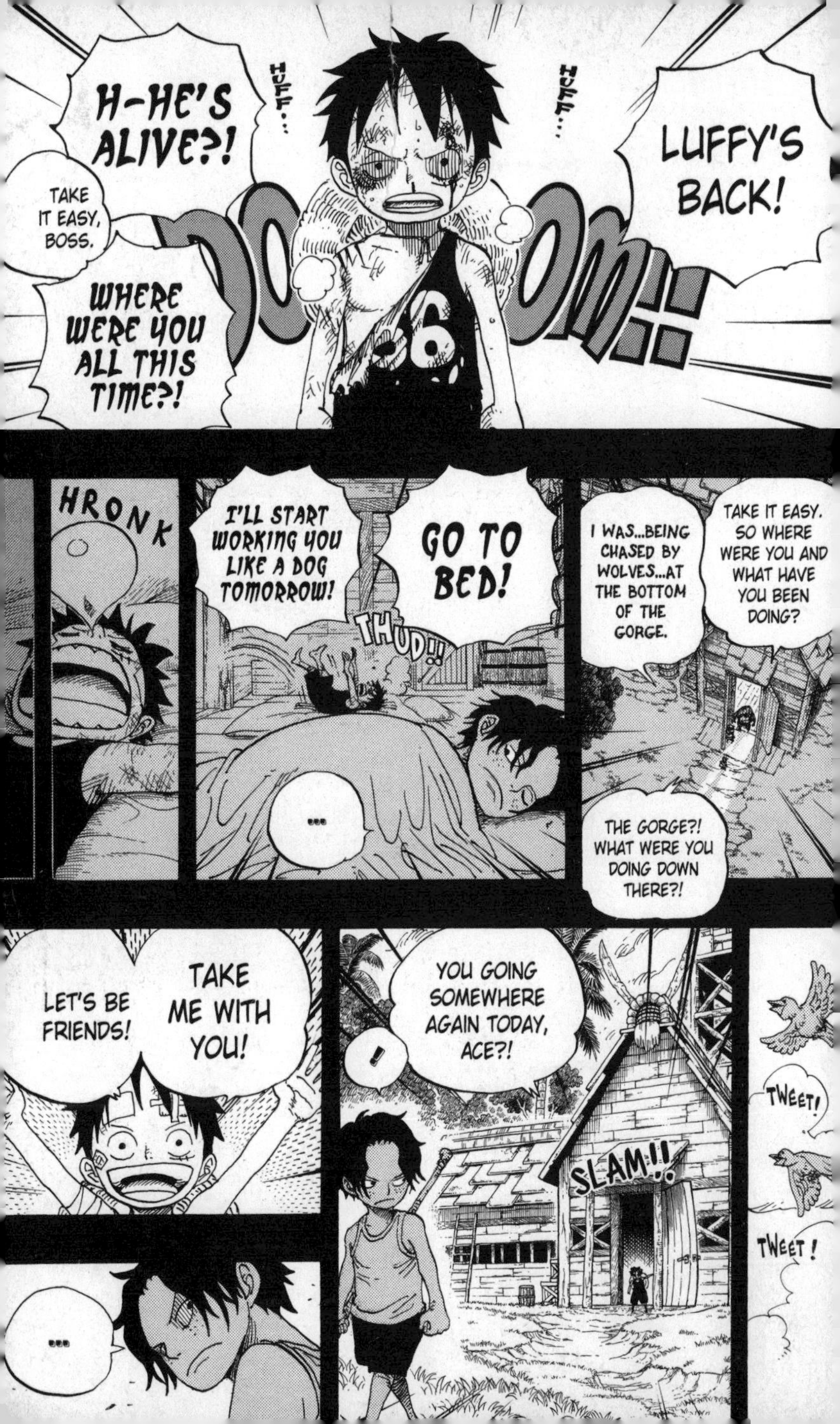
LUFFY'S BACK!
HUFF...
HUFF...
H-HE'S ALIVE?!
TAKE IT EASY, BOSS.
WHERE WERE YOU ALL THIS TIME?!
TAKE IT EASY. SO WHERE WERE YOU AND WHAT HAVE YOU BEEN DOING?
I WAS...BEING CHASED BY WOLVES...AT THE BOTTOM OF THE GORGE.
THE GORGE?! WHAT WERE YOU DOING DOWN THERE?!
GO TO BED!
I'LL START WORKING YOU LIKE A DOG TOMORROW!
THUD!!
...
HRONK
TWEET!
TWEET!
YOU GOING SOMEWHERE AGAIN TODAY, ACE?!
!
SLAM!!
TAKE ME WITH YOU!
LET'S BE FRIENDS!
...

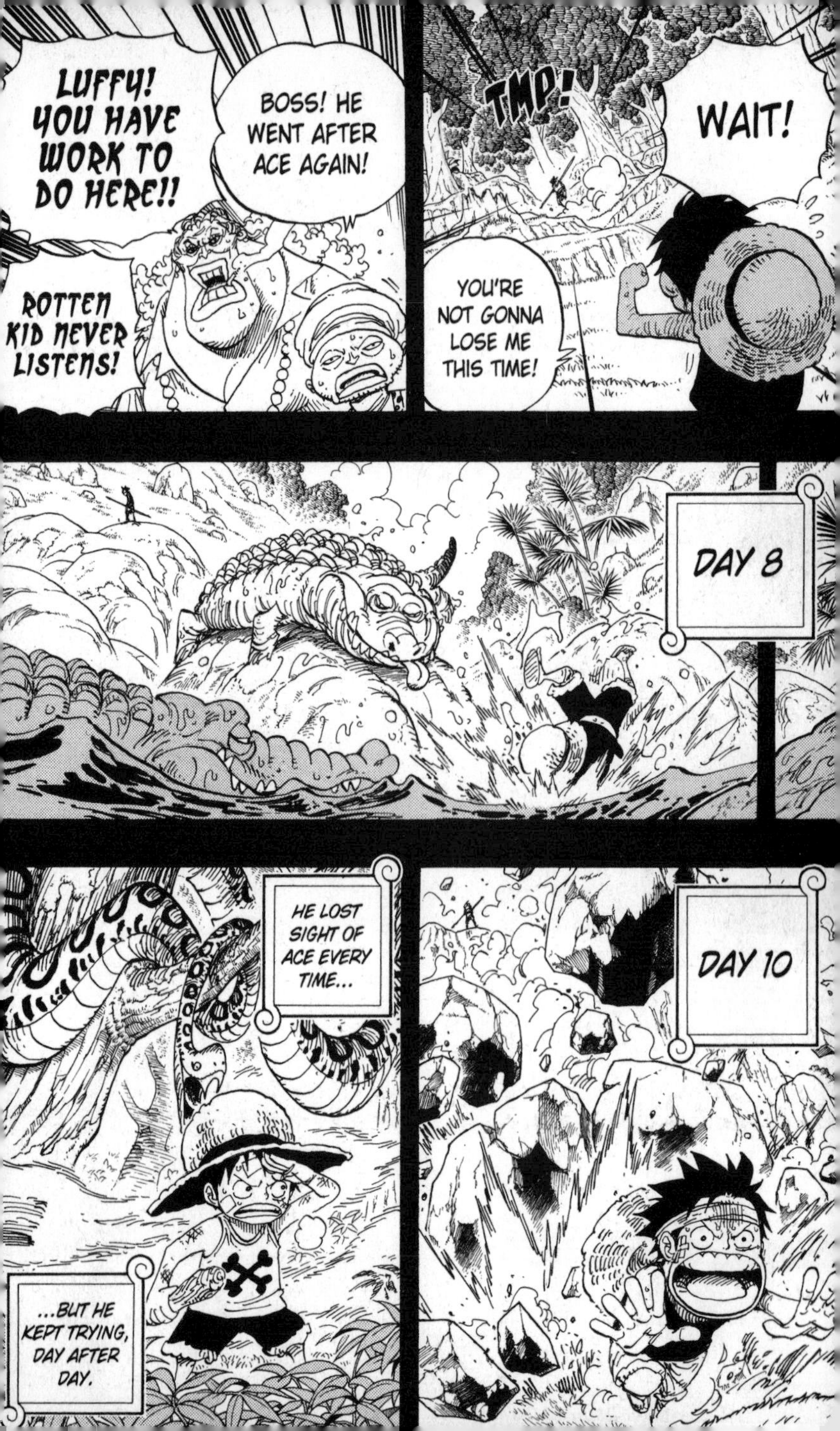
TMP!
WAIT!
YOU'RE NOT GONNA LOSE ME THIS TIME!
BOSS! HE WENT AFTER ACE AGAIN!
LUFFY! YOU HAVE WORK TO DO HERE!!
ROTTEN KID NEVER LISTENS!
DAY 8
DAY 10
HE LOST SIGHT OF ACE EVERY TIME...
...BUT HE KEPT TRYING, DAY AFTER DAY.

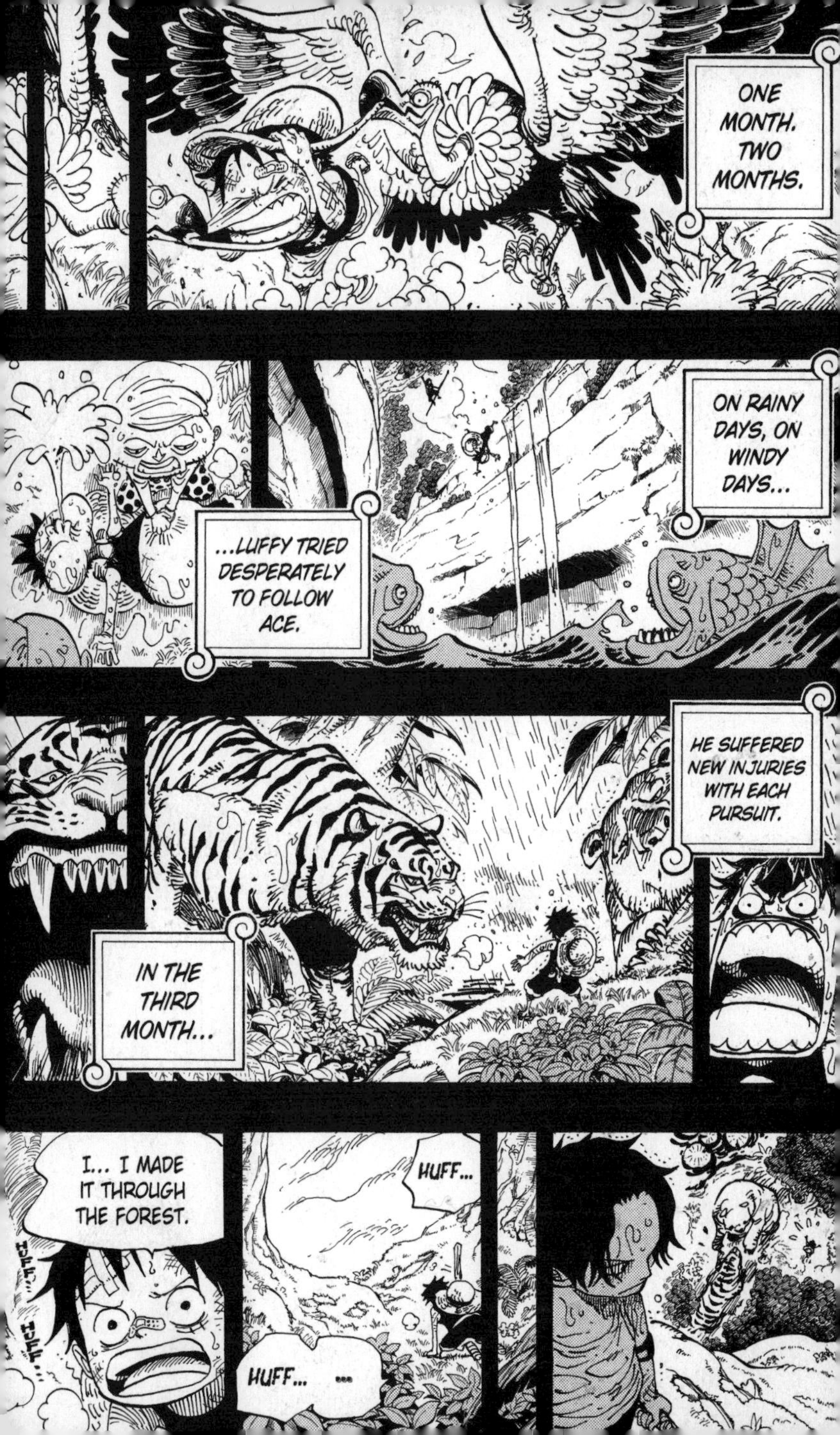
ONE MONTH. TWO MONTHS.
ON RAINY DAYS, ON WINDY DAYS...
...LUFFY TRIED DESPERATELY TO FOLLOW ACE.
HE SUFFERED NEW INJURIES WITH EACH PURSUIT.
IN THE THIRD MONTH...
HUFF...
HUFF...
...
I... I MADE IT THROUGH THE FOREST.
HUFF...
HUFF...

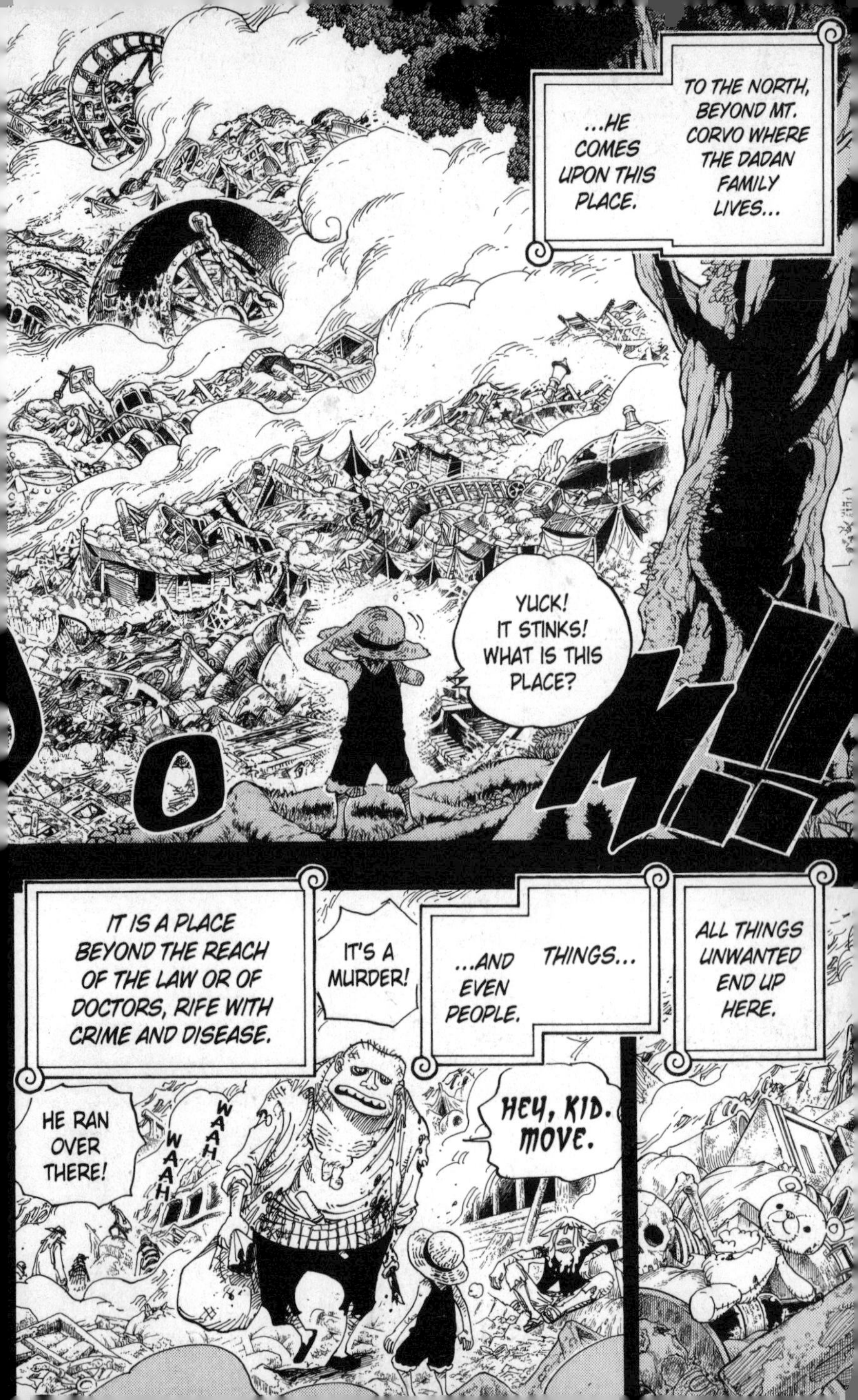
TO THE NORTH, BEYOND MT. CORVO WHERE THE DADAN FAMILY LIVES...
...HE COMES UPON THIS PLACE.
YUCK! IT STINKS! WHAT IS THIS PLACE?
ALL THINGS UNWANTED END UP HERE.
THINGS...
...AND EVEN PEOPLE.
IT'S A MURDER!
IT IS A PLACE BEYOND THE REACH OF THE LAW OR OF DOCTORS, RIFE WITH CRIME AND DISEASE.
HEY, KID. MOVE.
WAAH
WAAH
HE RAN OVER THERE!

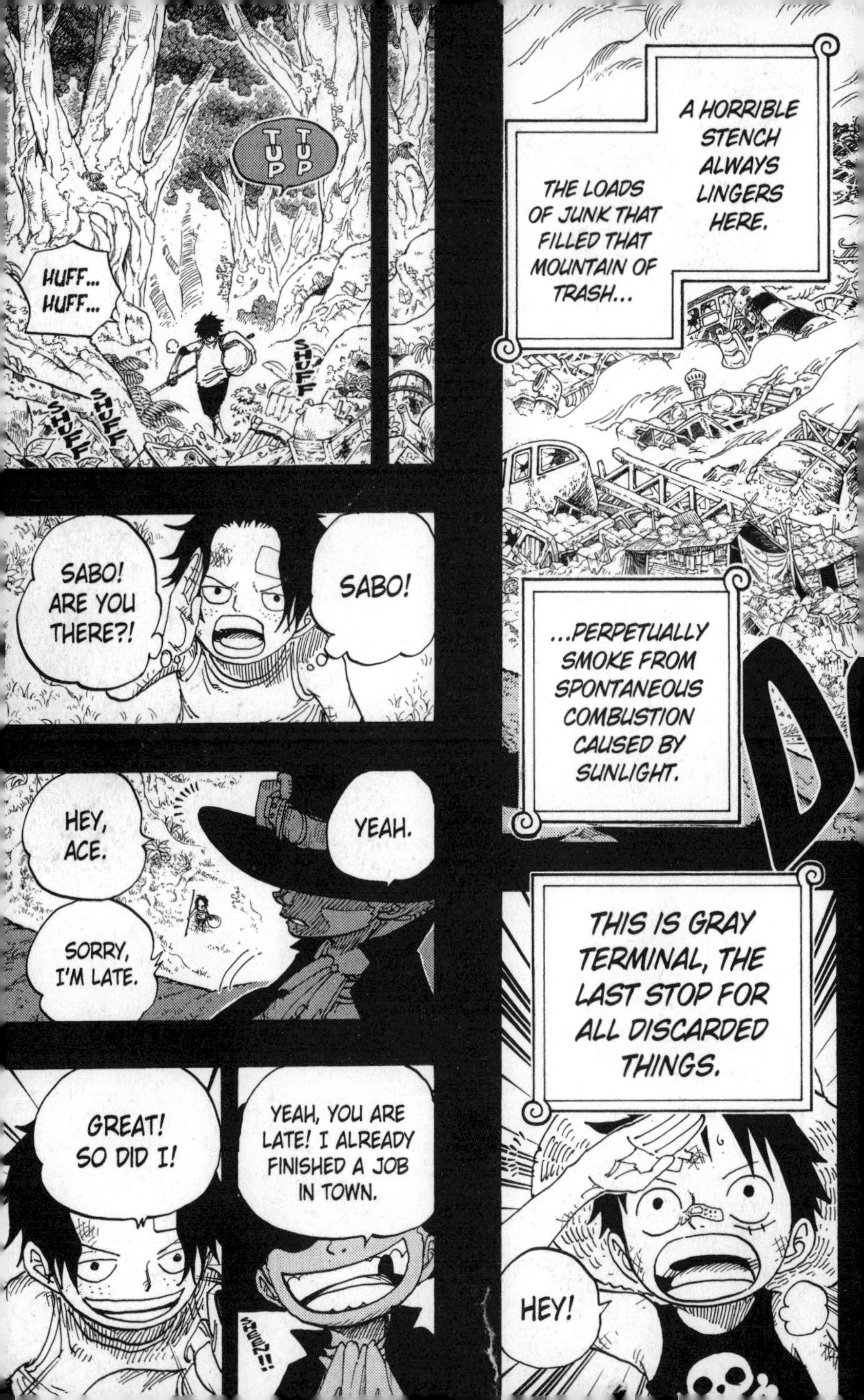
A HORRIBLE STENCH ALWAYS LINGERS HERE.
THE LOADS OF JUNK THAT FILLED THAT MOUNTAIN OF TRASH...
...PERPETUALLY SMOKE FROM SPONTANEOUS COMBUSTION CAUSED BY SUNLIGHT.
THIS IS GRAY TERMINAL, THE LAST STOP FOR ALL DISCARDED THINGS.
HEY!
TUP TUP
HUFF... HUFF...
SHUFF
SHUFF
SABO!
SABO! ARE YOU THERE?!
YEAH.
HEY, ACE.
SORRY, I'M LATE.
YEAH, YOU ARE LATE! I ALREADY FINISHED A JOB IN TOWN.
SHEEN!!
GREAT! SO DID I!

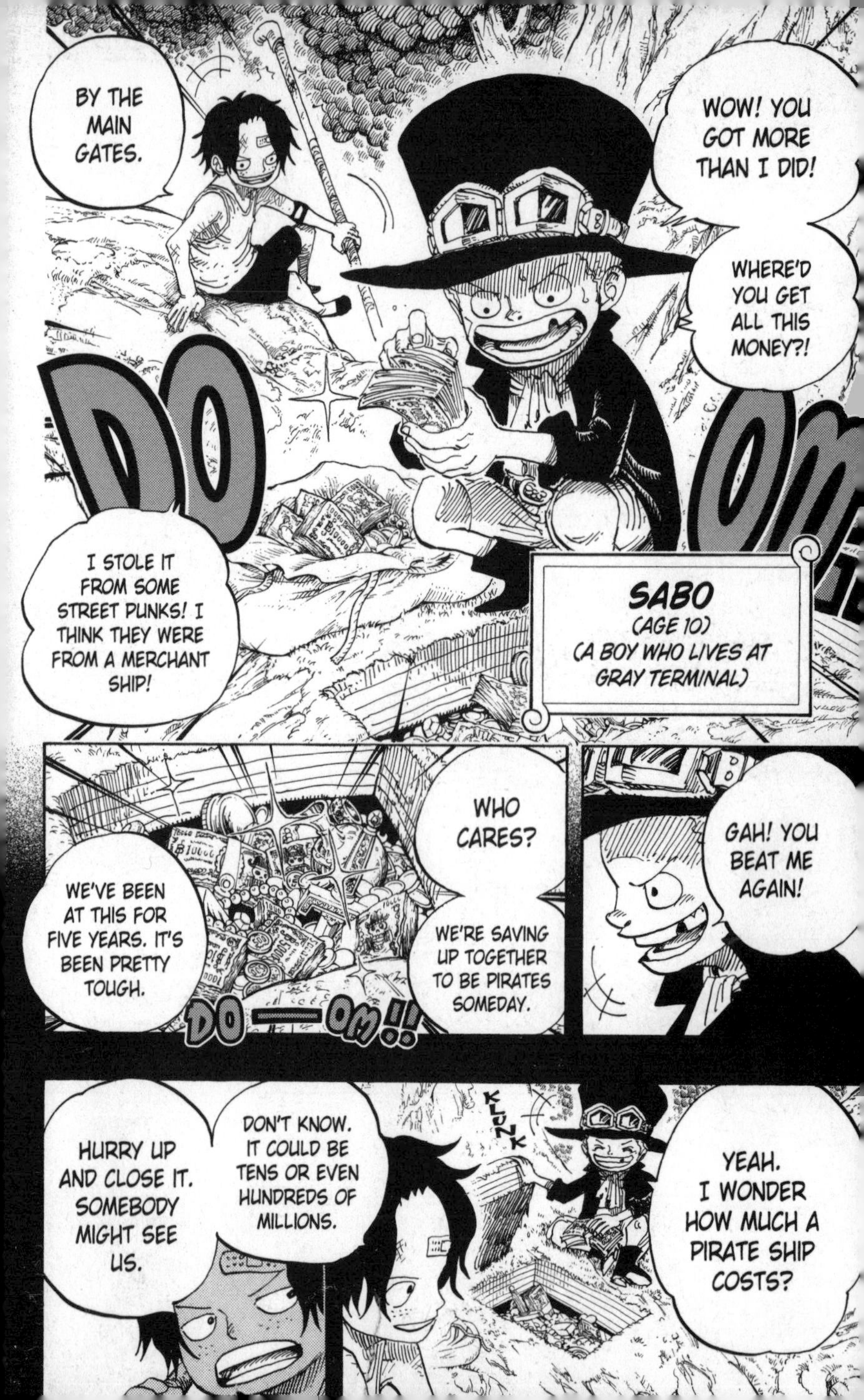
WOW! YOU GOT MORE THAN I DID!
WHERE'D YOU GET ALL THIS MONEY?!
BY THE MAIN GATES.
DOOM
SABO (AGE 10) (A BOY WHO LIVES AT GRAY TERMINAL)
I STOLE IT FROM SOME STREET PUNKS! I THINK THEY WERE FROM A MERCHANT SHIP!
GAH! YOU BEAT ME AGAIN!
WHO CARES?
WE'RE SAVING UP TOGETHER TO BE PIRATES SOMEDAY.
WE'VE BEEN AT THIS FOR FIVE YEARS. IT'S BEEN PRETTY TOUGH.
DO—OM!!
YEAH. I WONDER HOW MUCH A PIRATE SHIP COSTS?
KLUNK
DON'T KNOW. IT COULD BE TENS OR EVEN HUNDREDS OF MILLIONS.
HURRY UP AND CLOSE IT. SOMEBODY MIGHT SEE US.

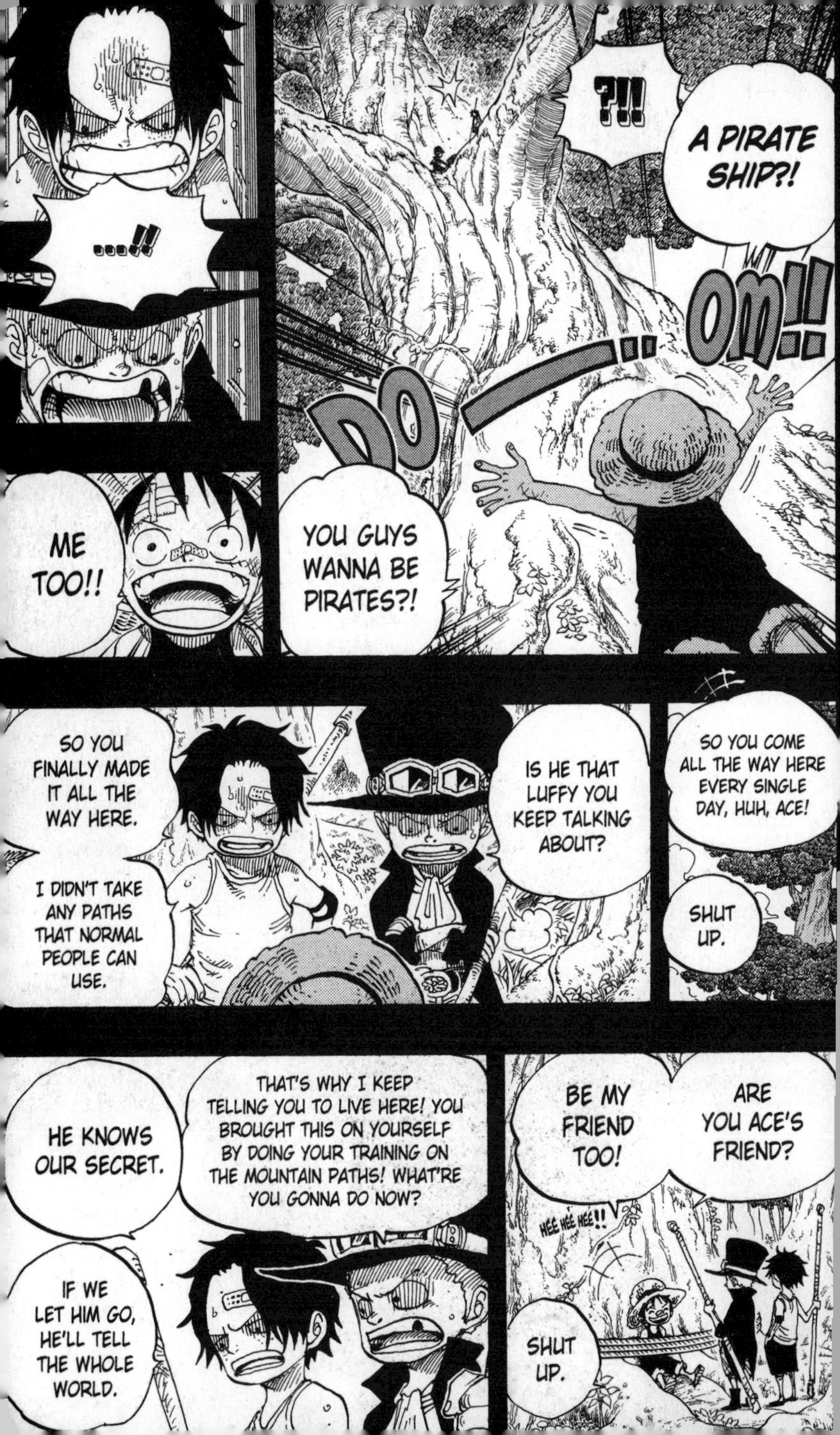
?!!
A PIRATE SHIP?!
DO—!!
OM!!
YOU GUYS WANNA BE PIRATES?!
...!!
ME TOO!!
SO YOU COME ALL THE WAY HERE EVERY SINGLE DAY, HUH, ACE!
SHUT UP.
IS HE THAT LUFFY YOU KEEP TALKING ABOUT?
SO YOU FINALLY MADE IT ALL THE WAY HERE.
I DIDN'T TAKE ANY PATHS THAT NORMAL PEOPLE CAN USE.
ARE YOU ACE'S FRIEND?
BE MY FRIEND TOO!
HEE HEE HEE!!
SHUT UP.
THAT'S WHY I KEEP TELLING YOU TO LIVE HERE! YOU BROUGHT THIS ON YOURSELF BY DOING YOUR TRAINING ON THE MOUNTAIN PATHS! WHAT'RE YOU GONNA DO NOW?
HE KNOWS OUR SECRET.
IF WE LET HIM GO, HE'LL TELL THE WHOLE WORLD.

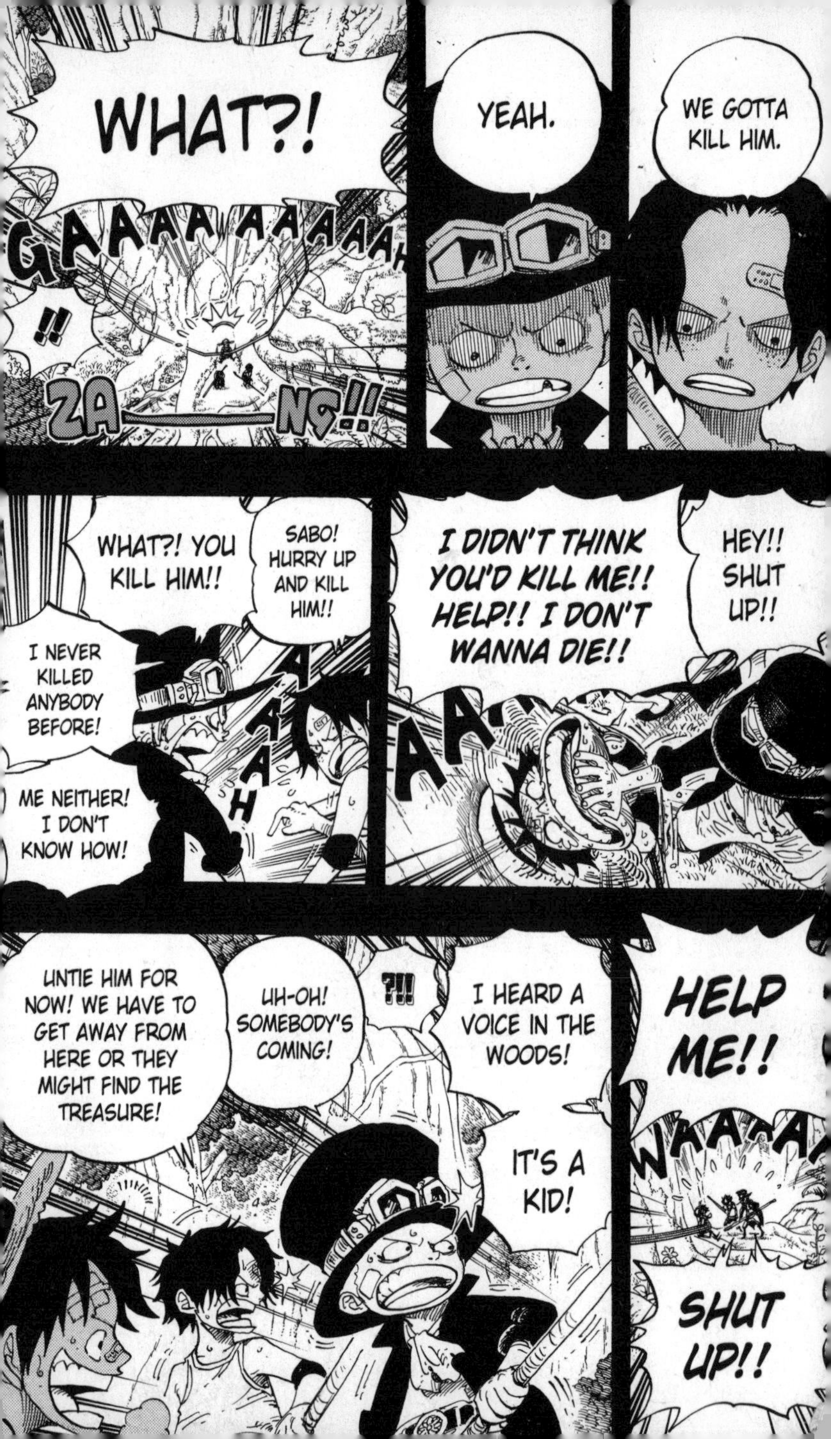
WE GOTTA KILL HIM.
YEAH.
WHAT?!
ZA—NG!!
HEY!! SHUT UP!!
I DIDN'T THINK YOU'D KILL ME!! HELP!! I DON'T WANNA DIE!!
SABO! HURRY UP AND KILL HIM!!
WHAT?! YOU KILL HIM!!
I NEVER KILLED ANYBODY BEFORE!
ME NEITHER! I DON'T KNOW HOW!
HELP ME!!
SHUT UP!!
I HEARD A VOICE IN THE WOODS!
IT'S A KID!
?!!
UH-OH! SOMEBODY'S COMING!
UNTIE HIM FOR NOW! WE HAVE TO GET AWAY FROM HERE OR THEY MIGHT FIND THE TREASURE!

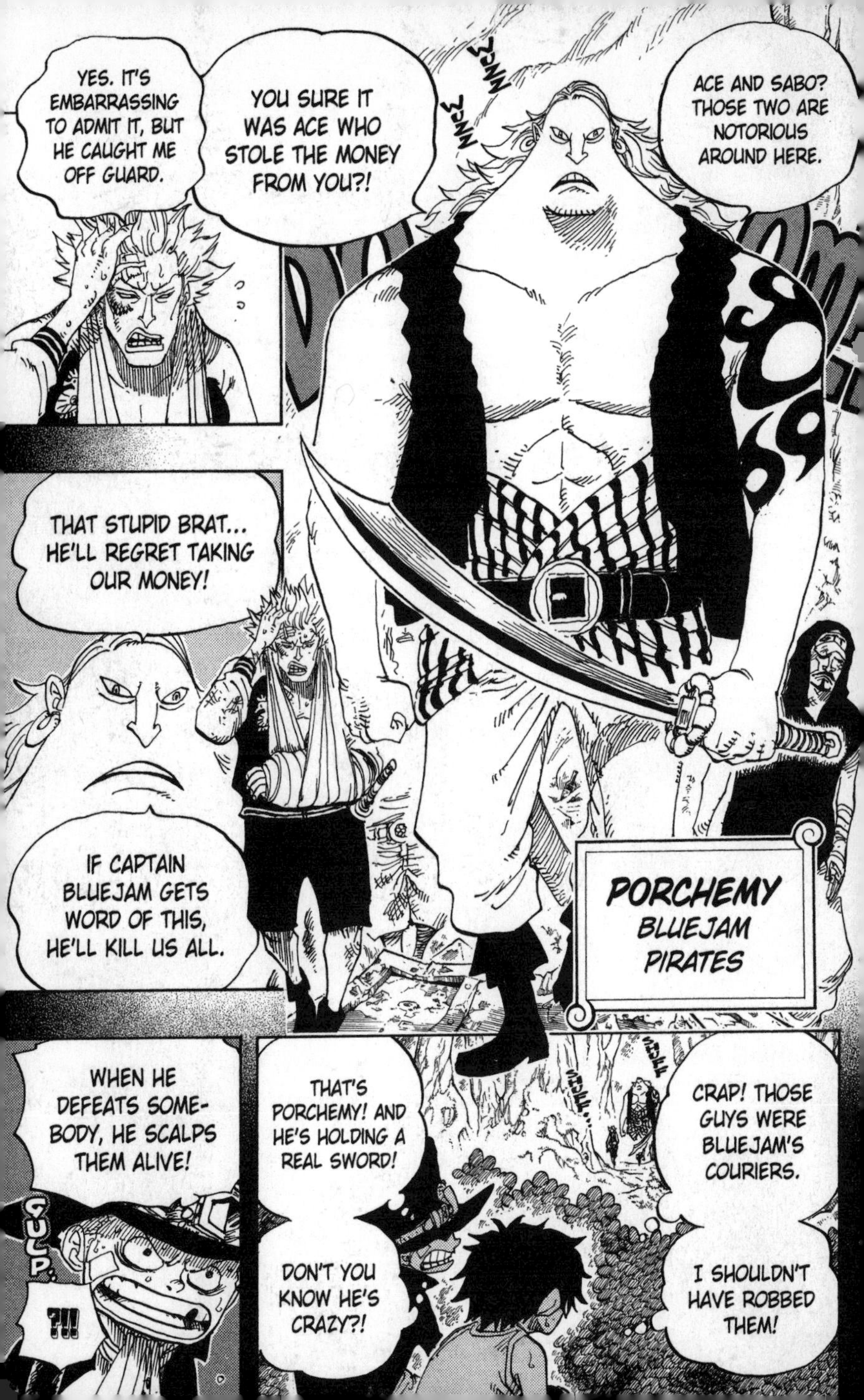
YOU SURE IT WAS ACE WHO STOLE THE MONEY FROM YOU?!
YES. IT'S EMBARRASSING TO ADMIT IT, BUT HE CAUGHT ME OFF GUARD.
ACE AND SABO? THOSE TWO ARE NOTORIOUS AROUND HERE.
PORCHEMY
BLUEJAM PIRATES
THAT STUPID BRAT... HE'LL REGRET TAKING OUR MONEY!
IF CAPTAIN BLUEJAM GETS WORD OF THIS, HE'LL KILL US ALL.
SHUFF
SHUFF...
CRAP! THOSE GUYS WERE BLUEJAM'S COURIERS.
THAT'S PORCHEMY! AND HE'S HOLDING A REAL SWORD!
I SHOULDN'T HAVE ROBBED THEM!
DON'T YOU KNOW HE'S CRAZY?!
WHEN HE DEFEATS SOMEBODY, HE SCALPS THEM ALIVE!
GULP.
?!!

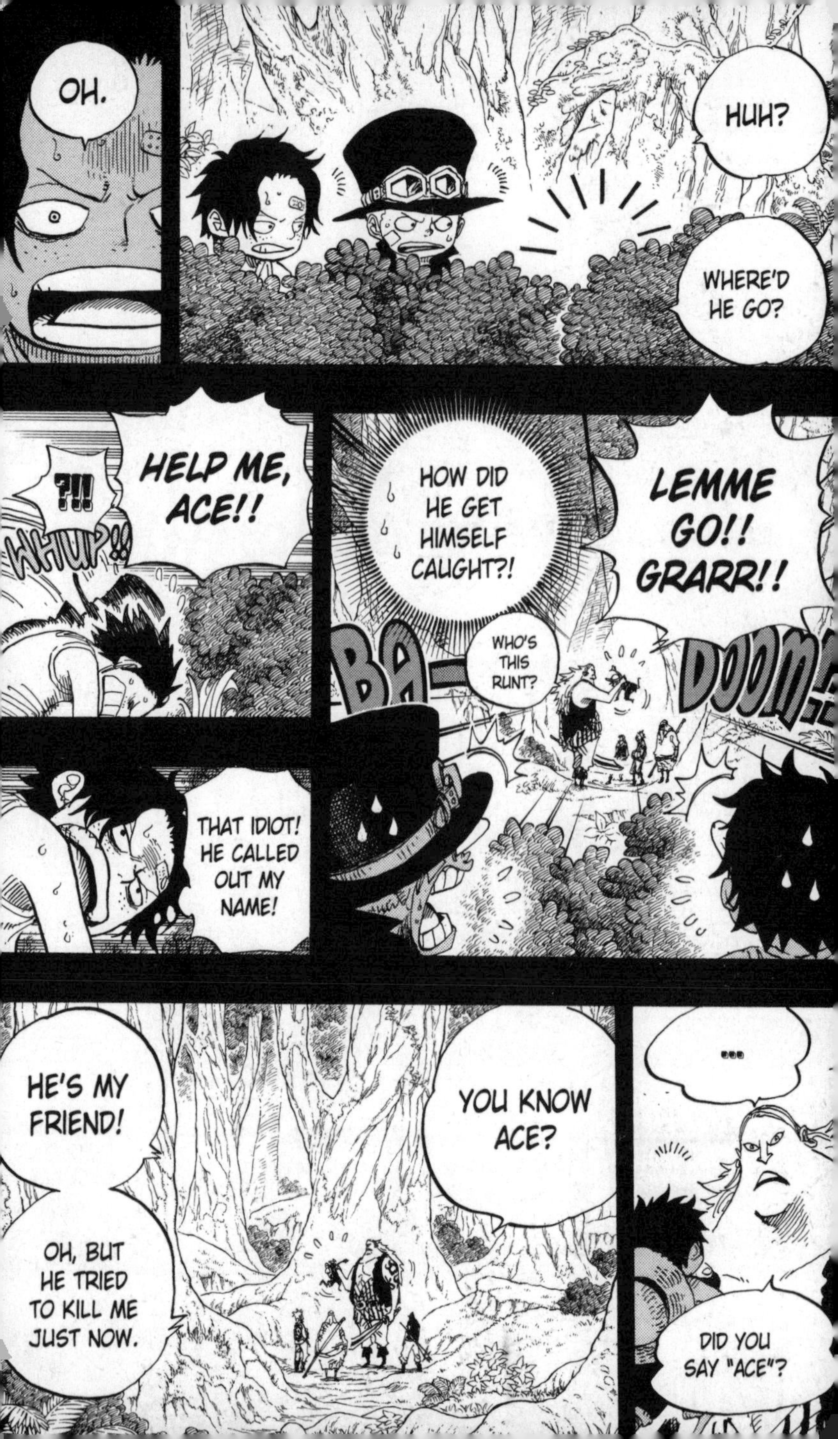
HUH?
WHERE'D HE GO?
OH.
LEMME GO!! GRARR!!
HOW DID HE GET HIMSELF CAUGHT?!
DOOM!!
WHO'S THIS RUNT?
BA-
HELP ME, ACE!!
?!!
WHUP!!
THAT IDIOT! HE CALLED OUT MY NAME!
...
DID YOU SAY "ACE"?
YOU KNOW ACE?
HE'S MY FRIEND!
OH, BUT HE TRIED TO KILL ME JUST NOW.

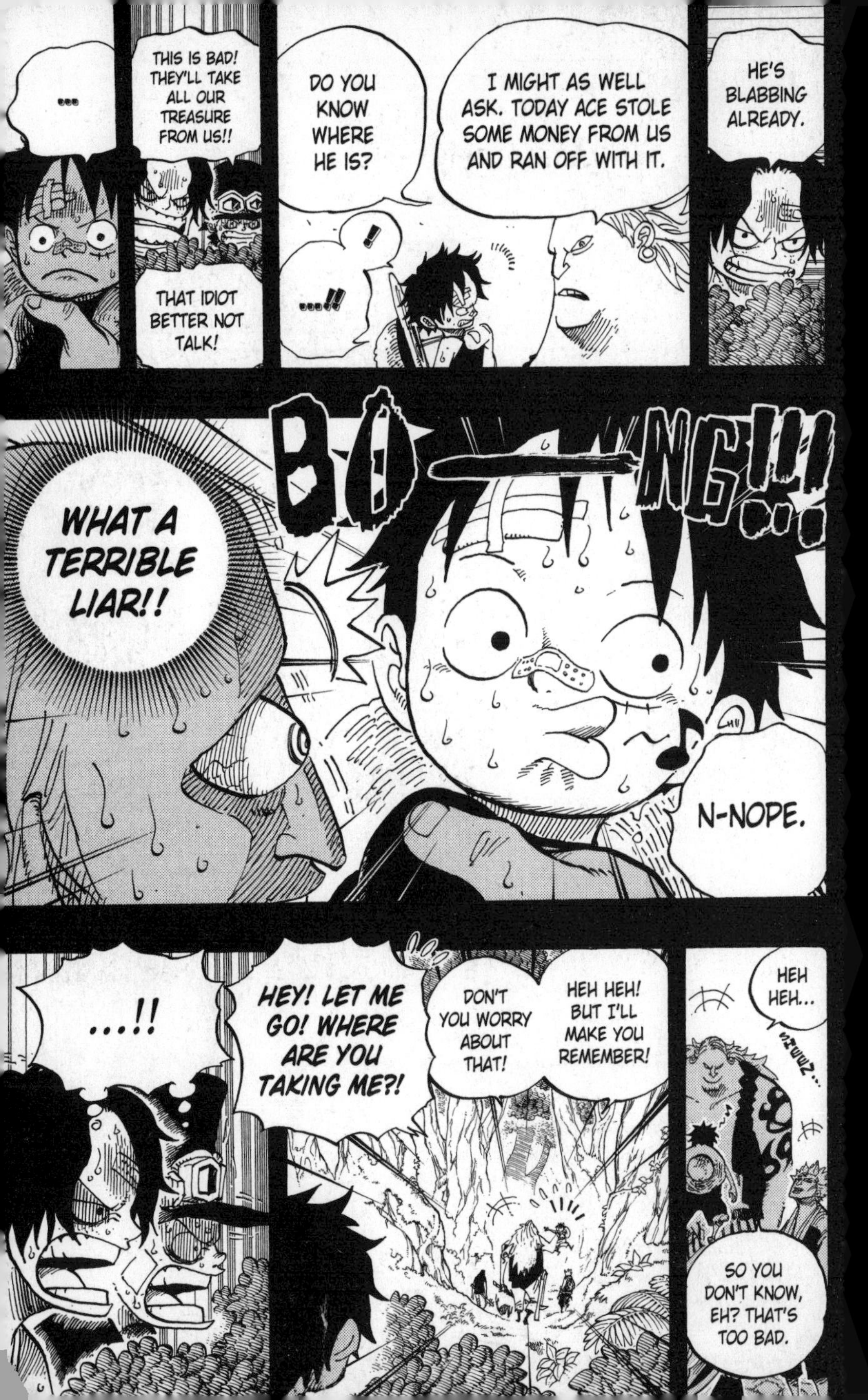
HE'S BLABBING ALREADY.
I MIGHT AS WELL ASK. TODAY ACE STOLE SOME MONEY FROM US AND RAN OFF WITH IT.
DO YOU KNOW WHERE HE IS?
!
...!!
THIS IS BAD! THEY'LL TAKE ALL OUR TREASURE FROM US!!
THAT IDIOT BETTER NOT TALK!
...
BO—NG!!!
N-NOPE.
WHAT A TERRIBLE LIAR!!
HEH HEH...
SO YOU DON'T KNOW, EH? THAT'S TOO BAD.
HEH HEH! BUT I'LL MAKE YOU REMEMBER!
DON'T YOU WORRY ABOUT THAT!
HEY! LET ME GO! WHERE ARE YOU TAKING ME?!
...!!

SBS Question Corner

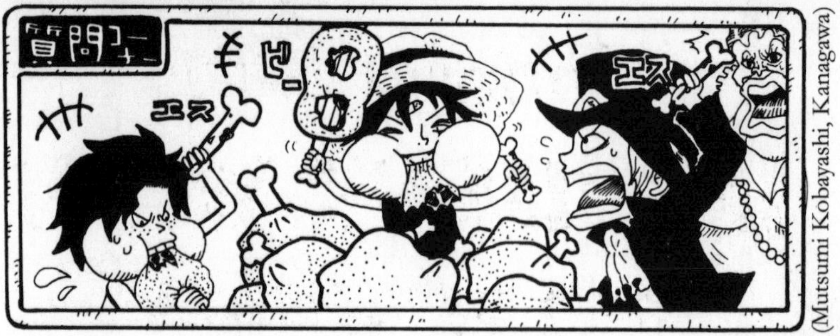
質問コーナー

(Mutsumi Kobayashi, Kanagawa)

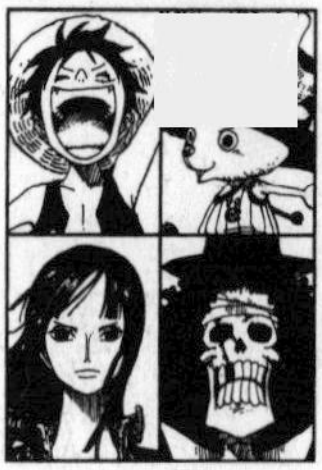

Q: Odacchi! I just realized something amazing! When you convert the Japanese names of the Devil Fruit eaten by the Straw Hat crew, they can go from 1-10! Luffy ➡ Gomu-Gomu (Go = 5, Mu = 6), Chopper ➡ Hito-Hito (Hi = 1, To = 10), Robin ➡ Hana-Hana (Ha = 8, Na = 7). Brook ➡ Yomi-Yomi (Yo=4, Mi=3) There's no 2, 9 in the crew, but Bartholomew Kuma's Nikyu-Nikyu (Ni = 2, Kyu = 9) would fit! Does that mean Bartholomew Kuma is going to join the crew?! Please tell me!

--SHANKUS LOVE

A: What?! That really surprised me! Why am I surprised?! No comment! Next!

Q: You can skip my letter and go to the next.

--Tomo

A: Uh... Sure. S-Sorry. Well, if you insist... Why the heck did you send this letter anyway?! (I'm sorry, that was immature of me.)

Q: I saw on the news the other day where they announced that they succeeded in turning a male eel into female by injecting female hormones into it. Was Iva also a part of this experiment?! Is it the "Emporio Estrogen?!"

--New Kama

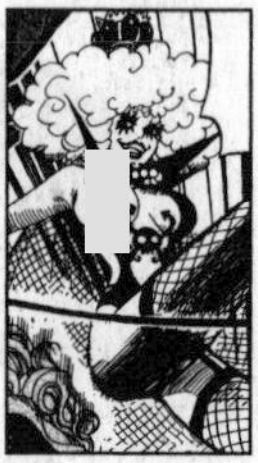

A: Without a doubt, yes. That is definitely "Emporio Estrogen." I believe that science will be able to make eels really excited in the future! Woohaa! I want to eat that eel!

Okay. I'm going to end this volume's SBS here. Because of the production period, there won't be a Voice Actor SBS this time. I'm really sorry about that. That thing actually takes a lot of time to prepare. We'll definitely resume next volume! Next up, we have...

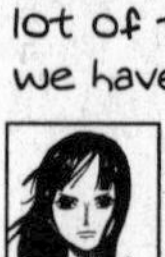

Yuriko Yamaguchi, who plays Robin

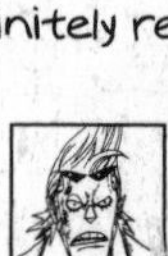

And Kazuki Yao, who plays Franky.

Thanks for sending in your questions! See you next volume!

Chapter 584:
INCIDENT WITH PORCHEMY

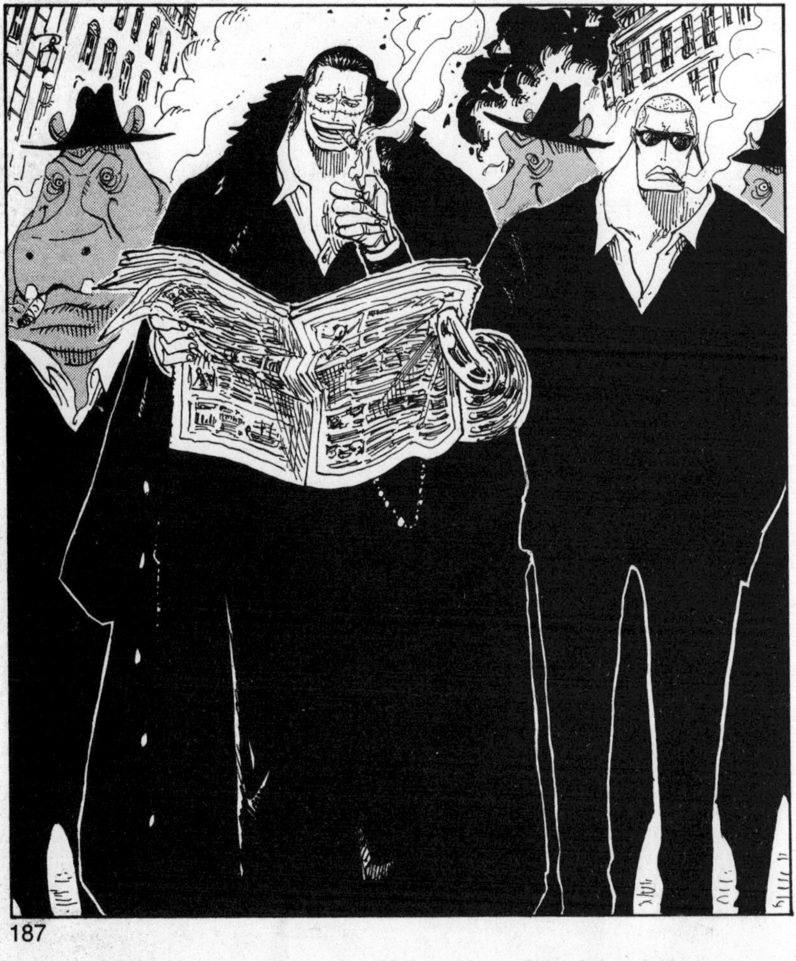

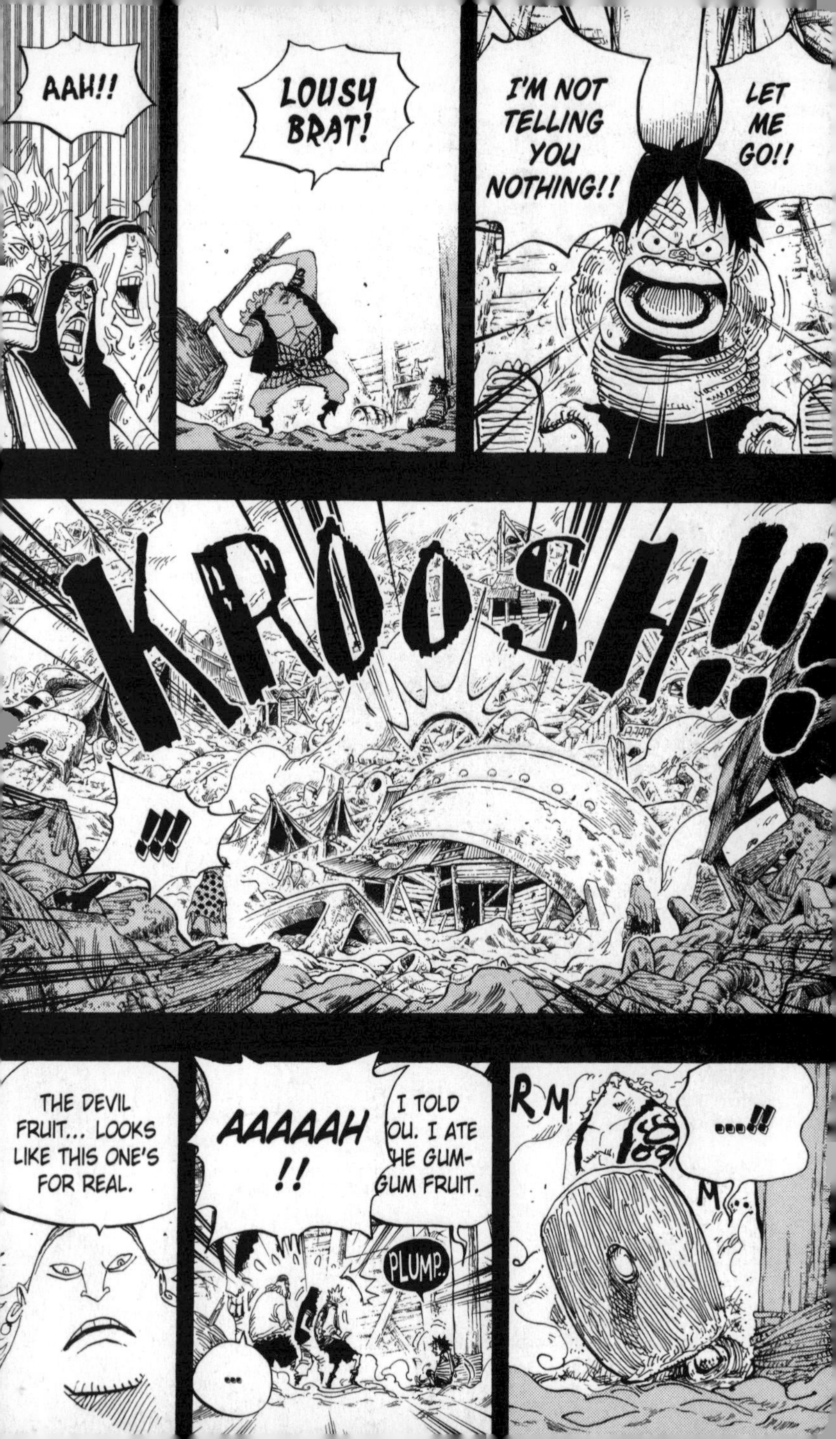

LET ME GO!!
I'M NOT TELLING YOU NOTHING!!
LOUSY BRAT!
AAH!!
KROOSH!!
!!!
...!!
RM
M
I TOLD OU. I ATE HE GUM-GUM FRUIT.
AAAAAH !!
PLUMP..
...
THE DEVIL FRUIT... LOOKS LIKE THIS ONE'S FOR REAL.

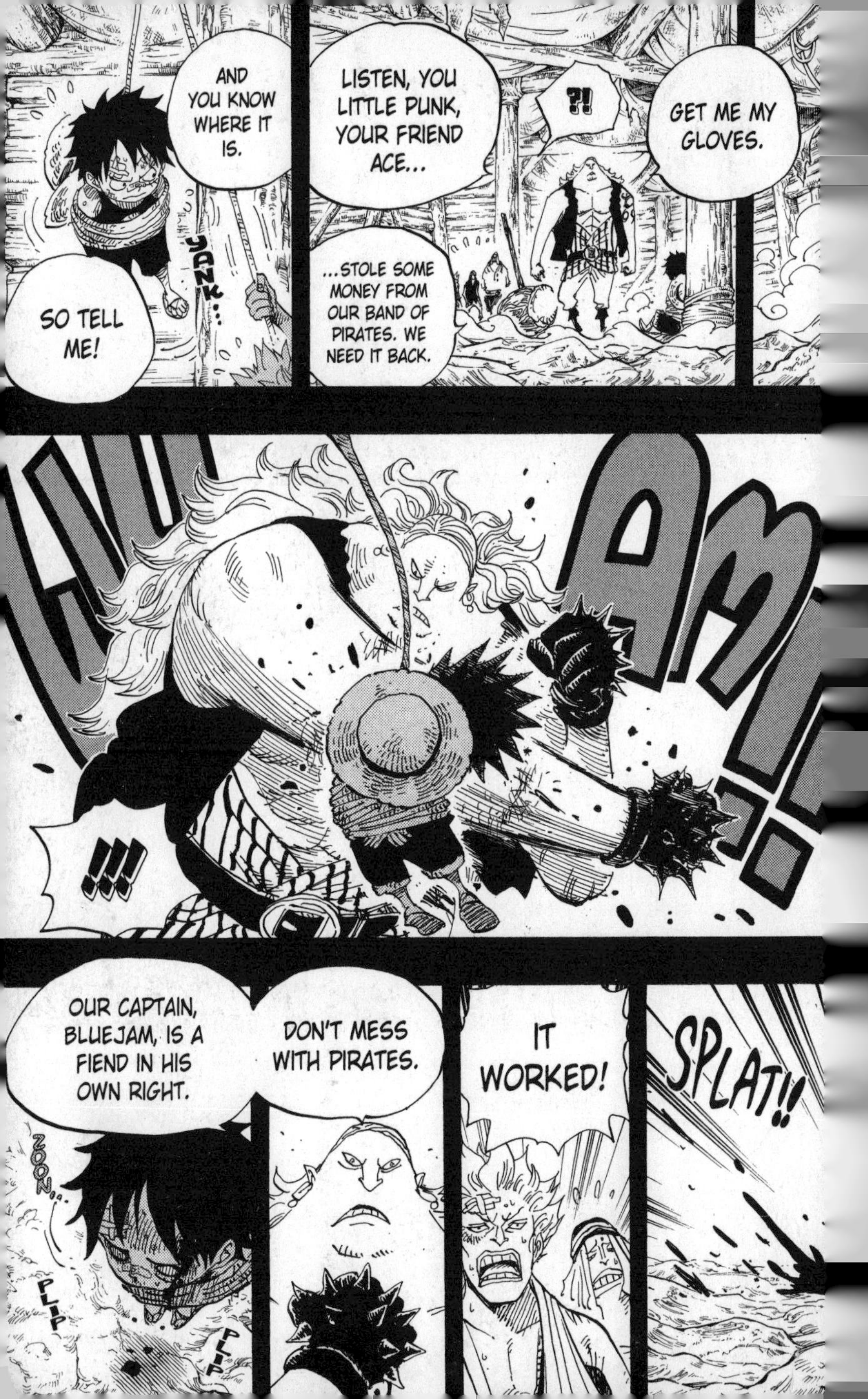
GET ME MY GLOVES.
?!
LISTEN, YOU LITTLE PUNK, YOUR FRIEND ACE...
...STOLE SOME MONEY FROM OUR BAND OF PIRATES. WE NEED IT BACK.
AND YOU KNOW WHERE IT IS.
YANK...
SO TELL ME!
!!!
SPLAT!!
IT WORKED!
DON'T MESS WITH PIRATES.
OUR CAPTAIN, BLUEJAM, IS A FIEND IN HIS OWN RIGHT.
ZOON...
PLIP
PLIP

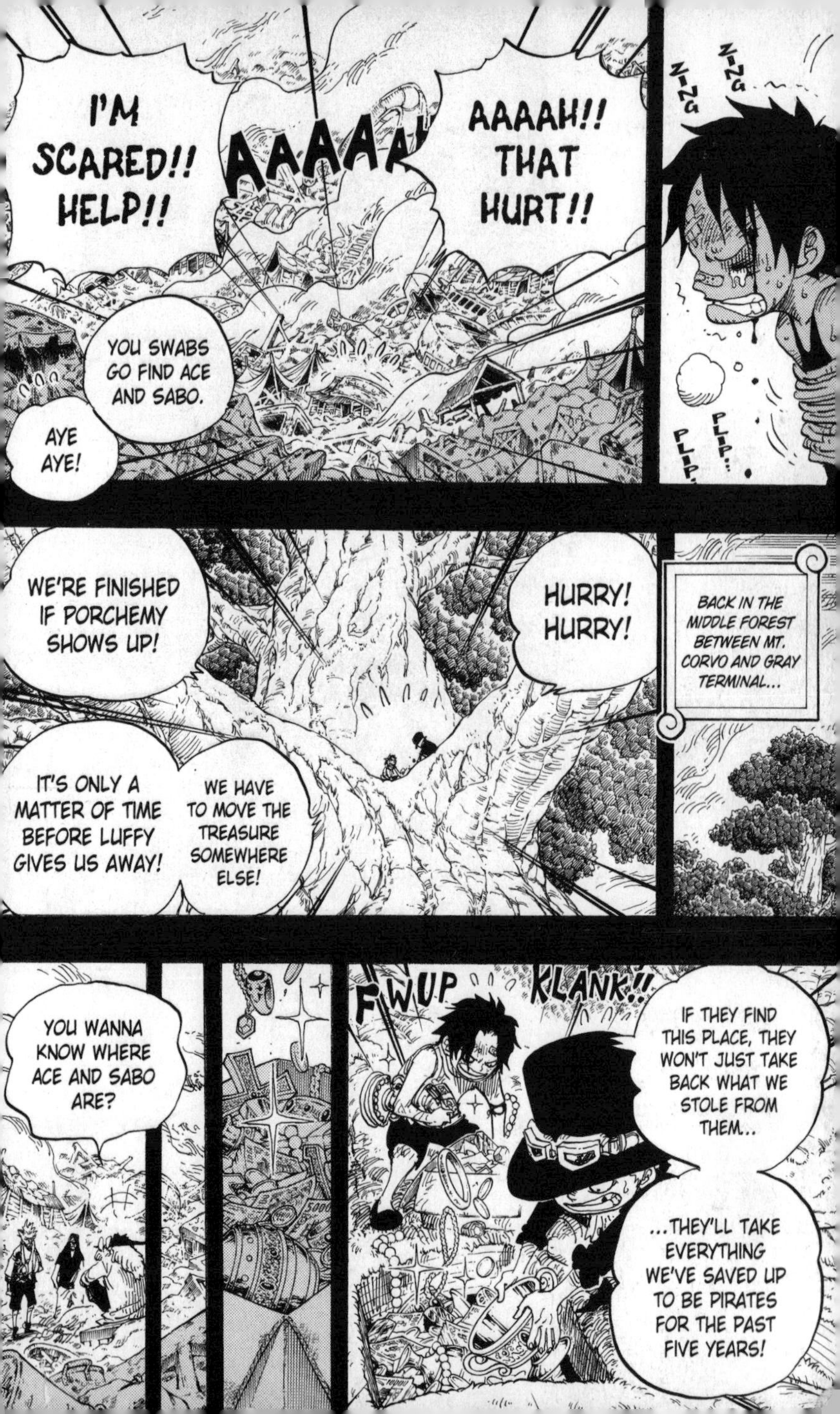
ZING
ZING
PLIP..
PLIP..
AAAAH!! THAT HURT!!
AAAAA
I'M SCARED!! HELP!!
YOU SWABS GO FIND ACE AND SABO.
AYE AYE!
BACK IN THE MIDDLE FOREST BETWEEN MT. CORVO AND GRAY TERMINAL...
HURRY! HURRY!
WE'RE FINISHED IF PORCHEMY SHOWS UP!
WE HAVE TO MOVE THE TREASURE SOMEWHERE ELSE!
IT'S ONLY A MATTER OF TIME BEFORE LUFFY GIVES US AWAY!
KLANK!!
FWUP
IF THEY FIND THIS PLACE, THEY WON'T JUST TAKE BACK WHAT WE STOLE FROM THEM...
...THEY'LL TAKE EVERYTHING WE'VE SAVED UP TO BE PIRATES FOR THE PAST FIVE YEARS!
YOU WANNA KNOW WHERE ACE AND SABO ARE?

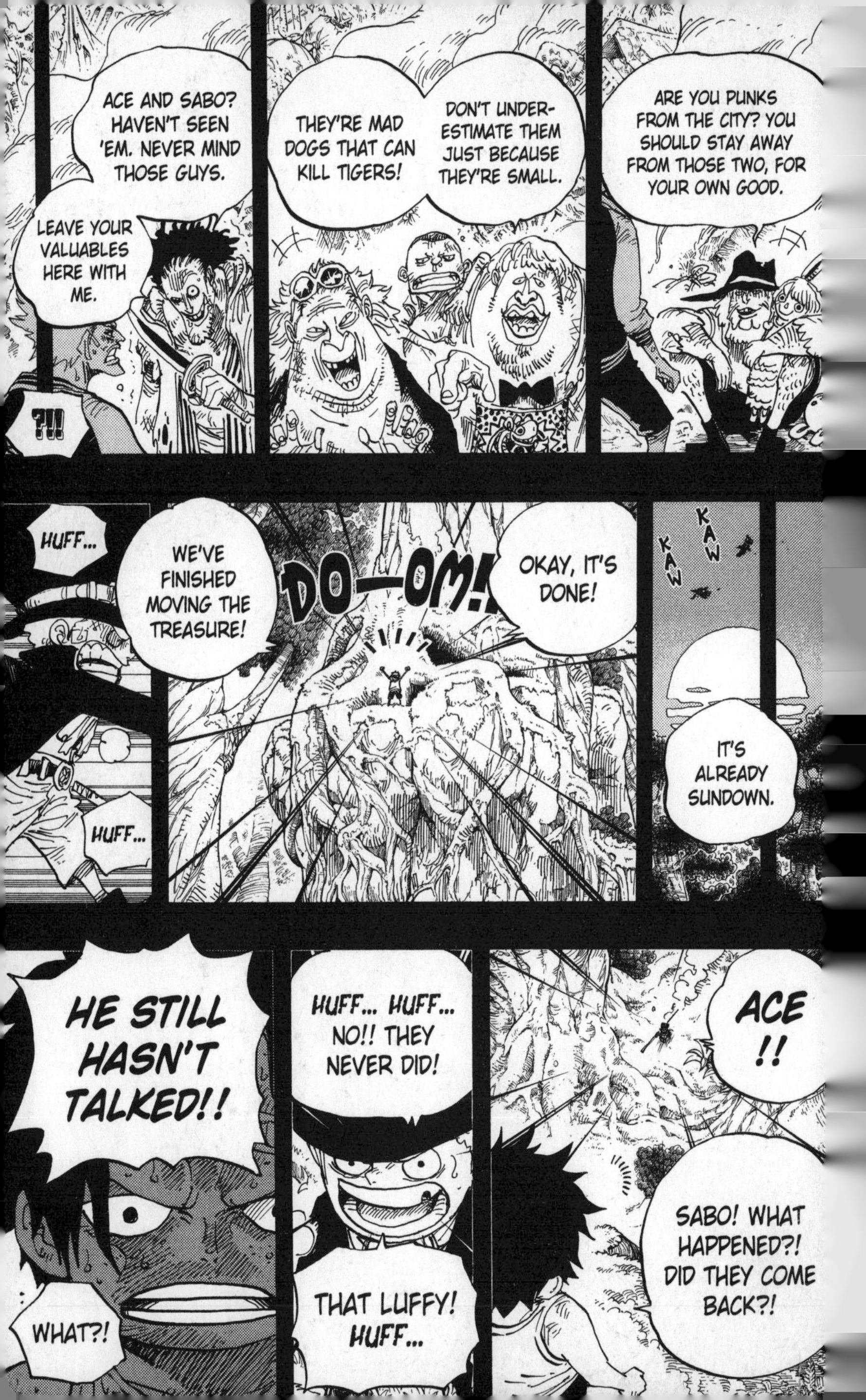
ARE YOU PUNKS FROM THE CITY? YOU SHOULD STAY AWAY FROM THOSE TWO, FOR YOUR OWN GOOD.
DON'T UNDER-ESTIMATE THEM JUST BECAUSE THEY'RE SMALL.
THEY'RE MAD DOGS THAT CAN KILL TIGERS!
ACE AND SABO? HAVEN'T SEEN 'EM. NEVER MIND THOSE GUYS.
LEAVE YOUR VALUABLES HERE WITH ME.
?!!
KAW
KAW
IT'S ALREADY SUNDOWN.
OKAY, IT'S DONE!
DO—OM!!
HUFF...
WE'VE FINISHED MOVING THE TREASURE!
HUFF...
ACE !!
SABO! WHAT HAPPENED?! DID THEY COME BACK?!
HUFF... HUFF... NO!! THEY NEVER DID!
THAT LUFFY! HUFF...
HE STILL HASN'T TALKED!!
WHAT?!

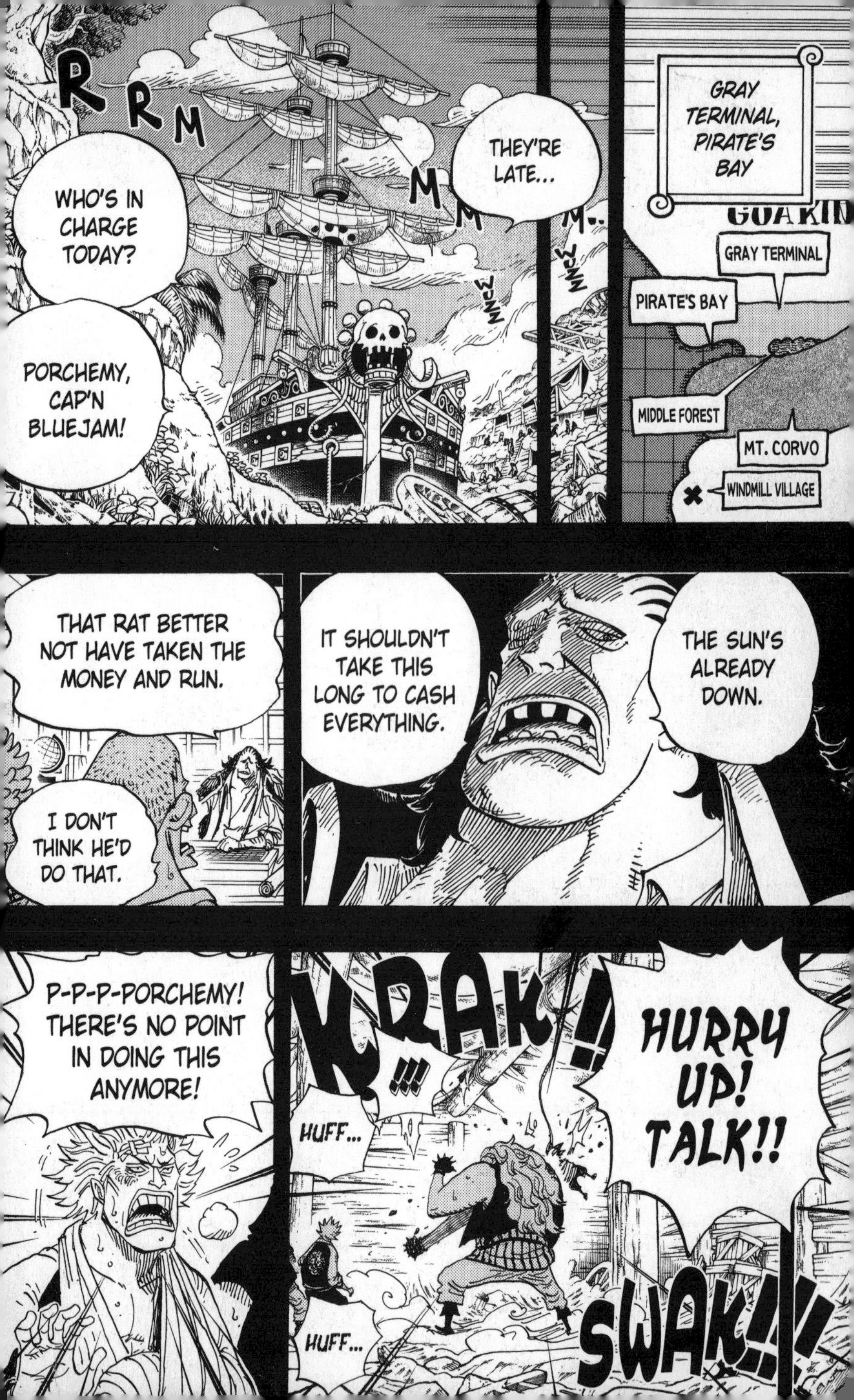
GRAY TERMINAL, PIRATE'S BAY
GRAY TERMINAL
PIRATE'S BAY
MIDDLE FOREST
MT. CORVO
WINDMILL VILLAGE
THEY'RE LATE...
RRRMMMM...
WHO'S IN CHARGE TODAY?
PORCHEMY, CAP'N BLUEJAM!
THE SUN'S ALREADY DOWN.
IT SHOULDN'T TAKE THIS LONG TO CASH EVERYTHING.
THAT RAT BETTER NOT HAVE TAKEN THE MONEY AND RUN.
I DON'T THINK HE'D DO THAT.
HURRY UP! TALK!!
KRAK!!
!!!
HUFF...
SWAK!!
HUFF...
P-P-P-PORCHEMY! THERE'S NO POINT IN DOING THIS ANYMORE!

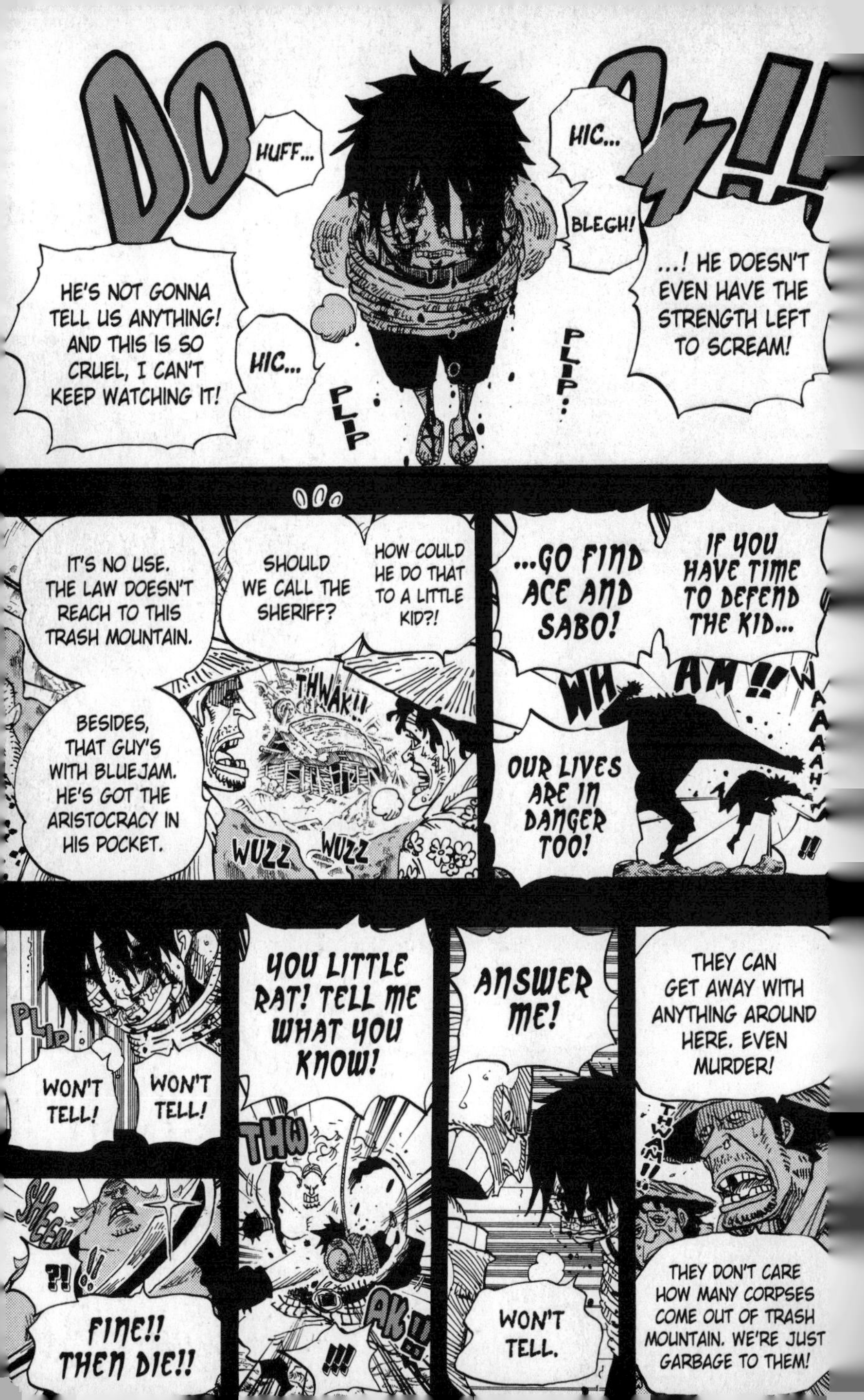
DO
HIC...
BLEGH!
...! HE DOESN'T EVEN HAVE THE STRENGTH LEFT TO SCREAM!
HUFF...
HIC...
HE'S NOT GONNA TELL US ANYTHING! AND THIS IS SO CRUEL, I CAN'T KEEP WATCHING IT!
PLIP
PLIP...
IF YOU HAVE TIME TO DEFEND THE KID...
...GO FIND ACE AND SABO!
WHAM!!
WAAAAH!!
OUR LIVES ARE IN DANGER TOO!
HOW COULD HE DO THAT TO A LITTLE KID?!
SHOULD WE CALL THE SHERIFF?
IT'S NO USE. THE LAW DOESN'T REACH TO THIS TRASH MOUNTAIN.
THWAK!!
BESIDES, THAT GUY'S WITH BLUEJAM. HE'S GOT THE ARISTOCRACY IN HIS POCKET.
WUZZ
WUZZ
THEY CAN GET AWAY WITH ANYTHING AROUND HERE. EVEN MURDER!
THWAM!!
THEY DON'T CARE HOW MANY CORPSES COME OUT OF TRASH MOUNTAIN. WE'RE JUST GARBAGE TO THEM!
ANSWER ME!
WON'T TELL.
YOU LITTLE RAT! TELL ME WHAT YOU KNOW!
THW
AK!!
!!!
PLIP
WON'T TELL!
WON'T TELL!
SHEEN
?!
!!
FINE!! THEN DIE!!

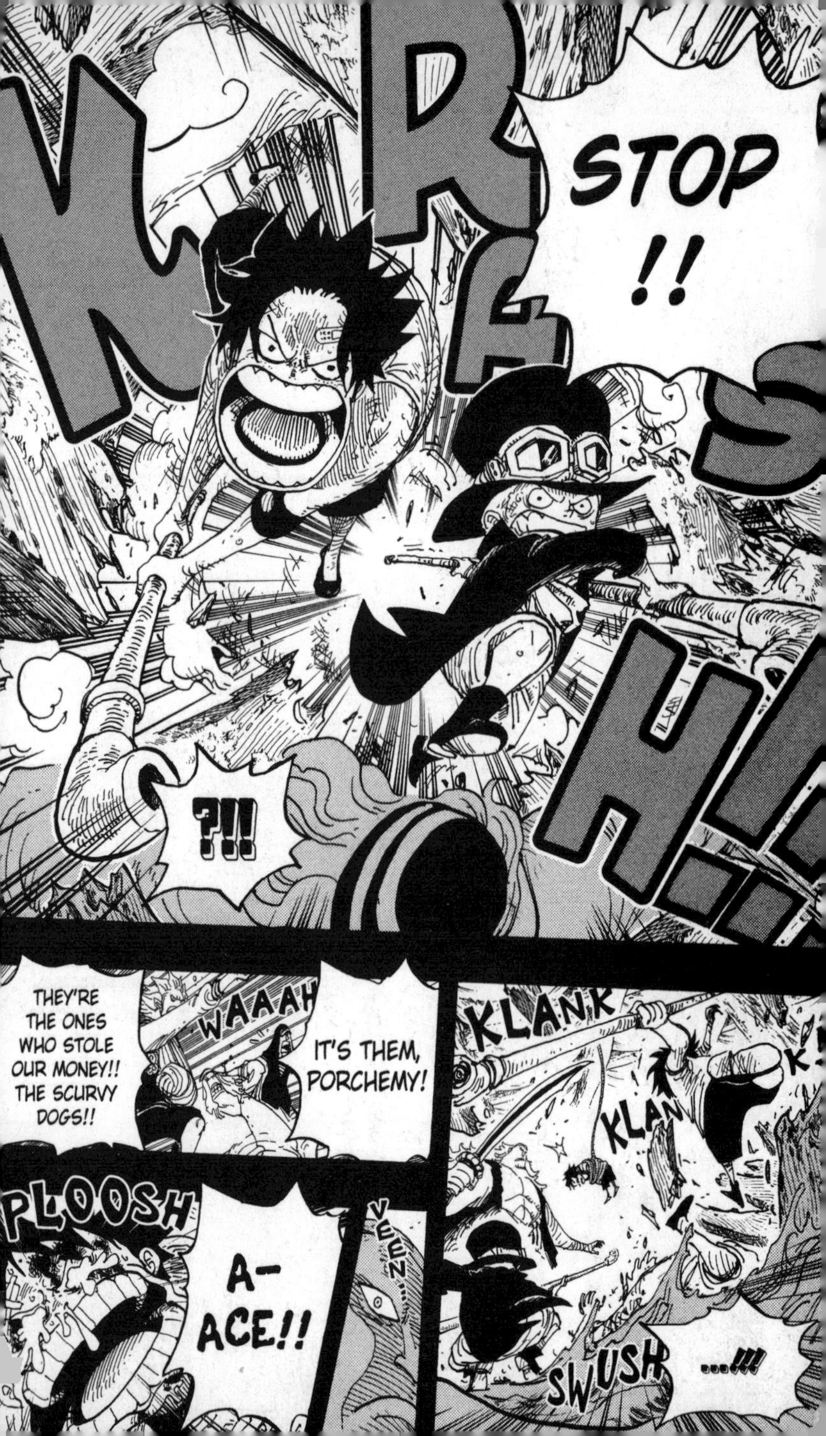
STOP !!
?!!
KLANK
K
KLAN
SWUSH
...!!!
IT'S THEM, PORCHEMY!
WAAAH
THEY'RE THE ONES WHO STOLE OUR MONEY!! THE SCURVY DOGS!!
VEEN...
A- ACE!!
PLOOSH

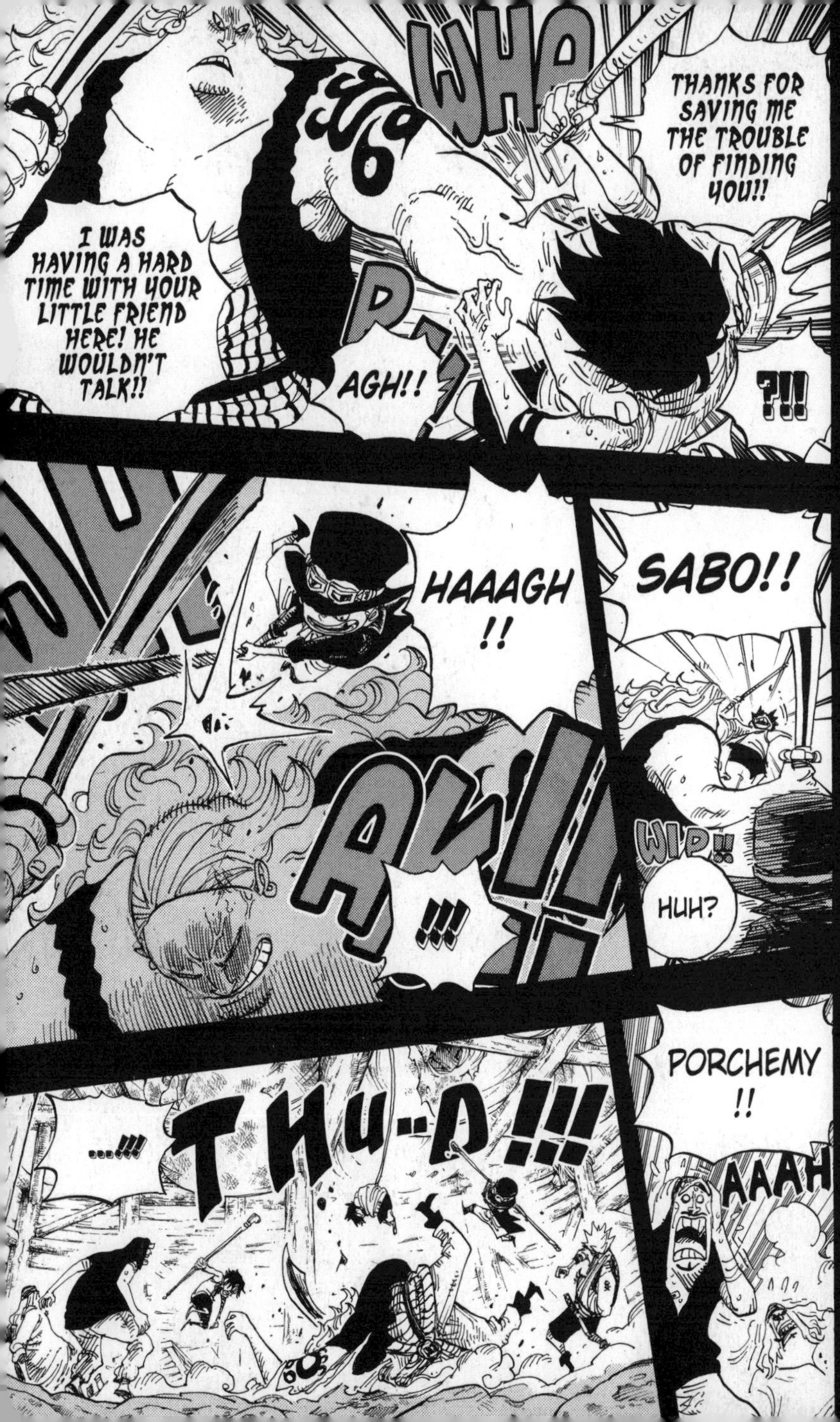
THANKS FOR SAVING ME THE TROUBLE OF FINDING YOU!!
WHA
?!!
I WAS HAVING A HARD TIME WITH YOUR LITTLE FRIEND HERE! HE WOULDN'T TALK!!
AGH!!
SABO!!
WIP!!
HUH?
HAAAGH!!
!!!
PORCHEMY!!
AAAH
THU-D!!!
...!!!

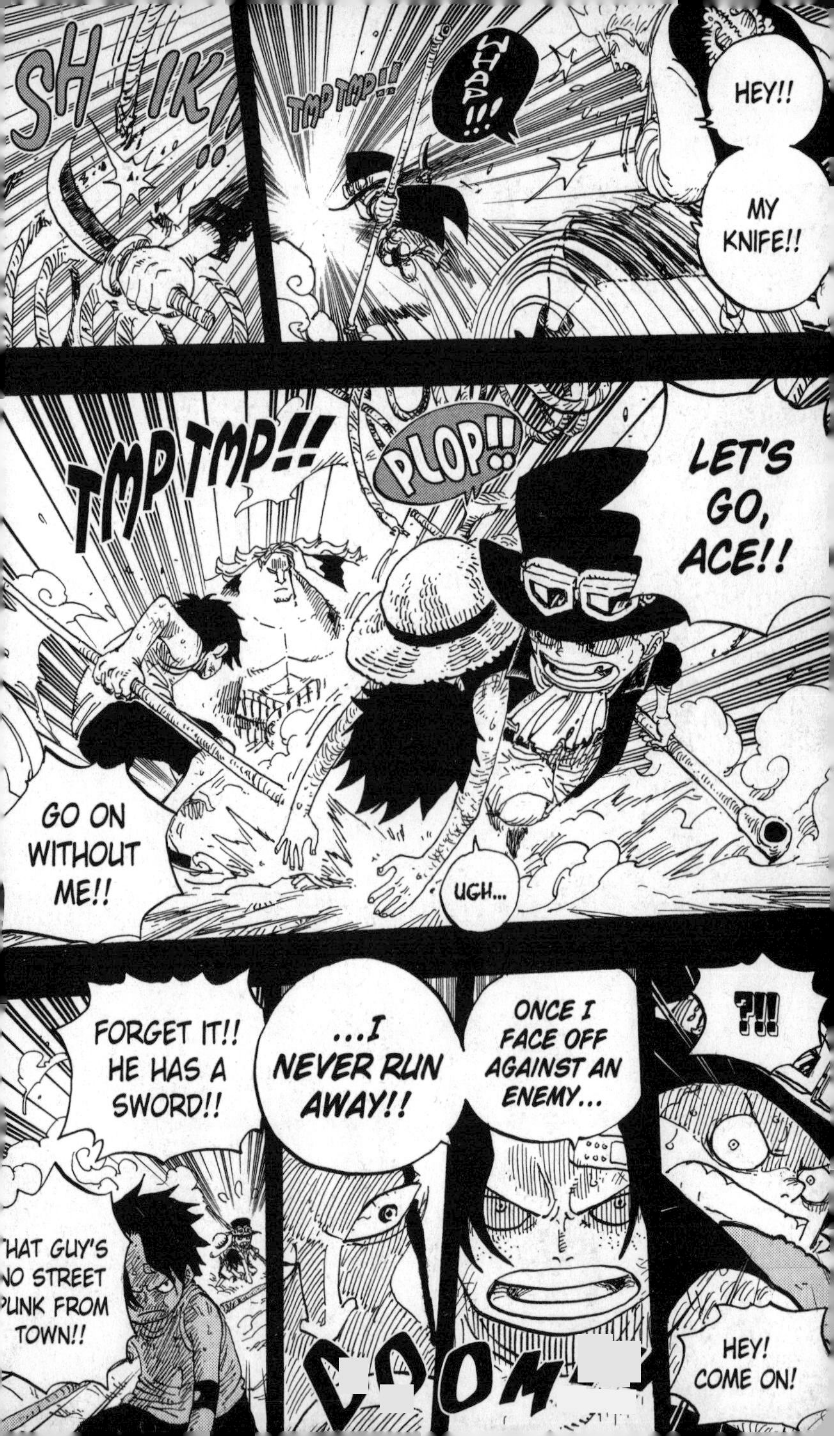
HEY!!
MY KNIFE!!
WHAP!!
TMP TMP!!
LET'S GO, ACE!!
PLOP!!
TMP TMP!!
UGH...
GO ON WITHOUT ME!!
?!!
HEY! COME ON!
ONCE I FACE OFF AGAINST AN ENEMY...
...I NEVER RUN AWAY!!
FORGET IT!! HE HAS A SWORD!!
HAT GUY'S NO STREET UNK FROM TOWN!!

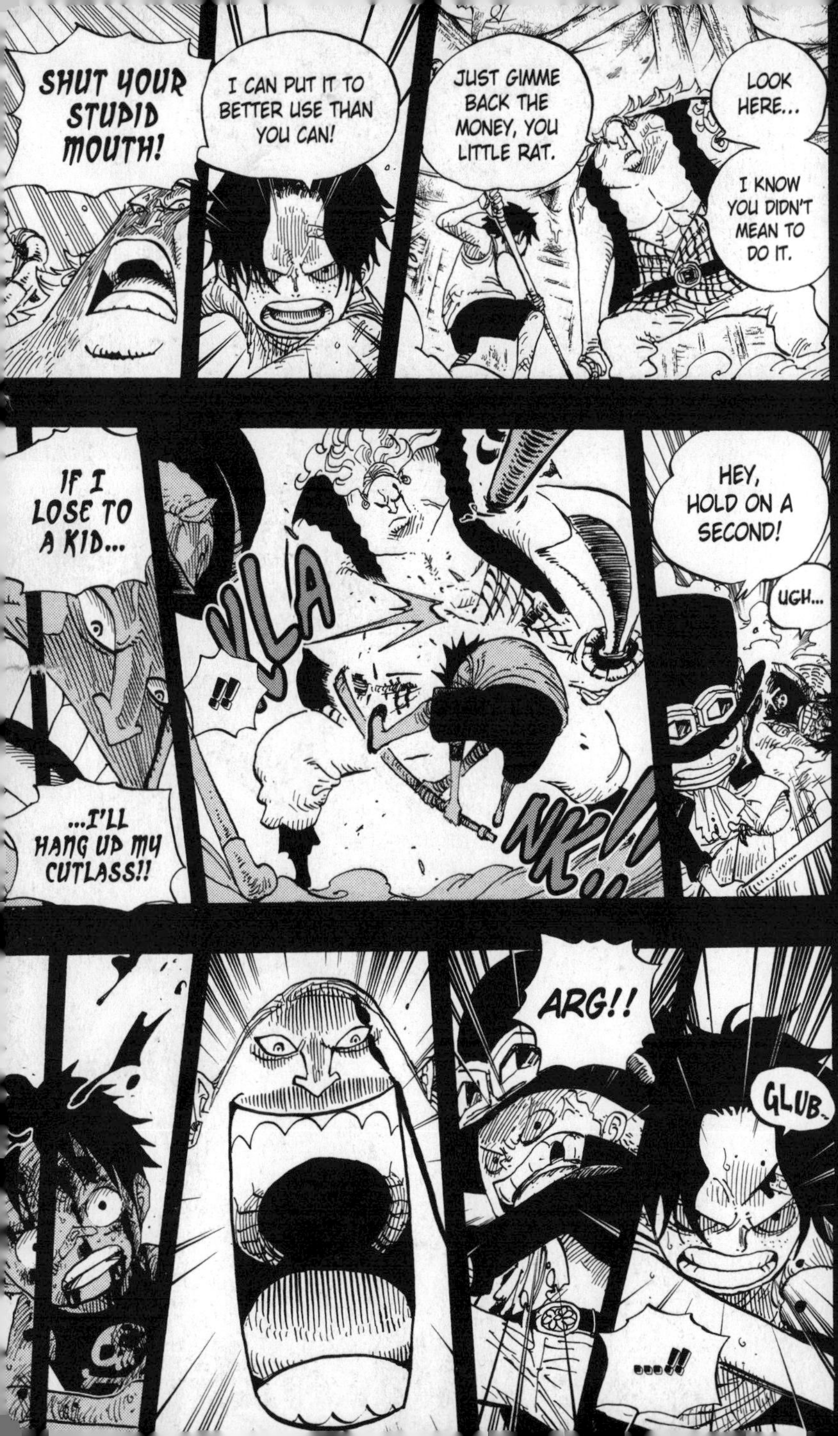
LOOK HERE...
I KNOW YOU DIDN'T MEAN TO DO IT.
JUST GIMME BACK THE MONEY, YOU LITTLE RAT.
I CAN PUT IT TO BETTER USE THAN YOU CAN!
SHUT YOUR STUPID MOUTH!
HEY, HOLD ON A SECOND!
UGH...
VLA
NK
!!
IF I LOSE TO A KID...
...I'LL HANG UP MY CUTLASS!!
ARG!!
GLUB
...!!

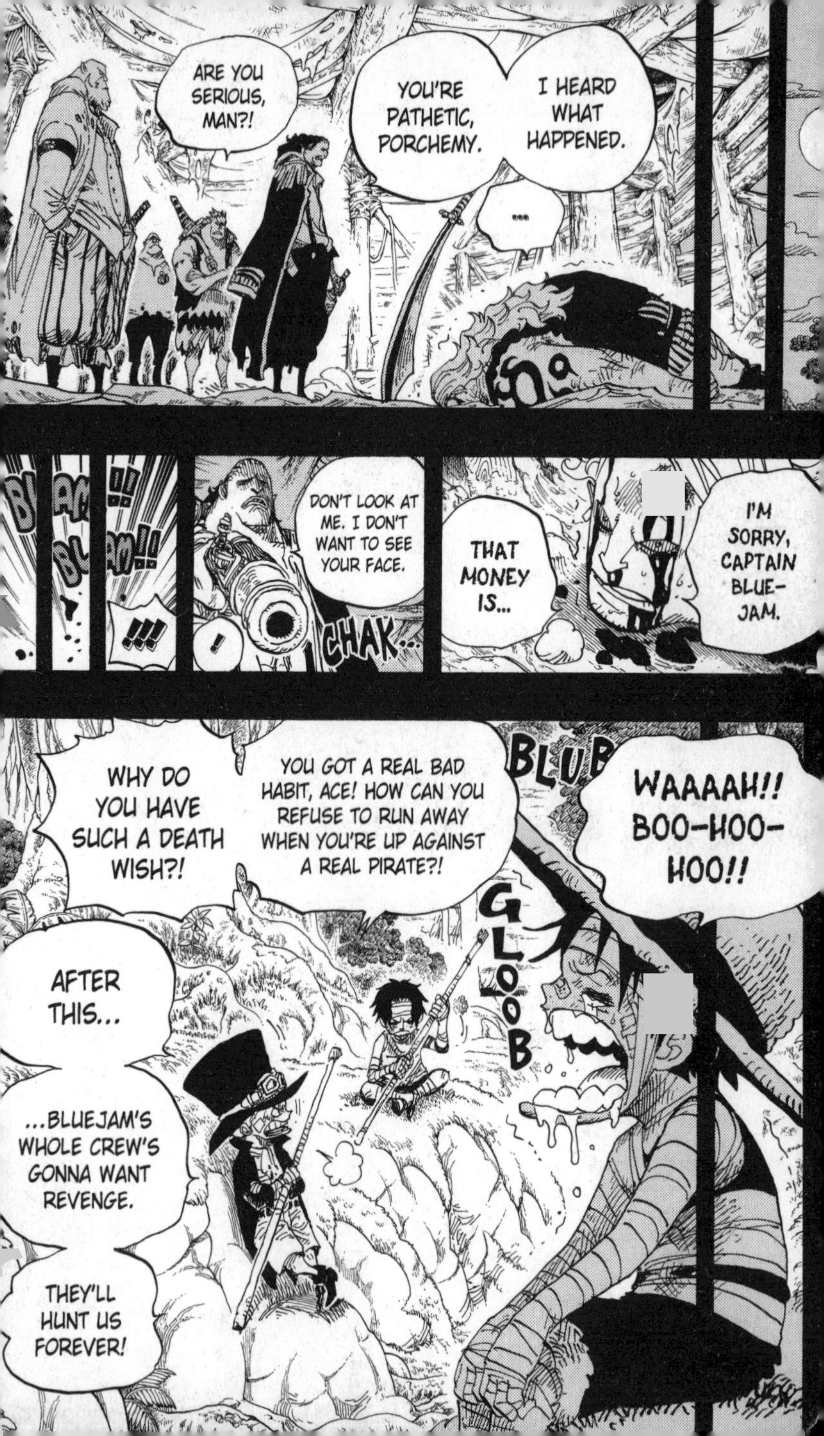
I HEARD WHAT HAPPENED.
YOU'RE PATHETIC, PORCHEMY.
...
ARE YOU SERIOUS, MAN?!
I'M SORRY, CAPTAIN BLUE-JAM.
THAT MONEY IS...
DON'T LOOK AT ME. I DON'T WANT TO SEE YOUR FACE.
!
CHAK..
BLAM!!
BLAM!!
!!!
BLUB
WAAAAH!! BOO-HOO-HOO!!
GLOOB
YOU GOT A REAL BAD HABIT, ACE! HOW CAN YOU REFUSE TO RUN AWAY WHEN YOU'RE UP AGAINST A REAL PIRATE?!
WHY DO YOU HAVE SUCH A DEATH WISH?!
AFTER THIS...
...BLUEJAM'S WHOLE CREW'S GONNA WANT REVENGE.
THEY'LL HUNT US FOREVER!

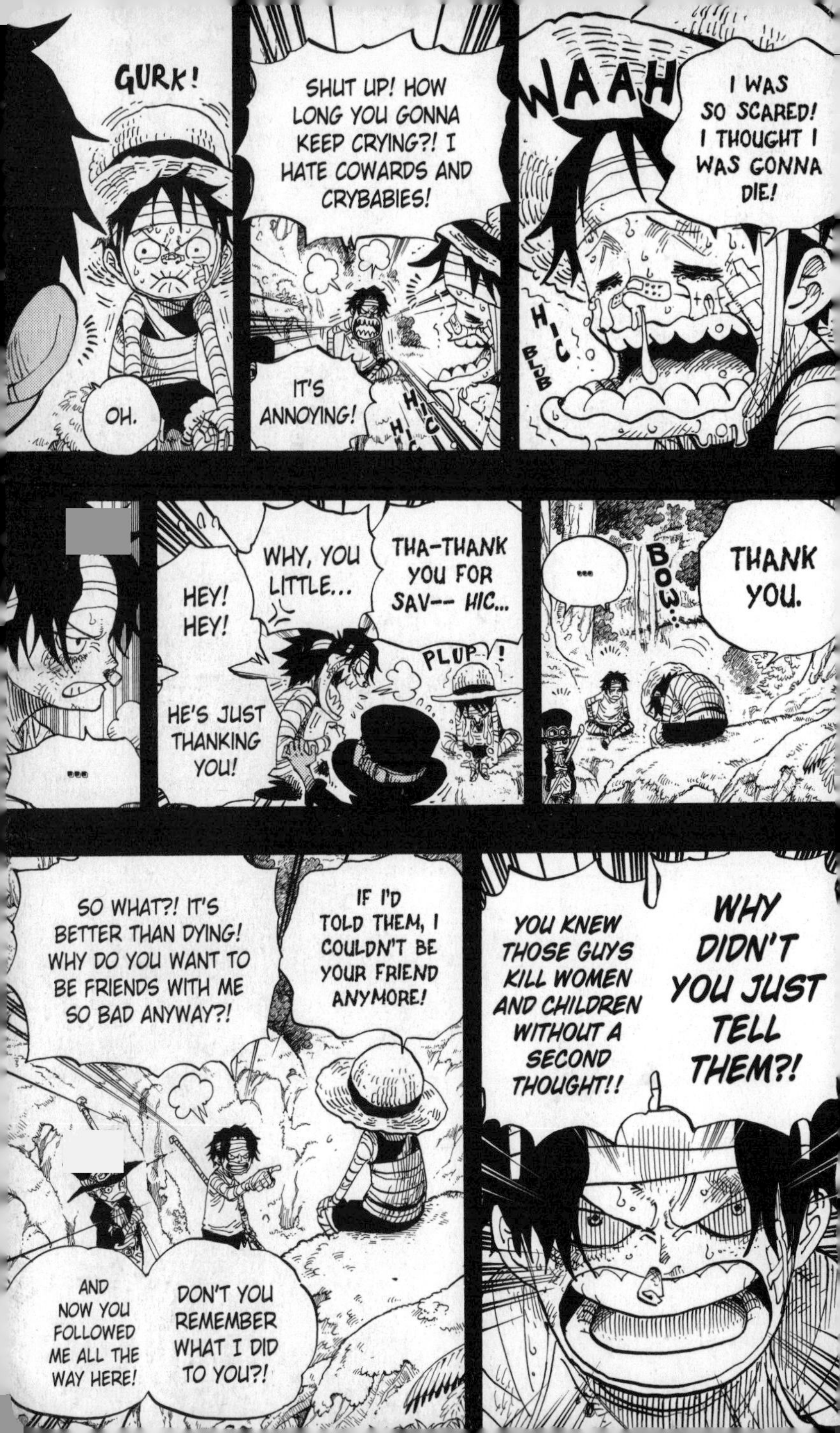
WAAH
I WAS SO SCARED! I THOUGHT I WAS GONNA DIE!
HIC
BLUB
SHUT UP! HOW LONG YOU GONNA KEEP CRYING?! I HATE COWARDS AND CRYBABIES!
IT'S ANNOYING!
HIC
HIC
GURK!
OH.
THANK YOU.
...
BOW...
THA-THANK YOU FOR SAV-- HIC...
WHY, YOU LITTLE...
PLUP!
HEY! HEY!
HE'S JUST THANKING YOU!
...
WHY DIDN'T YOU JUST TELL THEM?!
YOU KNEW THOSE GUYS KILL WOMEN AND CHILDREN WITHOUT A SECOND THOUGHT!!
IF I'D TOLD THEM, I COULDN'T BE YOUR FRIEND ANYMORE!
SO WHAT?! IT'S BETTER THAN DYING! WHY DO YOU WANT TO BE FRIENDS WITH ME SO BAD ANYWAY?!
DON'T YOU REMEMBER WHAT I DID TO YOU?!
AND NOW YOU FOLLOWED ME ALL THE WAY HERE!

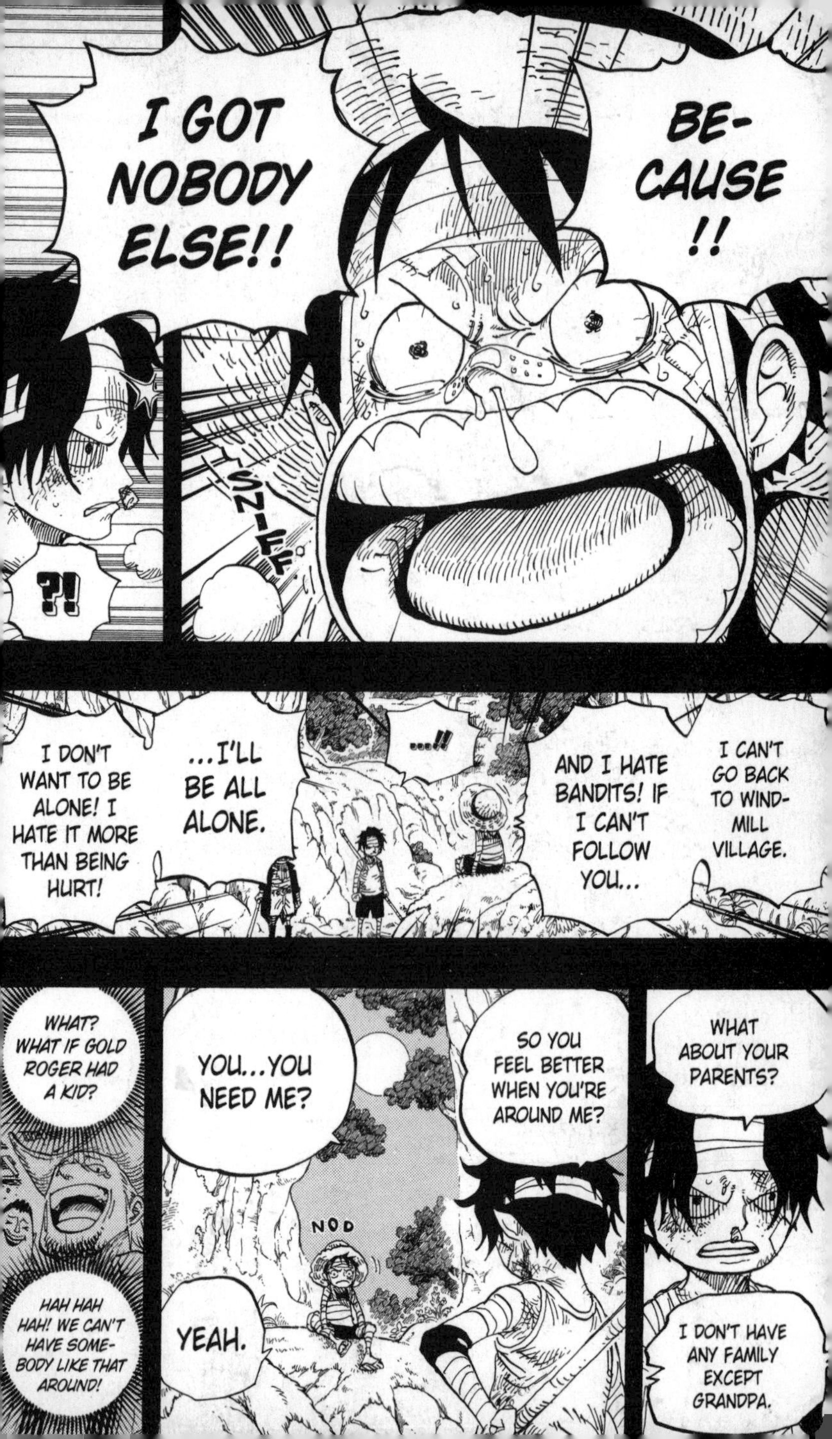
BE-CAUSE!!
I GOT NOBODY ELSE!!
SNIFF
?!
I CAN'T GO BACK TO WIND-MILL VILLAGE.
AND I HATE BANDITS! IF I CAN'T FOLLOW YOU...
...!!
...I'LL BE ALL ALONE.
I DON'T WANT TO BE ALONE! I HATE IT MORE THAN BEING HURT!
WHAT ABOUT YOUR PARENTS?
I DON'T HAVE ANY FAMILY EXCEPT GRANDPA.
SO YOU FEEL BETTER WHEN YOU'RE AROUND ME?
YOU...YOU NEED ME?
NOD
YEAH.
WHAT? WHAT IF GOLD ROGER HAD A KID?
HAH HAH HAH! WE CAN'T HAVE SOMEBODY LIKE THAT AROUND!

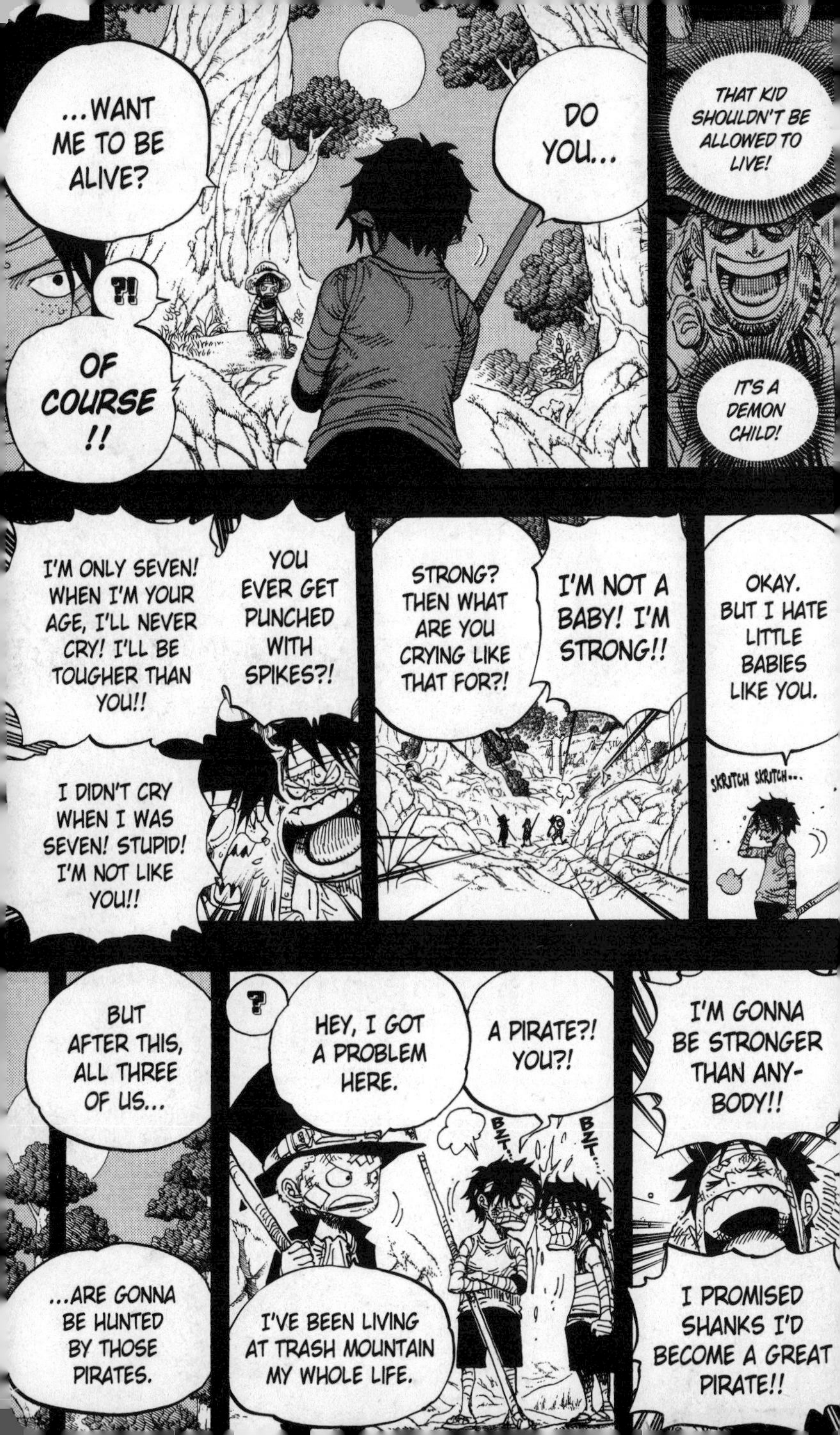
THAT KID SHOULDN'T BE ALLOWED TO LIVE!
IT'S A DEMON CHILD!
DO YOU...
...WANT ME TO BE ALIVE?
?!
OF COURSE!!
OKAY. BUT I HATE LITTLE BABIES LIKE YOU.
SKRITCH SKRITCH...
I'M NOT A BABY! I'M STRONG!!
STRONG? THEN WHAT ARE YOU CRYING LIKE THAT FOR?!
YOU EVER GET PUNCHED WITH SPIKES?!
I'M ONLY SEVEN! WHEN I'M YOUR AGE, I'LL NEVER CRY! I'LL BE TOUGHER THAN YOU!!
I DIDN'T CRY WHEN I WAS SEVEN! STUPID! I'M NOT LIKE YOU!!
I'M GONNA BE STRONGER THAN ANY-BODY!!
I PROMISED SHANKS I'D BECOME A GREAT PIRATE!!
A PIRATE?! YOU?!
BZT...
BZT...
?
HEY, I GOT A PROBLEM HERE.
I'VE BEEN LIVING AT TRASH MOUNTAIN MY WHOLE LIFE.
BUT AFTER THIS, ALL THREE OF US...
...ARE GONNA BE HUNTED BY THOSE PIRATES.

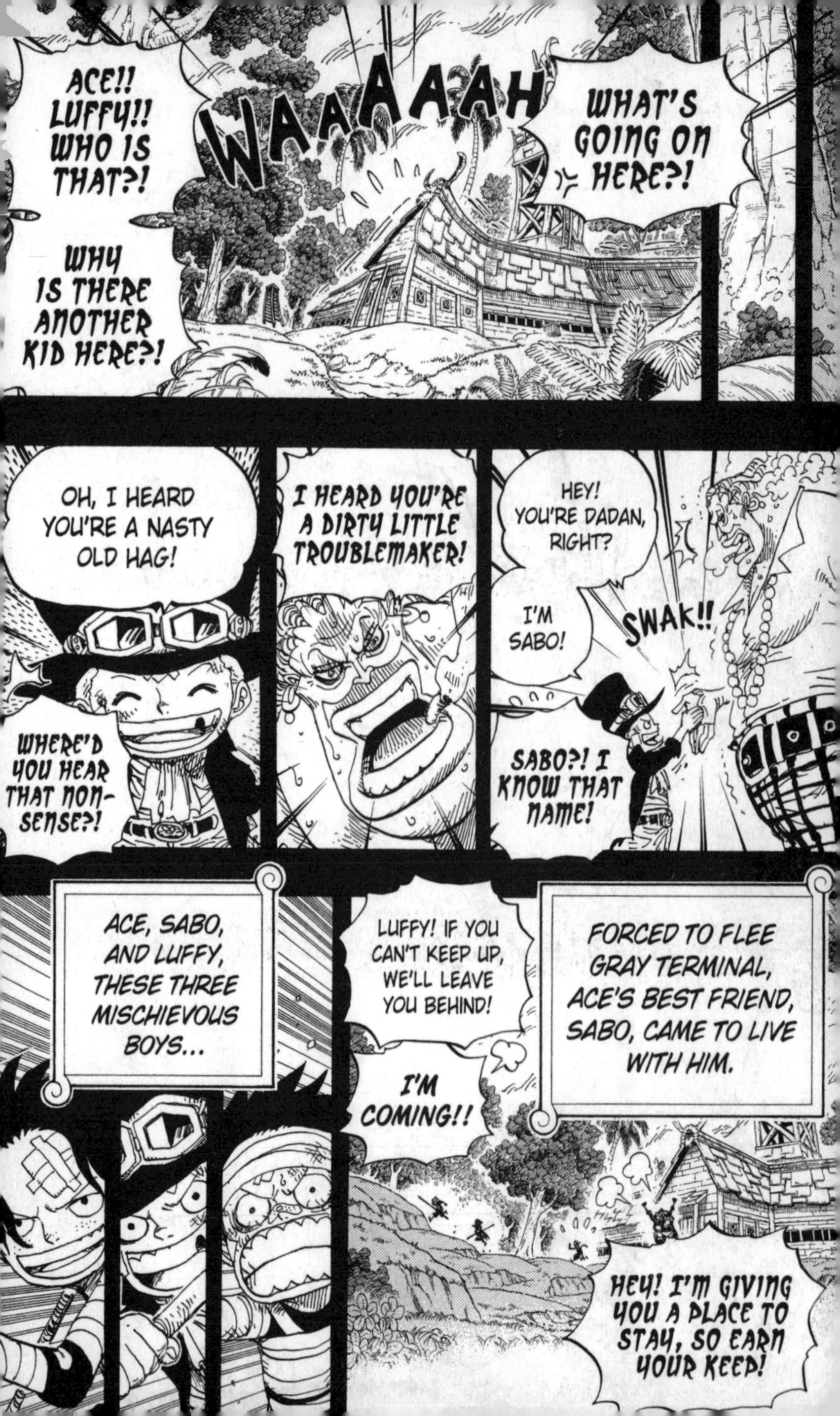
WHAT'S GOING ON HERE?!
WAAAAAH
ACE!! LUFFY!! WHO IS THAT?!
WHY IS THERE ANOTHER KID HERE?!
HEY! YOU'RE DADAN, RIGHT?
I'M SABO!
SWAK!!
SABO?! I KNOW THAT NAME!
I HEARD YOU'RE A DIRTY LITTLE TROUBLEMAKER!
OH, I HEARD YOU'RE A NASTY OLD HAG!
WHERE'D YOU HEAR THAT NON-SENSE?!
FORCED TO FLEE GRAY TERMINAL, ACE'S BEST FRIEND, SABO, CAME TO LIVE WITH HIM.
LUFFY! IF YOU CAN'T KEEP UP, WE'LL LEAVE YOU BEHIND!
I'M COMING!!
HEY! I'M GIVING YOU A PLACE TO STAY, SO EARN YOUR KEEP!
ACE, SABO, AND LUFFY, THESE THREE MISCHIEVOUS BOYS...

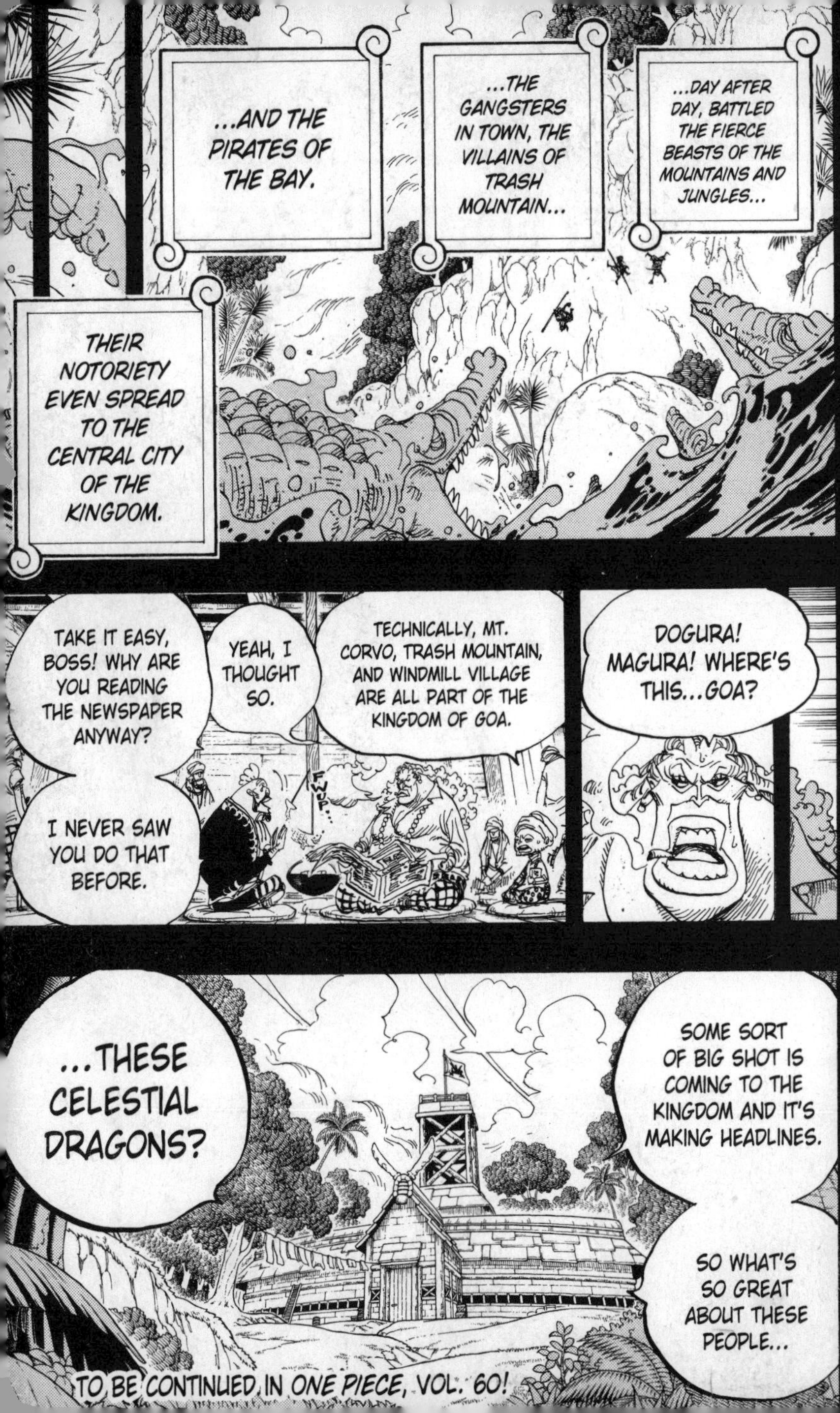
...DAY AFTER DAY, BATTLED THE FIERCE BEASTS OF THE MOUNTAINS AND JUNGLES...
...THE GANGSTERS IN TOWN, THE VILLAINS OF TRASH MOUNTAIN...
...AND THE PIRATES OF THE BAY.
THEIR NOTORIETY EVEN SPREAD TO THE CENTRAL CITY OF THE KINGDOM.
DOGURA! MAGURA! WHERE'S THIS...GOA?
TECHNICALLY, MT. CORVO, TRASH MOUNTAIN, AND WINDMILL VILLAGE ARE ALL PART OF THE KINGDOM OF GOA.
FWUP...
YEAH, I THOUGHT SO.
TAKE IT EASY, BOSS! WHY ARE YOU READING THE NEWSPAPER ANYWAY?
I NEVER SAW YOU DO THAT BEFORE.
SOME SORT OF BIG SHOT IS COMING TO THE KINGDOM AND IT'S MAKING HEADLINES.
SO WHAT'S SO GREAT ABOUT THESE PEOPLE...
...THESE CELESTIAL DRAGONS?
TO BE CONTINUED IN ONE PIECE, VOL. 60!

COMING NEXT VOLUME:

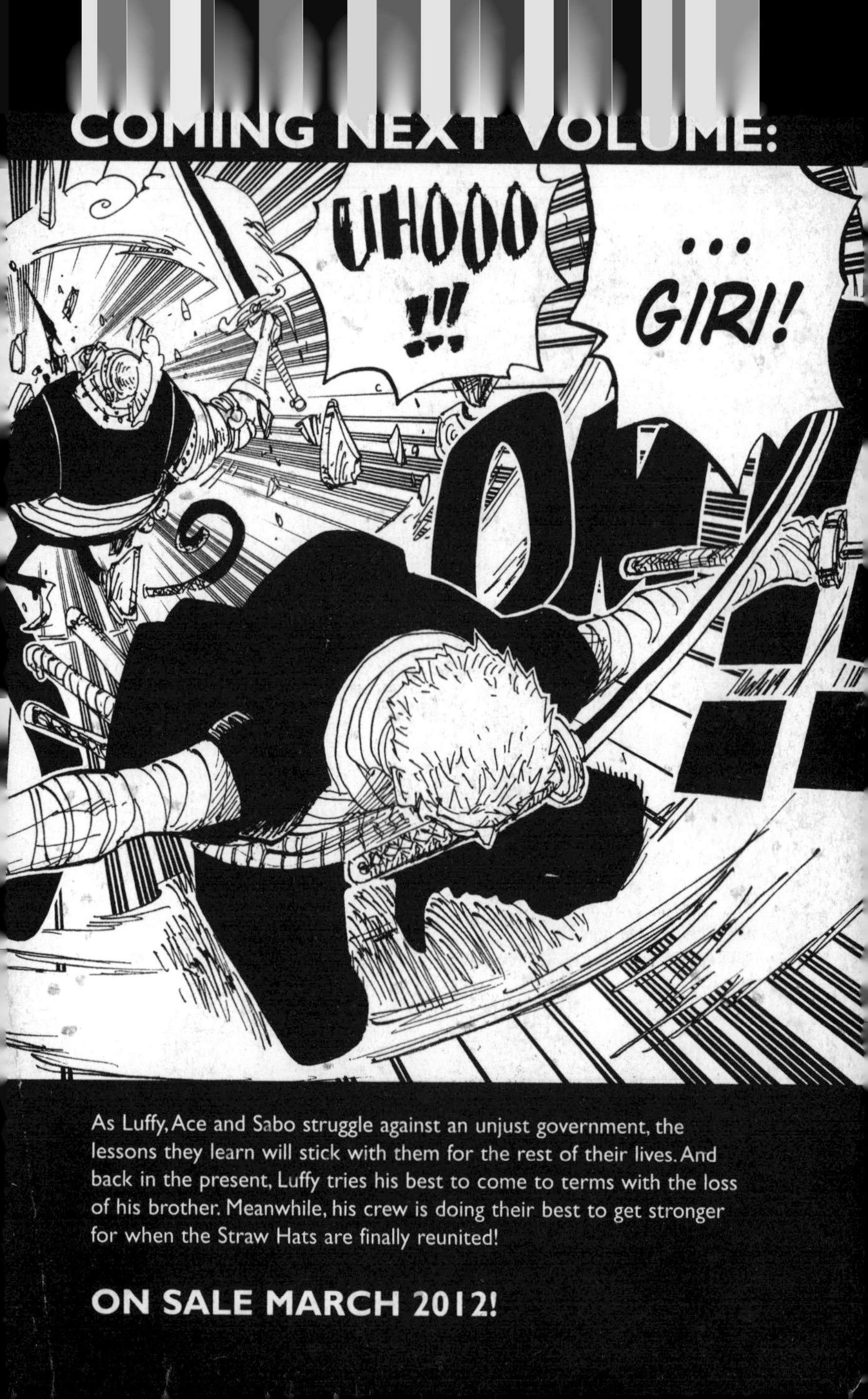
...GIRI!
UHOOO!!!

As Luffy, Ace and Sabo struggle against an unjust government, the lessons they learn will stick with them for the rest of their lives. And back in the present, Luffy tries his best to come to terms with the loss of his brother. Meanwhile, his crew is doing their best to get stronger for when the Straw Hats are finally reunited!

ON SALE MARCH 2012!

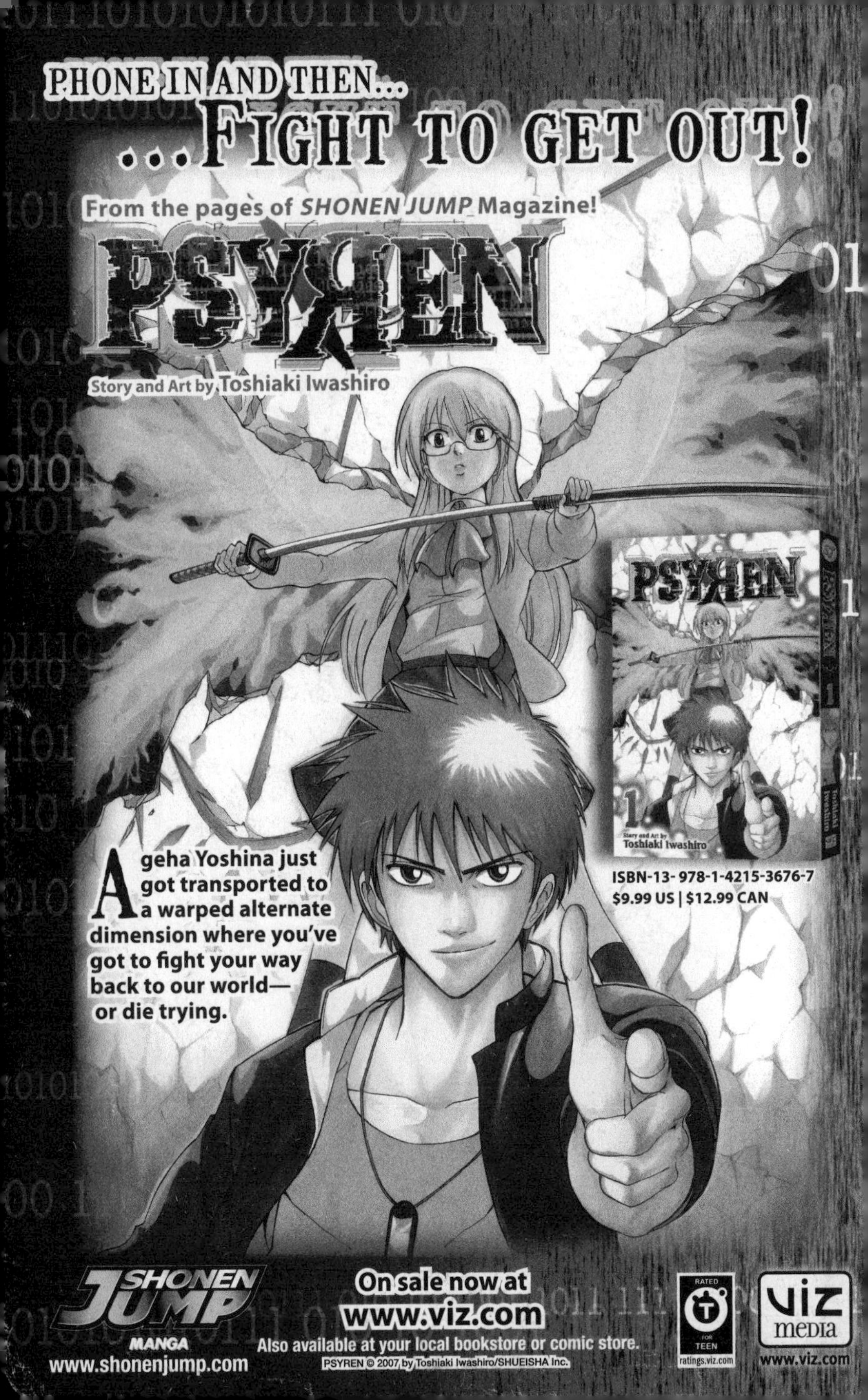

PHONE IN AND THEN...
...FIGHT TO GET OUT!
From the pages of SHONEN JUMP Magazine!
PSYREN
Story and Art by Toshiaki Iwashiro
PSYREN
1
Story and Art by Toshiaki Iwashiro
ISBN-13- 978-1-4215-3676-7
$9.99 US | $12.99 CAN
Ageha Yoshina just got transported to a warped alternate dimension where you've got to fight your way back to our world— or die trying.
SHONEN JUMP
MANGA
www.shonenjump.com
On sale now at
www.viz.com
Also available at your local bookstore or comic store.
PSYREN © 2007 by Toshiaki Iwashiro/SHUEISHA Inc.
RATED
T
FOR
TEEN
ratings.viz.com
viz
media
www.viz.com

BAKUMAN。

STORY BY TSUGUMI OHBA
ART BY TAKESHI OBATA

From the creators of *Death Note*

The mystery behind manga making REVEALED!

Average student Moritaka Mashiro enjoys drawing for fun. When his classmate and aspiring writer Akito Takagi discovers his talent, he begs to team up. But what exactly does it take to make it in the manga-publishing world?

Bakuman。, Vol. 1
ISBN: 978-1-4215-3513-5
$9.99 US / $12.99 CAN *

Manga on sale at store.viz.com
Also available at your local bookstore or comic store

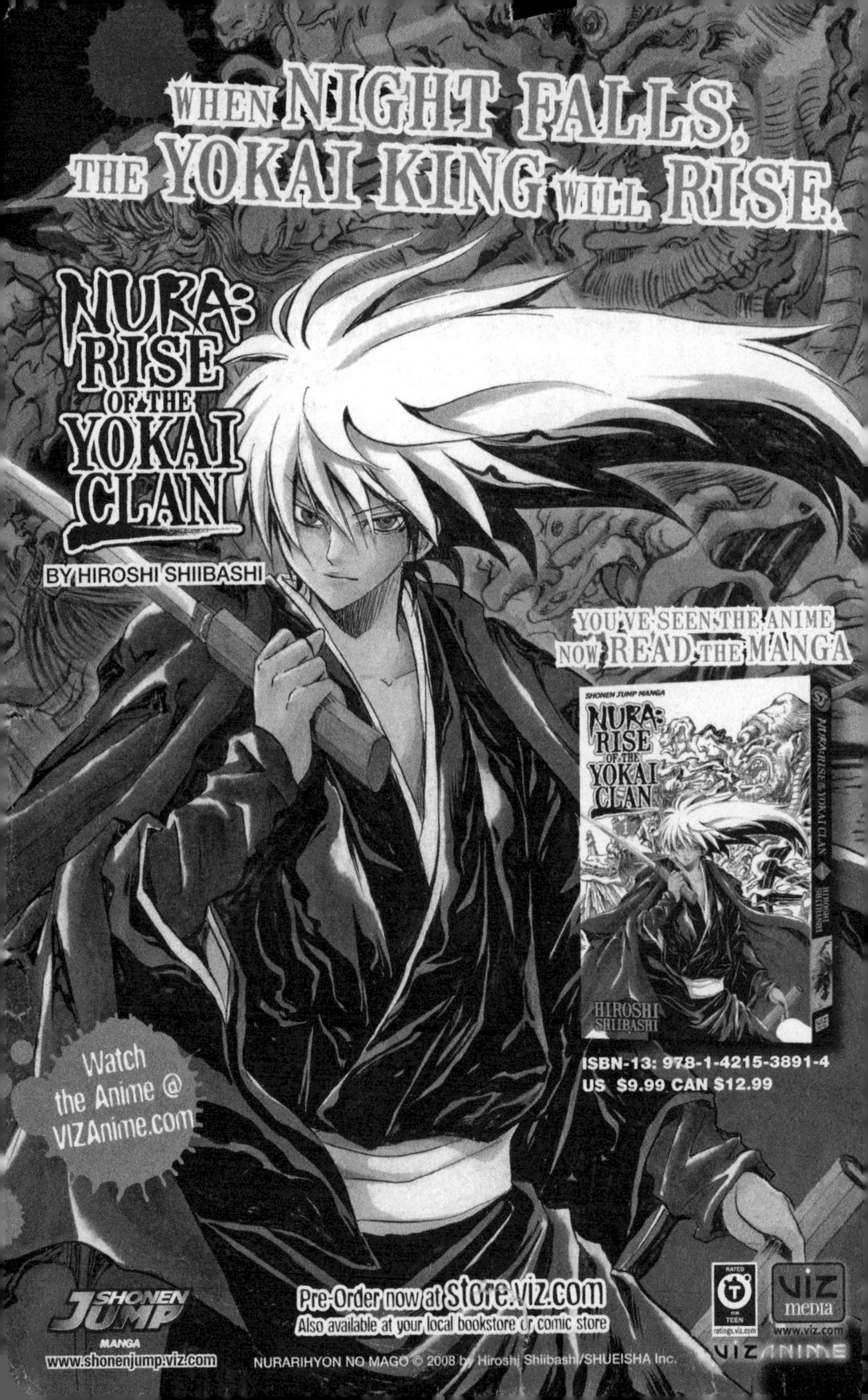
WHEN NIGHT FALLS, THE YOKAI KING WILL RISE.
NURA: RISE OF THE YOKAI CLAN
BY HIROSHI SHIIBASHI
YOU'VE SEEN THE ANIME NOW READ THE MANGA
SHONEN JUMP MANGA
NURA: RISE OF THE YOKAI CLAN
HIROSHI SHIIBASHI
ISBN-13: 978-1-4215-3891-4
US $9.99 CAN $12.99
Watch the Anime @ VIZAnime.com
Pre-Order now at store.viz.com
Also available at your local bookstore or comic store
SHONEN JUMP MANGA
www.shonenjump.viz.com
NURARIHYON NO MAGO © 2008 by Hiroshi Shiibashi/SHUEISHA Inc.
RATED T FOR TEEN
ratings.viz.com
VIZ media
www.viz.com
VIZANIME